IN THE

PAST
LANE

ALSO BY MICHAEL KAMMEN

*The Lively Arts: Gilbert Seldes and the Transformation
of Cultural Criticism in the United States (1996)*

*Meadows of Memory: Images of Time and Tradition in American Art
and Culture (1992)*

*Mystic Chords of Memory: The Transformation of Tradition in
American Culture (1991)*

*Sovereignty and Liberty: Constitutional Discourse in American Culture
(1988)*

Selvages and Biases: The Fabric of History in American Culture (1987)

A Machine That Would Go of Itself: The Constitution in American Culture (1986)

*Spheres of Liberty: Changing Perceptions of Liberty in
American Culture (1986)*

*A Season of Youth: The American Revolution and
the Historical Imagination (1978)*

Colonial New York: A History (1975)

*People of Paradox: An Inquiry Concerning the Origins of
American Civilization (1972)*

*Empire and Interest: The American Colonies and the
Politics of Mercantilism (1970)*

*Deputyes & Libertyes: The Origins of Representative Government in
Colonial America (1969)*

*A Rope of Sand: The Colonial Agents, British Politics, and the
American Revolution (1968)*

EDITOR

Contested Values: Democracy and Diversity in American Culture (1994)

The Origins of the American Constitution: A Documentary History (1986)

The Past Before Us: Contemporary Historical Writing in the United States (1980)

"What is the Good of History?" Selected Letters of Carl L. Becker, 1900–1945 (1973)

The History of the Province of New-York, by William Smith, Jr. (1972)

*The Contrapuntal Civilization: Essays Toward a New Understanding
of the American Experience (1971)*

Politics and Society in Colonial America: Democracy or Deference? (1967)

IN THE
PAST
LANE

Historical Perspectives on
American Culture

MICHAEL KAMMEN

OXFORD UNIVERSITY PRESS
New York   Oxford

Oxford University Press

Oxford   New York
Athens   Auckland   Bangkok   Bogotá   Buenos Aires   Calcutta
Cape Town   Chennai   Dar es Salaam   Delhi   Florence   Hong Kong
Istanbul   Karachi   Kuala Lumpur   Madrid   Melbourne   Mexico City
Mumbai   Nairobi   Paris   São Paolo   Singapore   Taipei   Tokyo
Toronto   Warsaw

and associated companies in
Berlin   Ibadan

First published by Oxford University Press, Inc., 1997

First issued as an Oxford University Press paperback, 1999

Oxford is a registered trademark of Oxford University Press

Library of Congress Cataloging-in-Publication Data
Kammen, Michael G.
In the past lane : historical perspectives
on American culture / Michael Kammen
p.   cm.
ISBN 0–19–511111–7
ISBN 0–19–513091–X (pbk)

1. United States—Social life and customs—Historiography.
2. Popular culture—United States—Historiography.
3. Memory—Social aspects—United States—History.
I. Title
E169.1.K293 1997   973'.072—dc21
97–21613

35798642

Printed in the United States of America
on acid-free paper

❧

For
Bamidele Fayemi Kammen
and
Daniel Merson Kammen
and
Douglas Anton Kammen

❧

✤

Volumes and vectors . . . angles and directions
Alexander Calder

✤

Contents

Introduction

During the past decade readers and writers of history have been intrigued, to an unprecedented degree, by three large and perplexing issues. One involves the nature of historians' personal commitments or concerns, and consequently the possible limits of their objectivity in reconstructing and understanding the past, especially in the realm of motives, beliefs, and modes of behavior.[1]

A second problematic issue has engaged legislators and policy makers at several levels along with people who manage cultural institutions and those who mobilize perceptions of the past for commercial or political purposes: What is the appropriate role of cultural programs in the civic sector and the relative responsibility of government, if any, to support or enhance cultural agendas and activities for the public?

A third problematic issue has generated an extraordinary range of publications during the 1990s. It concerns the nature and functions of collective (or social) memory in American life, particularly given the traditional propensity of this society for being present-minded and having an unreliable attention span—indeed, having a clear penchant for reconfiguring the past in order to make it comfortably congruent with contemporary needs and assumptions.[2]

The essays that constitute this volume address such issues from a perspective shaped by more than three decades of writing, teaching, and especially serving on the advisory boards of various history-oriented museums and organizations. The focus and emphases of my tripartite schematization in this book correspond directly to the three major issues outlined above. This is a work about the historian's vocation, about history and culture in American public life, and about changing perceptions of the past in the United States over a significant span of generations.

Such issues cannot be fully comprehended in a vacuum. Not only does their meaning involve contextual interdependence, it also requires comparison with the same matters when they are manifest in other societies. In addition to making such comparisons where it seems appropriate and whenever comparable information is available, Chapter 7 is entirely devoted to what I call the "problem of American exceptionalism." In my view that phrase does not mean superiority. It can and has implied, in a word, difference; but, above all, it has meant the *perception* that American culture is different, a perception long shared by residents of the United States and by foreigners alike—yet a perception that has been challenged and become controversial in the past fifteen years or so.

These essays have four interconnected themes. The first, exemplified in Part I, is that the history we read can best be understood if we have intimate knowledge of the people who wrote it. I am engaged by an observation made by Erik H. Erikson in the 1960s: "Everything that is new and worth saying (or worth saying in a new way) has a highly personal aspect. The question is only whether it is also generally significant for one's contemporaries."[3]

The second theme arises from my strong belief that historiography (knowledge of historical inquiry, broadly conceived) supplies important signs and clues that can enhance our understanding of culture generally. Because most of the chapters that follow are concerned with culture in one way or another, I feel an obligation to provide a definitional context—especially since E. P. Thompson warned not long before he died that "culture" was in danger of becoming a historical "catch-all." It is amusing to look back a century to someone like Charles W. Eliot, the president of Harvard (trained as a chemist), who regarded culture as marginally useful. He designated all courses lacking practical utility as "culture courses."[4]

For two decades now, historians of American culture have been reasonably careful in defining their subject. In essence, their common denominator declares that cultural history deals with human values, customs, practices, and their meaning understood in concrete historical contexts.[5] Raymond Williams shrewdly explained that during the nineteenth century the concept of culture came to be identified with high culture because of a desire by elites to separate certain moral and intellectual activities from society as a whole that was rapidly industrializing and (seemingly) becoming vulgar. As a socialist Williams insisted upon his own view that "culture is ordinary," by which he meant that its qualities were inclusive —aspects of everyday life that belonged to no one in particular because they were a common possession, a shared though shifting heritage.[6]

Ralph Waldo Emerson partially anticipated Williams in his famous "American Scholar" essay (1837) where he referred to a revolutionary process, "the gradual domestication of the idea of Culture." For purposes of the work gathered in this volume, which deals with public as well as personal manifestations of the past, I am especially obliged to various historians and anthropologists who acknowledge that cultural history can be persuasive, even compelling, despite its inability to be scientific or precise. As one practitioner has put it, the cultural historian must ultimately rely on "the gift of seeing a quantity of fine points in a given relation without ever being able to demonstrate it."[7]

Because quite a few of my essays concern recent trends and configurations, it may be helpful to differentiate between our contemporary, living culture, which cannot be perceived in its entirety because it is in process, and the historically cultural settings that also oblige us to perceive them selectively since all facts, tendencies, and patterns of meaning are not equally consequential. Because Americans are a heterogeneous people, moreover, we have a shared historical past that is political and constitutional at its core; yet we also have diverse particular pasts that tend to be ethnic, religious, and racial—in essence, cultural. Hence the continuing relevance of a remark made decades ago in a classic essay by Johan Huizinga:

> Cultural history has for the moment more than enough to do in determining the specific forms of historical life. Its task is to determine a morphology of the particular, before it can make bold to consider the general. There is time enough for description of whole cultures around one central concept. Let us for the time being be pluralists above all.[8]

Nevertheless, a number of these essays do, indeed, assume that a distinctive culture has developed historically in the United States, just as distinctive cultures have developed elsewhere. Some observers are disposed to skepticism on that score, for assorted reasons and because of certain universalizing predilections that are now fashionable. I can only say in response that foreign visitors have been noticing our distinctive configuration for generations if not for centuries. Ruth Benedict, an astute American anthropologist, never doubted that particular constellations of ideas and values gave a people a sense of sharing a culture and being different from those of other nations and societies. John King Fairbank, an American who devoted a lifetime to studying China and the Chinese, offered this assertion in 1971: "just as man is a creature of habit, so nations are creatures of history. One way to foresee their future conduct is to look at how they have behaved in the past."[9]

Readers will find that the third interconnecting theme in this volume, attention to collective memory (especially in Chapters 4–6, 8, and 9) emphasizes selective memory, distorted memories, and even amnesia.[10] The reasons why recollections are refracted or distorted have often been political and self-serving or else social and self-perpetuating in terms of cultural dominance. I have been especially concerned in recent years to explain a major cultural paradox: historical amnesia amidst so much apparent interest in the past displayed at museums, historic sites, and thematic historical places. These are not necessarily aberrations and they are significant even when they become national embarrassments. As William Faulkner once remarked, "we shall be judged by the splendor of our failures."

Because I use the phrase "collective memory" with some frequency, especially in Part III, a brief clarification of my meaning may be helpful here. I have in mind what might be called the publicly presented past: in speeches and sermons, editorials and school textbooks, museum exhibitions, historic sites, and widely noticed historical art, ranging from oil paintings to public sculpture and commemorative monuments.

Needless to say, collective memory is not merely fallible; it is also divisible. The more recent the memories, the more likely they are to become controversial when a provocation arises. Witness the contretemps over the Enola Gay exhibition at the Smithsonian Institution in 1994–95. A person who works in the past lane but lives in the present is well advised to recall two sentences from Finley Peter Dunne's Mr. Dooley: "Th' further ye get away fr'm anny peeryod th' betther ye can write about it. Ye are not subject to interruptions be people that were there."

Readers will find a fair amount of attention to iconography here, the fourth connecting theme, mainly historical art along with symbols placed on public buildings (Chapters 3 and 6). This represents a steadily growing engagement on my part for almost two decades now—one that will be even more evident in the years immediately ahead. I first began to "cultivate" an enthusiasm for art while in college. It then remained dormant for a considerable period of time; yet consistent with the beliefs of sociologist Pierre Bourdieu, my love of museums has not just been a purely aesthetic or instinctive experience. Rather, it has long since become a "trained pleasure," an "achieved aesthetic" that developed from a lengthy apprenticeship as a cultural historian.[11]

I am also tempted to say that readers will find in these pages varied approaches to the history of culture in the United States. More than half a century ago, however, Jacques Barzun casually mentioned in a brief essay that he had just read a half-baked report on "approaches to history." That prompted a chortling query from Charles Beard. "I am wondering whether you could let me know who is working on 'approaches to history'? I hope that it is some person who has studied a little history and tried to write a little also. I especially loved that blessed word 'approach.' Conceivably one could approach from any direction and on horse, on foot, or by plane!"[12]

The fact remains, though, that people who write about the past really do utilize numerous and varied approaches, not to mention having diverse intellectual dispositions. Although these essays offer many assertions and opinions, this is not a polemical book, not what the French would designate as a *livre à thèse*. I am fond of E. P. Thompson's maxim that "spleen is not a particularly effective cutting instrument," and I cherish the response to argumentation of Nathaniel Ward, a New England Puritan who was the very first public humorist in British North America. Writing as the "Simple Cobbler of Aggawam," Ward found it

> a most toylesome task to run the wild-goose chase after a well-breath'd Opinionist: they delight in vitilitigation: it is an itch that loves a life to be scrub'd: they desire not satisdiction, whereof themselves must be judges: yet in new eruptions of error with new objections, silence is sinful.

Several of the pieces that follow started out as oral presentations. All of them have been reworked into a form better suited to the eye than the ear, though I have not attempted to conceal the personal tone that some of them convey. The rationale for doing so will become evident in Chapter 1 (previously unpublished). Because each essay is of such recent vintage, there has not yet been time for new literature to emerge. So they are not yet dated, merely (in the case of some assertions, perhaps) unproved.

Certain kinds of ideas resist being readily tested or proved. As Henry Adams quipped in his *Education*: "the theory offered difficulties in measurement." I do not have many theories, actually, and even fewer measurements. My professional life has mainly been spent in the past lane. Where I have ventured an occasional prediction, or speculated about what lies ahead, only time will tell whether I hit the target. But I find solace in a sentence written by Thomas Reed Powell, a witty and wise constitutional lawyer from Harvard via Vermont. He said the following about Charles A. Beard in a book review: "Quite obviously Beard is not so well informed about the future as about the past. This will disappoint those whose assurances run along different chronological lines."[13] That's not a bad epitaph for those of us who have lived in the past lane.

≈

In 1928 two artisans were asked to repair the official yet well-used president's chair at Cornell University. In the small circular space behind a medallion displaying the carved bust of Ezra Cornell (located at the top of the chair, on the back), they discovered a closely folded slip of paper wrapped in tin-foil and tied with coarse thread. Translated from German, a single didactic sentence, written in script in 1868 when Cornell opened its doors to students, declared: "Go out into all the world and testify to what is born, even in prison walls, from strength, from patience, and from loving toil." The chair had been built on commission in a Prussian jail.

The writing of history has often come from the combined circumstances of confinement, patience, and compulsive affection for the historian's vocation. The most extreme cases are certainly memorable. Sir Walter Raleigh wrote his *History of the World* while confined for twelve years to a small room in the Tower of London. Napoleon wrote an *Outline of the Wars of Caesar* while a prisoner at St. Helena. William Smith, Jr., the last Chief Justice of colonial New York, completed volume two of his *History of the Province of New-York* while under house arrest in West Haverstraw (on the Hudson) during the American Revolution.[14]

During World War I the great Belgian historian Henri Pirenne was interned by the Germans at two successive prison camps. He passed the time by composing, entirely from memory, a stylish gem, his *Histoire de l'Europe des invasions au XVI siècle*, published posthumously in 1936. Lucien Febvre, cofounder of the Annales school in France, wrote his study of Rabelais while confined by the Nazis to his country house in 1942-44. Fernand Braudel, incarcerated by the Germans for four years during World War II, used his "enforced leisure" to compose (without access to notes) his masterpiece, *The Mediterranean and the Mediterranean World in the Age of Philip II* (1949). As Braudel recalled many years later, "it was in captivity that I wrote that enormous work, sending school copy book after school copy book to Lucien Febvre [his mentor]. Only my memory permitted this tour de force. Had it not been for my imprisonment, I would surely have written quite a different book."[15]

Historical projects composed under such vexed and inauspicious circumstances are virtually unknown in the United States. It might seem a stretch to suggest that my own pursuit of the past has meant a life of self-incarceration. The extraordinary freedom that I have enjoyed to pursue my own interests, however, has had its hostage-like obverse: the confining nonfreedom created by an enduring compulsion to compose historical essays about the American past. I recognize full well that I have shared that compulsion with many of my contemporaries.[16]

What truly separates us from those prisoners of the past cited above is that we enjoy remarkable networks of institutional and collegial support. Informational aids and modes of information retrieval have been revolutionized as our professional careers have occurred. Support from cultural foundations and from the government has increased dramatically since

1965. So, too, has public interest in the past despite our growing recognition of occasional public misperceptions and even ignorance of the past. As I try to suggest in Part I of this book, a period of enhanced professional freedom has been accompanied by an increase in personal candor about the historian's values in relation to the historian's vocation. Explanations of the American past have been presented to the public during the past generation accompanied by refreshingly candid assumptions about normative connections between the historian's commitments and the historian's craft.

Connections and commitments inevitably involve assistance, indeed patient support from friends and foundations. I am glad to acknowledge the debts that have been incurred in the process of producing these explorations.

I wish to express particular appreciation to colleagues who gave me constructive responses to chapter one: W. W. Abbot, David Brion Davis, Mary Maples Dunn, Jane Garrett, John Higham, James A. Hijiya, Linda K. Kerber, Walter LaFeber, and Paul K. Longmore. For the opportunity to write most of it under idyllic circumstances during the summer of 1995, I am indebted to the Rockefeller Foundation for a four-week "residency" at the Villa Serbelloni in Bellagio. Arthur Cameron Smith, then a Cornell undergraduate, helped me with research that summer.

For careful and critical readings of Chapter 2, my presidential address to the Organization of American Historians in 1996, I am deeply grateful to Thomas Bender, Paul J. DiMaggio, Alan Fern, Douglas S. Greenberg, Neil Harris, John Higham, James A. Hijiya, Arnita A. Jones, Stanley N. Katz, Walter LaFeber, Mary Beth Norton, Dwight T. Pitcaithley, Richard Polenberg, Joel H. Silbey, and David Thelen.

For astute assessments of the essay that became Chapter 7, I am deeply obliged to Stuart M. Blumin, David Brion Davis, Marianne Debouzy, John Higham, Akira Iriye, R. Laurence Moore, Richard Polenberg, Nick Salvatore, Rebecca Scott, and Laurence Veysey. Needless to say, I have not been able to satisfy all of their suggestions.

Michael A. Bellesiles of Emory University made a concerted effort to obtain for me the photograph of the Henry Grady statue in Atlanta, *History and Memory*; Paul S. Boyer and Stanley I. Kutler the photograph of Merle Curti; and Emmet Larkin the picture of Bessie Louise Pierce.

Jennifer DeMass, Jackie Hubble, and Yvonne Sims patiently prepared these essays for publication, often seeing more revisions than they wanted or needed to tolerate.

Sheldon Meyer at Oxford has once again been a wise, supportive, and generous senior editor. I am fortunate indeed to have had his counsel on this project prior to his retirement at the close of 1996. His assistant, Brandon Trissler, was always ready to help with matters of detail. Stephanie Sakson edited the manuscript with meticulous care. Helen B. Mules expedited the process of production at Oxford with her customary grace and good cheer.

For permission to reprint these essays I thank the *Journal of American History* for Chapter 2; Oxford University Press for Chapter 3; the Johnson School of Management at Cornell University for Chapter 4; *New York History* for Chapter 5; the Fraunces Tavern Museum for Chapter 6; *American Quarterly* and The Johns Hopkins University Press for Chapter 7; Harvard University Press for Chapter 8; and Simon and Schuster for Chapter 9.

Carol Kammen read each of these essays when it first emerged and provided candid, constructive suggestions. She also listened to several of them when they had their oral genesis. And she has graced a partnership, enriched by our mutual enthusiasm for life in the past lane, that began almost forty years ago. It has been a blessed partnership for me—a shared life in which the past has always been a vital and meaningful presence. This book is dedicated with love to three junior partners who joined us along the way.

Above Cayuga's Waters   M. K.
January 1997

PART I

The
Personal and the
Professional

Fig. 1.1   John Sloan (1871–1951), *Scrubwomen, Astor Library* (ca. 1910–11). Courtesy of the Munson-Williams-Proctor Institute, Utica, New York.

1

Personal Identity
and the Historian's
Vocation

The Personal and the Professional:
A Generational Approach

Perhaps I personify a curious paradox. Many years ago I developed a
strong admiration for such distinguished historians as Carl Becker
and Johan Huizinga, and noticed that, among other qualities, they
were notable for their intellectual detachment. Yet for decades now I have
also been a fascinated reader of historians' biographies and autobiographies,
their correspondence, interviews conducted with them, and lengthy necrolo-
gies. Consequently I feel something more than empathy with an observation
made by one senior historian (who has written an autobiography) and is
quoted approvingly by another, C. Vann Woodward, in his semiautobiog-
raphical essay. "Unless there is some emotional tie," H. Stuart Hughes
declared, "some elective affinity linking the student to his subject, the results
will be pedantic and perfunctory.[1]

That sentiment might appear, at least on the surface, to be somewhat at
odds with the professional goal of detachment. Could it be that the mind
and heart of this historian are not entirely in sync, that my vocational

practice does not coincide with my avocational pleasure? While seeking detachment in my own work without self-conscious effort, I have nonetheless wanted to know what makes other historians tick. I have assumed that in order to find answers one had to learn something about their subjective selves as three-dimensional people. I have never doubted that behind each historical text there is a flesh and blood person replete with "attitudes" waiting to be discovered. I feel somewhat reassured, therefore, by a recent pulsing of interest in notions of the "self" shown by historians of culture and literature, along with scholars in psychology and other disciplines.[2]

In the introduction to *That Noble Dream*, historian Peter Novick observed that "except with very good friends, it is considered tactless and discourteous to suggest that someone's views are a reflection of his or her background, prejudices, or psychic needs."[3] I do not wish to be either tactless or discourteous, but it seems to me that the key question is not whether personal concerns affect the historian's vocation. Of course they do, although in diverse ways and to varying degrees. The critical issue, in my view, is whether they are sufficiently important to warrant our close attention, and whether there are significant patterns that tell us something about the nature of history as a discipline and its intellectual dynamics.

My project here, consequently, is to pursue what one observer has referred to as "the reciprocity between the personal and the professional." When Pablo Picasso painted his portraits of weeping women in 1937–38, he linked the personal with the political. He was working on the *Guernica* at the time, his anguished response to brutal bombing in the Basque country by pro-Franco forces. But in the pictures of weeping women Picasso was also recording his intimate relationship with Dora Maar and *her* anguish at the Nazi invasion of Czechoslovakia. Consequently the personal, the political, and the professional became intertwined, a dominant motif in Picasso's art during a pivotal phase of its development. I wholeheartedly accept the feminist insistence that "the personal is political," and I agree that that perspective has helped to redefine the "private" as a realm of experience that should, in certain instances, at least, be subject to public inquiry.[4]

I do not for a minute deny that some historians have been exceedingly private—seemingly programmed, like Charles and Mary Beard, to destroy their papers so that subsequent snoops like myself would not be able to make such connections. The Beards, however, were rather extreme in their dogged determination to distance their professional work from their personal lives.[5]

Somewhat more representative, perhaps, is the response that David M. Potter made when he was invited to contribute an essay concerning professional autobiography to a fascinating collection of such essays that appeared in 1970 under the title *The Historian's Workshop*. Potter declined the invitation with this explanation: "I think my writing, like my metabolism, is something which I do not understand anyway, and I will make you the discouraging prediction that you will find this true of a number of contributors."[6]

The life of cultural historian Vernon L. Parrington is instructive for my purposes because he underwent a change that, ultimately, led him to anticipate a perspective I find more common in the quarter-century since 1970 than in the five decades preceding that time. According to Parrington's biographer, he initially sought to maintain a sharp separation between his private and his professional life. After he had been to Europe in 1903–04, however, a "consolidation of identity" occurred. In 1918 Parrington wrote an "Autobiographical Sketch," partially to explain and partially to assist the process of clarifying as well as consolidating his identity. He remarked at the time on the way historians do more than just inscribe themselves in their work. "We read the present into the past," he declared, "we guess at the lost facts, we seek to restore lifelikeness to the dimmed features; and we end by painting our own portrait."[7]

I have encountered endless actualizations of that theme. When Fawn Brodie agonized over her deeply skeptical biography of Joseph Smith, historian Dale Morgan, a remarkable man who served as advisor and alter ego to several Mormon historians—lapsed as well as faithful—explained why Brodie (a niece of David O. McKay, one-time president of the Church of Latter-day Saints) felt compelled to undertake such a controversial project: "the desire to interpret her own origins to herself."[8]

Wilbur R. Jacobs, who became a historian of the American West and of Indian–white relations, was born in Chicago but drove west with his family to California where he attended Pasadena schools and received his training at UCLA. Jacobs has acknowledged that his view of Western history is based upon "what has been called the development of 'self' in a lifetime of research and writing." Similarly, in a recent interview John Demos declared that his "personal experience, which clearly involved both family history and American history, has come together in some of my recent work." His advice to younger scholars? "Don't be afraid to use yourself as you study history."[9]

Now, at a fairly fundamental yet simplistic level, it is fair to say that historians—or at least some historians—have long acknowledged that link between the circumstances of personal identity and the nature of their professional vocation. Here is a representative extract from a letter left by the popular writer Bruce Catton in 1968:

About my early interest in the Civil War . . . I grew up amidst a regular flowerbed of Civil War veterans. In the small town that I infested as a lad [Benzonia, Michigan] I used to hear the old gentlemen tell war stories until I felt as if the whole affair had taken place in the next county just a few years ago. I remember especially, and maybe this is where the parade thing comes in, on Memorial Day when I was small there'd always be a meeting in the town hall, with the G A R veterans on the platform, with songs and speeches: then everyone would troop out to the village cemetery, to lay lilacs on the graves of the departed veterans. . . . I mention the whole business just to indicate how pervasive the Civil War thing was, in a small town 50 or 60 years ago.[10]

Similarly Robert G. Athearn, an influential historian of the intermountain West, published an autobiographical essay that made it seem virtually inevitable that he would one day become a historian of the United States beyond the 100th meridian. Athearn grew up near the engaging artist Charlie Russell and knew him: "the fact that he told stories of an earlier West with his brush left an impression."[11]

Thus far I have drawn illustrations from historians representing an array of sub-disciplines and originating in diverse regions of the United States. Moreover, I have not yet made crisp chronological distinctions. We have, therefore, in a sense, telescoped three generations, from Parrington and the Beards to John Demos, without qualification. We now must differentiate, however, for as Martin Duberman noted in 1969, "the way I have come to regard history as a profession is due at least as much . . . to my personal history as to my shared membership in a particular generation."[12]

I shall use Duberman, John D'Emilio, and Christopher Lasch to illuminate generational differences along two distinct lines. The first concerns motives and assumptions underlying the decision to become a historian. In two separate interviews conducted during the year before he died, Christopher Lasch (1932–94) remembered his apolitical life as a graduate student at Columbia during the 1950s. He recalled having no conversations with anyone about politics or international affairs. The history department that Lasch described was "very professionalized and all we ever really talked about was history, without much sense of its application to the present. . . . I was too busy with my studies to pay much attention to politics. . . . We were too preoccupied with the ordeal of the orals." Contrast those comments with the experience of John D'Emilio, also a Columbia Ph.D., also a student of William E. Leuchtenburg, but one passionately committed to history as an Archimedean lever. "I started graduate school in 1971," D'Emilio writes, "not to enter a profession, but to change the world." Developing the new subfield of gay history, he adds, appeared "inherently political."[13]

A second striking contrast involves the paths that brought Duberman and D'Emilio to the history of sexuality as a scholarly endeavor. Combining several autobiographical memoirs and interviews that Duberman has given, it becomes clear that his first major projects, biographies of Charles Francis Adams and James Russell Lowell, may have been remote from his private life as a closeted gay man, but they led him rather gradually and tentatively to a historical topic that really mattered to him: the antislavery movement and the history of racism in the United States. Only with the benefit of hindsight in 1991 could Duberman see that his interest in Lowell's opposition to slavery was "serving as a channel (not a substitute) for working my way into an awareness of my own oppression." [14]

Although D'Emilio initially felt that both he and gay history were professionally marginalized, he acknowledges that work on gay or lesbian topics is commonly treated as a de facto statement of identity. Despite the reality that Duberman and D'Emilio each passed through periods of disillusionment with the historical profession, in D'Emilio's case his sexual and vocational identities have always been fused, whereas Duberman endured decades of intensely difficult bifurcation. Duberman's history of Black Mountain, a personalized book in which he first "came out" publicly, was not very well received in 1972. D'Emilio's work, in contrast, has not been subjected to that kind of hostility, and the changing circumstances during the intervening years are highly instructive. [15]

Despite criticisms that were provoked by the overtly subjective aspects of Duberman's *Black Mountain*, and perhaps even because of them, during the last twenty years we have witnessed a dramatic transformation in what is regarded as acceptable or even, perhaps, as desirable. In 1975 when Henry F. May wrote the introduction to his innovative work on *The Enlightenment in America*, he concluded with these words of disclosure:

> One thing that has been forced on university teachers by their students in recent years is that they abandon the comforting pose of academic impartiality and declare their allegiances, even—contrary to all their training—admit their emotions. I am glad to try to do this, but in relation to this topic I find it simply impossible to escape a congenital ambivalence. . . . My sympathies are with those who are not sure that they understand themselves and the universe rather than with those who make hard things easy. [16]

The resonance of such candor, more commonly heard during the 1980s, has become a powerful cadenza in the '90s. "One of the things I'm trying to do in my writing now," Joan Jensen remarked in a 1994 interview, "is to talk more about myself, because it's important for historians and other scholars to let people know how their background might influence what they write." [17] I am astonished at the array of books by respected historians, published during the past decade, that begin with substantial (and sometimes deeply personal) autobiographical introductions. I find them utterly fascinating, and the roll call includes William Cronon, Anne Firor Scott, Christopher Lasch, August Meier, William M. Tuttle, Jr., Sacvan Bercovitch, Patrick H. Hutton, and Michael Zuckerman. [18] This simply was not done 25 or 30 years ago, and we can gauge the transformation in many ways.

Let's start with subjectivity. In 1933 when Charles A. Beard sought to explain to the American Historical Association that the historian's vocation was inevitably subjective—a belief that Mary Beard had already articulated two years earlier—his point was not very well received. Ten years later when Dixon Ryan Fox (formerly professor of American History at Columbia and then president of Union College) told Julian P. Boyd that "history more or less inevitably is subjective," he did so reluctantly and with a sense of disquiet. By 1970, however, the psychohistorian Robert Jay Lifton could speak positively of his field as "disciplined subjectivity [which] involves an ever expanding use of the self as one's research instrument." There were latter-day dissenters, to be sure, such as Jacques Barzun, but Lifton's comment hardly seemed heretical. [19]

It is essential for us to pause long enough to recognize the diversity of views among Beard's contemporaries about the practice of history. Otherwise my contrast between professional tendencies before and after 1970 (give or take a few years) melts down to a reductive distortion of the range of views held during the earlier twentieth century. Carl Becker, for example, believed that the value of history was ultimately moral. "Knowledge of history cannot be . . . practically applied," he insisted, "and is therefore worthless except to those who have made it . . . a personal possession. The value of history is indeed, not scientific but moral. . . . [It] enables us to control, not society but ourselves. . . ." W. E. B. Du Bois, writing from a different perspective, defined history as "an art using the results of science." [20]

Few among us would deny that members of that generation had opinions and biases, not to mention personal lives that shaped the histories they wrote. Based upon the research that sustains this project, however, I am persuaded that many among us have underestimated the extent to which they concealed or repressed personal concerns that today would be more openly acknowledged and expressed. Women historians like Bessie Louise Pierce of the University of Chicago who conveyed bitter resentment in personal correspondence and conversations about their shabby treatment by male colleagues rarely emphasized or discussed gender in their scholarship. On the basis of their published work alone, moreover, you would not have a clue that Charles S. Sydnor was a segregationist and a deeply committed Christian, or that Richard Hofstadter felt alienated from liberal democracy through the 1940s, or that F. O. Matthiessen was gay.[21]

In 1944 the young Hofstadter sent Arthur M. Schlesinger, Jr., a copy of his recently published essay, "U. B. Phillips and the Plantation Legend." One sentence from Schlesinger's response speaks volumes about the professional norms of Phillips's generation as well as Hofstadter's own cohort: "A whole series ought to be done on the concealed social presuppositions of our recent American historians as these presuppositions come out in the history." Four years ago, when I told Merle Curti (1897–1996) about the subject of this inquiry, he replied that "before identity and role had become as common in discourse and everyday language as is currently true, few historians among my contemporaries ever seriously verbalized these concerns." [22]

I am convinced that this commitment to discretion explains the incredible blandness of that first wave of book-length autobiographies written by historians of the United States late in their lives during the 1960s and 1970s. For Arthur M. Schlesinger, Sr., John D. Hicks, Roy F. Nichols, Dexter Perkins, and Thomas A. Bailey the watchword seems to have been, quite literally, don't bother to ask because I am not going to tell you anything truly revealing.[23]

It is highly symptomatic, I believe, that when Gilbert C. Fite (born in 1915) gave his presidential address to the Western Historical Association in 1986, he chronicled the dramatic failures of a South Dakota farm family living on the frontier many decades earlier. Only at the very end, and rather reluctantly, did Fite acknowledge that he had been describing his mother's family. Although Fite received his professional training at a time when detachment was considered a primary objective, at the age of 75 he conceded that he had written agricultural history in a particular way "because of my earlier years growing up on or near farms in South Dakota during the depression. . . . My personal involvement with the ups and downs of U.S. farming has contributed significantly to my work." [24]

Allan Nevins, on the other hand, rejected his personal origins in order to achieve professional objectives and a more congenial lifestyle. As he wrote to a colleague in 1928 when he decided to leave Cornell for Columbia, "after a laborious farm boyhood, I belong to the city, and not to the country." [25] (Cornell University, located on the site of Ezra Cornell's working farm, was even more pastoral in 1928 than it is today.)

One of the observations most readily remembered from Richard Hofstadter's last complete book, *The Progressive Historians* (1968), is summed up in this sentence. "If there is a single way of characterizing what has happened in our historical writing since the 1950's, it must be, I believe, the rediscovery of complexity in American history: an engaging and moving simplicity . . . has given way to a new awareness of the multiplicity of forces."[26] Although I believe Hofstadter was correct, that judgment has a misleading side effect: namely, the tendency to feel that historians active during the first half of the twentieth century were less complex people than ourselves. There is an inclination to assume, when we think about the issue at all, that it must have been easier and simpler to "do" history in those days. Having read their correspondence, their diaries, and their unpublished memoirs, I am not persuaded of that. In addition to feeling profound ambivalence, even uncertainty, about the relationship between their personal identities and their vocational productions, they suffered from a range of anxieties—sometimes verging upon despair—just as we often do.

Let me illustrate that point with instances from two prominent historians as different from one another as they could possibly be. Listen to the tones of blockage and frustration mingled with hope. The point, of course, is not

Fig. 1.2 Richard Hofstadter (1916–70). Photograph by Dwight W. Webb, courtesy of Alfred A. Knopf, Inc.

that these sentiments are unusual, only that we do not customarily connect them to the historian's vocation and sense of self two generations ago.

- Having read hither and yon in New England theology during 1935, Perry Miller reached the point where "I felt I no longer understood it because I had nothing that Henry James would have called a 'point of reference.'" Consequently for several weeks "I have been quietly reading St. Thomas Aquinas, with a sense of magnificent vistas opening before me, and a feeling that if I can get the time I shall, in the next five years, write really a great book on early New England." [27]

- "I no longer feel that I have anything urgent to say and that it makes very little difference to me or the world at large whether my books get written or not. No doubt this is a passing mood, but if you know how one makes such moods pass, do let me know." Richard Hofstadter. [28]

It seems highly appropriate here to quote a remark once made by Louis I. Kahn, the great architect: "No one ever really paid the price of a book, only the price of printing it." [29] And as historian Jonathan Spence has observed in an interview, each of his books "was written in response to a certain moment in my life. I don't know which was changing what. I'm never the same after a book. . . . I think I've been changed profoundly by each book." [30]

As provocative and as meaningful as those comments may sound—they make sense and they speak to us as authors—there is also a flip side, both literally as well as figuratively. T. S. Eliot once voiced its essence with penetrating charm:

> In our time, we read too many new books, or are oppressed by the thought of the new books which we are neglecting to read. . . . We are encumbered not only with too many new books: we are further embarrassed by too many periodicals, reports and privately circulated memoranda. In the endeavor to keep up with the most intelligent of these publications we may sacrifice the three permanent reasons for reading: the acquisition of wisdom, the enjoyment of art, and the pleasure of entertainment. [31]

Amongst all the extracts that I offer in this essay, that one, I believe, most nearly approaches being timeless.

I shall return, momentarily, to what we might call the complexity of so-called simpler times in the evolution of history as a profession, but first I want to draw attention to one more intergenerational contrast I find striking. Although it will not come as a major surprise, it needs to be noticed in this context. R. W. Southern, a distinguished English medievalist, offered the following observation in a presidential address to the Royal Historical Society in 1973: "So far as there is a central tradition in our historical writing, it arises from this recurrent need to understand and stabilize the present by reviving the experience of the past." If that sounded wise, or simply unexceptionable 24 years ago, it surely has become passé in our own time because currently we tend to speak of "an unstable past," not merely because we recognize the instability that existed in times past—as did Richard Southern's generation of historians—but because we also recognize, to a greater degree than our predecessors I believe, that the past is hotly contested in the present, and consequently that new knowledge and fresh interpretations of the past are more likely to throw our culture off stride rather than stabilize it.[32]

Although the past can, indeed, serve us as a compass, it is just as likely to lead us into dangerous shoals as it is likely to lead us beside still waters. Knowledge of the past may be precious, but it most certainly cannot assure stability. In Edward Albee's play, *Who's Afraid of Virginia Woolf?* (1962), there is a moment of hysteria when George, an associate professor of history at a small college, exclaims: "Read history. I know something about history." [33] The actual utility of his knowledge is unclear and unfocused. But it surely is not a source of stability for George, his wife, or his collegiate community. There is nothing inherently stabilizing about the past.

Religion, Ideology, and the Historian's Vocation

Throughout this essay I shall continue to make comparisons between historians' personal identities and their vocational practices before and after circa 1970. Although I am more impressed by the changes than by continuities, the latter most certainly exist and must not be minimized. I shall try not to. I also intend to suggest that the notion of simpler times when doing history was less complex—in the half-century prior to 1970, let's say—reveals a lack of perspective on our part based upon insufficient information. For professional people whose expertise is supposed to be the past, we live in a time-warp with some weird notions about our predecessors. Perhaps all that that means is that we are, after all, historians rather than genealogists. Most of us do not pursue the problematic nature of our work-related pedigrees.

In calling attention to the complexity of so-called simpler times, I will look first at the roles of religion and ideology. Then, in the third section, I will turn to other aspects of human experience in order to show how historians come to terms with the personal and attempt to resolve intimate concerns that affect their work. In the process we will look at race and racism, at gender-related discrimination, at sexual orientation, and at physical disabilities. In the fourth section we will turn to graduate and undergraduate teaching (the former involving ambivalent relationships more often than we recognize), and in the fifth section some of the ways historians have dealt with critical "feedback." I find this last category especially fascinating because intellectual contestation can be immensely stimulating and constructive, but also depressing and sometimes even dreadfully destructive. If I may post a roadsign here: Parables ahead, proceed with caution.

Religion

Richard W. Southern suggested many years ago that history attained stature as an academic field in the middle of the nineteenth century "on a wave of opposition to theological dogmatism and impatience with ancient restrictions, without anyone being clear whether the subject had a method, or a public, or indeed whether it was a recognizable subject at all." Not everyone, by any means, but many people turned to history because they grew weary of religious disputes.[34] So faith, or at least theology as a mode of understanding, came to be at least partially supplanted by history as a significant way of knowing.

That pattern of change carried over to the United States during the first half of the twentieth century in several ways, one of them being an initial but subsequently abandoned desire on the part of many historians, such as Parrington, John D. Hicks, and Thomas A. Bailey, to pursue the ministry as a calling. Among the documents that survive from Parrington's pioneering years at the University of Oklahoma is a small notebook labeled "Notes on the Old Testament" (dated 1901). Hicks wanted to be a Methodist preacher (his desire perhaps prompted by immense pressure from his parents), and as a Stanford undergraduate Bailey wanted to be a Baptist preacher. All of them eventually put fundamentalism behind them in favor of American history: cultural, political, and diplomatic. It may not be unfair to say that each young man replaced one kind of gospel with another.[35]

It is fairly dangerous to generalize in too facile a manner about the so-called crisis of faith during the later nineteenth and earlier twentieth century. Leopold von Ranke was a fervent believer and wrote that every age was "immediate to God." Many of his admirers subscribed to those sentiments. Cornell's first president, however, Andrew Dickson White, a founder of the American Historical Association, always felt torn between faith and doubt. Hence the stimulus for his best-known work, *A History of the Warfare of Science with Theology in Christendom* (1896, two volumes).[36]

One legacy of White's outlook, which was shared by many others, is that the history of religion came to be strikingly marginalized in the curricula of most history departments throughout the twentieth century. It almost feels as though the initial clause of the First Amendment of the U.S. Constitution had a kind of chilling effect upon religion being regarded as an appropriate subject for historical inquiry and instruction in higher education. Here is an intriguing extract from a letter written in 1919 by J. Franklin Jameson to a professor of history at Berkeley. It concerns "the general question of the teaching of church history in state universities":

> All over the country we have been very shy of bringing that discipline into secular institutions of education. In some places, heads of departments would only get themselves into trouble by suggesting such a thing to Philistine trustees. Here in Washington, the secretary of the Smithsonian Institution, in his capacity as secretary of the Bureau of American Ethnology, prints abundant material every year respecting the religion of the Pawnee or the Hopi or the Hidatsa, but if the publication committee of the American Historical Association presents to him in its annual report a paper relating in any way to the history of the Christian religion—which some would think quite as important as that of the Hidatsa—he cuts it right out, in deference to supposed congressional susceptibilities and the probability that some long-haired Member of Congress may object.
>
> You can judge how far the University of California can go, and I cannot, but I do feel that to exclude the history of Christianity and of the Christian churches from a university does limit to an unfortunate extent the appreciation of history as it really has been, by most students, and that it would be a good thing if circumstances everywhere permitted the introduction of organized courses in church history. Without them, young minds are not likely to get the whole story of the past; with them, they might make a better approach toward understanding the history of human thought and feeling, instead of confining themselves, as they are rather prone to do, to the history of politics.[37]

Residual patterns of unease concerning relationships between religion and the historical profession have persisted throughout the twentieth century. In 1975, to cite just one example, the Conference on Faith and History, an organization of scholars with a serious journal (*Fides et Historia*) that started in 1967, requested from the American Historical Association the status of an affiliated society. The AHA's Standing Committee on Affiliated Societies recommended against affiliation for the Conference on Faith and History "on the grounds that its purpose was not clear and, therefore, might not be consistent with that of the AHA." The AHA Council reversed that decision in 1979, yet we should not be startled to hear such cerebral historians as Stephen J. Tonsor, an ardent believer, observing that the sources of the "decay of a providential and universal historical idea lie in the desacralization of history and in the cultural relativism implicit in the historicist world-view."[38]

Although I have no sufficient explanation, I find it intriguing that similar tensions do not seem to exist in the realm of British historical scholarship. R. H. Tawney, for example, was an openly devout Christian, but that did not undermine his credibility or stature as a historian. As one distinguished economic historian remarked of Tawney in an autobiographical essay, "his religious faith was central to his work, even as an historian."[39] The same was true of Christopher Dawson and David Knowles (both Roman Catholic), and of Herbert Butterfield, a lay preacher in the Methodist Church who wrote *Christianity and History* (1949), and insisted that "diplomacy and power-politics could be understood in Christian terms and justified according to Christian categories."[40] Arnold Toynbee advocated the establishment of some sort of syncretist religion, and on more than one occasion he defined history as a vision of "God revealing Himself in action to souls that were sincerely seeking Him."[41]

Perhaps the most striking example of a British historian who not only felt comfortable infusing his religious beliefs into his scholarship, but did so without any loss of respect for the latter, was Roger Anstey (1927–79), an ardent Methodist who taught at the University of Ibadan in Nigeria and then at the University of Kent in Canterbury. Anstey emphasized the eighteenth-century intellectual and religious origins of antislavery thought in Britian. He stressed that many slaves were inspired by the "idea of Christian freedom." David Brion Davis has summarized the linkage between personal identity and the historian's vocation in an appreciative memoir written right after Anstey's untimely death:

> Because historical scholarship has become so thoroughly secularized, we generally consider it bad taste to discuss private and supposedly irrelevant religious beliefs, though of course we attach considerable significance to a historian's political ideology. Thus Roger's last book, *The Atlantic Slave Trade and British Abolition*, was generally interpreted as an anti-Marxist work because it demolished many of the premises of Eric Williams' *Capitalism and Slavery*. No one could deny Anstey's desire to discredit economic determinism and to counter Williams' contention that humanitarianism became convincing in Britian only when it served material interests. But it is a serious mistake, I think, to translate Anstey's arguments into political terms, for he was, as he once referred to himself, a "working historian who is also a believer." He scrupulously avoided sermonizing, being convinced that the truth, if once uncovered, would in the long run speak for itself. But if his professional writings seem to conform to the standards of secular history, every work reflects the world view of a devout Christian who literally *lived* the Protestant ethic.

Roger candidly affirmed his belief in history as the Providence of God under the lordship of Christ, observing that modern pretensions to "objective history" only conceal unconscious presuppositions which, "since we are all in some measure children of our age, usually consist of a varying mish-mash of woolly liberal, neo-Marxian, vaguely Weberian or vulgar Freudian ideas."

Davis then observed that Anstey lived in the same "spiritual world as the evangelical abolitionists. If this meant that he lacked some of the detachment of secular historians, it also gave him unrivaled insights into the historical meaning of sin, redemption, Providence, and retribution."[42]

It is noteworthy, I believe, that scholars like Anstey have had comparatively few counterparts among Americans who are historians of the United States. (Members of the profession are likely to differ, perhaps, as to whether or not that is a good thing.) Arthur S. Link comes to mind, for example, because he is a believing Presbyterian who openly declares that he and his work are instruments of God's purposes. But unlike Anstey, Link did not personalize his extensive work on Woodrow Wilson and the Progressive era. Instead, there is only one essay, appearing in a *theological* journal, not a historical publication, in which Link, perhaps paradoxically, declared that he

cannot escape the conviction that we cannot begin to know what it means to be Christians in our vocations until we have abandoned the absurd practice of compartmentalizing our lives and come to see that living by faith means living by faith as historians, economists, scientists, and so on, in every detail of daily work.

He went on to add that "God gives us power to fulfill our vocation's demands," and concluded with a rhetorical question: "What does God's lordship say to the historian in his daily vocation, in his work as a historian? I can be a true and faithful historian only as I remember that God, the Lord of history, is also the sole judge of history."[43]

To older members of our guild, and to his colleagues, Arthur Link's Christian commitment is not news. Younger members of the profession, however, who know Link only through his publications, will have almost no sense of that commitment from reading them.[44] If we reach back one generation to a comparable historian of Southern origins, Charles S. Sydnor (1898-1954), who specialized in U.S. political history from the mid-eighteenth century to the mid-nineteenth century, we find no published traces of his Christian commitment at all. From his papers at Duke University, however, we learn that he was quite active in the Presbyterian Church, and that he corresponded with people who taught Bible studies at colleges and in their respective congregations.[45]

At the very end of voluminous boxes of Sydnor's correspondence I found a handwritten schematization—fifteen small sheets in all, bearing this heading: The Christian as an Interpreter of History. Early in that text Sydnor made this arresting observation:

> In a sense, much & perhaps most of the written history of the Western world has been written by Christians—medieval chronicles, probably monographs [*sic*]. And yet if one reads at random in a library of American history he could seldom make an accurate deduction about the religion or lack of it of the author whose book was in his hand. Internal evidence would perhaps more often reveal whether the writer was American or foreign, N. Englander or Southerner, Negro or Jew, than whether he was Christian, agnostic or something else. Christians have written much history, but they had not in most cases, consciously & deliberately interpreted it as Christians. It is probably best that it has been as it has been. Historians seldom know the simple facts well enough to put them down in clear & proper order; much less do they have knowledge & wisdom to give a sound & sensible Christian interpretation to narratives of the founding of South Carolina, the Battle of Bunker Hill, or the presidential election of 1948.[46]

Sydnor then speculated ("perversely" he said) whether a genuinely good Christian could be a first-rate historian. Why not? Because "the man who believes in & whose life has been cast with people who attempt to live according to the principles is likely to have great difficulty understanding the motives that lie behind much human action. The forces that propelled Washington, T.J., Franklin, Napoleon, Caesar were in large measure non-Christian. The 'good' man is not likely to be the man best qualified to understand the ambition, selfishness, restlessness, & conventionalized codes of conduct" that motivated many of the most influential people in times past.

The remainder of Sydnor's sheets strike a much more positive note by enumerating qualities that Christianity can supply to the historian: a standard of values, compassion, "discrimination between sin & sinner," a broad view of human nature and human behaviors, a profound sensitivity to human fallibility, and, finally, "a thorough awareness of the high levels to which men ought to aspire" along with "the dignity & worth of each separate individual."[47]

We need not wonder here why a nonbelieving Christian or even a non-Christian could not also share these qualities. This is not the place to challenge Sydnor or even engage him in dialogue. I simply find it fascinating that he obviously devoted a lot of time and attention to such issues, that they mattered greatly to him, and yet he chose not to publish his reflections upon them. In each of those respects I am persuaded that he was highly representative of most historians in his generational cohort.[48]

It should be observed that among historians half a generation younger than Sydnor, a pattern emerged of explicitly acknowledging the intellectual and philosophical influence of theologian Reinhold Niebuhr. Whereas Henry F. May notes Niebuhr's actual impact upon his *religious* sensibilities, C. Vann Woodward was attracted to Niebuhr's emphasis upon irony, Arthur M. Schlesinger, Jr., felt affinity for Niebuhr's anticommunism, and Carl Schorske could build upon Niebuhr's "tragic vision." I am inclined to believe that the father of neo-orthodoxy would surely have mixed feelings about being so influential for predominantly secular reasons, however worthy.[49]

To the extent that one can suitably speak of a historian's faith during the 1940s, '50s, and '60s, it seems to have been a "faith" founded upon that trinitarian emphasis—irony, anticommunism, and tragic vision—rather than evangelical, ecclesiastical aspirations, or saving grace.[50] The principal exception? Perhaps historians of Europe who are observant Roman Catholics. Although their story is beyond the purview of this essay, their declarations of faith and their concern with the connection between personal identity and the historian's vocation must at least be acknowledged here.[51]

Among Catholics as well as Protestants, however, the primary sources that I have seen tend, more often than not, to reveal either/or situations, that is, religious faith may or may not create a problem for the practicing historian, but most of the time "not." (It can, on occasion, create an advantage.) Even in the case of Henry F. May, who has wavered between belief and doubt, his uncertainties have not fundamentally affected *how* he writes history. His interest in issues of belief has simply disposed him to be especially (though not exclusively) interested in the history of religion in the United States.[52]

Among Mormon historians there appears to be a pattern that is distinctive in some respects because it does not clearly follow the trajectory of generational change except in this regard: Contemporary scholars who are practicing Mormons are more likely than their predecessors to acknowledge openly the complexity of their particular vocational challenge. Richard L. Bushman explained at the very outset of his book *Joseph Smith and the Beginnings of Mormonism*,

> Believing Mormons like myself understand the origins of the book of Mormon quite differently than others. How can a description of Joseph Smith's revelations accommodate a Mormon's perception of events and still make sense to a general audience? My method has been to relate events as the participants themselves experienced them, using their own words where possible. Insofar as the revelations were a reality to them, I have treated them as real in this narrative. General readers will surely be left with questions

about the meaning of these experiences, but at least they will have an understanding of how early Mormons perceived the world.[53]

Juanita Brooks, a self-taught Mormon historian who became profession-alized (if I may use such a word) through intensive correspondence with Dale Morgan and contact with scholars at the Huntington Library, emerged a full generation before Bushman and faced a similar though somewhat more precarious situation. Charles S. Peterson has described that situation superbly in his introduction to Brooks's autobiographical *Quicksand and Cactus*. I cannot improve upon his intriguing account.

> Obviously her relationship with the church was of the essence. She was of the Mormon community, born to it, steeped in its tradition, and with a keen and loving sense of what it meant to be Mormon. Unlike many other Utah intellectuals of the era, she had no desire to leave Mormon Country either for distant centers or by way of close affiliation with institutions that would redefine or redirect her life. She remained a believer, on the other side of what she called the "philosophical Great Divide" from Morgan, who felt "absolutely no necessity to postulate the existence of God." "An unshakable conviction of the reality of God," he wrote her, "is basic in your whole attitude towards Mormonism. It gives an emotional color that subtly shapes all your thinking . . . The result is that when you contemplate Mormon history, there is a vast area of the probable and the possible that you accept without much question." She replied that not only would she have to make her own "judgements in the light of . . . the reality of God" but that the Church was "as much my church as it is . . . anyone elses [*sic*]" and that she was "loyal to it." Yet, in view of what she had come to know about the Mountain Meadows Massacre, she was unable to "yield unquestioning obedience" to the Church's efforts to suppress the Massacre's full and real history. In short, she was convinced that "nothing but the truth is good enough for the Church to which I belong, and that God does not expect us to lie in his name." As "an honest historian" she owed it to herself and "to my readers to tell the truth, for the truth suppressed is its own kind of lie."
>
> In her determination to examine the truth even if it was embarrassing, she met opposition in many forms. The social atmosphere itself was not inviting. In St. George [Utah] few understood her passion for opening the record. Although she longed to "write openly and unashamedly" her sense that her neighbors were unsympathetic became so strong that she did much of her research and writing under the closest secrecy.[54]

Brooks's study of the *Mountain Meadows Massacre* (1950) came to be regarded as an expression of the "profound emotional bond between . . . this quiet little woman . . . and the people of whom she writes." She had used history, as one biographical study puts it, for the elemental purpose of revealing "the emotional complexities" of her region and her church. For many Mormons Brooks had accomplished a "paradoxical alchemy whereby affirmation and belief arise from pain and despair."[55]

The dramatic story of Fawn McKay Brodie's tortuous relationship with the Church of Latter-day Saints will one day be told in its complex entirety. Half a dozen salient aspects of the story deserve to be mentioned here, however. Born in 1915 in Ogden, Utah, she was raised a Mormon at Huntsville, a small community in the nearby mountain valley. Following her undergraduate education at the University of Chicago in 1936, this precocious young woman became intensely curious about Joseph Smith, founder of her family's religion during the later 1820s and '30s in upstate New York. The more research she did, the more skeptical she became about claims that had been traditionally accepted by orthodox members of her faith concerning Smith's behavior and accomplishments.[56]

As an added push, her process of secularization accelerated when she decided to marry a brilliant young political scientist named Bernard Brodie in 1936. Her family objected to the match because he was Jewish, and his family objected because she was Mormon. Seven years later, however, when

Fig. 1.3   Fawn M. Brodie (1915–81). Courtesy of the Manuscripts Division, University of Utah Library, Salt Lake City.

she told her parents that she had won the coveted Alfred A. Knopf Fellowship in Biography for her work-in-progress on Smith, they were nervously supportive despite her warning that they would undoubtedly be criticized for "having reared a wayward daughter." In a second letter, knowing full well the consequences that she (and they) risked, Brodie sought to comfort if not reassure them by emphasizing the integrity that they had transmitted to her. "I want to spare you all the criticism possible. You have done nothing to deserve any. You brought us all up to revere the truth, which is the noblest ideal a parent can instill in his children, and the fact that we come out on somewhat different roads certainly is no reflection on you." One of her parents wrote on the bottom of that communication: "a sweet letter. She's a darling. Can hardly wait to see her." [57]

Dale Morgan warned Fawn Brodie in the autumn of 1943 that her situation was especially precarious because her uncle, David O. McKay, having become an Apostle in the LDS Church, was therefore a prospective president of the Church. As Morgan phrased it in his inimitably frank way, McKay must have felt that "it would be a hell of a note to be uncle to a naturalistic biographer of the Prophet; it would be a reflection on him. If he couldn't keep the members of his own family converted, what future was there for him as President of the Church?" In March 1946, in fact, five months following publication of *No Man Knows My History*, McKay attacked Fawn and her family publicly at a meeting held at Brigham Young University. The assault concentrated on Fawn's "upbringing" and harshly insulted her father. [58]

Throughout this intensely difficult period of crisis in Brodie's life, Morgan remained wonderfully supportive, both professionally and personally. He served as a combination of guru and therapist. He understood better than anyone else she knew, with the possible exception of her husband, just how intricately her personal identity was intertwined with her professional aspirations as a writer. A long letter that Morgan sent her in January 1946 is particularly forthright about her ambivalent feelings:

> I have an idea that you couldn't come full circle yet in liberating yourself from the church. You have an intellectual but not yet an emotional objectivity about Mormonism. You are still in certain of a mood of rebellion, and you sometimes give vent to a sharp intellectual scorn for the Mormon way of life which practically speaking is an intolerance for it. I suspect that you won't begin to have really generous feelings, a live-and-let-live philosophy, until you have finished disentangling [*sic*] yourself from the religion.

Five months later Morgan returned to his casually officious yet cordially received comments. "Your *criticism* of Joseph [Smith] is the reflection of your background, and your scholarly fairness about him is the counteracting effect of your effort toward objectivity. Your emotional rebellion tended to persuade you to write much more harshly about the Mormons than your mature intelligence would let you!"[59]

Fawn Brodie was ordered to appear before a Mormon Mission Court in Cambridge, Massachusetts, on June 1, 1946, "for investigation of alleged wrong-doing and to show cause . . . why you should not be excommunicated" for apostasy. She was, and Dale Morgan subsequently reported to her that devout Mormon women liked to say that in writing her book she had "committed suicide." Morgan then added, supportively, "I find this very interesting, for I never knew a corpse that had more energy and zest for living, or more interesting plans for the future. Tell me, do you sleep in a casket every night?" Right up to her death in 1981, after 35 years, *No Man Knows My History* remained a cause célèbre among Mormons. As one scholar told her after attending the annual Mormon history meetings in Independence, Missouri, "in all the talk with the historians, informally and in session, one is confronted constantly with 'Brodie' uttered with unmistakable passion in either respect or defiance. Can any other modern biography have so persistently potent a life and continue so vividly to symbolize so much to such divergent camps of people?"[60]

During the later 1960s Fawn engaged in an extended, frank, and revealing correspondence with a Roman Catholic priest assigned to the Newman Center at Utah State University in Logan. Monsignior Jerome Stoffel quite candidly wished to convert dissenting and lapsed Mormons to Catholicism, and in doing so became something of a dissenting authority on Mormon theology and historiography. Despite a curiously naive (yet earnest) quality in his letters, he managed to elicit revealing responses from Brodie—especially for purposes of the focus of this essay. Here are just two illustrative extracts. In the first she expresses her affection for the New Testament. "But I do reject the supernatural aspects of the Christian story," Brodie continued, "and I also stay away from organized religion of any sort. The 'agony' of disillusionment for me had to do with the pain I caused my family. The disillusionment itself was . . . a liberating experience."[61]

Brodie always retained a strong sense that the personal and the vocational were inseparable. Six months later she wrote the following to Monsignior Stoffel:

> I am fascinated by the close relationship between biographers and the subject or subjects they choose to write about. It is a deeply personal relationship, highly subjective, and difficult to analyze unless one knows the biographer well. One simply doesn't spend years delving into the intimate life of someone else unless it is to try to resolve some kind of inner conflict of one's own, or unless the subject of the biography reminds one in a compelling sense of

someone who has deeply influenced one's own life. Analysis of one's own motivations is extremely treacherous, since we are all so gifted at self-deception.[62]

Although Brodie was unquestionably ambitious, and undeniably had a penchant for flamboyant projects (the life of Sir Richard Burton, Jefferson and personal race relations, and a psychobiography of Richard Nixon), she explicitly considered herself a private person. Hence her sardonic response in 1980 when she received an inquiry from a graduate student writing a dissertation concerned with Mormon historiography. Because the student devoted an entire chapter to *No Man Knows My History*, he (or she) asked Brodie six direct questions:

The areas in which I would welcome your comments include:

1. The degree which Mormon authorities either facilitated or impeded your research efforts;

2. The state of your religious convictions at the time of your research and also at the time of your excommunication;

3. Any difficulties intellectually, psychologically, or emotionally which your Mormon background posed in your work;

4. Any other influences which had a bearing on your interpretation of Smith's life;

5. Your present ties to the Mormon intellectual community;

6. Whether or not you contemplate ever reentering the field of Mormon studies.[63]

Brodie's prompt response was curt yet candid. It is worth reading in its entirety.

I am rather amused at your letter, and also a little baffled by it. You say you are not invading my privacy, yet you ask the most intimate questions about my psychological and emotional state at crucial periods of my life. You do not tell me if you are male or female, or if you like or dislike my book.

You will forgive me, then, for being brief:

1. I was given permission to see published materials in the LDS Church library in Salt Lake City in 1944, also the Nauvoo Temple Record, in the Genealogical Library.

2. I was not a devout Mormon when I began the research on my book.

3. My Mormon background made me intensely curious about Joseph Smith, and particularly, in the beginning, the sources of the Book of Mormon. Had I not been brought up a Mormon I would have had no interest in Joseph Smith.

4. My classes in sociology, and my reading of anthropological literature convinced me before I began writing the book that the American Indians were Mongoloid in origin, and therefore the Book of Mormon must have been written by Joseph Smith and not translated from sacred plates given him by an angel.

5. I have many friends among "Jack-Mormons," especially in Salt Lake City.

6. I have no intention of writing in the Mormon field, save an occasional book review.[64]

And she didn't. Less than a year later she died of cancer.

Ideology

Historians have discussed at some length, and for many years now, the relative merits of detachment versus engagement or activism in their capacity as historians. I cannot begin to do justice to the diversity of their views or to the traces of their attitudinal odysseys. Nonetheless, to ignore the matter entirely in this context might be comparable to a consideration of *Hamlet* without the prince.

Ultimately, however, I must confess that my feelings about this topic are intellectually ambivalent. On the one hand, I am convinced that we cannot adequately understand, never mind evaluate, important historical scholarship without knowing something about the political or ideological dispositions of the men and women who produced that scholarship. On the other hand, though, I am also persuaded that there is no predictable relationship between ideology and quality. Carl Becker was comparatively apolitical, David Potter conservative, Richard Hofstadter essentially liberal after he rejected Marxism in the 1940s, and David Montgomery a radical—yet each one of them wrote (or continues to write in Montgomery's case) profoundly influential history. Ideology may enhance *or* detract from quality, but ideology alone certainly does not determine quality.

Let's start by putting on record positions that come fairly close to being polar opposites. J. H. Hexter wrote the following in 1954 in an essay that long ago came to be regarded as a classic:

For a small part of my day I live under a comfortable rule of bland intellectual irresponsibility vis-à-vis the Great Issues of the Contemporary World, a rule that permits me to go off half-cocked with only slight and occasional compunction. But during most of my day—that portion of it that I spend in dealing with the Great and Not-So-Great Issues of the World between 1450 and 1650—I live under an altogether different rule. The commandments of that rule are:

1. Do not go off half-cocked.
2. Get the story straight.
3. Keep prejudices about present-day issues out of this area.

In a presidential address given in 1976 to the Royal Historical Society, Geoffrey Elton used even stronger language. Those who would place history in the service of present-day needs "lead it straight to destruction and damnation."[65]

Contrast with those views a perspective John Higham offered in 1962 that I also regard as a classic formulation:

> Discussion has not ordinarily gone beyond the point of recognizing that the historian's own values inevitably color his writing. At best, we have acknowledged this coloring as a mark of our humanity. Professional historians have hardly begun to consider moral insight as something they can gain by skilled and patient historical study, not merely as something they cannot keep out of it. Historical method acquires a new dimension when we begin to speak of the criticism of life in addition to the technical criticism of documents. Then moral evaluation becomes a professional task, not just a predilection of our unprofessional selves.

We might add, for emphasis, these two sentences written by Henry Glassie in 1977: "If you cannot enter passionately into the life of your own times, you cannot enter compassionately into the life of the past. If the past is used to escape the present, the past will escape you."[66]

As I have already suggested, distinguished historians can be found on both sides of this dialogue. Partially, though *only* partially, the generational contrast that I proposed earlier is applicable here. It is undeniably true that historians of Hexter's generation, and especially its spokesmen, were committed to an ethos of detachment and politesse, even when they acknowledged in personal correspondence that what most concerned them was the *appearance* of detachment and politesse.[67]

Lest that sound suspiciously like a sweeping accusation of hypocrisy or insincerity, listen to Thomas Cochran's heartfelt letter to Merle Curti in 1948. Cochran did not care for the academic conservatism that he encountered in the vicinities of Boston and Philadelphia, so he worried that because of his particular scholarly projects he might, as he put it, "succumb to the environment":

> I have to understand businessmen as thoroughly as possible, which means I even have to associate with them to some extent, and it is a truism, judged by historical writing, that one comes to admire the people one studies. So far, however, I think I am still the same kind of mild, partial, compromising socialist that I always have been. That is, as nearly as I can figure an average of

my beliefs, I'd like a society that had enough socialized basic industry, transportation, communication and services to provide a stabilizing force in times of depression and provide a field for government enterprise; enough cooperative groups to encourage further development in that direction; but no prohibition on free enterprise in any field, even though it might compete with one of the other forms. In a way this is probably a have your cake and eat it too kind of program— although it's about what [Norman] Thomas has advocated. At any rate, I am sure that emotionally I favor the mixed society rather than the Orthodox Russian model, even if the latter were well governed.[68]

During the 1950s historians such as Richard Hofstadter and John Higham —both of them still rather early in their careers—gave a great deal of nuanced consideration to their political orientation and its implications for their work. Late in 1953 Hofstadter wrote privately what he called a "confession of faith":

I have grown a great deal more conservative in the past few years, whatever the cause. I do hope, at least, that my conservatism is libertarian in its bias. At any rate, I think I can say that I have not given up any significant portion of the human values I had 20 years ago when I was more "radical"— but I do have different ideas as to the extent to which some of them can be realized, and I think a lot of them have been (which takes some of the steam out of me).[69]

John Higham responded in 1954 to publication of a new essay by Merle Curti, his former Ph.D. mentor, with these striking reflections—prompted in part, perhaps, by the mindless wave of support at that time for McCarthyite anti-Communism:

I have gradually moved some distance from your point of view, but I am glad to be now—and I am quite sure for the rest of my days—in the broad liberal tradition for which you have spoken so eloquently. . . . An aristocratic liberal, who has come to think of the tyranny of mass opinion as the worst of the dangers confronting us, and whose faith in human intelligence is no longer anchored to a scientific philosophy but rather to shreds of traditional moral values and the hope of a new moral philosophy.[70]

When we turn from reflective liberals with assorted modifiers affixed—alienated in the case of Hofstadter, "aristocratic" in the case of Higham (yet prodded by a profound social conscience)—to historians on the left, we encounter the most divergent pattern of all because the trajectories of radical historians vary so widely. Christopher Lasch, for example, came from the Progressive tradition and was raised in a politically liberal home. Following his utterly apolitical career as a Ph.D. candidate at Columbia he turned against liberalism and coupled historical writing with the radical tradition of social criticism. By 1968, however, he was openly critical of the

New Left and opposed the views of Staughton Lynd in particular, a stance that he would regret toward the end of his life.[71]

Lasch remained empathetic to the socialist left and proceeded to mystify many people, admirers as well as skeptics, by trying to combine Freudian and Marxian insights, by differentiating between social criticism (a necessary good) and ideology (an unnecessary evil). Lasch wanted to believe that for himself, and for others, detachment and commitment were not merely possible but compatible. During the last fifteen years of his life (1979–94), Lasch turned away from his long-standing intellectual engagement with the Frankfurt School and European Marxism in favor of traditional American thinkers ranging from theologians to social theorists.[72]

Although historians on the left during the 1960s and '70s obviously shared a great many concerns—opposition to racism, sexism, the U.S. role in Vietnam, homophobia, corporate exploitation of workers, and so on—the differences and professional conflicts among them, which have not been adequately noticed, often had highly personal origins, as Lasch and Herbert G. Gutman acknowledged explicitly with reference to Eugene Genovese.[73] Sometimes the differences stemmed from their variations in emphasis upon domestic rather than international relations. Sometimes they stemmed from divergent emphases upon other variables, such as class, gender, or the desirability of politicizing professional associations.[74]

Equally important, I believe, in understanding fragmentation among New Left historians have been the divergent backgrounds in terms of social class and work experience that informed their activism. In conversation, for example, two interviewers observed that during the 1950s many intellectuals on the left "lost faith in the American working class as an agent of historical change." Why then, they wondered (and asked), did David Montgomery maintain a positive if not a sanguine view on this point? As someone who had been engaged in factory work and as a union organizer for years prior to graduate study in history, Montgomery did not hesitate to respond in terms of his personal history: "Simply being in factories around America every single day through the 1950s, involved in struggles along with other workers there, persuaded me that most of what was written in academic literature about the inherent conservatism or passivity of American workers in fighting to change anything was simply untrue."[75]

As for conservatism, it has become a form of "conventional wisdom," in some quarters at least, that the desire for professional detachment and objectivity, especially prior to the later 1960s, represented an affirmation of the status quo and consequently amounted to conservatism. That is surely valid in *some* instances, but not in many others. Those who chant that mantra need to be reminded of what a *real* conservative felt and said. I will illustrate my point with a complex exemplar, Charles Callan Tansill, an extremely productive scholar who specialized in diplomatic and political history.[76]

In 1947 Tansill told Harry Elmer Barnes that he had long been an "American Firster" [*sic*], "and it has made me furious the way Roosevelt drained our natural resources for a One World idea. Benedict Arnold only wanted to give up one American fort. The New Dealers gave away our future to foreigners and sold the birthright of future generations for a rotten mess of cosmopolitan cooking. I think Benedict Arnold was a patriot compared with F. D. Roosevelt."[77]

In 1953, after the *Mississippi Valley Historical Review* published a critical review of Tansill's book, *Back Door to War: The Roosevelt Foreign Policy, 1933-1941* (1952), Tansill became paranoid about the reasons why Ruhl Bartlett had been selected for the review assignment. So he wrote to Barnes: "I suspect that the Jewish nigger in the woodpile is that SOB Richard Leopold, of Northwestern University."[78] In 1956 Georgetown forced Tansill to retire prematurely at age 65 when the normal cut-off was 70.

> Because of my opposition to the integration of Negroes with White students in the Schools of the South I am to be punished. It is apparent to me that the Supreme Court decision on integration was merely an exercise in sociology and not in law. And it is damned bad sociology prepared by William E. Dubois [*sic*] and other Negro Commies.[79]

I believe that we need to be more careful in parceling out the label "conservative historian." Perhaps we simply need to differentiate between moderate conservatives, genuinely apolitical historians, and hard-line conservatives. I will concede, however, that the boundary between a hard-line conservative and a vicious reactionary may be elusive.[80]

Needless to say, David M. Potter was a very different sort of conservative: tolerant, extraordinarily subtle, and nuanced. Nevertheless, the fact that his conservatism was consistently firm and unwavering becomes apparent when one examines his recently opened papers at Stanford. In 1953, for example, Charles Madison, a historian who worked as an editor at Holt, Rinehart and Winston, asked Potter to evaluate for publication a chapter-length study of Associate Justice Hugo Black. After some weeks Potter decided that he could not do so in good conscience—that is, be sufficiently fair—because so much about Black was "uncongenial" to him. Potter then summarized his concerns in the form of four rhetorical queries. Their complexity almost defies ideological categorization.

> If I should try to formulate my criticisms, they would be principally as follows:
> (1) Was not Black one of the men who made the Congressional investigating committee the evil and inquisitorial thing which it is today? (2) Did not Black,

Fig. 1.4 David M. Potter (1910–71), later 1960s. Courtesy of the Stanford University News Service.

by his silence at a critical point, deceive his friends and permit them to support his confirmation as justice in the belief that he had never been a member of the Klan? Did he not even permit them to deny this for him? (3) Was there not a great deal more to be said on the side of Justice Jackson than your narrative recognizes? (4) and finally, was not Black harsh and unfair to loyal Americans of Japanese descent during the war, while he has been lenient with disloyal Americans during the period of undeclared war since the Soviet invasion of Korea?[81]

When Potter elaborated, however, his ideological position became unequivocal. "I regard Communists as public enemies," he wrote, "and I deplore classifying them in the same category with other 'dissidents,' partly because I feel that they are, in effect if not in purpose, the agents of an enemy power, and partly because they are committed to destroying all the liberties which may be invoked in defense of dissidents." If that seems hard-nosed and inflexible, Potter promptly resumed the judicious outlook that we long ago learned to associate with him:

I realize the great harm that is done by reactionaries who confuse liberalism with communism, and I realize the danger of hysteria; but I think reactionaries will continue to succeed in confusing the two in the public mind as long as liberals continue to treat communism as just another form of dissenting opinion, and I think it is as wrong to refuse to recognize the danger of Communism as it is to lose one's head and start striking about blindly at everyone who is left of center.[82]

When Madison attempted to defend Black, Potter stiffened and became more explicit. "Although I am not a liberal," he explained, "I feel great admiration for many of our liberals, such as Brandeis, Norris, La Follette, and others. . . . About Communism, I regard any Communist as a potential agent of the Soviet Union. . . . In all the furor about Communism, one of the things which concerns me most is the fact that reactionaries are seeking to brand any form of left-wing thought as Communism, and I feel that liberals have unwittingly assisted in this confusion by themselves failing to disavow the Communists, by apologizing for them and covering up for them."[83]

The outcome of this intense yet mutually respectful dialogue is fascinating. Later in the year, when Madison sent Potter his preface to be critiqued, Potter reluctantly explained his distress because the framework for this volume of biographical essays (in Potter's view) held that "the road of liberalism leads to the welfare state and that free enterprise must not be allowed to stand in the way." For Potter, however, "much of liberalism has been concerned with the defense of free enterprise both against public collectivism and against private collectivism. I feel that you do not give free enterprise its due." When Harvard University Press asked Potter for a confidential evaluation, though, he recommended publication on the grounds that the "public ought to have access to more material such as this. . . ." As it happened, Harvard decided not to accept the project, but another publisher eventually did. David Potter never compromised his intellectual integrity yet never, figuratively, ceased to bend over backward to be fair.[84]

I could proliferate illustrations of the careful, cautious, and astute ways in which Potter voiced his conservatism. While I do not accept or condone Potter's subsequent defense of U. S. policies in Vietnam, neither can I refute his critical assessment of Louis Hartz's *The Liberal Tradition in America* (1955). Potter contended in an interview that Hartz had "adopted an ideological emphasis that enabled him to overlook things that didn't fit in with his thesis. . . . Hartz did not allow for the fact that men can hold to the same ideological principle and yet fight bitterly about the construction they place upon it."[85]

Reading through Potter's correspondence, what seems most striking to me is that readers of all political or ideological persuasions listened carefully, almost always deferentially, to his critical advice about their works-in-progress, even peers who had achieved greater professional eminence than Potter at the time. C. Vann Woodward, for example, far more liberal than Potter in his views on social issues, public policy, and civic activism, heeded Potter's advice very carefully when the latter read a manuscript for him. If Carl Becker earned the title of Mr. Detachment, Potter surely deserves the sobriquet Mr. Judicious. He made this comment to Merle Curti in 1962: "I believe in the view that most people have the defects of their qualities and the qualities of their defects." [86]

Coming to Terms Professionally with Personal Identity

In contemplating various contingencies that affect personal identity and the historian's vocation it seems appropriate to ask what it must have been like, and perhaps even still be like, to sustain a professional life despite being marginalized, and in some instances even ignored, because of skin color, gender, sexual orientation, physical disability, or, believe it or not, being a successful popularizer of history (see below). My illustrative cases are fresh in particular even though they may feel familiar in general terms. In each instance the personal and the professional are so intertwined that they are virtually impossible to disentangle. (That is one of the realities I most want to convey.) If these episodes are somewhat embarrassing to historians as a guild, at least most of them are stories with heroes as well as villains.

Predictably, however, human nature being what it is, even some of my heroes commit serious lapses. Men who suffered horrendously from racism were nonetheless capable of unabashed sexism. Rayford W. Logan, for instance, who railed against every slight suffered by blacks at the hands of whites, inscribed the following in his diary in 1941. His wife, Ruth, had a beautiful voice and he was very proud of her when she sang in church or at informal gatherings. When she told him that she wanted to pursue a career, however, "I told her that I am not solving any problems now. Only one thing, if she wants a career we will have a friendly separation. I will not be married to a woman who has a professional musical career. There is no argument and there will be no discussion about it." [87]

Bessie Louise Pierce suffered many slights during her notable career at the University of Chicago, as we shall see below. She went there from Iowa in 1929 as an associate professor, and remained frozen at that rank for fourteen years because of her sex, despite being more professionally active and more prolific in publishing than most of her male colleagues. Perhaps as a survival technique, she learned to do things the old-fashioned way: the way the men did them. When the third volume of her history of Chicago was published in 1957 she wrote to the editor of a historical journal to suggest that Merle Curti, Thomas Cochran, or Ray Allen Billington be invited to review it. All three were her close friends and loyal supporters.[88]

Arthur M. Schlesinger, Sr., had been Pierce's dissertation advisor at Iowa and always remained one of her staunchest professional advocates. Perhaps it smoothed their relationship that she never married, however, because Schlesinger could not transcend his liberal yet traditional views concerning gender roles. When Curti consulted Schlesinger about the dynamics of balancing two careers within a marriage, Schlesinger replied that "people in your position must decide at some fairly early time which professional career is the more important, that of the husband or the wife. There is no escaping this, so far as I can see." And perhaps because Bessie Pierce was resilient and managed to cope in a profession dominated by males, Schlesinger even referred to her as a man! In 1936 they corresponded about Chicago's need to decide on what rank level to pursue in making a new appointment. "Everything considered," Schlesinger wrote, "it seems to me that the wisest policy to pursue would be to get a very promising young man who is on his way up. After all, you and [Avery O.] Craven give enough kudos to the department as the top men and it is always doubtful whether you can attract to Chicago first-rate full professors who are well located in the better universities."[89]

Finally, in this category that might be called "fallible heroes," consider the case of Douglass Adair, an early American historian who served for many years as the revered editor of the *William and Mary Quarterly*. The sensitive Adair did more than his share in raising the children that he and his wife brought into the world—some colleagues even felt that Adair did so to the detriment of his productivity as a scholar. Whatever the case, by the criteria of the 1940s and '50s he certainly was no sexist. When writing a strong letter of recommendation for a woman who wished to pursue a graduate degree in history, however, he explained that "she is a very bright, serious young woman who I could recommend wholeheartedly for a graduate program and a scholarly career if she didn't look like an early candidate for marriage, i.e., she is attractive enough so that the odds are all in favor of that institution . . . . I would judge she would be an outstandingly good research assistant or scholarly editor, and might become a good scholar/teacher if she steers clear of marriage."[90]

Race and Racism

On the basis of sources that I have seen, until the 1960s and '70s race was a greater barrier to full acceptance and participation in the profession than any other consideration such as class, gender, or even most manifestations of "marginal" European ethnicity. Although the essential story is familiar by now, its poignant particulars remain troublesome. Rayford W. Logan, who taught at Virginia Union, Atlanta, and Howard universities, battled with blacks as well as whites for explicit attention to be paid to Negro history. (In 1931–32, while working on his doctorate in U.S. diplomatic history at Harvard, Logan taught a course on Negro history at the Ford Hall Forum in Boston.)[91]

The year 1940 is especially interesting in Logan's life because it began with despair and ended in triumph, each instance proving illustrative. In March he participated in a panel discussion of American democracy at Miner Teachers College in Washington, D.C. Most but not all of the audience was black. Logan lamented in his diary that he could not get the panelists to discuss the mistreatment of Negroes as a serious blemish in the functioning of democracy in the United States. In December, however, when the American Historical Association met in New York City, for the first time in the organization's history an entire session was devoted to aspects of black history. W. E. B. Du Bois presided. Logan spoke on the American Colonization Society; Charles Wesley participated; and Vernon Wharton of Millsaps College in Jackson, Mississippi, who gave a fine paper on Reconstruction in Mississippi, told Logan that attempts had been made in his home state to prevent him from coming to New York to participate in the integrated panel.[92]

Logan was not an easy man. Just ask John Hope Franklin, who was his colleague at Howard. His arrogance tarnished his brilliance, and his inconsistencies compromised his genuine accomplishments. Nevertheless, to read through Logan's voluminous diaries is a numbing experience. It's not so much all of the slights and overt hostility that most of us cannot even imagine. Rather it is the frantic pace of teaching four classes every day with intensely politicized meetings in between; it is the staggering schedule of presentations that Logan made each year during Negro History Week; it is the unpredictable and capricious application of racial policies as Logan traveled from one city to another—a circumstance made all the more complicated because Logan was very light-skinned and spoke fluent French. When he had occasion to use French, white hostesses willingly seated him in segregated restaurants on the assumption that he must be foreign. Being

Fig. 1.5   John Hope Franklin (1915–) in 1981. Courtesy of John Hope Franklin.

foreign apparently forgave being colored! Is it any wonder that Logan once told an audience at Fisk University that segregation made him "regret that I was a historian and not a physicist," for then he could have produced an atomic bomb and coerced the government into terminating all Jim Crow policies.[93]

Although John Hope Franklin never contemplated quite such violent coercion of the government, he has spoken with eloquent anger of his treatment by the U.S. Army during World War II. I want to recall two other episodes in Franklin's career for which there is unnoticed documentation. The first concerns the annual meeting of the Southern Historical Association held at Williamsburg in 1949. C. Vann Woodward and Bell Wiley determined to have Franklin on the program despite the predictable resentment that would come from many members of the association as well as the staff at dining facilities in racially conservative Virginia. Douglass Adair and his wife invited Franklin to stay at their home. The reasons that Adair specified almost a decade later in recalling the occasion are fascinating:

> Virginia's and my decision to invite John Hope Franklin to stay with us was really quite selfish. We have three children, two boys and a girl, and like so many children growing up in a southern town, they had never met a Negro

gentleman with the educational background and the polish of gentility that makes for a gentleman. With our concern to keep them from being provincial, from falling into the rather nasty local prejudices, we thought of this as an opportunity for the children to meet in our home a colleague whom I knew and admired. The other element, of course, was the realization on my part that it would be embarrassing for John Hope, who was a distinguished speaker on the program to be shunted off with the kind of accommodations that were available.[94]

The second episode that intrigues me involves the reception of Franklin's important book, *The Militant South*, in 1956. A look at the professional journals will find rather bland reviews by well-known white southerners who are reasonably courteous even when they demur. Their private correspondence, however, reveals an astonishing degree of anxiety because they believed that Franklin was far too angry about racism to be fair; moreover, if his historical indictment of white southerners was correct, it tainted them, even at second hand. Wendell H. Stephenson, founding editor of the *Journal of Southern History* and subsequently editor of the *Mississippi Valley Historical Review*, wrote an anguished assessment for the *American Historical Review*. (At the time, Stephenson was teaching at the University of Oregon, a campus with virtually no black students.) He explained that in an effort to be fair he had read the book three times and that his review had gone through twelve drafts. But the extent to which his hackles had been raised is clear from a letter written to his friend Fletcher M. Green at Chapel Hill:

He [Franklin] seems almost unaware that there was an abolitionist crusade that contributed toward militancy in the South. He makes no effort to put the segment of southern history he narrates in the perspective of the total portrait of the southern people. I am very depressed about the picture he presents, which seems to me to be completely one-sided. If he is correct, then I am a prejudiced Southerner, unable to rise above my environment of nearly thirty years. If I am correct in thinking that the book is as much an autobiography of a mind as a segment of southern history, then he should turn his attention to a subject which his background will permit him to treat more objectively. Unfortunately for me, there seems to be growing up in the North and West a cult that believes a Negro can do no wrong.[95]

Green, who was reviewing *The Militant South* himself for the *Mississippi Valley Historical Review*, responded that "this is a very decidedly partisan book and that it shows as much of the mind of the author as it does of the subject he is attempting to develop."[96]

In 1951 the Mississippi Valley Historical Association (the maiden name of the Organization of American Historians) found itself in upheaval over whether or not a forthcoming annual meeting should be held in a Southern city, such as New Orleans, where segregated facilities prevailed. Paul W. Gates of Cornell, a member of the executive committee, laid out the issues clearly:

> The Association has conducted a vigorous membership campaign in recent years and has brought in a large number of young people who feel intensively on this question of discrimination. You may have noticed on the report of the chairmen of the membership committee that the greatest gains were made in the northeast. I think most northern liberals are aware of the progress that has been made in the South and look for continued progress but at the same time will not propose to give sanction to discrimination as we do if we go to a community that draws the line rigidly as does New Orleans. It is not just a matter of attempting to coerce the South as some have felt, and I think that most of our members have no such thought, it is a matter of maintaining our own self-respect. We want negro members as well as white membership and if the negroes are denied full equal rights in our meetings, we should not seek their membership.[97]

What is pertinent about this explosive episode to my focus here can be found once again in the correspondence of Southern members of the Association, particularly among the leadership. Wendell Holmes Stephenson called those who opposed meeting in New Orleans "holier than thou," and insisted that discrimination directed against a section was every bit as wrong-headed as racial discrimination. Frank L. Owsley agreed and explained that he had not supported the Democratic Party since 1940 because he felt that it had become a "Conglomeration of minorities—'Big Labor,' 'Big Nigger,' 'Big Jew' etc etc. who hold the balance of power in the big states between the 'Yellow Dog Democrats' and the 'Blue Bellied Republicans' and thus dictate national policy."[98]

Readers will recall that James W. Silver, Professor of History at the University of Mississippi (1936–64), was literally forced to resign and flee to Notre Dame as a safe haven after he published his devastating book-length critique, *Mississippi: The Closed Society* (1964). An intensely dramatic story, Silver's ostracism forms the centerpiece of his searing autobiography, *Running Scared: Silver in Mississippi* (1984). During the later 1930s Silver's colleagues at Ole Miss included young David M. Potter, an A.B.D. at that time from Yale; Bell I. Wiley; and Joe Mathews, a Europeanist from Penn who later moved to Emory and became the only historian of Europe ever elected president of the Southern Historical Association. Mathews's encounter with racism at Ole Miss is not common knowledge the way Silver's is, though it most certainly supports Silver's critique of the university as well as the state as a closed society.

In the autumn of 1959 the University of Mississippi invited Mathews to return from Emory to present the Claiborne Lectures during the following spring. On January 16, 1960, an essay by Mathews's wife describing her experiences as a part-time teacher at Morehouse College appeared in the *Saturday Evening Post*. "It was reportorial and reasonably objective in tone," Mathews told David Potter, "though her convictions on the race question were apparent." One of the illustrations showed an interracial student meeting. Within 24 hours of the publication of that issue the university administration decided to withdraw its invitation. Their reasoning, according to Mathews, "was that in the present inflamed state of opinion in Mississippi it would be unwise to antagonize the legislature or to give it any excuse for diminishing the forthcoming appropriations." [99]

It especially disturbed and annoyed Mathews when he learned that faculty members at Ole Miss were counting on Mathews's "friendship, etc., not to spread the story and hoped that it would be hushed up." According to Mathews, "this is such an unrealistic view that it bothers me almost more than the incident itself." [100]

One last example, different in nature and more recent, should be cited to indicate that the problem has not been confined to the Deep South and involves professional protectiveness of venerable reputations as well as racial conservatism. In 1967 *Agricultural History* published papers given at an AHA session the previous year evaluating the work of U. B. Phillips. Eugene Genovese offered the principal critique, followed by comments by David Potter, Kenneth Stampp, and Stanley Elkins. Potter called Genovese's paper arresting but suggested that Phillips's "Central Theme of Southern History" needed to be understood in the context of 1928, when it first appeared. According to Potter, "American liberals could and would easily have forgiven Phillips for asserting that many slaveholders were men of humane feeling, but they could not forgive him for saying that the obstacles to racial integration in Southern society (not to mention American society) were insuperable. . . ." [101]

The reactions to this forum of someone like Avery O. Craven, formerly of the University of Chicago but by then of Maryland, are symptomatic and instructive. The symposium reminded Craven of "a group of cannibals feasting on the body of a departed fellow man,—no! I should say 'carcus' [*sic*], that's more impersonal." After accusing Genovese of manipulating Phillips's language and concepts, Craven concluded by wondering

> whether, after all there is anything to history as a profession but the attempt to destroy, mostly by distortion, our fellows past and present. What simple persons Phillips, Turner, Beard and others must be to the bright young scholars (?) of today. Yet we knew them as gentlemen, kindly, generous, and only eager to do the impossible—discover historical truth. How I now regret

ever having turned from my first love, art, to enter a profession where I like the rest, am only a simple fool.[102]

We should note the poignant feeling of intergenerational misperception and conflict. That chasm may very well have been widest at the close of the 1960s.

A Problematic Time for Women

The generational contrast that I have been emphasizing, with the later 1960s as an approximately pivotal "moment," is notably applicable with regard to women. Fifteen years ago two scholars suggested that "the ambivalence of women historians about the meaning and consequences of professionalism in their own personal lives" may, among other reasons, explain the paucity of research on professional women. I will say little here about changes that have happened during the past three decades because they are fairly familiar. Jill Ker Conway, for example, tells us in the second volume of her autobiography that she chose her dissertation topic at Harvard during the 1960s because it was personally meaningful to her: specifically, Conway looked at how Jane Addams led women to seek higher education at a time when society had little expectation that women would use it "in any but a decorative sense." [103]

For purposes of contrast, let's turn back to the quarter-century following 1930, first noting briefly what males in the profession said privately about women. In 1946, when the editors of the multivolume *History of the South* series were seeking an author for their volume on the Revolutionary era, Thomas P. Abernethy of the University of Virginia, a very conservative person on racial issues, recommended Maude Woodfin of Westhampton College in Richmond. He called her a "sound scholar" and predicted that she would do a good job. The coeditors of the series, however, both Southern gentlemen, quite literally toyed with the idea. Wendell Holmes Stephenson asked E. Merton Coulter: "Frankly, do you wish to get involved with a lady? I mean in a historical way only? Is she a lady of parts, historically speaking?" Coulter responded three days later. "As for Maude, I know who she is, but I cannot remember much historical activity on her part; and as I do not remember her personal appearance, I fear at this stage of the game, I would not be overly desirous of getting involved with the lady, either historically or otherwise."[104]

It is not surprising that such attitudes and dialogues persisted for decades. In 1955, when Colonial Williamsburg decided to undertake an oral history project, Allan Nevins recommended a highly skilled woman to be responsi-

Fig. 1.6 Bessie Louise Pierce (1888-1974). Courtesy of the
University of Chicago Library, Special Collections.

ble for extensive interviewing. The head of the Division of Interpretation at
Williamsburg, a historian holding a Columbia Ph.D., responded with
self-defeating "realism" that was representative rather than an aberration:

> We have decided, however, that it is not wise for us to consider using a
> woman interviewer, even though she is as talented and attractive as Miss
> Hagedorn. There is no doubt in any of our minds that she may be more
> perceptive than any man we may find, but we do know that we are dealing
> with many men who have had a hand in constructing Williamsburg, who
> would feel somewhat under wraps in an interview with a woman. We fear
> that they would watch their language and feel bound to act in a way they
> would think proper. We deplore such a narrow-minded attitude, but we are
> inclined to think it exists in our situation.[105]

Rather than take a scattershot approach, I want to explore in some depth
the career of one fascinating woman, the above-mentioned Bessie Louise
Pierce (1888–1974), about whom very little has been written. An undergraduate at the University of Iowa, she earned her M.A. at Chicago and her
doctorate at Iowa in 1923, as noted, under the direction of Arthur M.

Schlesinger. After teaching at Iowa for a decade, where she was not treated well despite a strong record in publication, teaching, and service, she moved to the University of Chicago in 1929 where she taught until her retirement in 1953.[106]

During more than ten years at the beginning of her career Pierce carved out an enduring area of expertise: the controversial role of history in public education. She then turned to a massive project that occupied much of her scholarly attention for the rest of her life: a projected four-volume history of Chicago from the beginning in 1673 until 1933, of which she completed three volumes reaching to 1893. The thorough and patient reader of those three tomes will find scant traces of sympathetic interest in gender—occasional allusions to differences in treatment, exploitation, and praise for pioneering contributions by women—but nothing that would prepare the reader for the outspoken views that she expressed privately concerning the role of women in the historical profession.[107]

In 1932, for instance, when Schlesinger sent her a mint copy of *Historical Scholarship in America: Needs and Opportunities*, which he had edited for the AHA, she complimented him on the "format and printing," but then

> wondered why no women were included on any of the committees and when I found none were included I looked in vain for the report on the informal conference of women professors mentioned in your foreword. Please don't think I am getting militant, but I could not help wondering if women are doing so poor a job that in no case one should not have been taken into the membership of some one of the committees.

Schlesinger promptly replied that in planning the conference "I canvassed all the possibilities in the Eastern area and felt that the persons I finally invited were, for purposes of the conference, better than any women historians I could think of. Perhaps the chairmen of other conferences found themselves in a similar dilemma."[108]

Pierce then responded, as she invariably did, deferentially and somewhat less aggressively than at first.

> I am more sorry than I can say that I gave the impression in my letter regarding the Committee on Planning that I had "a feministical chip" on my shoulder. That, you know, I have never had, and I hope I shall not only be wise enough not to exhibit one if I ever do get it but also that I may avoid the hypersensitiveness which some of my sex have regarding rewards which they have not yet earned. My question was raised purely from the standpoint of an inquiry as to whether there were no women who ranked in the content field with men. As I survey the field, I, of course, would be forced to grant that I know of practically none. Certainly, not in the field of American History is there one which compares with the Committee meeting in the east.[109]

Pierce customarily reined herself in when an issue concerned sexism in the profession generally. Late in 1940, for example, Merle Curti wrote apologetically that a party at the forthcoming AHA meeting in New York was likely to be for men only. "I do hope that if you want a stag party," Pierce replied, "you will go ahead and have one. I do not think that women should ever intrude upon men when they aren't wanted or when it is inconvenient for the men to have them around. There are times when I don't want any of you men about, so I know exactly how you feel." [110]

When it came to her own professional treatment, however, Pierce was likely to be less tactful, and in a fracas that occurred in 1949, actually quite fierce. In 1941, having been frozen at the rank of associate professor for twelve years, she told Schlesinger that "the unwillingness to recognize a person chiefly because she belongs to the wrong sex, has almost 'gotten me down.'" When Merle Curti empathized with her on this matter, Pierce commented that because of her sex "the University feels it can keep me without doing anything because my market price is not as high as that of men.... The University of Chicago on the whole, I fear, thinks of women as an anomaly in a great university." [111]

In 1949, having suffered all sorts of professional slights for almost thirty years because of her sex, Pierce listened patiently when Curti explained why he really didn't deserve to become president of the AHA. Professional honors matter very little, he declared. "The things that mean most are helping the younger generation prepare themselves to carry on in the profession, and to have some understanding, at least, of what they are up against; and of making the rough road all our friends travel, a little the easier." [112] Pierce's candid reply endures because it speaks to the condition and the feelings of so many, and not just women. "I am in accord with your statement as to what honors really mean," she remarked. "I suspect, however, that someone might tell you that it is easy for you, who have had some, to speak so sensibly. You know those who do not get recognition would scarcely be able to be so philosophical." [113]

In 1949 Pierce became involved in a professional contretemps that truly enraged her, even though virtue was not entirely on her side alone. Having been urged to participate in a session at the annual meeting of the Mississippi Valley Historical Association, held that year in Madison, Wisconsin, she dispatched a copy of her paper, "Changing Urban Patterns in the Mississippi Valley," to her designated commentator. Although she may only have wished to disarm him, she acknowledged that "there is nothing new in the paper, but under the topic assigned I was unable to develop anything novel, even if I had known it, in a twenty minute period." [114]

Having conceded that it was not a very strong essay, she nonetheless offered it for publication to the editor of the *Mississippi Valley Historical Review* and he dealt with it in the traditional way. Not only did blind reviewing of submissions not yet exist, the editor's cover letter to a referee hinted at his own reservations about accepting the piece. Be that as it may, the reviewer, certainly no milquetoast, informed the editor, "I think it stinks. . . . Perhaps the review might print it as a masterpiece of fuzziness, historical and otherwise." The journal editor then sent Pierce the usual diplomatic boilerplate: "Since members of the guild will have an opportunity to follow your findings through volumes of your monumental *History of Chicago*, published and prospective, it might be well for us to reserve space for a study that had no other opportunity to reach the printed page except through a scholarly journal." [115]

Pierce then "went ballistic" and promptly submitted her resignation from the association. Her letter was courteous but curt. The following summer she vented her spleen to Ray Allen Billington of Northwestern and he conveyed her feelings to Stephenson in order to try to mollify both sides. "She felt strongly on the matter," Billington reported, "because this was only the second article she had submitted in the course of her long membership, and she felt that papers should be published, under those circumstances, unless there was something radically wrong with them. . . . Under the circumstances she believes that her resignation is necessary to preserve her self respect. . . . Could some other officer of the Association try to calm her down?" Stephensons's reply to Billington is very long and rather lame. His letter to Pierce asking her to reconsider resigning is equally so. [116]

Adding insult to injury, perhaps unintentionally, a staff member at the Mississippi Valley Historical Association office then wrote the following to Pierce: "You have been on our membership role [*sic*] for many years and we regret that you feel you must cancel. Perhaps you will consider a proposition for life membership. Your card shows that you have the Reviews from Vol. 5 to date. If you have this file we will give you a life membership in exchange for the Reviews. Some of the early Reviews are out of print and we can make good use of them." And then, putting even more salt in Pierce's wound in the form of a postscript: "If life membership does not appeal to you perhaps we can arrange to purchase your files [of the MVHR]." [117]

I have not been able to ascertain how matters came to be smoothed over, but in 1953 Pierce joined the association's executive committee for a two-year term, and in 1965, at the age of 77, she chaired a session at the OAH's annual meeting. Meanwhile she continued to network tirelessly with other women historians on behalf of women in the profession. She sponsored women when vacancies occurred elsewhere, and she told Viola F. Barnes in 1950 that "I am anxious to see a woman or women in the

Department here. My own time is getting short and, of course, Miss Gillespie's death a year ago left us with only me as the feminine representative of the historical craft."[118]

Frances E. Gillespie, who taught British history at Chicago, had been a close friend of Bessie Pierce, in part because they both felt very put upon—treated more like support staff than colleagues by some of their male peers. Nevertheless, Pierce liked the company of men and it is clear from conversations with those who knew her, and from remarks at her memorial service, that many men enjoyed working and interacting with her.[119] As William T. Hutchinson observed, "a mention of her name evokes a host of happy memories, both of her personality and her scholarship." Over and over, he remarked, "Aunt Bessie" (as she was called) "volunteered to perform tasks which her colleagues hesitated to assume [such as] taking over the tedious and complicated chore of preparing class-time schedules in such fashion as to aggrieve no graduate student majoring in a particular field of history because courses he much needed were listed to meet at the same hour."[120]

My inquiries have not extended to the professional lives and expectations of women historians who taught at colleges that were not coeducational and had faculties that were predominantly female. But it is clear that even through the end of the 1960s women in mixed-sex institutions and departments required a curious combination of qualities in order to survive, never mind flourish: They had to be "one of the boys" at the same time that they were expected to take on tasks that the "boys" preferred not to be bothered with.

Perhaps that dualism, or ambiguity if you prefer, was responsible for curious perceptions that existed and behavior patterns that persisted on the part of men. Fawn Brodie, for instance, remained a lecturer and then a senior lecturer at UCLA until 1971, when at the age of 56 she was finally promoted to the lowest rank of professor. Critical colleagues who had opposed her promotion from lecturer during the 1960s asserted that her work was "intuitive [that gender-loaded word], anecdotal, sensational, and that she seems to choose 'interesting figures' to write about and then to emphasize the sensual and exotic in their lives."[121]

The use of the word "intuitive" in conjunction with women historians is intriguing because it also came from persons who regarded themselves as sympathetic and supportive of women. When Fawn Brodie became involved with her interpretive biography of Thomas Jefferson during the 1970s, she engaged in a very cordial correspondence with Erik H. Erikson, the psychoanalyst and psychobiographer. He looked forward to her book because, in his words, "You have the concepts and the style to do this right."

He then added: "And (how does one say this these days) it takes a woman's intuition to respond both to the woman (and I don't mean the 'passive man'!) in Jefferson and to what he looked for in a woman." Despite Erikson's clear wish to avoid what could be construed as sexist language, he apparently knew no alternative to "woman's intuition." [122]

Sexual Orientation

I shall not say as much about sexual orientation and the historian's vocation because much less primary source material—interviews, autobiographical essays, and correspondence—is presently available. But three points, at least, seem clear. The first pertains to the generational shift that I have been emphasizing throughout. In the initial biographical work on F. O. Matthiessen that appeared, the authors made this striking observation.

> For most of his students and younger colleagues Matthiessen's homosexuality was suggested, if at all, only by the fact that his circle was more predominantly heterosexual than was usual in Harvard literary groups of the time and that he was unusually hostile to homosexual colleagues who mixed their academic and sexual relations. [123]

By contrast, John D'Emilio's personalized essays about his experiences during the 1970s and '80s clearly indicate that for himself, Allan Berube, and others, coming to terms with their sexual orientation, and being increasingly capable of contextualizing it with some detachment, made a world of difference in the quality and meaningfulness of their academic work. D'Emilio has written:

> Now, with my interest piqued by contemporary events, I began to search more deeply. Clues whose meaning had eluded me became significant. . . . I returned to New York [from San Francisco] not only with new friends and new insights but also with a much stronger commitment to history. . . . To understand this reaction requires the recognition that, at least in the 1970s and 1980s, the doing of gay and lesbian history has been more than a form of intellectual labor. . . . It was transforming, both for the doer and the receiver, and in the social context of those decades, inherently political. . . . For my generation and for cohorts both older and younger, the absence of self-affirming words and images and the cultural denial of our very existence made any kind of history a profound, subversive revelation. [124]

There is a third attitudinal perspective, however, at the very least, that transcends the covert self-protection of Matthiessen's era and the self-aware openness of D'Emilio's. Robert Dawidoff has insisted we should notice that historically

> gay men were secret about themselves, creating a secret world, and also gave

in tribute to the culture a defining and participatory energy that, stripped of its own interest, could make the culture see itself as it wished to be seen. To do this subject, you need to study the secret gay subculture and the selfless and often self-denying work gay men often did in the larger culture.

But then, he wonders with some anxiety, what could be the psychological or emotional costs of historicizing a phenomenon that is deeply felt in a personal way? What loss of intimacy or privacy must be paid in the quest for full disclosure? And conversely, particularly for gay and lesbian persons who do not teach or do research primarily concerning gay and lesbian history, "will I lose my professional identity in my subjective engagement in the scholarship?"[125]

I do not for a moment believe that one must be gay in order to write the history of persons with that sexual orientation and behavior, any more than I believe that only women can write women's history or blacks the history of African Americans. Nevertheless, I do find it rather difficult to imagine someone who is not gay or bisexual providing the poignant and deeply felt insights that Dawidoff has offered. As he observes, "the notion that the best history comes from a certain distance is a problem. Who but a gay would know to rewrite homophobic history to rescue the whispered voices of the closet? Actually some might and have done, but not many."[126]

He comments in this way, for example, upon the impact of AIDS on gay male culture. "One's interest in this history, whose writing it is in turn meant to serve, is sometimes at odds with professional scholarly history. As you turn it into the cadences of the profession, you feel a loss, you feel an anxiety, and those feelings are worth more than a moment's hesitation." Dawidoff concludes by reiterating the ambivalence he feels in seeking to negotiate between personal identity and vocational obligations:

> On the one hand, I am driven to historicize the Grace out of the Puritans and the "hotcha" out of Sophie Tucker; on the other, I am moved to protect the secrets and the activist consciousness of gay men from historicization—and probably from criticism. And the more history I attempt, the more intense the struggle between my training and my passions.[127]

Physical Disability

When we turn our attention to the physically challenged, to those who seek to surmount what some continue to call "handicaps" in order to teach and write history, we encounter a rather different psychological dynamic, and it is just that psychological aspect that interests me here. As a guild we have long been familiar, let's say, with Francis Parkman's perseverance in being prolific despite partial blindness, cardiac irregularities, arthritis, and insomnia. We know about Charles Beard's lonely deafness in his later years, which caused him to withdraw even more to the haven of his Connecticut farm, "in the silent hills where the birds keep on singing and the leaves murmuring even though I hear them not."[128]

Some readers may recall that Adrienne Koch courageously endured debilitating arthritis for most of her career. She also maintained her personal vibrancy and intellectual verve despite the amputation of a leg, and continued to attend the annual meetings of historical associations on crutches until she died of cancer in 1971. In each of these instances, however, and in the case of Charles McLaughlin, who successfully started the project of editing the papers of Frederick Law Olmsted despite contracting paralytic polio in 1955 while working on his dissertation in American Civilization at Harvard, their physical disabilities did not directly shape or color the particular historical work that they did.[129]

I want to situate in a somewhat different perspective those men and women whose physical disabilities caused them not merely to choose unconventional topics for historical inquiry, but in certain instances even to view familiar subjects in fresh ways because of their personal challenges. As an illustration of the first kind I would mention William Quentin Maxwell, who survived a terrible automobile accident, wrote his Ph.D. dissertation with Allan Nevins, and eventually published it as *Lincoln's Fifth Wheel: The Political History of the United States Sanitary Commission* (1956). As Nevins wrote in his foreword to that book, it treated "of almost the darkest side of the Civil War—the sufferings of the wounded and sick—and of the great philanthropic organization which did so much to save lives and alleviate agony during the four years of conflict."[130]

As an illustration of the second kind, consider the case of Paul K. Longmore, a scholar whose disability resulted from polio who has demonstrated unusual sensitivity (in several respects) to the role of physical disability, physical appearance, and psychological reactions to persons with disabilities in the American past. Readers of his first book, a study of the ways George Washington played a major part in shaping his own public image, barely noticed Longmore's subtle, unobtrusive attention to who could and could not participate in civic affairs in eighteenth-century Virginia. "Those regarded as having emotional, physical, or 'natural' 'disabilities' (women, slaves, minors, people with various handicaps) were thought incapable of real self-control and therefore incompetent for such involvement."[131]

Longmore also takes note, in a way that previous writers did not, of Washington's solicitude for disabled soldiers.[132] And Longmore is equally sensitive to the obverse: the political advantages of an attractive personal appearance, and then, in an elitist society where physical grace seemed to provide evidence of potential leadership, he frequently notes that Washington's presentation of self led people to make assumptions about his character and political ability. "It was undoubtedly George's skill as a dancer and horseman that, when added to his natural strength and prowess, made him lithe in all his movements. His physical grace was an important part of the personal presence that from early on so vividly impressed those who met him." [133]

During the past decade Longmore has done fascinating work in calling attention to the history of Americans with disabilities of diverse sorts. He has also examined images and stereotypes of handicapped persons in television and motion pictures. Above all he has taken a figure much written about in recent years, Randolph Bourne, and cast him in a fresh light. Longmore notes that the deficiency in all of the works on Bourne "is their explanation of his experience as a disabled person and its relation to his radicalism." Bourne's condition was highly visible: a twisted mouth, face, and ear because of a difficult birth; a severely curved spine; and stunted growth from spinal tuberculosis in childhood. [134]

Longmore persuasively re-examines Bourne's essay titled "The Handicapped," commenting that it has so frequently been quoted yet so poorly understood by his biographers. He goes on to observe that social scientists who have studied the "disability experience" no longer regard it as a fated and inevitable condition but rather as a "socially constructed identity and role triggered by a stigmatized biological trait. Bourne's lifetime of discrimination and rejection," Longmore insists, "was not inherent in his physical disability but part of that stigmatized social identity rooted in deep but unconscious social prejudice." Paul Longmore has effectively shown us that personal circumstances and empathy can enhance the historian's work in ways that have not been adequately explored. [135]

There is a poem that I like to share with my undergraduate students. In fact, I usually read it aloud at my last lecture of the term. It was written by a woman of wonderful intelligence and extraordinary courage. Josephine Miles earned her Ph.D. in English literature and became a Professor of English at the University of California, Berkeley. She wrote literary history and criticism as well as imaginative poetry, and she did all of that despite being stricken, initially as a teenager, with a rare and utterly constraining form of arthritis.

When she visited Cornell to give readings and meet with students in 1979, she was mobile in a wheelchair, from which she would be lifted and carried by a very strong and devoted assistant. Miles's degree of incapacity far exceeded, for example, our image of Franklin Delano Roosevelt. To be absolutely graphic, Miss Miles had a large head with an absolutely vital brain and temperament resting upon a small, withered, totally disabled body. When she talked or read her poems, however, people were spellbound by her conversation and her verse. The poem that I read at the end of my course was written by Miss Miles in 1974. It is called "Toward II."

Toward II

Go out a little from yourself as you sit here,
Maybe to the path outside the window
Maybe to an idea,
Or to in the next row an absorbing form.
Reject most of the lecture,
Most of your thought, most that the window bears,
Maybe the whole morning. There is being sifted
The sand of your time, turning as you turn.

I am beside you and we are exchanging
Several aspects of the ideas of history,
From their glosses there are being sifted
Sands of time only becoming yours.
Sift me away and sift the whole morning.
Some day, not accountable, you may look down
To see in your palm as on a field of history
The grain of time you recognize as yours.[136]

Students and Mentors

The graphic homily in that poem brings me to personal identity and the historian's vocation in relation to teaching, a central aspect of our careers because we all have been students for much of our lives and a great many of us teach. Most of us, in fact, teach quite a lot, albeit with varying degrees of self-awareness. Surely we have all had the experience of being told by returning alumni, often ten or twenty-five years after the fact, that we exerted a strong influence in some way that we never knew or even imagined. More often than not, I believe, our undergraduates avoid full disclosure prior to their graduation, either because it might be embarrassing or else because the nature of our influence is not yet entirely clear in their minds. And, almost invariably, when their reaction to us is not positive, we don't hear about it at all. In that respect, I suggest, our students are fairly kind. When it comes to teaching, no news at all, ever, is likely to mean that we failed.

On the other hand, it ought to be said that the incapacity or unwillingness to communicate feelings is certainly a two-way street, even when the "news," so to speak, is good news. After Carl Bridenbaugh had become director of the Institute for Early American History and Culture at Williamsburg, a friend repeated to him a complimentary remark that Arthur M. Schlesinger, his Ph.D. mentor at Harvard, had made. Bridenbaugh expressed gratitude because, as he explained, Schlesinger "never praises a student to his face; it is only through repeated [i.e., passed along] statements that we hear we are approved of." [137] I would like to believe that that, too, is much less true today than it was fifty years ago. But I may be wrong.

Perhaps this mutual caution in conveying compliments—or at least delaying them for decades—occurs because we are not at all sure the possible recipient, in fact, reciprocates our good will. Precise information on that point is so elusive that I won't pursue it any farther. It is also true that uncertainties arise from the reluctant realization that we have inherited students already steered to history by a hand (or a mind) other than our own. I want to say something more about that because egotism often prompts us to believe that we (or I) inspired so-and-so to love and pursue history as a vocation.

On the contrary, there is abundant evidence that many of our star pupils were attracted to Clio long before they entered our orbit. As Merle Curti wrote to me several years ago,

> like many children I loved history and knew before the end of high school in 1916 that studying and teaching it would be my central life interest. Two remarkable high school teachers encouraged me to think of history not only as puzzle-solving fun but as an exciting exploration of relations between "facts" and values, the efforts of agents, and of chance. This influenced my feelings about history from then on. [138]

I have seen similar statements about their high school history teachers from Gilbert Fite and Oscar O. Winther, one-time editor of the *Journal of American History* (1963–66), and on the European side from Lawrence Stone, the economic historian W. H. B. Court, Arnold Toynbee, and Fernand Braudel. Braudel's imagery is the most memorable. "I had a superb teacher," he recalled, "a man who was intelligent, considerate, authoritarian, and who recited the history of France as though he were celebrating Mass." [139]

And then, for those of us who teach graduate students, it is all too easy to forget, if we ever even knew, that these aspiring professionals were really

Fig. 1.7   Merle Curti (1897-1996) by Harold Hone (ca. 1954).
Courtesy of the University of Wisconsin-Madison Archives.

inspired to follow a career in history not because of ourselves but because of one or more inspirational teachers at the collegiate level. Carl Becker immortalized Frederick Jackson Turner's impact as a charismatic teacher of undergraduates at Wisconsin during the 1890s, and Merle Curti repeated that experience with Turner at Harvard College two decades later.[140]

Much less familiar to us is the transforming relationship of Robert Athearn with a devoted history teacher at a small college in central Montana, or John Hope Franklin's similar experience with Theodore S. Currier, who developed new courses expressly for Franklin at Fisk University, or intellectual stimulation enjoyed by H. Stuart Hughes from Laurence B. Packard at Amherst College during the 1930s.[141]

What is particularly notable in this context is that Franklin and Hughes regarded graduate study at Harvard as a far less nurturing experience than being a history major in college. More recently we have heard explicit echoes of that poignant concern from Christopher Lasch, who found the graduate program at Columbia a great let-down, and from John Demos, who so much enjoyed the close work with his undergraduate tutor at Harvard, William R. Taylor. Michael Zuckerman conveys a similar sense of loss and disorientation when he left a comforting relationship with Murray Murphy in the American Civilization major at Penn, as does Linda Gordon when she describes the transition from warm nurturance at Swarthmore to enigmatic instructors in European history at Yale. They were so disenchanting that she dropped out but subsequently returned as a novice to the field of American history.[142]

If a person has not had a positive experience as an undergraduate history major, he or she is not likely to pursue a Ph.D. in our discipline. But an inversion of that equation is clearly no guarantee of success. A glorious collegiate experience with Clio is commonly, though not inevitably, followed by disappointment at the graduate level. The fault does not always lie with the faculty, however. Sometimes undergraduates select the wrong institution, or a mentor unsuited to them, because of misinformation or simply inadequate information about a particular institutional or intellectual destination. At other times, however, such situations have happy endings. Does anyone recall, for example, that Richard Hofstadter's major teacher at Columbia was Merle Curti? Coming there in 1937 from Buffalo, Hofstadter simply assumed that Curti was a fellow Marxist. Curti wrote: "This astonished me. He was probably thinking of the emphasis on class and class conflict which did inform my book *The Social Ideas of American Educators* (1935)."[143]

It should come as no shock to anyone that, occasionally, professional historians have been known to turn against their former mentors and commit intellectual parricide. Ordinarily this is not a matter of deliberate cruelty or vengeance but a manifestation of the need to establish an autonomous intellectual identity.[144] Much less common, though not unknown, scholars have sometimes refused to acknowledge their dissertation supervisors, metaphorically erasing them from the personal chalkboard of experience when publishing a first book. Somewhat more surprising, at least to me, is the way former teachers have been known to take umbrage at revisionist or merely independent lines of thought taken by erstwhile students. Most astonishing of all is that the examples with which I am most familiar involve mentors who had become immortals in the sense that their reputations were exceedingly secure when they chose to take umbrage.

My first illustration involves Merle Curti, who learned in 1953 about a panel discussion concerning European and American intellectual history that took place at a meeting in Vancouver, Canada of the AHA's Pacific Coast branch. Curti was disturbed because rumors reached him that Henry F. May had been critical of his approach—that is, grounding the history of ideas in social history—and because John Higham, Curti's first Ph.D. student from the University of Wisconsin, also had seemingly deviated to some degree from Curti's application of an external/internal distinction to "the broad area of social thought in such a way as to reveal the thinking of great masses of people and to put these popular ideas in a sociological context."[145]

Higham closed his explanatory letter to Curti with these candid, engaging, and poignant sentences:

> Now if I may [be] as frank as you I will add that I think you are too darn sensitive. You have reached the highest pinnacle of the historical profession at such an early age that you still have great things ahead of you. Your reputation is secure. At the moment the danger seems to me to be not that you may be appreciated too little but that you may be criticized too little because of your influence. I have often noticed how the leading professional historians are hardly ever subjected to the kind of friendly but penetrating criticism that would stimulate controversy and generate new departures. One reason why you have always meant a great deal to me is that you always encouraged me to try something quite different from what others were attempting. This is the best side of you and the one I shall follow. I am a devoted friend and a deeply indebted former student but not a disciple.[146]

My second (and chronologically simultaneous) illustration of a mentor's tendency to be thin-skinned arises from Bernard Bailyn's lengthy published review of Perry Miller's book *The New England Mind from Colony to Province* (1953). After praising Miller's "brilliant technique," Bailyn, then an untenured assistant professor at Harvard just one year beyond the Ph.D., observed that

> new viewpoints and the social changes that underlie them are the real subjects of this volume, for they were the effects and the causes of the New England mind from colony to province. Difficulties arise from this fact . . . . In assessing the social changes to which he rightly assigns the main causative impulses, he is less successful. The mastery of detail and the soberness of judgment which mark all his work in intellectual history are occasionally lacking in his treatment of the social scene.

Bailyn ended this long review by commenting that Miller "wanders afield" as he approached the later seventeenth century, and that the final portions of the book were relatively "formless" in comparison with earlier sections. Because Miller broadened the scope of his inquiry as he proceeded, Bailyn felt that he found it increasingly difficult "to unify and harmonize his voluminous materials."[147]

Many years later Bailyn told a gathering of his own students that that review had made Miller "pretty sore." In 1961, when *Colony to Province* appeared in a paperback edition, Miller wrote a prickly new preface in which he answered Bailyn's review (without actually naming him) with this

Fig. 1.8 Perry Miller (1905-63). Courtesy of the Harvard University Archives.

defiant response, insisting upon the self-defining autonomy of intellectual history.

> The most charitable of my critics paid me a dubious compliment on my ability "to extemporize" the history of New England society, but he intended this courtesy to be a rebuke to the profession for not having yet built the foundation on which my account ought, by rights, to have been based. He implied that therefore that construct was floating in thin air, like some insubstantial island of Laputa.
>
> My unrepentant—or should I say defiant?—contention is quite the reverse. The terms of Puritan thinking do not progressively become poorer tools than were the concepts of the founders for the recording of social change. On the contrary, they are increasingly the instruments through which the people strove to cope with a bewildering reality. Unless we also approach that buzzing factuality through a comprehension of these ideas, it becomes even more a tumultuous chaos for us than it was for those caught in the blizzard. Unless we can do this, the writing of history ceases to be a work of the mind.[148]

Unlike Curti, who insisted that ideas must be understood in their social context, Miller regarded ideas as prime movers to which social realities were almost epiphenomenal.

Lest the graduate students who read these pages conclude that Ph.D. mentors must be mean-spirited monsters likely to repudiate their own progeny, let me close this section with an unknown narrative of kind nurturance. David M. Potter entered the graduate program in History at Yale in 1932. After four years in residence he left, his dissertation barely begun, and became an instructor in the history department at the University of Mississippi, where he took his teaching obligations very seriously. In 1938 he moved to the Rice Institute in Houston where he continued to be a conscientious teacher and while working at his dissertation established a life-long habit of perfectionism. Yale's regulations, however, stipulated that degree candidates who did not finish within seven years must be dropped from the rolls.

Precisely because the American historians at Yale regarded Potter so highly, in March of 1938 they began imploring him by mail to finish, regaling him with tales of first-rate former students who never finished their degrees because they procrastinated, perfected their work, or unwisely chose to teach summer school (as Potter did in 1938) rather than writing their dissertations. As Leonard W. Labaree (responsible for administering the graduate program) explained to Potter in a letter of warning,

> I would not sermonize you in this fashion if I thought you were just an average person, but I feel that you have capabilities and promise as a productive scholar which you must not allow to atrophy. I realize the value and broadening experience of your teaching but there is such a thing as overdoing it. You also have, perhaps, a tendency toward being a "perfection-ist" in your scholarly work—a quality admirable only if present in limited quantities.[149]

One year later, nearing the close of his seventh year of candidacy, Potter recognized that he would be unable to complete four remaining chapters in less than a month. Consequently, confessing his acute humiliation, he petitioned for a one-year extension. He explained that since leaving New Haven in 1936 he had never taught less than three courses per term and had never taught the same course twice! "I have thought all along," he told Ralph H. Gabriel, "and still think that these academic duties deprived me of any normal opportunity to push projects of my own. . . . But I am conscious that, with extraordinary diligence and judgment, I might have overcome the obstacles in question, and that I must forfeit your confidence for the present." He then made a pledge: "If granted an extension, I will either finish the business during the coming summer or abandon my doctoral aspirations altogether." [150]

Potter then received from the director of graduate studies a terminal date of May 1, 1940. Potter met the deadline comfortably and in 1942 the Yale University Press published his truly distinguished dissertation as *Lincoln and His Party in the Secession Crisis*. [151] In 1942 Yale promptly brought Potter back as an assistant professor of history. Five years later, even before being promoted to a tenured associate professorship, he went off to Oxford to serve a term as the Harmsworth Professor of American History. He achieved so much success there that Oxford pleaded with him to continue for another year, but Yale pulled him back, put him in charge of its American Studies program, made him a full professor in 1949 (responding to an offer from Northwestern University), and one year later advanced him to the Coe professorship. From high anxiety to the pinnacle of success within a decade. Sometimes virtue really is rewarded!

Coping with Criticism: Constructive, Depersonalized, and Deeply Personal

The historian's vocation is a collective enterprise—I like to call it lonesome mutuality—in which the quest for "truth" somehow moves along because we candidly offer searching criticism of one another's work. That's the ideal, at least, and sometimes it is actually fulfilled in practice. Often, though not always, criticism can be objective and detached. More commonly, however, critics are likely to assess the work of others through the prism of their own perspective and identity, and when that happens, obviously, the personal and the professional may become inextricably enmeshed.

In theory, perhaps, detachment is considered more desirable than personal engagement. Detachment is regarded as being more scholarly and judicious. Don't we all disdain the obtuse reviewer who seems to wish that we had written a different book than the one we actually set out to write? Be that as it may, our profession feeds on controversy. It is contestation that generates conversation at professional meetings. In their heart of hearts, book review editors yearn for the lively review that is likely to stimulate dialogue (though not a libel suit). After Douglass Adair had ceased to be editor of the *William and Mary Quarterly* he urged the book review editor to commission essay reviews of provocative books that would raise major issues for the profession. "I have a curiously old-fashioned prejudice," Adair explained, "that your magazine space is better devoted to the important piss and vinegar items that appear rather than the run-of-the-mill bland stuff that our profession squeezes out—lies flat on the brush, no odor, no taste."[152]

Historians cope with criticism and contestation in different ways because such conflicts occur under diverse circumstances in response to variable stimuli. I want to examine four such stimuli: one of them sought after; the second one unsought but conducive to intellectual growth even when it is dissenting; the third anticipated with fear, and consequently inhibiting; and the fourth engaged in reluctantly because it may very well lead to a slugging match. Needless to say, these four become progressively more fascinating to observers as we proceed from the first to the fourth. Therefore I will be briefest on the first two.

Criticism Solicited in Advance of Publication

This is the critical feedback that the profession reads about in our acknowledgments but almost never actually sees. We seek it from friendly colleagues with some kind of expertise on the subject of our work. We do not ordinarily send our projects in advance of publication to hostile competitors. I suppose Robert Fogel and Stanley Engerman did so with pre-publication copies of *Time on the Cross* in 1973–74, but that sensational episode is scarcely representative of how we customarily operate. Far more characteristic, by way of example, is Richard Hofstadter sending the manuscripts of his forthcoming books to such shrewd friends as Daniel Bell, David Riesman, and C. Vann Woodward in order to hone the conceptual aspects and eliminate potential gaffes.[153]

Trouble can arise, however, when someone whose judgment you value tells you that your manuscript has a serious flaw. Then you send the manuscript to a second friend for evaluation. If he or she does not mention the same flaw, then you are likely to assume that the first reader is having marital problems and as a result is irritable and hypercritical. If the second reader calls attention to the same problem as the first reader, however, then it's back to the drawing board.

So we love to get the kind of response that Hofstadter received from Woodward on the lengthy portion of *The Progressive Historians* (1968) dealing with Charles A. Beard:

> To tell you the truth, I rather dreaded reading you on Beard. I knew you would have to be crushingly critical of his history and I could not bear to see you be crushing about the man. There was just too much I cherished in the old codger, too much I loved him for. And I was afraid that these values would get battered in the critical process—and that I would have to tell you I didn't like it.

But I should have known better. You spared me any such embarrassment. You left me nothing to complain about on that score. You are as protective of those values as I could have wished. And without pulling your punches in the critical assessment. That to me is the most gratifying achievement of the whole treatment and I congratulate you. You make it possible to admire the man without endorsing his history. Those final pages about the "ruin" are as grand as anything you have written.

The critical assessments are far more than a synthesis of the monographic stuff and full of fresh apercus. The whole picture rounds out to a satisfying and authoritative judgment that should stand for a long time. . . . I got over my nit-picking impulses after the first few pages, but might as well pass on the trivialities I jotted down.[154]

It's very comforting to correct the trivialities and feel reassured that nothing major has gone awry. This is the kind of critical feedback that can lull us into a false sense of security, but it allows our gastric juices and our ulcers to lie low for about twelve to twenty months.

Dialogues Prompted by Perceptive Though Critical Reviews

A second kind of critical feedback is, in my view, by far the most rewarding yet also, perhaps, least germane to the focus of this essay. It usually occurs when some well-informed and fair-minded individual with a different ideological or methodological "take" than your own reviews your work, obliges you to think about it in an alternative way to the one you have chosen, and usually causes you at least to acknowledge that you have not communicated your views or your meaning with the clarity that you might have wished for. That is exactly what happened in 1963 when David M. Potter reviewed *The Radical Right: The New American Right* and as a consequence engaged in a serious, courtly, and intellectually sinuous dialogue with Richard Hofstadter concerning not only that volume of essays but, even more, Hofstadter's *The Age of Reform* (1955) as well.[155]

Reading their correspondence, one has the sense of two earnest scholars who had not previously met, swiftly developed rapport based upon genuine mutual esteem, modified their views in *some* respects, yet ultimately remained committed to incompatible positions. A few substantive extracts from their correspondence should convey the sense of what must have been a marvelous experience of intellectual growth for both men.[156]

R.H.: Whatever the justness of my characterization of the Pop[ulist] mentality —and it can certainly be argued with—I never at any time thought it important to attribute its qualities, as you say here, to status anxieties. I have searched my account of the Pops without being able to find the text that people must be drawing on to arrive at such an interpretation. . . . I never thought that status anxiety had any important bearing on the Pop movement. . . . The use of concern over status as an explanatory principle in my book was made only a propos of certain elite leaders of Progressivism and their forerunners in Mugwumpery. It was not applied to the entire Progressive movement. . . .

As to the closing point of your review, I can only say touché. Of course I didn't mean to say that most persons who have prejudices are pseudo-con., though that is not an unreasonable reading of the sentence you quote. I think what I meant to say was that as you find people have more prejudices, and more intense ones, you find the proportion of pseudo-c's among them rises. However, that's not what I said, unfortunately. But again, I never imagined that if the right is prejudiced, the left must be tolerant as you say in yr previous paragraph. Never. In fact a good part of the pt of the Age of Reform was to try to show that the two have more resemblances than is commonly recognized!

D.M.P.: When we come to the point . . . of whether *The Age of Reform* attributes status anxieties to the Populists, I must say that I think it does . . . . [It] speaks very pointedly about the status anxieties of the Populists and of the psychological manifestations which accompanied these anxieties. In fact it seems to me that all the way from p. 7 to p. 35 this theme is built up in an effective way and I might say, convincing way. . . . On p. 17, one meets the phenomenon of "psychic sprees that purport to be moral crusades," and the example given is a Populist one. . . . On p. 20, these psychic sprees have another significance for "Populism and Progressivism . . . particularly Populism" in seeming "very strongly to foreshadow some aspects of the cranky pseudo-conservatism of our time." On the next page, this involves "the choice of hatred as a kind of creed." . . .

As I tried to indicate in the review I am by no means unconvinced by the argument which I think I perceive and which you say is not there. This is perhaps the irony in this exchange of letters. What I felt in writing my review, was that the concept of status motivation is both basic and inescapable, but that it is also very tricky, and that perhaps the trickiest thing about it is that it tends to discredit any group to whom it is applied, while the concept of interest motivation tends to justify those to whom it is applied.

R.H.: Your letter was most helpful, and you make your point all too well. I don't know why my eye has glided over that passage about "Rank in society," but it can certainly be taken as justification of your reading of the Populist chapters. I think I said more than I meant, but it is of course impossible to recover just now what I had in mind. . . .

The use of status as an explanatory principle is, of course, tricky, and perhaps we would not be using it at all if it weren't for the fact that the generation of Beard and Turner made such heavy use of conflict and ec. interest that they ran them straight into the ground, and we had to turn elsewhere to find at least some supplementary principles of explanation.

I do confess that I am puzzled by the common feeling that somehow or other to be moved by a desire to protect one's status is a less rational or less creditable motive than pursuing one's economic interest. One can be irrational and outrageously demanding in the pursuit of either ec. or status considerations. And of course it is always possible to pursue them in a constructive way. I thought I had made it clear in my treatment of the Prog. leaders that their concern for protection of their status had led them into socially useful paths of protest—and then I was surprised at how many readers thought I was trying to discredit them.

However, I am more alarmed at some of the acceptance of my notions by students and young historians than I am by most of the criticism I get—particularly when I see people referring to the Status Revolution as though it were an established entity rather than an explanatory hypothesis.

I did not think that your review was in the nature of an intentional misrepresentation, or that it went beyond fair comment, and now that I have heard from you, I can see that you have read the book with possibly more care on this point than I wrote it! One can always tell the difference between the first-rate and third-rate spirits in our field by the manner in which points are made: people like yourself are interested in advancing our understanding of the subject, and the petty chaps are interested in scoring points against the author.

What we have in this superb exchange of letters, from which these are only selective extracts, is a prime example of intellectual contestation at its most constructive. Tragically, both men had less than eight more years to live. Each career was curtailed at its apogee by cancer. Both scholars left major works incomplete when they died on October 24, 1970 (Hofstadter) and February 18, 1971 (Potter). But the writing that remained to them after 1963 ripened and became even more sophisticated, nuanced, and self-aware, perhaps as a partial consequence of their epistolary encounter.[157]

Popular Historians' Fear of Academic Criticism

There is a genuine problem with terminology here because the kinds of writers I have in mind were not amateurs and they were not popularizers in any pejorative sense of that word. They worked very hard at their craft and they were, indeed, professionals because they made their living from magazine and book royalties, whereas for most of us such royalties are an adjunct to our institutional wages. Moreover, to designate people like Lewis Mumford, Bernard DeVoto, and Catherine Drinker Bowen as nonacademic historians would be to define them by what they were not rather than by what they were: namely, serious, professional writers who sought to reach a

Fig. 1.9 Catherine Drinker Bowen (1897-1973). Courtesy of the
Library of Congress, Department of Prints and Photographs,
Washington, D.C.

very broad audience. They wanted to tell a story that would be comprehensible and interesting to the nonspecialist reader; doing so required them to make compromises that most of us customarily do not worry about. They considered themselves as artists or authors first, and as historians second. They were determined to incorporate drama and develop tension.

But there seems to be a wrong-headed notion that they have been indifferent to the opinions of academic scholars—a notion that has circulated, I think, because we pick up second-hand fragments of their table talk rather than probing thoroughly what they said privately to their confidants and what they actually did as they brought their book manuscripts to completion.[158]

While Catherine Drinker Bowen (1897–1973) was working on *Miracle at Philadelphia* (1966), her best-selling history of the Constitutional Convention in 1787, her confidant was John H. Powell, also a writer of popular history and drama. She sent him segments of her text in draft form and talked through every problem that she faced, large and small. At one point early in the spring of 1965, when she was struggling, Bowen implored Powell to "please bear in mind I write NOT for the professors but for my usual audience, people like Bessie Evans who with her husband reads all kinds of history aloud. . . . One thing: The book simply HAS to move, to have pace, cannot sit down and inform. I want people to READ it—not to make money for me. . . ." She signed this letter "Love, misgivings, hopes," a clear indication of her anxious state of mind at the time.[159]

A little more than a year later, however, when *Miracle at Philadelphia* was almost ready to go into production, Bowen sang a rather different song to Edward Weeks, senior editor at the Atlantic Monthly Press. Now the levels of anxiety and ambivalence about audiences become more complex, and consequently more revealing:

> Actually, throughout these 25 years, since *Yankee from Olympus*, ["the professors"] have been wonderful to me. I have it's true a running feud with them on the subject of art versus scholarship. There shouldn't be a *versus* but there surely is. . . . Its true also that I have a mighty dread of making mistakes of scholarship and getting caught out. But this is a healthy fear, and is as it should be.

Following two pages describing the courtesies and honors that she had received from academic historians, Bowen closed with a postscript: "I hope this letter doesn't sound conceited. I am STILL scared of the professors. But I don't want them to know it except in my own terms."[160]

It should not be necessary to proliferate illustrations in order to persuade readers that beneath the bravura of professional writers who produce history for a lay or popular audience lies a deep concern about receiving hostile criticism from academics—a vocational cleavage that basically began, I think, in the 1920s. I do not find it in the previous generation when James Ford Rhodes, Theodore Roosevelt, and Woodrow Wilson wrote their multivolume histories aimed at the general public. A new psychological dynamic appeared in the '20s when Lewis Mumford said to Van Wyck Brooks: "Someday I must write a real history of American civilization and culture; treated as a whole; but I don't want to have my hand forced until I can do it with a grand gesture, and with a firmness that will win the reluctant assent of the professional historians."[161]

It may seem a somewhat peripheral point here, but I am struck by the disputes and volatile judgments rendered by nonacademic historians about the kind and quality of history being written among themselves. The point is germane, I believe, because so much personal animus (or approbation) lay beneath their intellectual judgments. Mumford and Brooks, for instance, intensely disliked the iconoclastic Bernard DeVoto because he had been critical of work by both of them. At Christmas time in 1932 Mumford informed his friend that he was using "the season of peace and cheer and goodwill to begin a murderous attack upon Mr. Bernard DeVoto. . . . [He] is, fundamentally, a jackass. Unfortunately jackasses live for years in our society, treated as pedigreed horses, and surrounded by all our outward marks of respect and admiration, and even their long ears are praised as an evidence of originality in horses."[162]

A few years later, however, when constitutional historian Thomas Reed Powell mobilized support from Felix Frankfurter and Kenneth B. Murdock to nominate DeVoto for membership in the Century Association, he composed the following endorsement:

His underlying major interest is American social history. The life and the outlook of varying groups in different localities and different periods are the focal points of his curiosity and his solid scholarly researching. His interest in literature is not from the standpoint of the Ivory Tower . . . . Perhaps some one can find an inner fundamental unity in what seem to me contradictory characteristics. Perhaps what seem to me the diversities of his own nature are merely the reflection of the diversities of culture in American social history.[163]

Reading through the correspondence of writers like DeVoto, Brooks, Mumford, Bowen, and others who worked outside of academe, I am struck by the personal intensity, length, and detail of their communications.[164] Such letters tend to be more animated, expressive, and have a different texture than most academic correspondence. In part that is because they were, above all, writers, but there is another reason that relates directly to the central focus of this essay, personal identity and the historian's vocation.

The position of independent historians, unaffiliated with an institution, is not only ill-defined in our society, it is precarious. Neither an adolescent nor an undergraduate history major declares that he or she wants to become a Bancroft, a Prescott, or a Parkman "when I grow up." For that matter, I don't believe that Barbara Tuchman or David McCullough could have imagined at age 20 or even 25 how their careers as independent historians would develop.

The principal point I wish to make here is that the lives of professional, *affiliated* scholars are no more isolated or lonely than we choose to make them. Just look at the proliferation of jointly taught courses, the multiauthored textbooks, the collaborative projects of people like Paul Boyer and Stephen Nissenbaum, Stanley Elkins and Eric McKitrick, or the team projects headed by the late Herbert G. Gutman or by Jacquelyn Dowd Hall, to select arbitrarily just a few of my favorite examples.[165]

By comparison the situation of independent scholars is quite different and rather difficult. A very few may eventually get big advances from publishers; but the vast majority labor under adverse circumstances without the alternative option and satisfaction of classroom contact when their muse fails to inspire or their money runs out.

Historical Contestation and Personal Destruction

There have been intense, even bitter controversies among and between historians of the United States that ultimately reflected little credit on any of the participants, nor did the conflicts particularly advance or improve the profession in some intellectually significant way. I have in mind, as examples, Samuel Eliot Morison and Charles A. Beard during the 1940s, or Oscar Handlin and William Appleman Williams during the 1960s.[166] There have been instances when historians actually committed suicide because of severe depression resulting, at least in part, from repudiation of their work, or else the inability to make progress with a particularly difficult project. I have in mind the tragic cases of Robert Starobin, John William Ward, and Gene Wise.[167]

It may surprise young and apprentice historians, but even senior scholars often find the presentation of a paper at a professional meeting an occasion for high anxiety. At a conference of early American historians in 1966, for example, when Douglass Adair first presented what became one of his two most distinguished essays, "Fame and the Founding Fathers," he barely made contact with personal friends of long standing because of anxious jitters. As Adair explained subsequently to Edmund S. Morgan, "as my speech time approached I became quite nervous and numb." A little more than two years later, in fact, following hospitalization for depression and alcoholism, Adair committed suicide.[168]

I want to explore a highly dramatic confrontation between two of the best-known historians in the Anglo-American world during the middle third of the twentieth century, Allan Nevins and Arnold J. Toynbee. I am going to talk about it because it exemplifies mutually critical confrontation at its destructive worst, and because it was totally unnecessary—having been staged like a human cockfight—and because it appears to be utterly unknown except to offspring of the participants. I also believe that it is an interesting event from the perspective of a historian because the accounts that have survived are so very different in their degrees of disclosure and tone. It barely seems as though Nevins, Toynbee, and the Los Angeles *Times* are describing the same event. Moreover, the personal as well as professional consequences for Nevins could not have been more serious. It effectively shut down his highly productive career.[169]

In 1958 Nevins retired from his professorship after almost thirty years at Columbia and became a permanent Senior Fellow in residence at the Huntington Library in San Marino, California, where he worked tirelessly on his multivolume history of the Civil War. (According to one memoir of Nevins written by a Los Angeles friend, during the course of public lectures Nevins would routinely recommend *The Ordeal of the Union* as an ideal wedding present. It's really not a bad pun when you think about it.)[170] Nevins swiftly became a dominating personality at the sequestered Huntington and something of a local celebrity among the affluent, well-educated denizens of the Pasadena area.

Born in 1889, Toynbee was one year older than Nevins and in 1956 retired as Research Professor of International History at the University of London. Still quite vigorous and prolific as a writer, Toynbee made annual visits to the United States in order to earn money by giving public lectures. Perhaps in this case familiarity bred contempt, but with each passing year he became increasingly disenchanted with U.S. government policies, more particularly the American role in international affairs. He endorsed unilateral nuclear disarmament, at least for the United Kingdom, even if that meant geopolitical concessions to the Soviet Union, and in an interview published in *Playboy* (April 1967) he said that communism had more to offer Latin America than anything ideological or economic that the United States could provide.[171]

In some respects, Nevins and Toynbee were temperamental twins. Each man possessed an astonishing work ethic. In 1969 Toynbee wrote in an autobiographical volume that "anxiety and conscience are a powerful pair of dynamos. Between them, they have ensured that I shall work hard." A few paragraphs later, however, he added the following, which Nevins might readily have subscribed to. "When I am asked . . . why I have spent my life on studying history, my answer is 'for fun.' I find this an adequate answer, and it is certainly a sincere one. If the questioner goes on to ask whether, if I could have my life over again, I would spend it in the same way again, I answer that I would, and I say this with conviction."[172]

Nevins certainly would have echoed that. His candid and detailed private journals provide abundant evidence. In the autumn of 1964, when Nevins made a teaching visit to Oxford University, he sent his full-time secretary at the Huntington a long, single-spaced list of directions, and concluded with

Fig. 1.10 Arnold Toynbee (1889–1975) and Allan Nevins (1890–1971) at the California Institute of Technology. Courtesy of the Archives, California Institute of Technology, Pasadena.

an admonition: "Please guard my study, my books, my typewriter, and my filing cabinets like a ferocious sabre-toothed tigress—if you can behave like one." In an unpublished interview that his secretary gave in 1970, after she had worked with Nevins for almost ten years, she said: "Well, he saw to it that I was very, very busy. I soon learned that if the typewriter stopped for a few minutes, he thought I wasn't working, and he'd be right out—'Oh, Mrs. Bean, are you busy? Have you got plenty to do?' " [173]

By 1967, however, the political differences between Nevins and Toynbee outweighed their temperamental similarities as workaholics. Whereas Toynbee ardently opposed the U.S. role in Vietnam, Nevins (always an American patriot) supported it. As he remarked a few years later while convalescing in Menlo Park, California: "I am much refreshed to see that Nixon is adopting some of the best Lyndon Johnson policies . . . and giving the Communists in Vietnam and Cambodia the hell they deserve. The silly students up here have quieted down a bit, and some arrests have helped. I hope that fines and prison terms will soon follow." [174]

Because Toynbee was in residence as a visiting professor at Stanford during the spring quarter of 1967, some antiwar Quakers managed to arrange for a public dialogue between the two men, and it took place on Saturday evening, April 29, before an overflow audience of 1500 at the

California Institute of Technology. Although a full-scale debate concerning Vietnam did not occur, the expectant audience apparently got its money's worth, and some of them paid scalper's prices to get in. Nevins, clearly quite nervous about this confrontation—he had suffered a heart attack in 1963 —tried very hard to establish clear ground rules well in advance, but Toynbee, behaving quite casually, acted as though they were headed for a genteel tennis match that required no warm-ups.[175]

Before we move on to the main event, it must be noted that Nevins was a veteran of highly visible public dialogues. In 1952, for example, NBC Television commissioned James Agee to write a series of scripts about Abraham Lincoln for "Omnibus." The completed film, which appeared early in 1953, ran four-and-a-half hours and was described at the time by one reviewer as a "personally addressed Passion play" in which Agee offered Lincoln as "a kind of American saint." Nevins attacked the program harshly for abusing poetic license in order to depict a legendary Lincoln rather than the historical man. NBC promptly arranged for a debate between Nevins and Agee that took place on "Omnibus" on March 29, 1953. Nevins was relentlessly overbearing in his fulminations against Agee: "He has tampered with the truth. He has taken a myth . . . and presented it to a great American audience as if it were verified truth." Agee writhed uncomfortably in his chair, and at the end his eyes filled with tears. The professorial Nevins left the poet/critic a numb ruin.[176]

Now let's turn to Nevins's own narrative of the Toynbee debate. As a compulsive journal keeper, his account is the fullest (though not the most substantive), and it includes most of the pertinent background. His entry begins on Friday, April 28, and continues seamlessly through April 30:[177]

A good many weeks ago a professor of politics at Cal Tech, named Langston, accosted me one day in the Huntington lunchroom, and asked me if I would hold a public talk with Arnold Toynbee sometime during the spring for the benefit of the Friends Service Committee. . . . As Toynbee is an old friend, and as I like to help out good causes, I said I would talk with him. . . .

This week I learned that all arrangements had been made. Beckman Auditorium at Cal Tech had been engaged and sold out, some tickets going at $25. Another hall a block or two distant had been half sold out to people who could listen, but not see. People were coming from goodly distances . . . . I began to feel nervous. After all, who am I to get into a discussion with this great historian. To be sure, I think a good part of his twelve volumes (including all the last four) tiresome, and other parts historically wrongheaded. He is far too much a determinist for me. . . .

So, nervously, I put my shoulder to some last minute preparations. I sent Toynbee in Stanford a brief outline of my ideas on the road the one-hour discussion ought to follow. He assented. I sent him a fuller exposition of my preliminary notions of the four or five principal problems we might attack. Our main theme is the probable progress and hazards of mankind through the remaining third of the present century. He assented to this, too. It was plain to both of us that if we got through one fifth of the subject-matter we laid out, we should do well. Declining his invitation to run (or fly) up to Stanford, I waited for him to come down.

This he did today, Saturday the 29th. In fact, he did not arrive until after three in the afternoon, and we were then interrupted by photographers and others. I gave him the head of five topics on which we seemed agreed as feasible bones to chew. He seemed to me much older than when I had seen him last, in Texas [at Rice] half a dozen years ago. No doubt I struck him in the same way. [They were 77 and 78 at the time.] But really he has aged rather distressingly. He walks with uncertain gait, has impaired vision, and even with the help of a hearing aid is plainly deaf. His mind, however, is active as ever. Mary drove me down to Cal Tech after a quiet dinner at home, and we had a few minutes of chat there.

Then suddenly we were propelled out upon the stage, where we seated ourselves at two tables, the twilit crowded hall before us, a battery of microphones around us. He threw some challenging observations at me on the tremendous disparity between the rapid advances of science and technology on one side, and the very uncertain and limping advances of mankind in controlling his ideas, prejudices, and emotions on the other. I responded with observations of my own. We were off! It was necessary to keep the ball moving, though we tried to maintain a relaxed bearing. Before I knew it the chairman was telling us our time was up. I thought we had but barely begun. We had covered but four of our five topics, and I had failed entirely to bring in some subjects I knew the audience would wish to hear Toynbee treat. . . .

The next day, Sunday, Toynbee and his wife had dinner at the Nevinses' home. Following a description of their table-talk, Nevins's journal summarized the episode in a single sentence: "On the whole, the Toynbee–Nevins talk was regarded by the auditors as a success—stimulating, provocative, [but] quite inconclusive." He may or may not have been correct intellectually; but in terms of Nevins's health, the event was literally provocative but scarcely inconclusive. More on that in a moment.

Toynbee summarized the entire episode in a single sentence. In fact, it is all that he seems to have said on the subject. The day after he returned to Stanford he wrote to a Scottish monk that he was back "from an expedition to Pasadena and Santa Barbara (at Pasadena a public dialogue—not dogfight, with Allan Nevins, for the American Friends Service Committee)." No verdict on win, lose, or draw.[178]

On Sunday the Los Angeles *Times* supplied the most substantive and therefore the most satisfactory account. In a discussion billed as "The Future of Man," it reported, the two mandarins "frequently disagreed in emphasis and gently needled each other." Although Vietnam was never mentioned by name, both participants clearly referred to it on several occasions. (Earlier in the day, at a press conference, Toynbee had lashed out at American policy in Vietnam as "morally wrong and unrealistic.") Toynbee urged that the United States and the Soviet Union should cooperate to establish a peaceful world order, and that China be granted a larger role in East Asia.[179]

The most heated exchange seems to have occurred early on when Nevins suggested that Americans had "a special sense of destiny" whereas the British no longer did. "Destiny is dangerous," Toynbee replied. "Japan believed she had the people of the Sun God and so did the Germans believe they had a destiny." Nevins answered that Americans felt they shared in a British tradition. "You didn't inherit the British tradition of losing a revolutionary war," Toynbee quipped, referring to British withdrawal from the colonies in 1781 in contrast to the American unwillingness to withdraw from Vietnam. "Our destiny is to preach liberty and free enterprise," Nevins shot back. "You should be very sure you have liberty and charity at home before you preach it abroad," Toynbee responded.[180]

Despite Nevins's unflustered journal account of the public dialogue followed by an amiable Sunday dinner the next day, the anxiety aroused by these issues and the rather personal nature of their confrontation evidently had a profound emotional and physical impact. A little more than five weeks later Nevins suffered a major stroke caused by a blood clot in his brain. In a second interview given a few years later by Lillian Bean, she made it very clear that stress precipitated the stroke and that Nevins had subsequently said so to her. When I interviewed Nevins's son-in-law in March 1994, he indicated that Nevins's wife and daughter completely agreed, and so does John Niven, a former Ph.D. student of Nevins who was teaching at the Claremont Graduate School, not far from Pasadena, in 1967.[181]

The blood clot gradually dissolved; Nevins eventually resumed work on *The Ordeal of the Union*; and on occasion even exchanged cordial notes with Toynbee. But he never regained the vigor and intense work schedule that had been his norm until June 1967. Within a year he left the Huntington for retirement in Menlo Park, where he died in a nursing home on March 5, 1971.[182]

Commitment and Contentment

An attempt to connect the personal with the professional might be more complete and perhaps inspiring if I listed historians who underwent vocational epiphanies, such as Edward Gibbon, Jules Michelet, Bernard Berenson, and Gershom Scholem. The difficulty there, however, is that I have encountered only two descriptions written by historians of the United States of their epiphanies: John Bach McMaster and Perry Miller.[183] (Amercanists are either more mundane or else less imaginative.) So that kind of arcane knowledge will have to await an increase in serendipity, which is the only way one collects this kind of information.

Consequently I will conclude with some comments on historians as "normal Americans," in part because some ideologically motivated politicians determined not long ago that liberals and intellectuals are not, in their view, normal Americans.* More important, perhaps, I sometimes wonder whether our *students* regard us as ordinary people who actually watch sports events on television, endure parenting crises, and, in the case of Frederick Jackson Turner, would much rather go fly fishing than go to the library.[184]

It may even be possible that among historians who labor for long years in libraries, in classrooms, and in committee sessions, the assumption exists that for those who manage to climb metaphorical mountains, nothing less than serene contentment awaits them. In my research, an examination of correspondence, diaries, and other personal papers demonstrates otherwise. It reveals a mix of anxiety and exasperation, occasional depression and even despair, accompanied by a modicum of self-satisfaction and serenity, sometimes.

A disabled historian, such as Robert V. Hine, who lost his sight for fifteen years but courageously continued to teach (superbly), do research, and write, provides us with a fresh awareness of what we can do despite adversity, of the diverse ways we accomplish our tasks, and why it matters — sometimes enormously, to ourselves and to our students.[185]

For disillusioned graduate students who loved the study of history when they were in college, there ought to be some kind of solace in the knowledge that their own mentors as well as historians whose work they read and

---

* When Republican ideologues announced in 1994 that liberal intellectuals were not "normal" Americans, they (perhaps unwittingly) followed the lead of John Sumner, advocate for the New York Society for the Suppression of Vice, who had expounded exactly that view in 1933 while attempting to censor Erskine Caldwell's novel *God's Little Acre*.

admire underwent many of the same experiences that they have. Professional training is tough and it can be demoralizing. Just remember the plight of David M. Potter between 1938 and 1940, or the disillusionment that Richard Hofstadter underwent during the 1940s. Remember the travail that began for Fawn Brodie in 1945 when she published her first book, a travail that really did not end until she died. Remember the mean slights and difficult circumstances that John Hope Franklin endured as an apprentice historian and journeyman. Each one of them climbed a mountain nonetheless; and yet, there is a sense in which we only (or only we) know that now. Did they feel that they were climbing a mountain back in the 1930s, '40s, and '50s? Perhaps, but I suspect that their emotional sense of what they were doing and how it would turn out must have been inchoate, partial, and tentative at best.

In Raymond Williams's wonderful essay, "Culture Is Ordinary," he uses family stories and autobiographical information to illustrate some of his points.[186] Professional historians actually do that rather infrequently. Both literally as well as figuratively, it just isn't "done." And as I have tried to indicate, prior to the 1970s a virtual taboo existed against it. *The Education of Henry Adams* is the most engagingly unrepresentative book that I have ever read. It is sui generis, of course, because Adams himself was.

Albert Einstein was also sui generis, obviously; but in the "Autobiographical Notes" that he wrote in German in 1946 at the age of 67, he made observations that seem to me illuminating in this context:

> What I have here said is true only within a certain sense, just a drawing consisting of a few strokes can do justice to a complicated object, full of perplexing details, only in a very limited sense. If an individual enjoys well-ordered thoughts, it is quite possible that this side of his nature may grow more pronounced at the cost of other sides and thus may determine his mentality in increasing degree. In this case it is well possible that such an individual in retrospect sees a uniformly systematic development, whereas the actual experience takes place in kaleidoscopic particular situations. The manifoldness of the external situations and the narrowness of the momentary content of consciousness bring about a sort of atomizing of the life of every human being.[187]

Almost forty years ago, by chance in the very year that I began graduate study, Michael Polanyi argued that much of the scientist's success depends upon knowledge that is acquired through interaction as well as serendipity, and therefore is very hard to articulate explicitly. Although the self-aware scientist must participate personally (i.e., as a particular person) in acts of understanding, that does not necessarily mean that the knowledge achieved is subjective. Learning and knowing and communicating, Polanyi wrote, involve a kind of fusion of the personal and the professional, the subjective and the objective.[188]

James D. Watson's famous memoir, *The Double Helix: A Personal Account of the Discovery of the Structure of DNA*, caused such a sensation in 1968, I believe, because it exemplified in astonishingly explicit ways just what Polanyi had been saying in more abstract terms.[189] Polanyi's revelation, if I may call it that, prompted him to reject the ideal of scientific detachment, and he moved from physical chemistry to the philosophy of science and social studies.

Not having had a revelation, not even having had an epiphany, I shall continue to pursue history as a vocation. It is the only one that I have ever known, and I enjoy it more than I can say. John Updike recalls his grandfather as having been, like himself, "bookish and keen to stay out of harm's way." Updike then offers an autobiographical observation about the reciprocal nature of his life as an observer. "The price that we pay, we Americans who shyly wish to live by our eyes and wits, at our desks, away from the frightening tussle of human strength and appetite and intimidation and persuasiveness, is marginality: we live chancily, on society's crumbs in a sense, as an exchange for our exemption from the broad brawl of, to give it a name, salesmanship."[190] Marginality is not an exorbitant price to pay if one finds value in serving as the synapses of memory to a society.

PART II

Perceptions
of Culture and
Public Life

Fig. 2.1 *The Navy Needs You* (1917), poster by James Montgomery Flagg. Courtesy of Department of Prints and Photographs, Library of Congress, Washington, D.C. James Montgomery Flagg (1877–1960) was appointed Military Artist for New York State during World War I. He made about fifty posters for the United States government.

2

Culture
and the State
in America

During 1989–90 the National Endowment for the Arts (NEA) underwent a fierce attack because it indirectly funded allegedly anti-Christian work by Andres Serrano and a Robert Mapplethorpe photographic exhibition considered pornographic by some.* In 1991 a revisionist, didactic display of Western art at the National Museum of American Art (part of the Smithsonian Institution) aroused congressional ire, yet that latter episode now seems, in retrospect, a fairly calm fracas compared with the controversy generated in 1994–95 by "The Last Act," a long-planned exhibition concerning the end of World War II in the Pacific that was canceled by the Secretary of the Smithsonian because of immense political pressure and adverse publicity emanating from veterans' organizations and from Capitol Hill.

Throughout 1995 those who hoped to eliminate entirely the National Endowment for the Humanities (NEH) and NEA, the Institute of Museum Services, and the Corporation for Public Broadcasting, and to reduce

* This essay was delivered as the presidential address at the annual meeting of the Organization of American Historians in Chicago, March 29, 1996.

support for the National Trust for Historic Preservation did not succeed, although they did achieve devastating budgetary cuts. Moreover, Speaker Newt Gingrich insisted in a two-page essay in *Time* magazine that "removing cultural funding from the federal budget ultimately will improve the arts and the country."[1]

All of these controversies and attacks, taken together, have had me wondering for years why it is that most nations in the world have a ministry of culture in some form, whereas the United States does not. Indeed, the very notion seems politically inconceivable in this country. It has actually been proposed from time to time, most notably in 1936–38 (offered in Congress during Franklin Roosevelt's second term as the Coffee–Pepper bill), but each time abortively.[2] It has been considered and rejected by several presidential administrations. Comparative investigation of state support for cultural projects, examined in historical perspective, provides grist for the mill of anyone inclined toward a belief in American exceptionalism, by which I mean difference, not superiority.[3]

The purpose of this essay, therefore, is to examine, in several different ways, the development of a historical context that has shaped contemporary relationships between government and culture in the United States along with contested attitudes concerning those relationships. I am persuaded that our controversies (as well as our current options) cannot be understood without historical perspective.

As a historian who entered the profession in the mid-1960s, my own views on this subject have been formed by essential legislation and events that occurred in 1965, a year that seems to me the pivotal turning point (in a positive sense) for the relationship between government and culture in the United States. I personally do not believe that the federal government should have or seek a national cultural policy in the French sense, meaning a specific agenda for a ministry of culture and related agencies determined in a highly centralized fashion.[4] I do, however, believe in governmental funding at all levels, sometimes on a collaborative basis, for cultural programs and institutions of many different sorts. Although I certainly cherish and applaud support from foundations, corporations, and private individuals, there are cultural imperatives, ranging from preservation to scholarly innovation, that will be achieved only with encouragement and help from the state. Although he carries the idea to an extremist conclusion that I do not share, I am intrigued by an assertion once made by the philosopher Horace Kallen: "There are human capacities which it is the function of the state to liberate and to protect in growth; and the failure of the state as a government to accomplish this automatically makes for its abolition."[5]

Complexities, Ironies, and Anomalies

Numerous complexities, ironies, and historical anomalies are evident in the relationship between government and culture in the United States. Three of them seem especially noteworthy. First, it has not simply been persons uninterested in cultural programs and those with a reflexive distrust of federal expansion who oppose government support for culture in the United States. To be sure, such conservative politicians as congressmen George A. Dondero of Michigan, H. R. Gross of Iowa, and Howard W. Smith of Virginia were frequent and formidable opponents. When legislation creating the two endowments neared passage in 1965, it was the irrepressible Representative Gross who offered an amendment that would have expanded the definitional scope of arts activity to include belly dancing, baseball, football, golf, tennis, squash, pinochle, and poker.[6]

A year later, when the Historic Preservation Act moved haltingly toward approval, Representative Craig Hosmer of California presented a comic version of the time-honored argument in opposition, using Al Capp's America as his point of reference. "Let us keep the hands of Washington, its resources, and its politics out of the arena of local historical interest," he declared. "In short, if Jubilation T. Cornpone's birthplace is to be preserved, Dogpatch should do it." [7]

Gross and Hosmer provide familiar voices of protest. Much less expected, however, is the opposition, mainly before 1965 to be sure, of such creative figures in American culture as Edward Hopper and Thomas Hart Benton, Duke Ellington and George Jean Nathan, Gilbert Seldes and John Cheever.[8] The painter John Sloan said that he would welcome a ministry of culture because then he would know where the enemy was. And in 1962 Russell Lynes, a widely read cultural observer, warned that

> those who administer the subsidies first must decide what is art and what is not art, and they will have to draw the line between the "popular" arts and the "serious" arts, a distinction that is increasingly difficult to define.... Having decided what is serious, it will follow that those who dispense the funds will also decide what is safe ... able to be defended with reasonable equanimity before a Congressional committee.[9]

From a historian's perspective, then, there really has been an astonishing reversal. We tend to forget that in 1964–65, when NEA was being hesitantly created, some of the most prestigious artists, art critics, and arts institutions felt suspicious of politicians and believed that they had more to lose than to gain from any involvement in the political process. Three decades later that pattern of mistrust has been turned inside out. Now it is numerous politicians who regard artists and arts organizations as tainted and unreliable. Consequently the former feel that they have much to lose if they endorse government backing of cultural programs.

A second anomaly worthy of attention arises from the fact that the United States actually does not lag behind all other industrialized countries in *every* respect where preserving the national heritage and environmental culture are concerned. We were the very first to set aside large and spectacular natural areas as national parks, a precedent followed by Canada and eventually by other countries.[10] Moreover, the United States created a precedent in 1917–18 when it became the first nation to allow federal tax deductions for cultural gifts to museums and nonprofit cultural organizations. The pertinent legislation has been altered several times since then, sometimes in ways that seem inconsistent to the point of being bizarre, but the operative principle has been an immense boon to cultural institutions. Moreover, the principle has become increasingly attractive to quite a few European countries during the past decade or so.[11]

A third complexity verges upon anomaly in the eyes of some, but is not widely or well understood. In accord with our commitment to a federal system of government, we have had since the early 1960s state agencies for the arts, and a network of state humanities councils since the mid-1970s. Their existence is reasonably well known to scholars, to nonprofit organizations such as local historical societies, and to civic leaders. Less familiar, though, are the quite separate state offices of "cultural affairs" (in some but not all states) that frequently have as their primary mission the promotion of tourism and related commercial activities within the state. Quite a few of these agencies, however, have been created in recent decades to do at the state level, and with little or no controversy, what many Americans apparently mistrust at the national level. In North Carolina the Department of Cultural Resources was the first such cabinet-level entity to be established in any of the United States. It emerged from the State Government Reorganization Act of 1971 as the Department of Art, Culture, and History. Its name was changed to the present designation a few years later.

The legislature of West Virginia created a Division of Culture and History in 1977 that includes five sections: Archives and History, Historic Preservation, Arts and Humanities, Museums, and an administrative unit. The state museums of New Mexico are run by the Office of Cultural Affairs. In Iowa the Cultural Affairs Advisory Council's mission is to advise the director of the Department of Cultural Affairs on "how best to increase the incorporation of cultural activities as valued and integral components of everyday living in Iowa." Wyoming now has a Division of Cultural

Resources, and in Hawaii the State Foundation on Culture and the Arts prepares programs designed to promote and stimulate participation in the arts, culture, and humanities.

As more American states create such governmental departments and programs, the process suggests a gradual, almost evolutionary (rather than revolutionary) departure from the long-standing preference for leaving to private and local groups the determination of decisions affecting the creation and conduct of cultural institutions. It has to be acknowledged, however, that in some states these bureaus cooperate harmoniously with the state arts and humanities councils, while in others a sense of rivalry exists; in a few the bureaus keep one eye nervously on the state legislature and the other warily on the arts and humanities councils that really ought to be their natural allies.

Thoughts on Not Having a National Cultural Policy

At the end of the 1960s UNESCO mobilized in Monaco a Round-Table Meeting on Cultural Policies and commissioned a series of booklets about state cultural programs in diverse nations of the world. The United States paper that was prepared for presentation in Monaco opened with this categorical yet somewhat enigmatic statement: "The United States has no official cultural position, either public or private." The author of the American booklet that resulted, Charles C. Mark, called his opening chapter "Cultural Policy within the Federal Framework" and offered this explanatory definition:

> The United States cultural policy at this time is the deliberate encouragement of multiple cultural forces in keeping with the pluralistic traditions of the nation, restricting the federal contribution to that of a minor financial role, and a major role as imaginative leader and partner, and the central focus of national cultural needs.[12]

Simultaneously, Roger Stevens, the first chairman of NEA (1965–69), declared that his agency did not have a cultural policy as such, and his successor, Nancy Hanks, reiterated that position. By the autumn of 1977, however, spokesmen for the Carter administration asserted that by means of special task forces in tandem with state and national conferences, a cultural policy for America would be forthcoming. The following year Joan Mondale led a concerted effort to activate the Federal Council on the Arts and the Humanities, which had been inert since its legislative creation in 1965. One of the council's first responsibilities would be to review "the arts and cultural policy of the United States."[13]

Ambivalence and uncertainties ensued, though. In 1980 Representative Sidney R. Yates of Chicago, chairman of the House Appropriations Subcommittee on Interior and Related Agencies, requested a full-scale review of both NEH and NEA operations. The report that emerged more than eight months later concluded that NEA had failed to "develop and promote a national policy for the arts." When Yates called for clarification of NEA's objectives, its chairman, Livingston Biddle, was distressed on the grounds that compliance would require him to become a "cultural czar" and exercise control, a role highly inappropriate in a democratic society. After two intense days of hearings, Congressman Yates shelved the committee report and did not subsequently mention the need for a national cultural policy. Former Congressman Thomas J. Downey puts it this way, semifacetiously: "We have a cultural policy by the seat of our pants. We do it ad hoc." [14]

I am persuaded that what emerged during the Carter years—namely, the desire by a few people to articulate a national cultural policy—represented an aberration, albeit a recurrent one in the American past. For the most part we have not had such a policy because it seemed inappropriate in such a heterogeneous society as well as a potential flashpoint in the view of many political leaders. (The 1965 legislation creating the two endowments explicitly advocated "a broadly conceived national policy of *support* for the humanities and the arts. . . ." [my italics].) Ever since the administration of John F. Kennedy, despite very significant changes in the visibility of cultural activities in public life, it has remained essentially inexpedient or imprudent to advocate a full-blown national cultural policy. [15]

A notable exception to that generalization, however, involves Nelson A. Rockefeller, a man who once remarked that "it takes courage to vote for culture when you're in public life." Rockefeller remained a staunch advocate of government support for culture. New York created the first state council on the arts in 1960, a major precedent, during Rockefeller's first term as governor, and not by happenstance. Nancy Hanks served her apprenticeship as an arts administrator when Rockefeller hired her as a member of his advisory staff. [16] It has not been adequately recognized that John F. Kennedy, Lyndon B. Johnson, and Richard M. Nixon all accepted the idea of federal support for culture rather reluctantly because Nelson Rockefeller loomed as a potential threat for the presidency. Political consultants warned them that the active governmental role envisioned by Rockefeller appealed to an increasing number of major campaign contributors and influential local elites as well as voters. That was the advice given to Nixon, for example, by Leonard Garment, his closest advisor on cultural matters. It is revealing that directly following his reelection in 1972, Nixon no longer felt any need to keep pace with Rockefeller's freewheeling agenda for cultural programs. "The arts are not our people," Nixon told his aide, H. R. Haldeman. "We should dump the whole culture business." [17]

Nixon unleashed his cynicism once he knew that he would never again have to compete with Rockefeller for the White House. When John F. Kennedy campaigned in 1960 he refused to commit himself to federal support for cultural programs. During his presidency, according to August Heckscher, Kennedy always used the word "marginal" when questions of federal funding arose. And considering Lyndon Johnson's rage at writers and artists as a result of their critical reaction to his foreign policy and, more particularly, their negative response to the White House Festival of the Arts in June 1965, it seems almost a miracle that only a few months later he actually signed the legislation that created NEH and NEA. [18]

~

So the United States government has never had a national cultural policy—unless the decision *not* to have one can, in some perverse way, be considered a policy of sorts. (Unquestionably, creation of the national endowments in 1965 marked a notable break with tradition and legitimized the concept of *federal* support for culture.) Two partial exceptions to my assertion ought to be acknowledged, however.

It became apparent during the first half of the nineteenth century that public architecture would follow the classical revival model, a policy strengthened and extended between 1836 and 1851 when Robert Mills served as Architect of the Public Buildings in Washington, D.C. Having been a student of Jefferson, James Hoban, and Benjamin H. Latrobe, Mills mingled Palladian, Roman, and Greek motifs. By the end of his tenure a pattern had been firmly established that would endure. Although Mills certainly did not create the classical revival, he made it ubiquitous in prominent public structures. In this particular instance, the government's architectural policy turned out to be the lengthened shadow of one man's drafting board and engineering skills. [19]

The second partial exception, in my view, occurred during the Cold War decades, most notably 1946 to 1974, when a pervasive concern to combat and contain Communism prompted an unprecedented yet uncoordinated array of initiatives by the federal government to export American culture as exemplary illustrations of what the free world had to offer Europe as well as developing nations. A new position was created, Undersecretary of State for Cultural Affairs, with Archibald MacLeish as the first incumbent—America's closest counterpart, perhaps, to André Malraux of France. The State Department actually purchased and sent 79 works by contemporary artists abroad for exhibitions. [20] The Fulbright Scholarship Program emerged. The United States Information Agency came into being in 1953, and soon had jazz bands like Dizzy Gillespie's making international tours. Such exports achieved undeniable popularity wherever they went, and they were perceived as the music of individualism, freedom, pluralism, and dissent—fundamental qualities obliterated by Communism.[21]

From 1950 until 1967 the CIA covertly funded the Congress for Cultural Freedom, whose publications ranged from the widely admired monthly magazine *Encounter* to a slew of foreign language journals. What their editors and authors held in common was a liberal or even a radical hostility to Communism. Although Allen W. Dulles and other leaders of the CIA did not exactly share the values of such men as Dwight Macdonald and Melvin Lasky, they assumed that anti-Communist statements coming from the Left would carry special credibility.[22]

After 1963, when rumors of CIA support for the Congress for Cultural Freedom began to spread, the Congress gradually became discredited, especially following the escalation of U.S. bombing of North Vietnam in the spring of 1965. Stalwarts like George Kennan, however, defended the millions of dollars used by the CIA to disseminate Western values, and he based his support on curious yet symptomatic grounds. "The flap about CIA money was quite unwarranted," Kennan wrote. "This country has no ministry of culture, and the CIA was obliged to do what it could to try to fill the gap. It should be praised for having done so, and not criticized."[23] I find it intriguing that an American ministry of culture, rarely considered politically viable by anyone, might be envisioned by George Kennan as an appropriate vehicle for anti-Communist and ideologically related literature.

Culture and the State before 1965

Taking the long view, there were some unsuccessful efforts at government support, some highly expedient initiatives, and some embryonic moves that provide historical context for the major breakthrough that occurred in 1965, yet also help to explain why many participants in the polity still have ambivalent or even negative feelings about the existence of NEH and NEA.

Let's begin late in 1825, when President John Quincy Adams sent Congress his recommendations for a national university, astronomical observatories, and related programs. Congress scornfully rejected his initiatives and they never even reached the stage of serious consideration. Martin Van Buren and John C. Calhoun led the opposition with contemptuous charges of "centralization," a catchphrase that would become a standard rallying cry for more than a century among opponents of federal support for cultural projects.[24]

The federal government did fund exploring expeditions at intervals throughout the nineteenth century, the best known being the ones led by Lewis and Clark, Captain Charles Wilkes, Ferdinand V. Hayden, and John Wesley Powell. Although each of their ventures had assorted scientific objectives, including ethnography on some occasions, they received validation primarily because they served the national interest and, in the trans-Mississippi West especially, they also opened entrepreneurial vistas, ranging from railroad routes to water use for agriculture and ranching.[25]

The early history of the Smithsonian Institution provides us with a symptomatic object lesson for the subsequent story of government and culture in the United States: uncertain, politically troubled, and contentious. In the very year of the Smithsonian's inception, 1846, a Princeton scholar offered these rhetorical warnings to Joseph Henry, the first secretary (director):

> Is there any adequate security for the success or right conduct of an Institution under the control of Congress, in which that body have a right and will feel it to be a duty to interfere? Will it not be subject to party influences, and to the harassing questionings of coarse and incompetent men? Are you the man to have your motives and actions canvassed by such men as are to be found on the floor of our congress?[26]

As for inconsistency and uncertainty, Joseph Henry spent much of his tenure as secretary, 1846 to 1878, trying to *prevent* any merger between a proposed National Museum and the Smithsonian. His successor, Spencer Baird, however, promptly reversed that policy.[27] There would be many other vacillations and reversals in years to come. Cultural institutions, like any other kind, are bound to redirect their course, but the Smithsonian's prominence, and its peculiar circumstances as a privately endowed public institution, meant that its policies would be closely scrutinized. Unpredictability in those policies, especially under Baird's successor, Samuel P. Langley, made it all the more likely that the Smithsonian would come to be regarded as the "nation's attic," an institution of memory rather than its guiding gyroscope or compass for cultural affairs.

In 1904, two years before his death, Secretary Langley included at the outset of his annual report an upbeat assessment of the Smithsonian's political autonomy. He even specified the principal sources of that sheltered status: Congress and the Institution's Board of Regents.

> The appreciation of the work of the Institution by the American people is best testified by their representatives in Congress. This has been clearly demonstrated through many successive terms regardless of political change; by the judgment with which their representatives upon the Board of Regents are

selected; by the care by which they protect the Institution in its freedom from political entanglements. . . .[28]

Moving forward swiftly, as I must in this survey, we find that the American film industry received major federal support during the 1920s, a decade prior to the one we customarily emphasize in terms of federal support for cultural activities. It should be acknowledged, however, that the film industry's "angel" was the Commerce Department, which assumed that it was helping to sustain a fledgling but potentially important international industry, rather than "culture" as such. When World War II cut off the extremely lucrative European market that provided half of the income for Walt Disney's corporate enterprises, the U.S. government helped Disney develop audiences in Latin America. In 1941, moreover, when Disney was on the verge of bankruptcy, the federal government began to commission propaganda films that became Disney's mainstay for the duration of World War II.[29]

The proliferation of cultural programs during the New Deal—almost entirely for reasons of economic relief rather than as a result of any sudden epiphany about the importance of art for its own sake—has been so well documented that it requires no more than a mention here. Writers and painters, sculptors and photographers, folklorists and dramatists were able to feed their families, sustain or even launch careers, and they made some innovative as well as enduring contributions to the arts in America.[30]

We cannot ignore, however, the lingering hostility that led Congress to end these programs in the years 1939–41. It was not simply that the programs had already served their purpose, or that funds and human resources had to be redirected to a global military struggle. A great many politicians didn't believe the products had justified the expense. Congressmen had not been converted to the notion that government had a permanent role to play as a cultural entrepreneur or advocate. And theatrical productions, in particular, came to be regarded as leftist critiques of traditional American values. Representative Clifton Woodrum of Virginia, chairman of the House Appropriations Committee, expressed his determination to "get the government out of the theater business," and he succeeded.[31]

Nevertheless, the mid- and late 1940s, not customarily regarded as a propitious decade for governmental support of culture, produced promises of changes to come. Discussions of a national portrait gallery occurred even as World War II drew to a close. (The initiative for such a gallery actually dated all the way back to Charles Willson Peale, was raised again when the British Portrait Gallery was created in 1856, resurfaced once more after

World War I when paintings of the Versailles peace treaty negotiators and war heroes like Pershing were commissioned, and was envisioned by Andrew Mellon during the 1930s when he purchased works specifically for a portrait gallery that would be a separate entity from the projected National Gallery of Art.) As an illustration of how indirect support for the arts could occur, in 1949 Alan Lomax got Woody Guthrie a job writing and singing songs about venereal disease for a radio program on personal hygiene sponsored by the U.S. government. (Guthrie produced at least nine songs, a few of them clever and moving but most of them considered raunchy or outrageous.)[32]

During the 1950s the long-standing pattern of hesitancy and inconsistency persisted. In 1954 a special subcommittee of the House Committee on Education and Labor considered bills to establish arts foundations and commissions, including a proposed national memorial theater. A majority recommended against the bill, explaining that it would be an inappropriate expenditure of federal funds. "It is a matter better suited for state, local, and private initiative," they said.[33]

A forceful minority report, however, called attention to the propaganda value to the Soviet government if the United States stopped participating in international festivals of art, music, and drama. A New Jersey Democrat warned that the Soviet Union and its satellite states "picture our citizens as gum-chewing, insensitive, materialistic barbarians." Albert H. Bosch, a Republican from New York City, responded and probably spoke for many Americans at that time: "We are dubious, to say the least, of the contention that people abroad are drawn more easily to Communism because we have failed to subsidize, or nationalize, the cultural arts in the United States."[34] No one involved in that dialogue, however, had said anything about *nationalizing* the arts.

Change was clearly in the air by the later 1950s—most notably for our purposes an awakening sense of popular pride in American cultural activities, broadly defined, and the proliferation of cultural centers all across the country that could house those programs. The renaissance in American cultural awareness customarily identified with the Kennedy years actually had its genesis several years before Kennedy took office. In 1960, for example, *Life* magazine devoted a laudatory two-page editorial in its twenty-fifth anniversary issue to "The New Role for Culture."[35] Simultaneously, the American Assembly, based at Columbia University (created in 1950 by Dwight D. Eisenhower while he served as president of Columbia), invited August Heckscher, a patrician long prominent in New York's cultural life, to contribute an essay concerning "The Quality of American Culture" to a volume published in 1960 under the title *Goals for Americans:*

Programs for Action in the Sixties, Comprising the Report of the President's Commission on National Goals. Pieces like Heckscher's and the widely noticed editorial in *Life* suggest a new peak of interest and enthusiasm at all taste levels: highbrow, middlebrow, and mass culture.

The penultimate section of Heckscher's essay, called "Government and the Arts," acknowledged that "where government has entered directly into the field of art, the experience has too often been disheartening. Political influences have exerted themselves. ... The art which has been encouraged under official auspices has almost always favored the less adventurous and the more classically hide-bound schools." Heckscher then proceeded to turn the discussion in a new direction, however, one that would be followed during the Kennedy and Johnson administrations, and beyond. "From this experience," Heckscher observed, "leading figures in the art world have drawn the conclusion that anything is better than the intrusion of government."

> It may be questioned, however, whether such men are not thinking too narrowly as professionals, without adequate understanding of the governmental methods and institutions which in other fields, no less delicate than art, have permitted the political system to act with detachment and a regard for the highest and most sophisticated standards.[36]

(Heckscher clearly had the National Science Foundation in mind.)

During 1961 and 1962, when John F. Kennedy and his advisors briefly considered the creation of a cabinet-level department of fine arts or cultural affairs, August Heckscher was envisioned as the secretary of such a department and served JFK as Special Consultant on the Arts in 1962–63.[37]

Meanwhile, in the spring of 1960, eight months before moving from Harvard to Washington as Special Assistant to the President, Arthur M. Schlesinger, Jr., published a short piece titled "Notes on a National Cultural Policy." Much of it addressed what he called "the problem of television," and revealed a very different perspective when compared with the hands-off stance of cultural critics from Gilbert Seldes's generation. Schlesinger insisted that "government has not only the power but the obligation to help establish standards in media, like television and radio, which exist by public sufferance." There seemed to be no other way, he continued, "to rescue television from the downward spiral of competitive debasement." Much in this vigorous piece anticipated the famous address given by Federal Communications Commission (FCC) head Newton N. Minow in May 1961 to the National Association of Broadcasters, the well-remembered "Vast Wasteland" speech in which Minow threatened government regulation in order to improve quality control of television. (Late in 1960 Walter

Lippmann called for the creation of a federal television network because he felt that program quality on the commercial networks was so low.)[38]

In his final two pages Schlesinger moved more expansively to the difficult issue of broad responsibility for cultural policy in general. He acknowledged that compared with regulation of the media, "the case for government concern over other arts rests on a less clear-cut juridical basis." He reminded readers that John Quincy Adams had "clearly stated that a government's right and duty to improve the condition of the citizens applied no less to 'moral, political, [and] intellectual improvement.'" Schlesinger did not mention that most Americans had ignored President Adams. He did concede, however, that "the problem of government encouragement of the arts is not a simple one; and it has never been satisfactorily solved."

Schlesinger's closing remarks anticipated the new endowment initiatives implemented in 1965 and whose emergence has been fully described in several histories and memoirs:

> Government is finding itself more and more involved in matters of cultural standards and endeavor. The Commission of Fine Arts, the Committee on Government and Art, the National Cultural Center, the Mellon Gallery, the poet at the Library of Congress, the art exhibits under State Department sponsorship, the cultural exchange programs—these represent only a sampling of federal activity in the arts. If we are going to have so much activity anyway . . . there are strong arguments for an affirmative governmental policy to help raise standards. . . . Whereas many civilized countries subsidize the arts, we tend to tax them. [A series of recommendations followed.] . . . As the problems of our affluent society become more qualitative and less quantitative, we must expect culture to emerge as a matter of national concern and to respond to a national purpose.[39]

The extent to which Schlesinger's recommendations (along with those of Robert Lumiansky of the American Council of Learned Societies and others a few years later) were implemented during the mid-1960s and after surely must have exceeded even the wildest dreams of any wistful or visionary academic historian.

Some Problematic Developments Since 1965

The history of governmental support for cultural programs and related activities during the past three decades is familiar in certain respects yet obscure and sorely misunderstood in many others.[40] Although space does not permit even a cursory survey, I want to call attention to four problematic matters.

First, because the perception of a tension between "quality and equality" has been troublesome, most of the conferences and blue ribbon reports that have appeared since 1965 emphasize, *pari passu*, the goals of "supporting excellence" and "reaching all Americans." One rubric that has resulted from these dualistic goals is "excellence and equity." Many of the key figures in the post-1965 period have believed that they could square the circle and achieve both. Hence Ronald Berman at NEH and Nancy Hanks at NEA both loved the so-called blockbuster museum exhibits during the 1970s because they brought first-rate materials to audiences of unprecedented size. When Joan Mondale led the Federal Council on the Arts and the Humanities late in the 1970s, she made this declaration: "If being an elitist means being for quality, then yes, I am for quality. If being a populist means accessibility, then yes, I am a populist. I want the arts to be accessible."[41]

Quite a few of the key participants in this narrative have insisted over the past twenty-five years that "excellence versus equity" is a false dichotomy, a nonissue, a diversion that obscures more important matters. As I read through pertinent texts and historical records, however, the fact remains that keen observers have regarded the tension as real and problematic. Many crucial policy makers, moreover, are divided, explicitly advocating either more emphasis upon excellence or else greater attention to the democratization of resources and opportunities.[42]

I find it curious that in so much of the discourse (including speeches, testimony, and commission reports) "excellence" is casually used with positive implications while "elitism" has pejorative connotations. Yet many of the advocates of excellence are essentially elitists in terms of wanting quality control, and many of the so-called elitists are guilty of nothing more than insisting upon rigorous peer review procedures because they believe that taxpayers' money should be used accountably to support those projects most likely to have enduring value. Livingston Biddle, who drafted much of the 1965 legislation that created the endowments, recently clarified for me his vision at that time: namely, that excellence would be made available to the largest number of people, which is not the same thing as "trying to make everyone excellent," an unrealistic goal.[43]

My second observation about the past three decades is that the art forms that are most distinctively American—musical theater, modern dance, jazz, folk art, and film—had to struggle very hard indeed to achieve recognition as genuine cultural treasures. For many years, for example, the NEA was not notably supportive of jazz, a pattern that changed in 1977-78 because Billy Taylor, the jazz pianist, played a persuasive role on the National Council for the Arts.[44]

My third observation in the problematic category is that the two endowments have sparred with each other on occasion, competing in ways that were not constructive for the politics of culture in the United States. It is no secret that Nancy Hanks and Ronald Berman (respectively the heads of NEA and NEH) had different agendas during the 1970s and developed a cordial disdain for one another, despite the fact that each endowment, at different times, has done so much to sustain its sibling politically. Moreover, relations have not always been optimal between NEA and the National Assembly of State Arts Agencies. Ever since the mid-1970s many of the state arts agencies have really wanted something closer to *partnership* with their federal parent, and not just patronage. They have sought, even demanded, a larger role in policy formation.[45]

My fourth observation concerns a phenomenon that may, in the long run, be just as significant as the much-noticed politicization of the endowments: the proliferation of state humanities councils as well as state and local arts agencies. State arts agencies first appeared early in the 1960s, were then mandated by the federal legislation of 1965, and became a complex, architectonic reality by the mid-1970s and a major source of cultural funding by the 1980s.

The structural and funding differences between the state agencies and councils are significant but not widely or well understood. All arts agencies are funded by their states as well as by NEA (at a higher percentage of its annual budget than what NEH is required to provide for its dependents). They are much broader in their operations than the state humanities councils, and collectively they now receive four times the amount of funds, per annum, as NEA itself. State arts agencies fund institutions, organizations, and individuals. They are the single most important source of support for the arts, and their work is supplemented by local arts agencies that are funded by the states, mayors' offices, small foundations, businesses, and county boards.[46]

State humanities councils, on the other hand, are not state agencies. They are comparatively small nonprofit organizations that fund projects, usually involving one or more appropriate scholars along with other expenses associated with a program. Because they do not fund institutions, they tend to be mission- and theme-driven. More often than not, their objective is to shape a civic culture in their respective states by providing support for humanities programs that engage public (i.e., nonacademic) audiences. A fundamental distinction also remains as true today as it was thirty years ago: Most people who are at all interested in culture understand what the arts are and mean far better than they understand what the humanities are all about. According to a catchphrase that some administrators have been known to use: "If they do it, it's art. If they talk about it, it's humanities."[47]

The unwanted aspect of this bilevel, yet asymmetrical federal structure, as I have noted, is that rivalries and tensions occasionally occur between the state and national bodies. (For those with historical knowledge reaching back to New Deal cultural programs, this offers a vivid sense of déjà vu. The state-based writers' projects during the 1930s chafed at the degree of control exercised by officials in Washington.[48]) The competitiveness and occasional resentments are more serious on the arts side than on the humanities side. There has also been a lot of cooperation, to be sure; during 1995 the state bodies did a great deal that was politically efficacious in helping, quite literally, to save, the national endowments.[49]

The endowments and their state programs have gone far beyond the New Deal arts projects in terms of intellectual coherence and enduring value. New Deal relief programs improved people's cultural lives in ways that were positive yet utilitarian and largely passive in terms of public engagement. There were guidebooks, murals, and plays for viewers to enjoy. But America's cultural heritage was more often romanticized than preserved, and the New Deal programs provided scant basis for the public to become culturally interactive, except perhaps to protest some murals that they did not want in their local post offices and courthouses.[50]

In contrast, engagement has been a major success of government support at several levels over the past thirty years: preservation, creation, dissemination, and interaction. We recognize, for instance, that museum attendance and activities have reached unprecedented and unanticipated levels during the past quarter-century. Diverse stimuli are responsible, but a very major one, surely, has come from initiatives supplied by both endowments.[51]

Essential though they were at the time, New Deal projects did not sustain exhibits of history and art (accompanied by conferences and symposia) that enlarged understanding of American culture in multifaceted ways. They did not support seminars for the enrichment of teachers and the overall improvement of education. They did not sustain humanistic research, especially long-term projects that require collaborative efforts, such as bibliographies, encyclopedias, dictionaries, and critical translations. They did not launch interactive public programs by promoting partnerships among libraries, historical societies, universities, and schools. They did not engage the public culture through innovative films with compelling humanistic content, up-to-date interpretation of historic sites, and stimulating occasions that bring scholars together with lay audiences.

Despite some slips of judgment, despite some inevitable elements of trial and error, despite some unhelpful competitiveness and bureaucratization, the two endowments, the Smithsonian Institution, the Institute of Museum Services, the National Park Service, and the National Trust for Historic

Preservation, along with an array of state cultural agencies that have emerged or else been transformed during the past generation, all have redefined their mandates and modes of operation as circumstances dictated. In doing so they have altered not merely the nature, but the very meaning of public culture in the United States.

If we believe that culture is a necessity rather than a luxury, if we feel that public dialogue and comprehension of a heterogeneous social heritage are essential, if we are committed to a more inclusive audience for scholarship, then there simply has to be sufficient governmental support for such an agenda.

What our historical experience has shown, beyond any doubt, is that public money spent on cultural programs has a multiplier effect—in terms of *participation by people* as well as in economic terms.[52] What the critics of state support for culture dismally fail to understand is that a diminution or elimination of public support will not prompt an increase in private support. Quite the contrary, it leads to a loss of private support. That, in turn, impoverishes the nation, with implications and outcomes that are truly lamentable.[53]

Comparisons and Explanations

Most industrialized nations, and many of the so-called developing ones, have a cabinet-level ministry of culture. Poland, Denmark, Argentina, Haiti, and France are among the notable range of highly diverse examples. André Malraux really wrote the script for such a department in France, and the actress Melina Mercouri made it quite visible in Greece some years ago. In Spain the Minister of Culture played an important role in 1992–93 when his country arranged a genuine coup: the acquisition for $350 million of a phenomenal art collection belonging to the Swiss industrialist Baron Hans Heinrich Thyssen-Bornemisza.[54]

Because a full-scale comparative study of these ministries has not yet been made, however, those of us in the United States who think about them at all tend to assume that they must do pretty much the same kinds of things because they have fundamentally similar titles and mandates. In reality there is far more variation than we recognize. (The European Economic Community even has a commissioner of cultural affairs, and the European ministers of culture meet regularly on a monthly or sometimes a bimonthly basis to discuss their differences and possible modes of cooperation.)

The French Ministry of Culture, created in 1959 under Malraux, who earnestly wished to democratize culture, is probably the best-known and surely the most publicized. A four-page explanation of the government's cultural policy, prepared in 1983, begins with this paragraph:

> France has long had a tradition of supporting the arts. French monarchs considered themselves protectors of the arts, and since the republic was founded the public sector has viewed "culture" (the arts and the humanities) as its responsibility to encourage. And though private support for the arts and the humanities has existed, the major thrust most often has come from the central government if only to preserve the heritage of the country.[55]

Although particular projects or initiatives of the minister may turn out to be controversial, the ministry itself normally is not.[56]

In Germany, by way of contrast, because it is a Federal Republic but also owing to pressure from the Western Allies following World War II, the establishment and maintenance of most cultural facilities is the responsibility of provincial government (*Länder*). The Allies wanted an end to state-controlled culture as propaganda. All legislation pertaining to cultural matters, therefore, with a few exceptions, is the prerogative of the separate federal states. There is no federal ministry of culture.[57]

In Great Britain, where the Department of National Heritage enjoys cabinet-level status, the most significant connections between culture and the state for more than four decades have been found in national museums and archaeological sites, in broadcasting, in arts councils, and in historic preservation activities. Curiously, however, the Department of National Heritage under Prime Ministers Thatcher and Major has been quite candid about its entrepreneurial aspirations. It also happens to run the National Lottery (a modest portion of the "take" goes to support cultural programs), it advocates "sport and recreation," and lists as its sixth objective on page one of its informational brochure that it seeks to "encourage inward [from abroad] and domestic tourism so that the industry can both make its full contribution to the economy and increase opportunities for access to our culture and heritage."[58]

In a country such as Botswana (formerly Bechuanaland Protectorate), the Ministry of Culture deals primarily with the preservation of aboriginal culture because the Bushmen of the Kalahari are a diminishing presence. In many other so-called developing nations the ministry of culture enjoys an autonomous existence at times, is sometimes combined with the ministry of education, and often is mainly concerned with tourism. In Brazil individual states have a secretary for cultural affairs. In Bahia during the early 1990s, for example, that position was held by Gilberto Gil, an immensely popular musician and advocate of Afro-Brazilian culture.

To the best of my knowledge, virtually no historian has systematically examined two closely related questions: Why is the United States so distinctive in not having a ministry of culture? And why is that office comparatively noncontroversial in some nations yet politically or ideologically problematic in others—above all, in our own? Although I cannot answer those questions exhaustively, I would at least like to propose a plausible hypothesis.

Suppose we consider those countries of continental Europe where the ministry of culture not only is ordinarily noncontroversial, but where the cultural authority of the state is highly centralized—a concentration of control long feared and resented by so many in the United States. We can illuminate the contrast if we look back more than three centuries to a period when the consolidation of royal power occurred in such sovereign entities as France and what became the Austro–Hungarian Empire.[59]

Because the appearance of royal strength and attendant splendor mattered a great deal, patronage of the arts developed in an uncontested manner that was regarded as perfectly natural. The Habsburgs seem to have sponsored music because the Roman Catholic Church had done so. The Bourbons were more attracted by theater, and the French were especially partial toward regally supported architecture as well as music. The Louvre, which became the model for all state art museums, had its origins in the French royal picture collections. It opened as a public museum in 1793, at the height of the French Revolution. Whatever their pet projects may have been, however—and they changed from one ruler to the next—all of these regimes established and sustained cultural institutions on a grand scale: opera houses, theaters, museums, and so forth. Equally important, perhaps, they created an enduring environment in which support of the arts came to be widely accepted, both among those at the very apex of the social pyramid as well as among those who aspired to be. Even municipalities felt a sense of civic reponsibility for culture. In 1767, for example, the City of Paris decided that it would make an annual subvention to the Opéra.[60]

What seems notable and significant for our purposes, moreover, is that such supportive attitudes survived the overthrow or decline of absolute monarchy, enlightened or otherwise. Moreover, the diverse regimes that succeeded those absolute rulers continued to support the cultural institutions that had been lavishly established by the dynasties they replaced. (It should be acknowledged that in nineteenth-century France a struggle took place between church and state for control of cultural patronage.) The blurred lines of distinction that dated back to the later Renaissance—did cultural patronage truly come from the state, or from the private purse of a monarch or some noble grandee?—remained ambiguous, albeit less so, even in the nineteenth and early twentieth centuries.

By contrast, in countries whose destinies were determined by the Protestant Reformation and by the evolution of constitutional monarchy, such as Great Britain and the Netherlands—which happen to be the nations that founded the colonies that became the original United States—kings and queens did not find themselves in such an absolute position to spend quite so lavishly on cultural projects as a means of glorifying their reigns. Consequently they relied more heavily on what we would consider the private sector, both as a matter of policy and of necessity. Moreover, the appearance (if not always the reality) of austerity required by Calvinism, even in historically modified forms, would not allow for the kinds of cultural luxury and artistic life that continued to flourish in Roman Catholic countries such as France and Austria–Hungary.

The constitutional monarchies were not exactly abstemious, to be sure; they also provided varying amounts of cultural patronage. But compared with the courts of central and southern Europe, conspicuous consumption in the realm of culture was not commonplace. Historian Janet Minihan, for example, demonstrated how stingily Parliament supported the British Museum during the nineteenth century, and as a consequence that national treasure grew in a haphazard fashion. Although the government eventually purchased those notorious Greek marble reliefs from Lord Elgin, it did so reluctantly and ungraciously.[61]

In sum, it is obviously the case that state support for cultural endeavors has been much weaker in the United States than in Europe. It should surprise no one that we can locate the antecedents of our own reluctance to spend public money on artistic and humanistic programs in the eighteenth- and especially the nineteenth-century cultural costiveness of the very countries that colonized what became British North America. We also know that Congress looked carefully at the Arts Council of Great Britain as a kind of model when launching the two endowments in 1964-65, especially in order to maximize protection for the endowments from political interference. In 1946 Britain became the first country to create a quasi-autonomous nongovernmental organization (QUANGO) to be the primary conduit for government support of the arts.[62]

In closing this section devoted to comparisons, it is essential for us to acknowledge a major irony.[63] For more than a decade now there have been clear signs that European countries are increasingly interested in and attracted to the American model. Without exception they all insist that they would like a policy of decentralizing support for art and culture. More particularly, as governmental budgets grow leaner, political leaders abroad express envy for the American tradition of private support. They are especially fascinated by the matching grant concept even though there have been only modest attempts thus far to implement that mechanism in Europe. Matching grants have worked successfully at the provincial level in Canada.[64]

Owing to economic contraction, moreover, Europeans are becoming more inclined to emphasize excellence above equity, and to insist that cultural creativity can be encouraged but not purchased. We now hear echoes of a letter written by Flaubert back in 1853:

> Have you ever remarked how all *authority* is stupid concerning Art? Our wonderful governments (kings or republics) imagine that they have only to order work to be done, and it will be forthcoming. They set up prizes, encouragements, academies, and they forget only one thing, one little thing without which nothing can live: the *atmosphere*.[65]

When budgets shrink in our own time, encouraging an optimal "atmosphere" looks like a prudent yet easy alternative. Mere encouragement is not sufficient, however.

Conclusions

Anxiety at the prospect of a Leviathan state—ranging from social services to cultural programs—has been a persistent legacy in American political culture for a very long time. Fears about centralization prompted the opposition of Van Buren, Calhoun, and many others to the cultural and scientific agendas of John Quincy Adams. Those concerns resurfaced prominently during the later years of Franklin D. Roosevelt's second administration, once again during the early Reagan years, and in 1995 when Republicans sought to fulfill their Contract with America.[66]

I believe that those nagging concerns can be turned to the advantage of those who value cultural growth, achievement, and institutions—in particular, those of us who are persuaded that NEH has been the single most important source of support for humanistic endeavors in the United States during the past generation. Major cultural organizations and significant, broad-gauge scholarship must be sustained at the national level. Federal dollars are absolutely indispensable in order to leverage local and private funds. The federal imprimatur has meant legitimacy for cultural programs at all levels.

An important rationale for fostering closer collaboration between federal and state entities (meaning consultation and the sharing of resources) is that it might help to depoliticize culture. Support at the state and local levels is less likely to provoke controversy. Cultural localism and regionalism may not make a big splash, but neither do they ordinarily alienate citizens and suffer from distortion or sensationalism in the national media. Increased cooperation among levels and sources of government support simply makes sense in a country that everyone acknowledges is diverse in terms of taste levels, opinions, and what is perceived as being in the public interest. It is worth bearing in mind that Nancy Hanks's phenomenal success as the chair of NEA owed a great deal to her carefully organized network of support at the grass roots. Moreover, former Congressman Thomas J. Downey, who chaired the Congressional Arts Caucus from 1982 until 1987, regarded the state arts agencies as "invaluable" because they constantly pressured members of Congress and made them aware that support for cultural programs was both essential and politically viable. As Downey put it, they provided validation from the districts on economic as well as cultural grounds. They also undercut those who contended that federal support for the arts was elitist.[67]

It is particularly noteworthy, I believe, that during the 1995 campaign to save NEH and NEA, advocates scored effective points by constantly calling attention to positive achievements made at the state and local levels. Those are the levels most appealing to members of Congress, and we cannot escape the reality that we are discussing a highly political process. Congressional supporters of cultural programs are partial to the phrase "building from the bottom up." That's a crucial reason why the state councils and agencies are so essential.

From the perspective of historians, state programs have had, and will continue to have, the salutary effect of broadening the audience for history. They transmit far beyond academe new historical interpretations and an understanding of what American history is all about—something that many scholars have long been saying needs to be done. State councils transmit money to local historical societies and discussion groups that meet at public libraries, and professional historians play a prominent role on state humanities councils. They can have a profoundly influential impact by determining what kinds of history will be disseminated and discussed at the grass-roots level.

I do not for a moment mean to suggest that the state agencies and councils are prepared or able to resolve all the vexed issues involving culture and government in America. Historical experience has demonstrated their limitations. Generalizations about fifty-six different entities are dangerous, but overall they are more oriented to the contemporary than to the historical. They do not *directly* support scholarship. Their assistance to museums goes for public and educational programs rather than for basic curatorial, cataloging, or even exhibition needs. On occasion, some members of the state councils have even been disdainful of scholarship.[68]

The obvious point, therefore, is that state and local cultural organizations do things that complement what only the national entities are able to do. We need *all* of them, working in concert, if we genuinely hope to achieve excellence *and* equity. It is imperative that we strengthen the connective links of cultural federalism because that is the way American governmental politics works most successfully in so many instances.

Earlier, when I supplied cursory descriptions of the state humanities councils and arts agencies, I emphasized contrasts between the two because their histories are so asymmetrical and not clearly understood. There is, however, a key area in which they have been moving in sync. In more than thirty states (by the mid-1990s) the state agencies and councils do some kind of cooperative or shared programming. Several states now have a joint standing committee on the arts and the humanities, a collaborative arrangement in which Ohio has been the leader.[69]

For about two decades the humanities councils have emphasized a concept that they call the public humanities. Basically, that means disseminating fresh perspectives to a broad, nonacademic audience. As the philosopher Charles Frankel phrased it: "Nothing has happened of greater importance in the history of American humanistic scholarship than the invitation of the government to scholars to think in a more public fashion, and to think and teach with the presence of their fellow citizens in mind."[70]

Similarly, both NEA as well as the state arts agencies have promoted what is called "the new public art," meaning art put in public places for its own sake rather than the commemoration of some politician or military hero. Doing so entails a vision of art that can humanize and enliven public places—art to be enjoyed. Needless to say, Richard Serra's *Tilted Arc* certainly did not achieve such an outcome in lower Manhattan; but responsibility for that debacle rests with misunderstanding on all sides. Alexander Calder's *Grand Vitesse* commission for Grand Rapids, Michigan, provides an illustration of communication and explanation eventually leading not merely to acceptance but pride.[71]

~

It may help to clarify our thinking if we reflect comparatively on the historically determined nature of our situation. During the eighteenth century, what later became Germany was a fragmented set of societies partially bonded by a common culture. A *Kulturvolk* existed rather than a cohesive polity. In the nineteenth century, after the fall of Napoleon, when Germans wanted a political structure worthy of that rich culture, and commensurate with it, they regarded the nation that emerged as a

Kulturstaat: a state defined by the vigorous presence of a common culture.[72]

In striking contrast, when the United States emerged as a nation in 1789 it came to be defined by its distinctive *political* structure and by the founders' desire and rationale for that republican structure. Unlike Germany, a common culture had not yet been defined, and it might very well be argued that the task of defining a common culture in the United States has become more difficult, rather than less, in the intervening two centuries.

Henry Adams perceived that problematic reality more than a century ago when he wrote an open letter to the American Historical Association, which he served as president in 1894. He fully anticipated the flowering of intellectual and cultural diversity in the United States. Efforts to "hold together the persons interested in history is worth making," he wrote. Yet his candid realism followed directly: "That we should ever act on public opinion with the weight of one compact and one energetic conviction is hardly to be expected, but that one day or another we shall be compelled to act individually or in groups I cannot doubt." [73]

I feel certain that solutions to the complex interaction between culture and the state in the United States can be found in improved institutional and organizational relationships—connections that belong under a rubric that might be called cultural federalism. The state now has a strong tradition of encouraging and supporting cultural activities when doing so seems to be in the interest of the state. That is exactly why federal support for culture accelerated during the Cold War decades.

It is no coincidence that a broadly based acceptance of government support for culture waned precipitously once the Cold War ended in 1989. Many of those who had long feared alien ideologies have subsequently projected their anxieties on to domestic "enemies" such as artists, intellectuals, and institutions who communicated unfamiliar views or unconventional positions critical of orthodox pieties. The historic hostility toward unusual, dissident, or revisionist views described so forcefully by Richard Hofstadter in 1963 resurfaced with renewed political potency after 1989, resulting in mistrust of artists, intellectuals, and many cultural programs because they appeared elitist or else unpatriotic.[74]

Cultural federalism—government support for cultural needs along with collaboration *at all levels*—could go a long way toward minimizing anti-intellectualism, fear of innovation, and mistrust of constructive cultural criticism. That is why the notion of public humanities really matters. It is an idea whose time has come because it is sorely needed at this juncture.

3

Temples of Justice:
The Iconography of
Judgment and
American Culture

Nineteenth-century Americans tended to be tardy in their commemorative observances, and the centennial of the Judiciary Act of
1789 turned out to be no exception.* In September 1889, a
committee formed by the New York City Bar Association finally got around
to discussing a celebration planned for February 2, 1890. All the nation's
federal judges as well as New York State's appellate judges were invited to
attend. Better late than never. Then, on December 7, 1889, the Judiciary
Centennial Committee met at the Federal Building in New York City to
adopt a plan that had been submitted for festivities honoring the hundredth
anniversary of the first sitting of the Supreme Court of the United States. It
would take place on February 4, 1890, at the Metropolitan Opera House in
Manhattan. Former president Grover Cleveland consented to preside over
ceremonies attended by the entire Supreme Court. Following remarks by
the chief justice, President Benjamin Harrison would give an address. The

* This essay was presented in Washington, D.C., on September 22, 1989, at the Bicentennial
Conference on the Judiciary Act of 1789.

New York City Bar Association would hold a reception the next day in honor of the justices.[1]

By that time the bar had become thoroughly professionalized—no longer did poems like Philip Freneau's "The Pettifogger" (1797) appear[2]—and the power of the bench was considerable. As James Bryce observed in 1889, for example, one "fact which makes the function of an American judge so momentous is the brevity, the laudable brevity, of the Constitution."[3] The fact that judges did not have to overcome nearly so much social prejudice as lawyers is perhaps indicated by the prestige that judges clearly enjoyed in 1789.* Eight of the delegates to the Constitutional Convention at Philadelphia in 1787 not merely were sitting judges, but held seats of distinction; three others had been judges sometime earlier in their careers. Three or four others became judges subsequently.[4]

More significant, however, yet surprisingly neglected by historians of political culture, is the concern felt generally by the founders for justice. (Given the frequency with which they talked about justice, I am amazed that we do not have a single treatise concerning the history of the idea and ideal of justice, whereas we have at least half a dozen monographs on their conceptions of property.) The only quotation that easily comes to mind, almost as a cliché, is James Madison's assertion in *The Federalist*, Number 51, that "justice is the end of government. It is the end of civil society. It ever has been, and ever will be pursued, until it be obtained, or until liberty be lost in the pursuit."[5]

Madison's well-known words actually came as the culmination of an important development in American political thought, rather than as a visionary notion that appeared from nowhere in 1788. Writing as "Novanglus" on March 6, 1775, John Adams had expressed similar sentiments. In 1783, George Washington wrote the following to a friend: "We now have a National character to establish; and it is of the utmost importance to stamp favourable impressions upon it; let justice be then one of its characteristics, and gratitude another." In 1786, when the quality of life under the Confederation government seemed to have reached its nadir, Washington lamented to John Jay, then Secretary for Foreign Affairs:

> From the high ground we stood upon, from the plain path which invited our footsteps, to be so fallen! so lost! It is really mortifying; but virtue, I fear has, in great degree, taken its departure from us; and the want of disposition to do justice is the source of the national embarrassments.[6]

Although the roots and continuity of such sentiments extend well beyond

---

* We should, however, bear in mind the old adage that a judge is a lawyer who once knew a politician.

the scope of this essay, it should be noted that in the Republic of Venice a newly installed doge would publicly repeat in three different places his pledge to promote peace, prosperity, and justice. In the late seventeenth century, John Locke wrote in his *First Treatise of Civil Government* that "justice gives every man a title to the product of his honest industry." [7] Explicit echoes of Washington and Madison recurred from the debates over ratification in 1787 and 1788, through John Jay's concern for a "due Distribution of Justice," right on to the views of radical as well as conservative jurists and political theorists in the middle third of the twentieth century.[8]

Given that cultural context, it should scarcely come as a surprise that Justice appeared as a popular and highly visible motif in American decorative arts and architecture during the generation that followed 1789. Simon Willard, for example, the legendary Connecticut clockmaker (1753–1848), built around 1819 an eight-day, weight-powered brass timepiece on which he arranged Miss Liberty and Miss Justice, holding her scales, standing beneath the American Eagle.[9] Around 1824, William Rush carved from pine a figure of Justice bearing the traditional sword and scales. The Shelburne Museum in Vermont has a ten-foot-tall figure of Justice that was carved from white pine (and elaborated with metal) around 1825. This "statue," which is blindfolded and holds the scales and sword, originally stood atop the Barnstable County Courthouse on Cape Cod in Massachusetts. A remarkably similar figure, also carved from white pine (and gilded), was made in 1827 by an anonymous artisan and placed on top of the cupola of the Old State House in Hartford, Connecticut. Both state and federal court sessions took place in that building, which was common at the time, and in 1979 the statue was repaired, brought within the state supreme court chamber, and replaced on the cupola by a replica.[10]

The personification of Justice as a female holding scales in her left hand and a sword pointing downward in her right had become a fixture of Western iconography since the late Middle Ages and the early Renaissance. Examples are especially abundant from Renaissance Venice (where Justice ranked second in importance only to the winged lion of Saint Mark as a symbol of the republic), from sixteenth-century Siena, and from cities and towns along the Dalmatian coast of what used to be Yugoslavia.[11] They may or may not be blindfolded, and they may be sitting rather than standing. The figure of Justice (made of plaster in 1817 by Carlo Franzoni) in the "old" Supreme Court chamber (1810–60), located in the basement of the Capitol, is seated and wears no blindfold, for example.[12]

As we have already noted, and soon will do so in greater detail, most of these icons of Justice were made either to surmount or to decorate the interior of a courthouse. How fortuitous, therefore, that James Wilson, associate justice of the Supreme Court from 1789 until his death in 1798, used the following image when he presented his *Lectures on Law* in 1790: "According to the rules of judicial architecture, a system of courts should resemble a pyramid. Its base should be broad and spacious: it should lessen as it rises: its summit should be a single point."[13]

The Changing Symbolism of Nineteenth-Century Courthouses

This essay explores symbolic aspects of judicial art and architecture, especially in the early republic—a subject that has received some attention in Europe, but very little in and for the United States.[14] The "bad news," for our purposes, is that early courthouses built exclusively to serve that purpose were not common, and few have survived. Court sessions were held in various sorts of public and private buildings, ranging from the statehouse (where other branches of government also met) to taverns and barns.[15] In architectural terms, the judiciary was very much the neglected branch prior to the third decade of the nineteenth century. There is a symbolic sense in which "doing justice" received a relatively low priority and therefore transmits to us a low profile.[16] The "good news," however, is that the judiciary had certain prominent emblems—widely recognized and well understood—that were therefore culturally meaningful, much more so than any iconography associated with the executive and legislative branches of government. In addition to Justice, for example, folk artists created other vivid icons, such as a large handcuffed figure carved from wood, called *Felon*, which used to be prominently displayed at the Kent County Jail in East Greenwich, Rhode Island.[17]

The particular symbol that provides the primary focus for this essay, however, is the American courthouse perceived as a "temple of justice," which takes us back to James Wilson's metaphor of judicial architecture. I do not know when the image made its initial appearance in American discourse, but there are some notable clues. During the French Revolution, of course, churches were deconsecrated, put to secular purposes, and renamed temples of reason. When the Marquis de Lafayette made his triumphal return visit to the United States in 1824, one feature of the elaborately festooned Castle Garden in New York was a pavilion reserved for Lafayette's exclusive use. It consisted of thirteen columns supporting a dome that was surmounted by an eagle; it contained a great amount of red, white, and blue gauze illuminated from within; and it was called the

Temple of Liberty. A cartoon (concerning anti-Chinese attitudes) drawn by Thomas Nast in 1882 includes a castle sardonically designated as the Temple of Liberty. That rubric had become commonplace in nineteenth-century public discourse and iconography.[18]

Sir Frederick Pollock used the phrase "Temple of Justice" in a letter to Oliver Wendell Holmes, Jr., in 1890, and from the opening of the present home of the Supreme Court of the United States in 1935,* it was commonly referred to as a temple of justice.[19] When we look at the neoclassical statehouses erected after independence, such as the jewel that Thomas Jefferson designed for Richmond, Virginia, and if we recall that both the federal circuit courts and the state courts met there on a regular basis, it certainly seems appropriate to view those structures as temples of justice.[20]

With the coming of the nineteenth century, an increasingly prosperous society began to be able to afford discrete structures devoted exclusively to the administration of justice—especially at the county level. And even there the grand image of a temple of justice seemed suitable. In Eudora Welty's enchanting memoir of her early years, she recalls her grandfather's role in dedicating a new courthouse in Nicholas County, West Virginia (following the Civil War), and she quotes from a copy of his speech that her mother had saved:

> The student turns with a sigh of relief from the crumbling pillars and columns of Athens and Alexandria to the symmetrical and colossal temples of the New World. As time eats from the tombstones of the past the epitaphs of primeval greatness, and covers the pyramids with the moss of forgetfulness, she directs the eye to the new temples of art and progress that make America the monumental beacon-light of the world.[21]

That episode, replete with appropriate enthusiasm, must have occurred hundreds, if not thousands, of times in antebellum America. And when we look at the Chenango County Courthouse in Norwich, New York (Fig. 3.1), built in 1837, with its elegant statue of Justice standing on top of the cupola (Fig. 3.2); the courthouse in Petersburg, Virginia (Fig. 3.3), built between 1838 and 1840, which has Justice on a double pedestal above a clock that surmounts no fewer than two cupolas; or the Ontario County Courthouse in Canandaigua, New York, with its gilded dome (Fig. 3.4) and Justice of Amazonian proportions (Fig. 3.5), we surely feel that we are indeed gazing at temples of justice.[22] What phrase could conceivably be more appropriate?

The arresting answer to that question—or at least a logical response for historical reasons—is temples of *in*justice; so we must back up two generations to the age of the American Revolution in order to appreciate why the

---

* In October 1935, one of the justices, uncomfortable in the Court's awesome new abode, called it the Temple of Karnak.

Fig. 3.1 Chenango County Courthouse, Norwich, New York (1837). Photograph courtesy of Milo V. Stewart, Cooperstown, New York.

proud construction of these handsome buildings presents us with a problematic anomaly. For various reasons, more often than not courts and courthouses had been viewed by the populace as symbols of oppression in the eighteenth-century colonies. Viva voce voting took place on election day in front of courthouses, and because intimidation of the voters frequently occurred, the courthouse as a venue was not perceived as a place where the rights of ordinary folks were protected.[23] The colonists regarded prerogative

Fig. 3.2 Chenango County Courthouse, Norwich, New York. Cupola detail. Photograph courtesy of Milo V. Stewart.

courts, dominated by royal governors and their creatures—courts that dealt with unpopular matters and sat without juries—with a distaste that commonly verged on overt hatred. A pamphlet that originated in Virginia in 1701 referred to "the Crooked Cord of a Judge's discretion in matters of the greatest moment and value." [24]

Given that background, it should come as no surprise that the North Carolina Regulators vented their frustration and anger in 1769 and 1770 by harassing lawyers and judges and shutting down local courts that favored planters and merchants over debtors and persons who felt aggrieved for assorted causes. Many Whig colonists attacked the courts once again during the crisis years of 1775 and 1776. [25]

The same thing recurred between then and late in 1786 when Shays's Rebellion erupted in western Massachusetts. And in April 1787, a little more

Fig. 3.3 Petersburg Courthouse, Virginia (1838–40). Photograph by William Clift, Seagram County Court House Archives, © Library of Congress, Washington, D.C.

than a month before the Constitutional Convention opened, the people of Caroline County, Virginia, made an agreement to purchase no property sold at auction. Just as the delegates were convening in Philadelphia, in fact, a mob committed arson at King William County Courthouse in Virginia and destroyed all the legal records there. In August, James Madison learned from a letter written in Richmond that about 300 men in Greenbrier County, Virginia, "have signed an Association, to oppose the payment of the

Fig. 3.4 Ontario County Courthouse, Canandaigua, New York (1858). Photograph courtesy of Milo V. Stewart.

Fig. 3.5 Ontario County Courthouse, Canandaigua, New York. Cupola detail. Photograph courtesy of Milo V. Stewart.

Fig. 3.6 First courthouse in Greene County, Ohio. Courtesy of Department of Prints and Photographs, Library of Congress, Washington, D.C.

certificate Tax, & in genl. of all debts; & it is apprehended there, that they will attempt forcibly to stop the proceedings of the next court." Late that summer, Madison informed Thomas Jefferson in Paris that

> the people also are said to be generally discontented. A paper [money] emission is again a topic among them. So is an instalment of all debts in some places and the making property a tender in others. The taxes are another source of discontent. The weight of them is complained of, and the abuses in collecting them still more so. In several Counties the prisons & Court Houses & Clerks offices have been willfully burnt. In Green Briar the course of Justice has been mutinously stopped, and associations entered into agst. the payment of taxes.[26]

That sort of action—simultaneously symbolic and substantive—continued intermittently through the nineteenth century and even in the twentieth when intense feelings arose over lost land grants, mortgage foreclosures, and so forth.[27]

Given the intense animosity directed at courthouses in diverse locations between the 1760s and the end of the eighteenth century, how can we explain the expense and labor lavished—not to mention the community pride exuded—on new temples of justice starting in the second quarter of the nineteenth century? (For a prototypical early county courthouse on the frontier in post-Revolutionary times, see Fig. 3.6) Americans might plausibly have been expected to erect *un*attractive courthouses roughly comparable as "judicial architecture" with the grim Italian Renaissance *bargello*, meaning "home of the jailer," a structure that also housed the civic courts of law.[28]

I believe that the answer is to be found in rapid demographic and economic growth in general, but more particularly in patterns of intense rivalry between neighboring communities to be designated as the county seat—with all the implications that that status conveyed in terms of political clout, social prestige, and, above all, entrepreneurial and professional possibilities. Competition to be the county seat had indeed occurred during the colonial period—witness the case of Winchester versus Stephensburg, Virginia, in the later 1740s—but the power of decision lay with royal officials or local elites who commanded deference. Economic development was not yet flourishing, moreover, and thus much less seemed to be at stake.

By 1807, however, when Newark and Elizabeth, New Jersey, staged a donnybrook over the location of their county seat and consequently a new courthouse, much had changed and a pattern began to emerge that occurred so often that folklore specialists—who love typologies—have assigned the phenomenon a number and a name: stealing the county seat. Waterloo, New York, stole the seat from Ovid in Seneca County, and then had to fend off Seneca Falls for hegemony.[29] Principal prizes involved patronage for county jobs and possession of the primary bank in the county. Subsequently, in Michigan's Upper Peninsula, Crystal Falls stole the courthouse from Iron River, a classic episode; and in California, Santa Rosa snatched the Sonoma County seat away from the town of Sonoma.[30]

After all the scheming and all the physical energy had been expended, victory invariably meant very tangible benefits. Consequently, erecting a handsome county courthouse became a logistical necessity, a victory trophy, and a matter of local pride. Communities renamed the appropriate thoroughfare Court Street. Political processions, rallies, and ritual celebrations started out at diverse points of origin but invariably culminated at the courthouse square.[31] And political activity, electioneering, and social interaction soon converged on the county courthouse as a focal point (Fig. 3.7).[32]

Judicial architecture underwent a diffuse transformation during the century that followed the Civil War. Although county courthouses no longer resembled Greco-Roman temples, remnants of the usual iconography persisted. Justice will be found perched above the entrance to the Pitkin County Courthouse in Aspen, Colorado (Fig. 3.8), which was built in 1890 and 1891, and she was placed within a window niche in the façade of the Monroe County Courthouse, which was built in 1894 and still serves Rochester, New York (Fig. 3.9). A fair number of Victorian structures, such as the courthouse in Hampton, Iowa (Fig. 3.10), continued to display Justice on the tippy-top, regardless of whether the building was bastardized Romanesque, Italianate, or whatever.[33] And a few did away with Justice but retained just her scales as an ornament, such as the St. Lawrence County Courthouse in Canton, New York (Fig. 3.11).

Fig. 3.7 A mountain courthouse scene. Knox County Courthouse, Barbourville, Kentucky (January 30, 1930). Courtesy of Department of Prints and Photographs, Library of Congress, Washington, D.C.

Many courthouses ceased to display Justice prominently, if at all, which may or may not be symptomatic of a certain ambivalence about American justice that we shall note in the next section.[34] Others perpetuated neoclassical frontal columns on buildings that are otherwise banal or nondescript (Fig. 3.12). And in a few situations, when a genuine temple of justice burned or ceased to be functional, its modern replacement keeps company with a reminder of once-upon-a-time.[35] The juxtaposition of judicial architectural styles can create bizarre effects (Fig. 3.13).

One finds in the press occasional notes of nostalgia for structures that could not be saved despite the richness of their historical associations. In 1888, for example, workmen demolished the old United States Courthouse in New Orleans. It had been a public building when the French governed the city. After 1803, it became a federal district courthouse—the one where Andrew Jackson was fined $1000 for contempt of court because he had refused to obey a writ of habeas corpus.[36]

In October 1889, the residents of Bedford Village, New York, gathered in the remodeled courthouse, which henceforth would serve as a town hall, to celebrate their successful effort at historic preservation. The plain structure had been erected in 1787, that *annus mirabilis*, when Bedford Village was the Westchester County seat. It became a major center of social and political

Fig. 3.8 Pitkin County Courthouse, Aspen, Colorado (1890-91). Photograph by William Clift, Seagram County Court House Archives, © Library of Congress, Washington, D.C.

Fig. 3.9 Monroe County Courthouse, Rochester, New York (1894). Photograph courtesy of Milo V. Stewart.

Fig. 3.10 Hampton County Courthouse, Hampton, Iowa (pre–1910). Courtesy of Department of Prints and Photographs, Library of Congress, Washington, D.C.

Fig. 3.11 St. Lawrence County Courthouse, Canton, New York (1895). Photograph courtesy of Milo V. Stewart.

activity for decades, but in 1868 the state legislature moved the county seat to White Plains. For twenty years, the eighteenth-century building simply sat and deteriorated. But when the citizens of Bedford decided to renovate it for use as a town hall, Albany permitted the requisite taxing power for the project. On October 23, 1889, the Honorable John Jay, whose forebears had served as judges in the former courthouse, presided over the town meeting and spoke about Bedford's founding back in 1681.[37]

In the twentieth century, despite our familiar image of the United States Supreme Court building as the ultimate temple of justice, judicial architecture in county courthouses has become increasingly eclectic, ranging from the Art Nouveau Reno County Courthouse in Hutchinson, Kansas (Fig. 3.14), to the weirdly modified Hispanic-Islamic mosque that constitutes the Pima County Courthouse in Tucson, Arizona (Fig. 3.15).

Some still resemble temples of a sort, but others range from movie-palace *moderne* to a modified country-club style in Santa Barbara, California. The nation as a whole may have become culturally more homogeneous, but its courthouses certainly offer greater diversity than ever before in our history. It is not surprising that recent artists who have chosen to depict American courthouses, such as Horace Pippin and Whitney North Seymour, Jr., have been attracted to the older, more traditional temples of justice.[38]

Fig. 3.12 Moniteau County Courthouse, California, Missouri (1867–68). Photograph by William Clift, Seagram County Court House Archives, © Library of Congress, Washington, D.C.

Fig. 3.13 Floyd County Courthouse, New Albany, Indiana (1960–61). Columns from the courthouse built between 1865 and 1867. Photograph by Bob Thall, Seagram County Court House Archives, © Library of Congress, Washington, D.C.

Fig. 3.14 Reno County Courthouse, Hutchinson, Kansas (1931). Courtesy of Department of Prints and Photographs, Library of Congress, Washington, D.C.

Fig. 3.15 Pima County Courthouse, Tuscon, Arizona (1928). Photograph by William Clift, Seagram County Court House Archives, ©Library of Congress, Washington, D.C.

The Iconography of Frontier Justice in America

If we look beyond judicial architecture to the iconography of American justice in general, we encounter a subject and an expanse of documentation that is too broad for comprehensive coverage in this chapter. It seems appropriate, however, at least to suggest the nature of that material and some of the motifs that resonate from it. I want to call attention to two themes that are complementary—opposite sides of the same coin, if you will—and note that both of them wind up as ambiguous elements in American art and literature.

Both take the same point of departure: the quality of justice in frontier America, a subject that has inspired a considerable amount of folklore and folk art. One "tradition" suggests that justice was done, or at the very least that a good-faith effort was made. When Sam Houston appointed "Three Legged Willie" Williamson to be district judge for the Upper Brazos district in Texas, Williamson is supposed to have sent the community a signal when residents informed him that they had no use for Houston's courts. Williamson came to court, placed a rifle at one elbow, a pistol at the other, and declared: "Hear ye, hear ye, a court for third district is either now in session or by God somebody's going to get killed." [39]

Such paintings as *Missouri Courtroom* (no date, antebellum) by William J. Brickey and *General Andrew Jackson Before Judge Hall, 1815* (1858–60) by Christian Schussele suggest that justice was achieved despite primitive or difficult circumstances. The latter picture concerns the trial of Jackson on charges of illegally declaring martial law and defying civil authority in New Orleans at the close of the War of 1812. In a contemporary explanation of the painting, Jackson is quoted as saying, "I now set you an example of obedience to its constituted authorities." [40]

On the west wall of the chamber of the Illinois Supreme Court there are three panels—*Continuity of Law*—created between 1907 and 1911 by the Chicago artist Albert Henry Krehbiel. A decade later, when 92-year-old Ezra Meeker recalled what life had been like on the Oregon Trail in 1852, he made this assertion:

> The American instinct for fair play and a hearing for everybody prevailed, so that while there was no mob law, the law of self-preservation asserted itself, and the counsels of the level-headed older men prevailed. When an occasion called for action, a "high court" was convened, and woe betide the man that would undertake to defy its mandates after its deliberations were made public! [41]

In 1929, a few years after Meeker wrote those words, Henry Ford bought and brought to Greenfield Village in Dearborn, Michigan, the Logan

County Courthouse from Postville, Illinois, where Abraham Lincoln had served as a young trial lawyer in the early 1840s. The image that we have been conditioned to conjure up is that justice was achieved despite the crude physical setting of that courtroom. In *Young Mr. Lincoln* (1939), filmmaker John Ford conveyed an enduring memory of Lincoln defending the Clay brothers on the charge of having committed a murder at a Fourth of July celebration by undermining the validity of the only damaging testimony. Lincoln also manages to calm a lynch mob, and following the trial, when he steps awkwardly from the courthouse into the bright sunlight, a grateful crowd cheers Lincoln for having saved them from their lethal impulse to lynch.[42]

Late in his career, George Caleb Bingham (while serving a term on the St. Louis Board of Police Commissioners) painted an intriguing canvas that also suggests a rustic judicial system functioning fairly well. Titled *The Puzzled Witness*, it was effectively described by an art critic who viewed it on exhibition in November 1874:

> "Puzzling a Witness" is one of these pictures of western life, recognizable at once as faithful to the circumstances as art could make it. We are in the office of a country justice of the peace. There is the "court," the opposing lawyer, the defendant, the jury and the witness on the stand, all taken from the streets of a country town, as familiar as the post office itself, and in the homespun which we all know so well in the land of the granger. The artist has seized upon the strong moment. The witness for the prosecution is up, and the attorney for the defense has just put a puzzler to him. It is a stunner. The witness is, in point of fact, stumped. He scratches his head for the answer, but it don't seem to be there, or perhaps it is a neat bit of acting. . . . Then there is the lawyer on the other side. He is satisfied with his witness, and smiles as if to say, "well, when you have made anything of that witness, just call around and tell me, will you."[43]

Both William J. Glackens and Thomas Hart Benton had a penchant for painting courthouse scenes. Benton's *Trial by Jury* (1964) was composed late in his life. Although we know from Benton's autobiography that he had some interest in judges and the law, it is not evident from either Glackens's or Benton's courthouse scenes what sort of attitude is being conveyed about justice in America. Perhaps the very phrasing of *Trial by Jury* rather than, let us say, *Jury Trial* is meant to suggest something like ordeal by jury, trial by combat, or "J'accuse." Perhaps. It is not clear.[44]

The alternative or counter-theme concerning the quality of justice in frontier America is epitomized by the euphemism used in California in the mid-nineteenth century to describe violence as a means of resolving a dispute: "Judge Lynch." It is conveyed with equal force by the words of an African-American in Richland County, South Carolina, during the 1920s: "Justice is a stranger in them precincts."[45]

The Ox-Bow Incident (1940) by Walter Van Tilburg Clark may provide the most memorable example in American fiction of justice denied, of lawlessness perpetrated in the name of justice. Set on the Nevada frontier in 1885, it describes the vigilante murder of three suspected cattle rustlers who turn out to have been innocent. There are recurrent dialogues involving Reverend Osgood, Judge Tyler, and a man named Davies, all of whom plead for genuine justice administered in a court of law, and the hard-nosed impatient, self-appointed "jury" members, who contend that "law, as the books have it, is slow and full of holes" (p. 223). Osgood admonishes the vendetta-bound vigilantes early on that "we desire justice, and justice has never been obtained in haste and strong feeling" (p. 43); but it soon becomes clear that Osgood will be ignored. When one of the mob is asked directly to define "real justice," he replies, "It's seein' that everybody gets what's comin' to him" (p. 62). Davies gives the group a little homily:

> True law, the code of justice ... is the conscience of society. It has taken thousands of years to develop, and it is the greatest, the most distinguishing quality which has evolved with mankind. None of man's temples, none of his religions, none of his weapons, his tools, his arts, his sciences, nothing else he has grown to, is so great a thing as his justice (pp. 66–67).

The words fall on deaf ears and go unheeded.

What Clark and his characters take 309 pages to convey, the nineteenth-century artist David Gilmour Blythe achieved in three paintings. In *Justice* (ca. 1859–62), workers who have apparently been beaten by the police are brought before a magistrate. An eagle holds the scales of justice over his head, but they are not in balance. An elderly black man holding a banjo sits on the shadowy bench. The likelihood that any of these defendants will receive justice seems to be very dim, and the concept of justice itself appears in a murky light. The same is true of Blythe's *Courtroom Scene* (ca. 1860–63), in which members of the jury are asleep, bored, or inattentive, or have the facial expression of imbeciles. A similar impression is conveyed by Blythe's *Trial Scene* (1860–63), based on an episode involving the Molly Maguires, a secret association of Irish miners who violently resisted being drafted during the Civil War.[46]

The tradition of cynicism toward American justice is exemplified in the twentieth century by Jack Levine's painting *The Trial* (1953–54), in which sober formality affords masks for the gravity of scandal in high places,[47] and, returning to a temple of justice, by Eugene Savage's 1940 mural for the Fountain County Courthouse in Covington, Indiana (Fig. 3.16). The folded papers in the barrel are labeled "Bonded Debt," "Public Bond," "Public Debt," "Refund Bond," and "Public Loan," and the wall sign reads "No Men Wanted." Like the courtroom scenes painted by Glackens and Benton, there appears to be a deliberate element of ambiguity in both of these sardonic paintings. Clearly, neither one is an "upbeat" statement concerning human nature, yet a categorical verdict has not been rendered in or about *The Trial*. Justice may not have been done, but perhaps one might say that judgment has been suspended.

Icons of Justice in Comparative Perspective

In the famous colloquy between Oliver Wendell Holmes and Learned Hand, the latter was rebuked for offering the exhortation to "Do justice!" because Holmes seemed to have a greater realism about the judge's role in

Fig. 3.16 Mural by Eugene Savage (1940). Fountain County Courthouse, Covington, Indiana (1936). Photograph by Bob Thall, Seagram County Court House Archives, © Library of Congress, Washington, D.C.

relation to the law. (Holmes responded, "My job is to play the game according to the rules.") If, however, we find Madison's assertion that "justice is the end of government" at all compelling, then Learned Hand seems less naive and one must wonder whether "doing justice" is not in fact an appropriate activity for those whose vocational role is played out within a temple of justice.[48]

We may also wish to reconsider the debate between Lawrence Friedman and others as to the issue of just how litigious American society is.[49] Perhaps what matters is not some quantitative measure of litigation per person, or even the cost of litigation, but the process of litigation itself and how members of the culture feel about it. To clarify this matter, a comparative look at the iconography and artifacts of judgment may be stimulating, if not definitive, for purposes of resolution.

John T. Noonan, Jr., has utilized the notion of judicial masks in a metaphorical way as a means of arguing for a genuine alliance between law and history, and as a means of looking at the law in terms of actual persons and human responses rather than abstract analyses of jurisprudential rules.[50] I would like to invite consideration of judicial masks not as metaphors but as actual instruments of judgment.

Among certain West African tribes, for example, such as the Toma in Liberia, when a member of the Poro Secret Society was selected to put on a mask with a long nose and beak (Fig. 3.17), he lost his personal identity and became an awesome judge commanding authority beyond any challenge. The immense fear evoked by this mask would, for instance, ensure the prompt payment of debts.[51]

Or consider the Nail and Blade Oath-Taking Image (*nkisi n'kondi*) made in coastal Zaire (Congo) during the nineteenth century (Fig. 3.18). The figure is poised in a condition of acute alertness, thereby indicating its potential role in the settlement of law suits or other serious disputes. It is regarded as a living presence and conversed with by clients or litigants. Each nail or blade that is driven into the figure symbolizes the words and oaths that will resolve a legal controversy.[52]

Perhaps we should look more closely at cultures in which the law itself is less complex and less mysterious, and that lack a sacred text (or texts) that require interpretation by trained "priests." Perhaps we should look more closely at societies that make the judge and the process of judgment (rather than the law itself) mysterious.[53] In purely functional terms, the outcome seems to be broad acceptance of the *results* of adjudication. There are no appeals from the verdict rendered by a masked judge or a nail-and-blade fetish figure.

By contrast, when a judging body divides 5 to 4 with some frequency, when some justices concur in part and dissent in part from the principal

Fig. 3.17 Mask, Toma of Liberia (nineteenth century). Carved wood with original encrusted patina. Courtesy of the Toledo Museum of Art. Gift of Edward Drummond Libbey (1970).

opinion, or when justices are openly critical of one another's opinions, we do not achieve finality of judgment, the law is likely to become needlessly politicized, and the Temple of Justice surely loses some of its luster.

No one understood that lesson better than Chief Justice John Marshall, although Chief Justice Earl Warren ranks fairly high on the list of those who appreciated the importance to a political culture of judicial cohesion concerning moral issues.[54] It fascinates me that John Marshall never had a temple of justice to call his own. The Marshall Court labored in comparative obscurity; its quarters were truly inconspicuous. Of course, that did not prevent some decisions of the Marshall Court from becoming extremely controversial, as Gerald Gunther has shown so well in *McCulloch v. Maryland*. But when John Marshall wrote as a partisan and attacked Judge Spencer Roane of Virginia, he carefully put on masks of anonymity, masks called "A friend of the Union" and subsequently "A Friend of the Constitution."[55]

John Marshall used various techniques and devices to enhance the legitimacy of judicial decision making. They have been described in detail

Fig. 3.18 Nail and Blade Oath-Taking Image, Congo (coastal Zaire) (nineteenth century). Wood, textile, iron, bronze, twigs, glass, and horn. Courtesy of the Fine Arts Museums of San Francisco, Museum purchase, gift of Mrs. Paul L. Wattis, and the Fine Art Museums Foundation.

by others.[56] It is sufficient for me to say that credible and consensual judgments are far more vital to the integrity of a political culture than its temples of justice—however elegant, however awesome, however austere. Although John Marshall lacked a temple of justice, his greatest legacy may very well have been a template of justice—a gauge and a guide that successors might use in rendering judgments that achieve legitimacy and endure.

4

"Our Idealism Is Practical": Emerging Uses of Tradition in American Commercial Culture, 1889—1936

To understand the relationship between commerce and the American sense of heritage, consider for a moment the holiday that commemorates George Washington's birthday.* On that day we remember and honor the accomplishments of the Father of Our Country. Right?

Wrong. We usually think about George Washington (and now other presidents) on his birthday because it's a great day to go shopping: to get two snow tires for the price of one, or carpet remnants at 80 percent off, or a third television set (a small one for the kitchen, perhaps) at a large discount. It has become an American tradition to observe Presidents' Day by slashing prices (if you are in business) or by stockpiling things you may or may not really need (if you are a consumer), just because "you will never see such prices again."

* This essay was presented on February 17, 1986, as part of the Johnson Distinguished Lecture Series at Cornell University. It appeared in *Cornell Enterprise* (Fall 1986), 18-27.

How old is that American tradition? Did they hold special sales on February 22, 1800, the first occurrence of Washington's birthday after he died? Perhaps his very last words, barely audible to Alexander Hamilton, were, "Tell them to cut inventories and slash prices." Washington was, after all, a practical man. He believed that prosperity would be good for the national character and that an economic depression might actually subvert our virtuous way of life and our republican form of government. That's why he presided over the Constitutional Convention of 1787, a body that exceeded its authority and chucked out a legitimate government that was doing poorly in favor of a questionable one (at that time) that has had a winning record, more or less, ever since. Back in Revolutionary times they treated governments the way we treat football coaches: Losers must go.

At any rate, if we look back a century or so, we will find no buggy wheels or telephones being offered at irresistible prices on George Washington's birthday. In New York City on February 22, 1887, the Society of the Sons of the Revolution held a Washington's Birthday dinner at Delmonico's, and there were a lot of toasts drunk and tributes spoken. The Hebrew Sheltering Guardian Society's Asylum for Children held an afternoon reception in honor of Washington, the "father of his country." Throughout the land, by and large, according to the *New York Times*, Washington's birthday was celebrated in a "quiet way." In Washington, D.C., Congress convened even though government offices were closed. Grave-side ceremonies were held at Mount Vernon, and parades took place in some cities.[1]

Not much had changed by 1888. Most businesses actually *closed* on Washington's birthday. People decorated their homes with leftover red, white, and blue bunting from the Fourth of July. Some folks took strolls along the avenues or through their local parks. It was a day of leisure rather than frenzied commerce.[2]

The next year, the centennial of Washington's first inauguration as president, things began to change. Many New Yorkers still went out for a stroll. The chimes at Trinity Church, near Wall Street, rang out patriotic songs like "Yankee Doodle" and "Hail, Columbia." The Sons of the Revolution met at Delmonico's as usual, and the Society of the Cincinnati, the Order of United Americans, the Harlem Democratic Club, and the Sagamore Club all held birthday dinners and raised their glasses time after time.

As commercial advertising began to play an important role in American culture, however, the image and name of our first president came to be exploited in the sale of ice cream, canned vegetables, and steam radiators, as well as many other goods. Somehow, an association with George Washington seemed to make products more attractive. Manufacturers thought so, at

Fig. 4.1 Martha and George Washington advertising stove polish. Trade card (chromolithograph on paper) printed by Donaldson Brothers, Brooklyn, New York, late 1880s. Courtesy of the Margaret Woodbury Strong Museum, Rochester, New York.

least, and the commercial link between Washington and your wallet was established (see fig. 4.1). It has endured for decades. A 1937 advertisement for Mount Vernon Straight Rye Whiskey, for example, explained that "from George Washington's day, it has been accepted among gentlemen that to show special hospitality one serves Mount Vernon, the patrician of American ryes."[3]

A century ago American enterprise seems to have had a rather ambivalent attitude about the effectiveness of using the past in general, and the American heritage in particular, as stimuli in sales promotion. Leaders in the realm of advertising tended to rely on an "ideology of improvement." Insofar as the past was presented at all, it was deployed to contrast primitive predecessors with dazzling improvements, as in AT&T's 1912 campaign, which compared the telephone to earlier, inferior forms of long-distance communication.[4] In 1889 a window display at J. S. Conover and Company in New York City showed a "colonial style" room from the eighteenth century, rather Spartan and bare, alongside another room "furnished most elaborately in the colonial style of 1889." The chairs and tables were made of the finest mahogany. The tapestries were silk. Silver and ivory artifacts abounded. Obviously, ersatz American colonial was preferable to the real thing: more comfortable, more luxurious, a measure of higher status if you could afford it. The present could reproduce the past but improve upon it as well. Once upon a time, to some people, reproductions were worth more than originals.[5]

At about the same time, however, businessmen began to use the American heritage to good advantage. In 1887–88, for example, the Grant Monument Association became active in raising funds for a memorial to Ulysses S. Grant. Mr. O. P. Dorman, president of the Gilbert Manufacturing Company, announced that he intended to donate all the profits from a particular grade of dress linings to the Grant Monument Association. Women were therefore urged to ask for "Grant Memorial Twills." The press gave that promotion a lot of free publicity. One article began, "Although the ladies of the republic have no share in electing a president, it now rests wholly with them whether or not a suitable memorial shall be erected to General Grant."[6]

Just five weeks after the promotion was announced, Mr. Dorman declared that because Grant Memorial Twills were selling so well, the company would double the number of looms engaged in their production. Two months later such stores as Altman's, Bloomingdale's, and Lord & Taylor had reordered. In April 1888, eight months after the public-spirited enterprise got under way, the Gilbert Manufacturing Company presented a $2500 donation to the Grant Memorial Fund. Considering all of the hoopla, that seems a modest purse indeed. But the free publicity certainly didn't hurt the Gilbert Manufacturing Company, and the Grant Memorial Fund had $2500 more than it would have had if Mr. Dorman hadn't dreamed up the promotion.[7]

Commercial and patriotic motives have commonly been intertwined throughout our history. At times the love of country and the love of profit

are compatible, even mutually reinforcing. It gets more complicated, however, though perhaps more interesting, when celebratory and mercenary
instincts come into conflict—which was a frequent occurrence, for example,
at the centennial celebration of George Washington's first inauguration,
held in New York City in April 1889. Merchants feared that if the fête
became an official three- or four-day holiday, too much business would be
lost. Those who rented apartments feared that if every truck was pressed
into service for the several parades, people would be unable to move to new
locations on May 1, the traditional moving day in the city. Would landlords
extract an extra pound of rental flesh? Would the railroads extend their
special excursion rates into the early weeks of May, when out-of-town
businessmen customarily came to New York City on buying trips? That
became a very hot issue. And ultimately, why did the city's business
community not reap the bonanza that had been anticipated? That turned
into a topic of bitter debate during May of 1889.[8]

The centennial celebration of the ratification of the Constitution, which
continued from September 1887 until May of 1889, required a lot of red,
white, and blue bunting. In February 1889 the Protective Tariff League's
mouthpiece publication, *American Economist*, condemned as unpatriotic
anyone who opposed a new 80 percent tariff on foreign-made bunting. The
People's Cause, a tariff-reform magazine, complained that "the duty of 80%
was imposed in order that the American people might be compelled, in the
name of patriotism, to buy all of their bunting from General Butler's
factory." An editorial in the *New York Times* expressed skepticism about the
recent decision by Congress to raise the duty, and particularly disliked the
linkage between that issue and patriotism. "Where does patriotism end and
treachery begin," the *Times* asked, "as measured by a descending scale of
duties on bunting?"[9]

Be that as it may, the success of the Constitutional centennial whetted
New York City's appetite for more. The business community began to think
ahead, and decided that it wanted to host a grand exposition in 1892 to
celebrate the 400th anniversary of Columbus's epochal discovery of the New
World. The big question, however, was whether the $15,000,000 needed to
finance such an exposition could be raised from commercial firms and
private individuals. Another *New York Times* editorial explained that contributors need not be inspired by "patriotism and public spirit," because such
an exposition surely would "pay, if that must be regarded as the controlling
consideration in everything American." Contributors would become stock-
holders in the venture and receive a proportionate share of the profits. Even
if there were no direct profits, the indirect ones would be terrific for hotels,
restaurants, transportation companies, merchants, and local industry.[10]

As it happened, local enthusiasm and venture capital turned out to be inadequate. An upstart city, Chicago, outhustled and outbid New York, produced the great Columbian Exposition, and reaped bundles for the Windy City, even though the fair had to be delayed until 1893, the 401st year after Columbus's arrival.[11]

For almost twenty-five years thereafter, merchants and city fathers, hither and yon, seized on commemorative occasions to promote major expositions that benefited everything from real-estate development and the construction trades to taffy sales and ticky-tacky souvenirs. The American heritage could be exceedingly good for tourism and business. Hence, for example, the Pan-American Exposition, held in Buffalo in 1901. (When it became clear that the electricity for that affair would be provided by the American power plant at Niagara Falls, the American Exhibitors Association became very interested.)[12] Hence the Louisiana Purchase Exposition, set up in St. Louis in 1904, and the Jamestown Tercentenary Exposition, held in Norfolk, Virginia, throughout most of 1907.

It must be conceded, moreover, that even the Janus-faced exhibits at those great fairs fostered an interest in American history. The dominant theme at such extravaganzas, other than pride of place, was invariably progress. What better way to demonstrate progress than by displaying the quaint yet primitive life-style of your ancestors? In addition, the sponsors shared, as an article of faith, the belief that history could best be taught to ordinary folks by means of objects rather than books.

The success of those massive expositions, which usually remained open for six to eight months, helped stimulate a related form of municipal promotion—the urban historical pageant, a popular phenomenon during the second and third decades of the twentieth century.

In 1913, for example, business and civic leaders in St. Louis decided to risk $125,000 on a large pageant to celebrate the 150th anniversary of the founding of the city. The leaders felt "shamed" by Chicago's growing dominance in midwestern commerce, by the apparent ineffectiveness of municipal improvement campaigns, and by a series of articles that had appeared in *McClure's Magazine*, written by the prominent muckraker Lincoln Steffens, exposing political corruption in St. Louis. The leaders hoped that a successful historical pageant would achieve two goals: cleanse St. Louis's tarnished reputation in the nation at large and promote a coherent civic identity around which the city's diverse ethnic groups and social strata could unite to enact reforms. A letter that was sent to local businessmen, seeking their support for the pageant, warned that unless St. Louis showed the nation (even the world) that it could sustain productions in a grand manner, the fourth largest city in the United States would soon suffer the "humiliation" of being surpassed by Cleveland and Boston. Heaven forbid![13]

At this point it may seem that a strong trend was taking shape: civic and business leaders teaming up to promote commerce and the American heritage simultaneously—what Tom Lehrer, the irreverent songwriter, once called "doing well by doing good." Some of the participants saw it that way, too, and articulated what seemed to them a clear rationale. In 1923, for example, the executive officer of Steves Sash and Door Company in San Antonio explained to an avid pro-Confederate history buff that although businessmen and educators had different points of view, they were not necessarily incompatible. "We possibly may believe in idealism just as much as the educator does," he wrote, "but our idealism is practical." [14]

It would be easy to enumerate a long list of ventures, some successful and others less so, in which business leaders have sought to exploit some aspect of the American past for personal profit and municipal promotion. But that is not my purpose. Instead, I prefer to call your attention to occasions when business leaders have done well by the American heritage, and vice versa. Positive examples do come to mind. When J. P. Morgan accepted the presidency of the Metropolitan Museum of Art in 1904, he had a grand design for the artistic enrichment of the United States, and to a remarkable degree he succeeded in implementing it. (In that same year, by the way, he gave $100,000 to help establish the American Academy in Rome.)[15]

R. T. H. Halsey, the man most responsible for developing the American Wing of the Metropolitan Museum of Art, is a different sort of exemplary figure. He was born in Elizabeth, New Jersey, to a wealthy family that traced its American ancestry back to 1630 through "generations of bankers and merchants." As a Princeton undergraduate, Halsey developed a fascination for Revolutionary America that he never lost. After Halsey's graduation in 1886, his father bought him a seat on the New York Stock Exchange. Young Halsey became a very successful broker and was a member of the board of governors of the New York Stock Exchange for twenty-five years. In 1899, the very year of his election to the board of governors, Halsey also published his first book, *Pictures of Early New York on Dark Blue Staffordshire Pottery*. He had become a devoted collector of Americana and in 1914 was elected a trustee of the Metropolitan Museum of Art, where he soon became chairman of the Committee on American Decorative Arts. Nine years later he sold his seat on the stock exchange in order to devote full attention to the American Wing, which opened late in 1924. Halsey remained chairman of the Committee on American Decorative Arts and continued to be actively involved in major decisions affecting the purchase of period rooms and furnishings for them until his death in 1943.[16]

Fig. 4.2   Thomas Hart Benton (1889–1975), *Independence and the Opening of the West*
(1959– 62). Courtesy of the Harry S. Truman Library, Independence, Missouri.

~

Let us now shift from individuals to institutions and organizations in order
to demonstrate the potential of American traditions to improve the quality
of life, educate the populace, and stimulate economic growth. A most
intriguing case study of what a business enterprise can do to educate
Americans about their heritage occurred in 1925–26 and is today virtually
unknown. Because I regard it as a parable for business leaders who want to
do well by doing good, I shall discuss the episode at length.

Seventy years ago, during the summers of 1925 and 1926, the Great
Northern Railway conducted two rather remarkable historic expeditions.
That company, established by a major entrepreneur of the upper Middle
West, James J. Hill, was based in St. Paul, Minnesota.[17] The president of the
company throughout the twenties, Ralph Budd (1879–1962), had been the
brilliant chief engineer of the Panama Railroad after 1906. Budd happened
to have a strong interest in the history of French pioneers in the American
Northwest as well as in the general development of that vast and romantic
region.

In 1924 he sent an inquiry to the Travel Club of America, whose home base was on Madison Avenue in Manhattan, asking what the organization did to carry out its "stated aims to assist in the preservation of sites of historic interest and all that which is of historical value." Budd discovered a strong bias toward early American sites along the East Coast, and even toward Sulgrave Manor, regarded as George Washington's ancestral home in Great Britain.[18] Consequently, Budd used some of the rolling stock and other resources of the Great Northern Railway to conduct the Upper Missouri Historical Expedition in 1925 and the Columbia River Historical Expedition in 1926. As he put it in letters to various members of the Upper Missouri Historical Expedition in July 1925, the company's initiative was intended to stimulate "the revival of public interest in the historical background of our country."[19]

Budd fulfilled that objective to a remarkable degree and made quite a contribution to the nation's self-knowledge and sense of its heritage. First and foremost, the expeditions were to be commemorative and educational. If they enhanced the Great Northern Railway's visibility and reputation, that would be desirable, too. But Budd was sensitive to matters of dignity and propriety. He refused to allow anything that smacked of crass commercialism. His correspondence with W. R. Mills, a public-relations man whose title was general advertising agent for the company, makes that clear. As Budd wrote early in July 1925: "As to the sale of souvenirs, of course, the railroad does not want to sell any, but if the local people want to put some on sale, I do not see any objection to it. What do you think of letting the Elks Lodge take charge of all the concessions?"[20]

Although the Great Northern Railway did not exactly maintain a low profile throughout the two expeditions, much of its success resulted from appropriate planning that engaged the leadership of several state governors and the joint sponsorship of all appropriate state historical societies. The participants who attended as guests of the company were also shrewdly picked: prominent historians, writers, and artists, as well as politicians, jurists, businessmen, and bankers. The 1925 expedition included, for example, Major General Hugh L. Scott (United States Army, retired), a member of the United States Board of Indian Commissioners and "considered the greatest living authority on the North American Indian" (according to an official brochure); Pierce Butler, associate justice of the United States Supreme Court; Charles M. Russell, of Great Falls, Montana, the beloved artist who depicted cowboy and Indian life on the old frontier; Lawrence F. Abbott, prominent New York editor and president of a widely read monthly called the *Outlook*; and the directors of the state historical societies of Minnesota, North and South Dakota, and Montana.[21]

Budd's gracious approach worked well. By including various organizations in the planning and giving them a stake in the success of the ventures, he could be sure that they would do much to enhance publicity on their own initiative. The librarian of the Historical Society of Montana wrote the following to Budd:

> I must compliment you upon the preparation of the program, which is certainly unique and tastily [*sic*] gotten up and certainly every pioneer of the north-west is indebted to you for this timely action in dedicating and preserving to future generations the history of the great north-west. . . . I have put out some good publicity matter through the Associated Press as per the inclosed clipping and this matter will have wide publicity, and I am sure you will have one of the greatest gatherings of noted men and women on historical matters ever congregated in the great west.[22]

A brochure prepared by the Great Northern Railway called the 1925 expedition a pilgrimage, the word customarily used for more than half a century when referring to visits to historic sites and shrines. It concluded with a claim—plausible, though excessively inflated—that the expedition "marks an innovation in the development of public interest in the preservation of historic records concerning any region. This is the first expedition of its kind recorded in the United States."[23] Although the first part of that assertion may have been "hype," the second part was true.

What, in fact, was the program all about? Where did the 1925 expedition go, and what did it do when it got there? A special train left St. Paul at 9:00 p.m. on July 16 and made its first stop at Verendrye (formerly Falsen), North Dakota, a town east of Minot. Pierre de la Verendrye, a French Canadian explorer, had in 1738–39 penetrated into what became North Dakota, and he is considered the first white man to reach the upper Missouri River. (In 1742–43 two of his sons pushed on to the foothills of the Rockies. They are said to have been the earliest white men to see "the snowy magnificence of that range.")

Governor Sorlie of North Dakota presided over ceremonies that included an address by Lawrence J. Burpee, a distinguished Canadian historian, on the explorations by Verendrye, plus another address about David Thompson, an English explorer who had surveyed and mapped the area in 1797–98 and gathered a great deal of valuable scientific information. A monument to Thompson was presented to the state of North Dakota by the Great Northern Railway. A typical North Dakota farmers' picnic followed, sponsored by the Minot Association of Commerce, after which the party drove in a caravan to Minot for an evening banquet.

The expedition then reboarded its special train to head for old Fort Union, located on the Missouri River (close to its confluence with the

Yellowstone River) about twenty miles west of Williston, North Dakota, near the Montana border. Members of the expedition met with representatives of all the tribes that had traded at Fort Union, and smoked a peace pipe together. (Between the 1820s and 1860s Fort Union became the center of fur-trading activity for the entire region drained by the upper Missouri and its tributaries, which extended west to the Rockies and north into Canada. Eventually it became the largest trading post in the United States.) On the morning of July 18 a "series of teepee villages housing the tribes of yesterday who will have convened for the congress" suddenly appeared along the banks of the Missouri. For those gazing through the windows of their railway cars, the experience must have been roughly comparable to Catherine the Great's review of her Potemkin villages.

One of the very few lapses of judgment and taste to be found in the whole affair resulted from the patently ambivalent feelings that some of the whites felt toward the Indians. The Great Northern Railway's brochures are filled with statements that seem incompatible to us, but must have looked just fine in 1925. One paragraph in a brochure that praises Major General Hugh L. Scott as a "famous Indian fighter who engaged in more than one important campaign" goes on to say that after Scott's address the American flag at the July 18, 1925, congress would be raised "on a giant flag staff erected on the exact site over which Old Glory waved little less than one hundred years ago, when the guns of Fort Union boomed a friendly salute to the tribesmen coming to trade." It was easy to boom a friendly salute after the savages had been devastated, but General Scott had killed a lot of Indians many years—in fact decades—after Fort Union had boomed those "friendly" salutes.

What helped to make Americans of European descent feel good about the historical record, of course, was that so much progress had been made in "civilizing" the natives. Consequently the afternoon of July 18 and all of the next day were devoted to Indian "contests and ceremonies." Tepee-raising contests, horse races, and a competition for the most appropriate old-time costume were held. Various tribes exhibited their arts and crafts "of sixty years ago" and demonstrated "the progress that has been made by those tribes in industry and agriculture since that time."[24]

From Fort Union the special train proceeded to Glacier National Park, near the Canadian border in western Montana. En route the expedition made a trip to the battlefield, fifteen miles south of Chinook, Montana, on the high bluffs above Snake Creek, where the rebellious Nez Percé Indians led by Chief Joseph were "overtaken" late in 1877 after a forced march of more than 160 miles. Then, on July 20, the expedition moved on to Meriwether, Montana, the northernmost point reached by Lewis and Clark, where the Great Northern Railway presented a permanent monument to the state of Montana in honor of Captain Meriwether Lewis.

The official program lists other highlights of the trip: a band concert in Verendrye by the Minot Great Northern Employees' Band; hymns and songs at various spots presented by the Great Northern Songsters; selections played by the Great Northern Railway Orchestra after the banquet in Minot; speeches following the banquet by Lawrence F. Abbott ("Imagination in American Life") and by Miss Stella M. Drumm ("The Preservation and Recording of History"); the competition at Fort Union for the "best medicine pipe in the possession of a full-blooded Indian delegate"; the Great Northern Songsters singing "Carry Me Back to Old Virginny" in Meriwether, Montana; and the grand finale in Summit, situated at Marias Pass on the Continental Divide, where the Great Northern Songsters gave their rousing rendition of "I've Been Working on the Railroad."[25]

Actually, the enterprise was carried off with less hype and more good will than my selective emphasis might suggest. An editorial about the expedition in the *Minneapolis Journal* was entitled "Pride in Prairie History." The *Record-Herald* in Helena, Montana, quoted Lawrence F. Abbott as saying that the Old Northwest had its pilgrim fathers, too. (There might also have been pilgrim mothers, but no one mentioned them.) An editorial in the *Anaconda Standard* of Anaconda, Montana, was entitled "Business Teaching Us Romance." It said:

> Sentiment has indeed come to be an integral part of the modern business structure. Sentimental considerations observed by many business institutions bring to them a measure of respect and sympathy—a comradeship from the public—that mere success and fair dealing cannot alone engender. Recent action of the Great Northern Railway company in leading the way toward a more general dissemination of knowledge of the early history of Montana and the Northwest is a sentimental business activity which is bound largely and vitally to benefit this commonwealth while redounding to the credit and increasing the respect for the railway company.[26]

Like the official brochure of the 1925 expedition, that editorial includes some unintended ironies. Nevertheless, however self-serving the venture may have been and however insensitive to the realities of Native American history during the preceding century, it can stand as an exemplary instance of American business leadership taking a genuine initiative and playing a major role in history education. The only "commercial," so to speak, in the Great Northern Railway's official literature on the 1925 expedition appeared in paragraph three of the foreword to the program:

> The Northwest really was settled from emigrant trains moving into the territory on the great steel highways—the railroads. In this part of the United

Fig. 4.3 Ralph Budd (right), president of the Great Northern Railway, receiving a peace pipe from Yakima Chief Minninick during the Columbia River Historical Expedition of 1926. The expeditions of 1925 and 1926, which included such veteran Indian fighters as Major General Hugh Scott (on Budd's right), were insensitive to the realities of Native American history yet gave fresh attention to a region that had been neglected by historians and tourists. Courtesy of the Great Northern Railway Company Records, Minnesota Historical Society, St. Paul.

States the railroad builders were the pioneers who made possible the rapid and complete occupancy of the country.

Tones of crass commercialism do appear in letters and memoranda from W. R. Mills, the company's general advertising agent, to Ralph Budd. Here are a few excerpts from a letter dated May 1, 1925:

> I believe the interest in this occasion at Fort Union would be greatly stimulated, and we would get much greater returns in the form of national publicity if we were to hold an Indian congress there for two days. . . . We are confident that the Indians would enter into the spirit of this occasion with great enthusiasm, and that we could count on their hearty cooperation in putting on a sort of an Indian pageant of frontier fur trading days that would be wonderful copy for magazines and newspapers, particularly publications that use pictorial material. By carefully organizing it and securing the right list of newspaper and magazine representatives, motion picture representatives, etc., we could count on blanketing the country with Great Northern publicity as a result of this effort.[27]

If we focused our attention exclusively on the general advertising agent, we would be obliged to second-guess the *Anaconda Standard* and say that sentiment must have been secondary to self-interest. Looking at the 1925 expedition in terms of its consequences, however, we reach a rather different verdict that emphasizes neither sentiment nor self-interest. The expedition genuinely honored a cluster of key figures in Canadian history and was consequently good for Canadian–American relations. It gave a whole batch of youthful historical societies, state and local, a true shot in the arm. It gave the occupants of a region that had been relatively neglected by historians and tourists a new feeling of identity and pride based on a brightened sense of their heritage. As the railroad summarized the matter in its own house publication, the *Great Northern Semaphore*, "this is said to be the first time in the history of railroading that a 'common carrier' has taken the initiative in preserving the historical features within its territory."[28] I see no reason to reject that claim.

Nothing succeeds like success, it has been said, so Budd and his staff conducted a more elaborate venture in the summer of 1926: the Columbia River Historical Expedition. The initial part of the route was roughly similar to that of 1925, with stops at Grand Forks and Fort Union in North Dakota and at Fort Benton and Great Falls in Montana; but from Glacier National Park the Great Northern Railway's special train wound its way up to Bonners Ferry on the Kootenai River in northern Idaho, then southwesterly to Spokane and on down to Wishram (once Fallbridge), Washington, on the Columbia River, where a monument was dedicated to the pioneers of that region. The train then followed the Dalles of the Columbia River to Portland, Oregon. From there the participants moved on to their ultimate destination, Astoria, Oregon, where they dedicated a large column on Coxcomb Hill (the site of old Fort Clatsop) to commemorate the discovery in 1792 of the Columbia River by Robert Gray in the ship *Columbia*, along with the subsequent achievements of Lewis and Clark and John Jacob Astor. As Ralph Budd explained to secretary of war Dwight F. Davis, the basic purpose of the 1926 expedition was to celebrate the exploration of the Pacific Northwest by Lewis and Clark in 1805–06 and the occupation of the territory in 1811 by Astor's Pacific Fur Company.[29]

The whole venture in 1926 was on a grander scale than the 1925 expedition. There were more miles, more days, more invitations to more prestigious people, more sight-seeing and speeches along the way, and more publicity. Parts of the expedition were even filmed. It became an extravaganza.

In a retrospective essay about both expeditions, the distinguished Harvard historian Samuel Eliot Morison observed that "they mark a new chapter in historical synthesis in which the actual sites, and often actual participants, give unique vitality to our past." The prominent scholar also had lavish praise for the Great Northern Railway's president: "Mr. Budd's primary purpose was in the broadest sense educational. He is attempting (1) to promote knowledge and appreciation of their regional history by the people of the Great Plains and the Northwest, (2) make them better acquainted with Easterners, and give Easterners better knowledge of them." [30]

Theodore C. Blegen, then a professor of history at Hamline College, in St. Paul, provided more detached praise. Unlike Morison, he had not been a member of the expedition, but his use of the word "exploitation" in a most complimentary manner indicated that Ralph Budd had done something valuable:

> A private enterprise has become a matter of public importance, for an effective object lesson has been given in the exploitation of historical background as a means of furthering interest in and understanding of a vast region. . . . Now alert business men are becoming alive to the fact that land and people must be observed in conjunction, that the two are inexplicable save in the light of historical development. [31]

At the close of his essay Morison remarked that "other transcontinental railroads would do well to follow the example of the Great Northern." That did not happen, however, nor did the Great Northern Railway perpetuate what it had so nobly begun. I don't know why. The expense surely must have been steep, and perhaps after two stunning successes there was nowhere to go but down. [32] Why not bask in the glow of work well done and much praised?

~

During the past seventy years business leaders have continued to use the American heritage in various ways, among them to promote products and even a way of life. But exploitation of that heritage primarily for commercial purposes, rather than for educational ones as well, has been the dominant motive. Two highly significant exceptions should be acknowledged, however. Early in the 1930s the Henry Ford Museum and Greenfield Village in Dearborn, Michigan, and Colonial Williamsburg, in Virginia, opened to the public. As far as I know, the institutional embodiment of Henry Ford's passion for Americana has not been seriously tainted by commercialism. The same might also be said of Williamsburg, which John D. Rockefeller, Jr., spent some $75,000,000 to restore. Both Ford and Rockefeller always regarded the primary purpose of their projects as educational, and they said so repeatedly.

The case of Williamsburg is a bit different, however, because in the late 1930s the corporation that administered Williamsburg began to manufacture and sell reproductions of early American furniture. The administrators simply could not resist the nationwide enthusiasm for colonial material culture and decorative arts, a trend that began soon after the highly successful opening of the American Wing of the Metropolitan Museum of Art. By 1933 W. and J. Sloane, a furniture manufacturer, had begun to copy early American pieces from the American Wing and also from the private collection of R. T. H. Halsey.[33]

In February 1937, five hundred people (mostly women) attended a Colonial Williamsburg restoration conference held at the Hotel Astor in New York City. They heard Kenneth Chorley, the president of Colonial Williamsburg, Incorporated, announce that several craft shops would open in Williamsburg that spring. By May a story that appeared in the *New York Times Magazine* commented on the popularity of reproductions of eighteenth-century furnishings. "The fine antique furniture displayed in museums and historical shrines has become a potent source of inspiration to designers and manufacturers."[34]

Yet few, if any, critics screamed "commercialism." After all, Wallace Nutting, a pioneer collector and eminent authority on the "Pilgrim Century," had begun to make and sell reproductions of his seventeenth-century pieces in 1917, and Eleanor Roosevelt, along with two friends, started a company that from 1927 until 1936 made reproductions of early American furniture.[35]

Manufacturers of clothing for men as well as women wanted to cash in on the craze, too. Macy's, for example, advertised homespun suits made by Chatham in 1936. Three years later Franklin Simon introduced a new line of printed dresses "inspired by America's colorful history" called "The American Way." An advertisement explained that the designs were based on drawings recently discovered at what once had been the George Washington Print Works, founded at Philadelphia in 1816. The designs bore names such as "Jamestown Belle," "Mount Vernon," "Washingtonia," "Salem," and "Colonial Daughter."[36]

During the 1950s and 1960s, museums and major restoration sites, such as Colonial Williamsburg and Old Sturbridge Village, in Massachusetts, started to sponsor forums on antiques and collectors' weekends that certainly increased attendance and stimulated sales generally for antique dealers as well as the manufacturers of reproductions. By the time of the national bicentennial, in the mid-1970s, prices of authentic originals as well as imitations had virtually climbed out of sight. It was a sign of the times that materialism in the name of patriotism could be justified so easily. The secretary of Iowa's State Bicentennial Commission confessed that "principles are nice, but they don't make the cash register ring." [37]

Two incidents that occurred more recently provide an epilogue to our story. In 1980, in Ithaca, New York, the Lagrand E. Chase Company announced the construction (across from the Ithaca Country Club) of early American homes. A printed invitation to inspect "The Patrick Henry" urged potential buyers to "experience the charm and elegance of Colonial America tastefully united by expert craftsmen with the exciting luxuries of today."

Also, in late 1985 an announcement appeared concerning the use to be made of 137 acres that Averell Harriman had donated to Woodbury, New York. Because the land is situated where several major highways intersect in Orange County, it was considered a potentially lucrative commercial site that could return a lot of revenue to the town if it was sold and developed. The successful bidder, who paid $10,000 an acre for 105 acres (the other 32 acres were sold to Waldenbooks), plans now to construct a 300,000-square-foot open-air shopping center for up to eighty factory outlets, discount stores, and restaurants. The whole ensemble is supposed to resemble an early American village, except for two eighty-foot towers, visible from the nearby highways, that would serve as bus stops and information booths. Woodbury Common, as the project is called, follows the pattern of Liberty Village in Flemington, New Jersey, another conglomerate of discount outlets with a colonial motif.[38]

Before we know it, this country will be studded with early American shopping villages spouting eighty-foot towers. Ralph Budd, where are you now that we really need you?

But perhaps there is still hope. In September 1985 a feature story in the *New York Times* pointed out that the corporate headquarters of companies situated in New York City and its suburbs were buying art on an extraordinary scale and were becoming "working museums." In 1985 alone the Chase Manhattan Bank bought 1,200 paintings and prints. On the grounds of Pepsico, in Purchase, New York, there are more than 30 prestigious works of sculpture. The property, which is open to the public daily, resembles a large park in which sculptural forms sprout from the landscape everywhere you turn.[39]

If our business leaders can become patrons of the arts, perhaps they can do something similar with our historic past. For example, preserve, and find ways to use, significant structures that might otherwise be torn down.[40] Subsidize television programs and films of a historical nature that have educational value. Sponsor essay contests emphasizing themes and issues about which public knowledge is weak, such as the Bill of Rights, the origins of federalism, the meaning of republican government, and the nature of leadership when we have needed it most and it has served the nation well.

I realize that some of that has been done and is being done. Some of it. A lot more could be done, however, and more imaginatively. *Are* there Ralph Budds in our future?

5

The Enduring
Challenges and
Changing Role of
Cultural Institutions

Although I have been an enthusiastic museum visitor for some forty
years, a personal episode that occurred more than twenty years ago
memorably altered my thinking about such places and left me with
the inescapable feeling that museums must be very much in the eye of the
beholder.*

In March of 1969 my wife and I and our two young sons made a
long-planned, much discussed weekend trip to Manhattan in order to see
close friends and visit such places as the American Museum of Natural
History. The museum was frequently mentioned in table talk as an
incentive to pique the enthusiasm (and perhaps the good behavior) of our
younger son, then a little more than three years old.

When the great day came, a crisp but clear Saturday morning, six of us
descended into the subway to catch a train for Central Park West and

---

* This essay was first presented on October 28, 1990, in Princeton, New Jersey, as the keynote
address at the annual conference of the Mid-Atlantic Association of Museums.

Seventy-ninth Street. Because it was Saturday, the trains were running on a slower schedule. So the four adults stood on the platform chatting while the seven-year-old and the three-year-old remained very quiet and looked wide-eyed at the tracks, at the curious tiles, the other would-be passengers, and a combination news stand-candy counter. Keeping in mind that neither child had ever set foot in a Manhattan subway—in fact, neither of these country mice had ever been in New York City—it may not surprise you too much that after five minutes of rapt fascination the younger lad looked up and said (in a bell-clear voice): "This is a *very* nice museum." Lacking any preconceptions about what a museum is and does give the guise of innocence a good deal of flexibility, not to mention perspective.

When it was explained to me that the focal theme of this conference would be cultural diversity in the United States and the so-called mainstream canon, I had several reactions. First, I noted that the issues presently facing the museum world are being discussed in a variety of disciplines that serve scholarship and the public. The question of multiculturalism is currently very sensitive, for example, in the Regents' mandate to revise radically New York State's history curriculum for primary and secondary schools.

The whole business of reformulating the canon, or even abandoning it, has been agitating the folks in literature for several years now. So it may or may not be soothing to report that museum curators and administrators are part of a pervasive phenomenon, and that they are not alone in searching for answers to very difficult questions.

When I asked myself what I could contribute on this occasion—what I might say that would be informative and useful—I gave the only answer that I possibly could: historical perspective. I am a historian of American culture and that is my sole claim to expertise. When it comes to museums, I know what I do and do not enjoy; but basically I am a voyeur.

Having chosen to offer historical perspective, however, I swiftly recognized that I faced a problem. Until a few years ago museum history was a musty and rather neglected field. But that all changed in the later 1980s and we have recently seen a spurt of valuable, well-informed, intelligent new publications, including *History Museums in the United States: A Critical Assessment*, edited by Warren Leon and Roy Rosenzweig (1989); *Past Meets Present: Essays about Historic Interpretation and Public Audiences*, edited by Jo Blatti (1987); many shrewd essays by Michael Wallace that have appeared in assorted books and journals; *Museums of Influence* by Kenneth Hudson (1987); and the provocative "Common Agenda for History Museums" that appeared in *History News* (May 1989), the magazine of the American Association for State and Local History.[1]

Having learned a lot from these publications, I still feel that historical perspective is appropriate, especially in the form of a longer view that dips back to the 1920s, at least. So the essence of my homily is really twofold: First, that the more things change, the more they remain the same; and second, although multicultural realities require a considered response characterized by intellectual integrity, there is a genuine risk of *over-reaction* that could result in presenting the public with visions of a segmented society utterly lacking in cohesion, any history of cohesion, or any potential for cohesion.

The United States has commonly been called a nation of nations. If the inclination of American museum policies has traditionally tilted in the direction of a mainstream consensus, one present danger is that curators and administrators may overemphasize the parts and lose sight of the whole. They are surely not alone in trying to come to terms with that problem. For instance, from what I know about diverse plans for the Columbian quincentenary in 1992, there is a serious prospect of fragmentation verging upon chaos because every Caribbean and Central American nation where the proud admiral made a landfall wants to conduct its own celebration (or else a lamentation for the indigenous peoples). The rivalry between Spain and Italy, however, is even more competitive; and that between Italian Americans and Hispanic Americans is the hottest of all. The quincentenary is potentially a boilerplate invitation to commemorative bedlam. I look forward to watching it unfold. After it stops being nasty, it may seem very amusing indeed.

∾

I would like to call to your attention half a dozen major themes in American museum history that illustrate just how persistent the present challenges actually are. I shall then abandon my safe haven of history, where I feel relatively secure, and offer six suggestions or gratuitous pieces of advice, which is probably madness on my part. But keep in mind that these will be no more than recommendations.

Let's begin, then, with historical perspective, and more specifically with the first major theme—multiculturalism. As a significant challenge for museum professionals it is more than seventy years old, at least. At the Newark Museum in 1916, for instance, a New Jersey textiles exhibition highlighted a "Homelands Exhibit" that displayed articles made in the countries of origin of hyphenated Americans (borrowed by means of the Newark schools). Children who attended the show were taught "how the poorest immigrants from a distant land may have talents and ideals of art capable of transforming crude articles of daily use into things of beauty." Visitors were also informed that "with the coming of peasants from Europe the virtues of the past still live among us." [2]

A few years later, in 1919, a series of Exhibitions of Arts and Crafts of the Homelands, held in Buffalo, Rochester, and Albany, supplied models for subsequent such events. Undertaken unabashedly as a joint Americanization effort by New York State and the American Federation of Arts, these exhibits featured Old World arts and crafts, with skilled artisans demonstrating their work, as well as native music and dance. So professional forebears in museums confronted ethnic pluralism in the past, and have often met with a fair amount of success even when their motives seem more "ulterior" and less altruistic than our own.

For theme number two I call attention to a thoughtful essay that appeared a year ago in *Museum News* titled "To Collect or Educate?" prepared by two top administrators at the Henry Ford Museum and Greenfield Village in Dearborn.[3] My point here is that the educational mission of American museums has been stressed repeatedly in their charters and other statements of purpose ever since 1870 when the Metropolitan Museum of Art began. Public reaffirmations of that educational responsibility recurred even when trustees, curators, and staff all privately agreed that the great unwashed posed a threat to decorum and perhaps even to the security of works on display.

Every so often an article appeared in print to assert that "the multiplication of young art museums is creating in the country a great educational power" (1922). That particular writer, a curator at the Cleveland Museum of Art, acknowledged that in the past collections "tended to express the interests of scholars and the enthusiasms of donors, resulting in a certain aloofness from common interests and common needs." Responsiveness to community interests, he insisted, did not mean an inevitable dilution of standards. "In cultivating public taste," he explained, "it is not necessary to begin with the poor and progress toward the excellent. One can begin with the easily comprehended and progress toward the more difficult—more complex and subtle, always on a high plane."[4]

Although that sounds wonderfully uplifting, a few pages later the author revealed his underlying rationale. Precisely because industrialization had caused a decline in the quality of American life, museums were essential in order to occupy leisure hours with diversion. The time had long gone when laborers derived pleasure from their work. Therefore, "the factory town has the greatest need of the museum of art to supplement its schools, not primarily as a factor in vocational training, but as a stabilizing influence among the laborers."[5]

Transforming collections into genuinely educational institutions is currently high on our agenda, and it is being done with considerable success. But the rhetoric (if not always the same modern rationale) has been around for 120 years, biding its time. In the decades following World War II many American museums began moving to make the rhetoric much more of a reality than it had been.

Theme number three on my list is closely related to the issue of educational mission: the historical democratization of culture by means of more populistic exhibits, or being open on the Sabbath (a big issue at Colonial Williamsburg during the 1930s), and especially by emphasizing everyday life and the history lived by mere mortals of both sexes rather than brilliant statesmen, heroic generals, and legendary woodsmen. In 1939, when Francis H. Taylor was about to take over as the Metropolitan's dynamic new director, he explicitly called for the democratization of American museums generally.[6]

The past quarter-century has witnessed a remarkable though belated response to that appeal, and it surely deserves our applause even though symptomatic anecdotes make us wince and wonder why *some* people go to museums. One example should suffice. When the King Tut exhibition opened at the Los Angeles County Museum of Art in 1976, people were told to line up in order to obtain tickets for particular days and times. One woman arrived at a ticket booth, was asked for her preference, and responded: "I want my ticket for the day that the King will be there." We may all be Federalists *and* Republicans, as Thomas Jefferson once declared, but I guess we are *not* all Egyptologists.

Theme number four concerns the customary distinctions between elite and popular culture, or between high and mass culture. A currently problematic and trendy question is whether meaningful distinctions can be made between them. After all, didn't Ralph Waldo Emerson travel the lyceum circuit and serve to connect disparate segments of society?[7] Didn't the Beatles have fans from every social stratum? The issue of stratification is not new, however, and neither is a closely connected one: whether the objects displayed in museums should be the very best of their kind or ought instead to be representative. If one collects on the scale that Henry Ford or Margaret Woodbury Strong of Rochester did, it is really not a dilemma because they bought quantity as well as quality. For most museums, though, the issue is not so simple. Nevertheless, in a country containing thousands of diverse museums, it ought to be possible for several of them to show a breathtaking display of Tiffany glass while others install exhibitions about everyday life in the age of homespun.

Even so, I find it fascinating to notice that seventy years ago an essayist in

Scribner's pleaded for the abolition of distinctions between high art and designed (or machine-made) art, urged that mass-produced objects based upon unique original designs be placed in the Metropolitan Museum of Art, and insisted above all that museums should cooperate with the production and display of American industrial art.[8]

Joseph Downs, on the other hand, who presided over the American Wing of the Met during its early decades, perpetuated quite a different position that endured well past World War II:

> The American Wing presents an aspect that is disappointing to certain visitors who believe that the everyday life of the average early American should be represented. . . . We can rightly judge a cultural period by its greatest achievement rather than its mean average. The American Wing is not ethnographical, concerned with the habits and customs of man, but is the esthetic expression of artisans even before painting, sculpture, and other graphic arts found a foothold.[9]

The contrast in perspective between a Joseph Downs and a Henry Ford, let's say, is quite remarkable. For despite all of Ford's well-publicized eccentricities (displaying Thomas A. Edison's last breath in a test tube, and a dead cat under glass at Botsford Tavern), and despite his anti-intellectualism, he felt determined to present the evolution of material culture in the United States, primarily as it pertained to the lives of ordinary folk: not the very rich and not the very poor, but middling people in between. As he explained to a journalist in 1936, three years after his Dearborn museum complex opened to the public:

> This museum has been organized for the purpose of teaching. In it we show the development of many things we use today. . . . Whatever is produced today has something in it of everything that has gone before. Even a present-day chair embodies all previous chairs, and if we can show the development of the chair in tangible form we shall teach better than we can by books.[10]

Many in the museum field may not be comfortable with the idea of Henry Ford as their professional progenitor, but in certain ways he was.

Theme number five on my déjà vu chart concerns the decentralization of significant museums and their varied contents, a phenomenon that really dates from the 1930s. It is no longer necessary to travel to the northeastern corridor of the country in order to view the high-quality handicrafts of colonial America. When John D. Rockefeller III died in 1978, he left his superb collection of American art to the Fine Arts Museum of San Francisco because the great institutions east of the Mississippi already had works by most of the artists whose pictures Rockefeller had collected, whereas the Bay area did not.[11]

Improving the geographic distribution of museums and their holdings has meant more than finding Copley portraits and Philadelphia-made Chippendale highboys at the Bayou Bend mansion of Miss Ima Hogg of Houston, Texas. It has meant an increase in local and regional pride derived from museums that highlight local and regional subcultures, themes, ethnic groups, industries, and episodes.

Closely tied in with that trend has been a parallel development: the decentralization of commemorative observances over the past thirty years or so. I am persuaded that the Civil War Centennial (1961–65), the Bicentennial of the American Revolution (1975–76) and of the U.S. Constitution (1987–88) were far more successful and meaningful at the grass-roots level than they were as national anniversaries. People who cannot recall anything about the nationwide celebration can tell you what their particular communities did. And in many instances, where some sort of historic preservation and adaptive re-use resulted, what occurred at the community level remains as an enduring legacy.[12] The decentralization of American survivals and revivals antedates the push for multicultural recognition in institutions of memory. Surely that pattern of local enthusiasm has made it somewhat easier to achieve multiculturalism as a goal and gain acceptance for it.

Theme number six on my agenda concerns the role of ethnicity in American life and its explication by museums. The point that I want to make is that ethnicity and Americanism are not necessarily at odds. Nor are assimilation and the so-called "mainstream canon" antithetical to the culture generated by "marginal" or minority groups. I vividly recall a remark made by New York's Mario Cuomo on March 3, 1990, while doing his weekly radio interview called "Meet the Governor." Referring to presidential chief of staff John Sununu, Governor Cuomo said that "He is very proud of his ethnic heritage, and even prouder to be an American, as I am." Tension between the two identities is not inevitable. Consequently, for museum personnel ethnicity or race and Americanism should not present insuperable, either/or exhibition issues.

Take, for example, the Weeksville Project that began in 1968 in the Bedford-Stuyvesant section of Brooklyn, New York. An urban renewal project there revealed the remains of an affluent nineteenth-century black community called Weeksville. After archaeological investigations in the area turned up artifacts, household objects, photographs, and records of business organizations and benevolent societies, attendant enthusiasm led to the creation of a Society for the Preservation of Weeksville and Bedford-Stuyvesant History in order to protect and present these physical remains. Soon thereafter the Soulard neighborhood in St. Louis was carefully studied and designated as a historic district because it had been home to *successive* waves of Germans, then to immigrants from eastern Europe, and then African Americans.[13]

Similarly, the Ethnic Heritage Studies Act of 1972 acknowledged that "in a multi-ethnic society a greater understanding of the contributors of one's own heritage and those of one's fellow citizens can contribute to a more harmonious, patriotic, and committed populace," and it therefore provided assistance primarily aimed at enhanced educational programs in ethnic studies. It authorized the U.S. Commissioner of Education to make grants to, and contracts with, public and private nonprofit organizations and institutions in order to assist them in "planning, developing, establishing, and operating ethnic heritage studies programs." By 1973–74 the results could be seen nationwide: courses in Italian-American, Polish-American, German-American, and Greek-American studies swiftly appeared, among others, at universities and high schools, alongside curriculum development for African Americans, Hispanics, Chicanos, and Native Americans. Some of these programs have quietly disappeared, especially the so-called "white ethnic" studies; but many of them have also expanded.[14]

∾

The point of my presentation thus far, and the principal thrust of my six themes, has been to suggest that historical background and context can be helpful because they place what appear to be difficult current problems in a meaningful and less daunting perspective. If the issues are not so unprecedented as they seem, if our predecessors wrestled with them and even devised viable solutions, then surely we can too.

It helps, moreover, to pay attention to local and regional museums in other societies, and to the presentation of varied subcultures in such institutions as the Museum of French Popular Arts in Paris. One of these days someone is going to undertake a comparative study of museums in the United States and those elsewhere. There are striking similarities to be sure. France, for instance, has an intriguing assortment of topical museums, ranging from posters to costumes to wine; and the Netherlands does a fine job with local historical museums and regional ones like the Museum of the Zuyder Zee.

It is my impression that for more than six or seven decades American museums borrowed heavily from the planning and design strategies of Old World counterparts. The influence of Skansen, the outdoor museum at Stockholm, to mention one example, is well known. Nevertheless, I have a hunch that in recent decades American museums have contributed much that is distinctive to institutional developments around the world.

Using the notion of a "museum" in its broadest possible sense, so as to include historic sites, living farms and villages, and even entire towns ranging from the industrial exemplar in Lowell, Massachusetts, to the Chinese enclave in Locke, California, we find some clear patterns that help to make a case for American exceptionalism in presenting history, art, and artifacts to the public. I have in mind, for example, the use of costumed guides and craft demonstrations, which most foreigners are not accustomed to; or interpretive "street theater" which has been used effectively in different ways at Colonial Williamsburg and Plimoth Plantation; or the lively presentations by National Park Service personnel at such places as Ford's Theater in Washington, D.C.; or the vivid social history conveyed in conjunction with the network of lock canals that demonstrates how water power was controlled and utilized in Lowell, Massachusetts.

Above all, though, I have in mind the astounding diversity of American museums, especially in terms of their topical specialties: some concern particular aspects of national or regional commerce (such as the Museum of Tobacco Art and History located in Nashville) or else a specific vocation (such as Fred Hunter's funeral museum in Hollywood, Florida, which displays old embalming tools, a 1917 Ford model T hearse, intricately braided wreaths of human hair, and a 1500-pound glass coffin).

In a nation that numbered more than 6500 museums by the end of 1988, a commonly voiced concern called attention to their predominantly pastoral nostalgia for preindustrial serenity.* Agricultural museums and villages are numerous, to be sure, but the balance is steadily being redressed. Baltimore has its Museum of Industry, for example; and Waterloo Village in Stanhope, New Jersey, which opened in 1965, shows an ironworking community on the old Morris Canal and serves as a reminder that many American industries developed in the countryside. Since 1983 the American Labor Museum has been open near Paterson, New Jersey, in the former home of Pietro Botto, an Italian silk weaver who died in 1945. Paterson has several other museums, of course, that explain the silk manufacturing process and also describe the comfortable lives of those who controlled the industry.

I could continue with the enumeration of new thematic museums almost indefinitely, ranging from Steamtown, U.S.A., in Scranton, Pennsylvania, to institutions that stress the sea as a way of life, to a museum of trash located near Lyndhurst, New Jersey, proximate to the Hackensack Meadowlands where trash has been dumped by the ton for more than half a century.

---

* By 1996 the total had risen to 8200. When the last national survey was conducted in 1991, 55% of the 7500 museums in the United States were historic sites (2,083) or history museums (2,401).

Visitors to this unique "facility" will walk through a cross-section of a dump, surrounded by a depressing accumulation of household junk: old telephones and milk containers, broken toys and rusted car fenders, bald tires, empty bottles, and discarded magazines. Needless to say, the trash museum is meant to be especially didactic. Then there is the McDonald's Museum at Des Plaines, Illinois, created in 1985, where Ray Kroc opened his first drive-in restaurant three decades earlier.

I could go on and on—the Dog Museum of America (1982), the salt museums in Syracuse and Watkins Glen, New York. My point is very simply that for sheer diversity, the panorama of museums in the United States is phenomenal.

~

My conclusion, as I indicated earlier, comprises six suggestions. My first suggestion in dealing with multiculturalism relates to one of the assumptions underpinning Common Agenda: Museums as particular places of work are not solo acts; therefore, in terms of social responsibility to the community or to a region, what matters is for each museum to build upon its own strengths and do what it can do best. Diversify collections and exhibitions, of course (within fiscal constraints and realities), but try to complement rather than compete with the efforts of other museums in a given area. What ultimately matters is the overall *configuration* of exhibits accessible to the residents of a state, section, city, or neighborhood. People who enjoy museums go to more than one. For a fine example of cooperation, see "Home: A Place in the World," a related series of exhibits planned by five New York City museums (including the Jewish Museum and the Studio Museum in Harlem) in conjunction with the New School for Social Research.

When I read about the fierce hostilities that occurred between Albert C. Barnes and Fiske Kimball back in the 1920s, or the ongoing rivalry between the National Gallery in Washington and the Metropolitan Museum in New York City, I think wistfully of the extraordinary cooperation that took place during the 1930s between Henry Ford and John D. Rockefeller, Jr., who exchanged all sorts of information ranging from potential acquisitions to management policies. Both of their institutions benefited as a result of this genuine collegial courtesy. It succeeded, in part of course, because each man had somewhat different objectives.

My second suggestion in dealing with multiculturalism: When special exhibits are devoted to particular ethnic or racial groups—and I very much value such exhibits—they should not convey an impression of absolute social autonomy or be presented in vacuo. Rather, they should be cognizant of *relationships* (positive and negative, reflecting mistreatment, scorn, or benevolence) to the so-called "mainstream" as well as other ethnic groups. If we have a responsibility to acknowledge the diverse subcultures that compose our society, and to note the ways and degrees to which they have shaped their own destinies, we also face an intellectual imperative that is the obverse.

The attributes and aspirations that we share in common are certainly as significant as those that differentiate us. The dynamics that have made us a nation or region with a distinctive culture, however flawed, cannot be ignored or minimized. It is my impression that the Valentine Museum in Richmond, for example, has been very successful in this regard since the mid-1980s. Displays pertaining to the old white elite that dominated nineteenth-century Richmond have not disappeared. But they have been richly supplemented by thorough attention to communities of slaves, free blacks, and freedmen after 1865, with special emphasis upon discrimination, hostility, and economic interdependence as well as autonomy.[15]

My third suggestion in dealing with multiculturalism: Take a cue from the growing popularity of theme parks and do more thematic or topical exhibits. That is, organize them along the lines of: How did diverse groups respond to (or were affected by) the Great Depression, or World War II, or the Cold War? How do various subcultures in American society regard the young, the aged, and diverse authority figures? How are cultural values transmitted among them?[16] Some of these thematic issues may be more viable as photographic exhibits, or with video introductions. But that's all educational, and, especially important, it enables one to present a totality composed of connected parts rather than scattered pieces of a segmented society (which only caricatures American pluralism).

From 1991 until 1995 we commemorate the fiftieth anniversary of U.S. participation in World War II. Whereas television specials may lend themselves to remembering major military actions, such as the Battle of Midway or the Normandy invasion, I would urge museums to focus on the home front, particularly because there was such a strong and positive emphasis at the time upon American pluralism—except for Japanese Americans, needless to say. By 1938–39, for instance, a representative series of twenty-six radio broadcasts titled "Americans All . . . Immigrants All" stressed the contributions of diverse ethnic groups to American development.

When Winston Churchill visited Franklin D. Roosevelt in Washington during the winter of 1941–42, Churchill seemed obsessed with the notion of an Anglo-Saxon alliance of homogeneous people with historically shared

Fig. 5.1 John Cotton Dana (1856–1929), director of the Newark Art Museum (1909–29). Courtesy of the Newark Public
Library.

values. Roosevelt urged Churchill to read books by Louis Adamic, the
Yugoslavian American who wrote so much about the United States as a nation of nations. Roosevelt even invited Mr. and Mrs. Adamic to dine with
Churchill at the White House, and complained to them subsequently that
Churchill seemed oblivious to American multiculturalism. "My friend
doesn't realize fully," FDR said, "what a mixture of races, religions and
nationality backgrounds we are, and that our backgrounds persist." [17]

I strongly believe that World War II served as a major turning point in
the history of America's recognition of its heterogeneity, and that museums
can build upon that awareness in very effective ways.

My fourth suggestion: Welcome outsiders as colleagues, consultants, or
even (just imagine) as museum directors. We need to look no farther than
the fascinating example of John Cotton Dana, founding director of the
Newark Museum (1909–1929; fig. 5.1), a librarian with no background in
the realm of museums yet a man who turned out to be ahead of his time in
highlighting exhibits pertaining to folk culture and New Jersey's historical
and aesthetic heritage. The astounding depth and range of Newark's

collections and the museum's record of pioneering exhibits owe a great deal to this innovative Yankee's vision and flexibility.

Let me cite just one delightful and droll example. In 1912 and 1913 Dana initiated a show titled "Modern German Applied Arts." When it finished in Newark it traveled to the City Art Museum in St. Louis, the Art Institute of Chicago, the John Herron Art Institute of Indianapolis, the Cincinnati Art Museum, and the Carnegie Institute in Pittsburgh. The Metropolitan Museum of Art, however, archly declined to borrow the show because it seemed to have commercial overtones. Such hauteur irked John Cotton Dana immensely, and he derived no satisfaction in 1917 when the Metropolitan reversed its policy and held several exhibitions that touched upon industrialism, thereby acknowledging Dana's foresight and pragmatism. A decade later, in fact, when the Met made extravagant claims for the installation of a Swedish show, Dana wrote an acerbic letter of correction to Robert Weeks deForest, President of the Metropolitan Museum.

Dear Mr. deForest:

In opening the Swedish exhibition on January 17th, you said that "It is the first one country exhibit of industrial art ever held in this country."

I am sure that when you said this you had forgotten that the Newark Museum held a one-country exhibition of industrial art, from Germany, a full fifteen years ago. This exhibition was gathered under the direction of Mr. Osthaus of Hagen, a wealthy patron of the arts, who had given a beautiful museum and its contents to his native town, Hagen. He was one of the moving spirits of the Werkbund, the organization which had much to do with the development of the industrial arts in Germany, and beyond question was, through the astonishing results of its activities, an immediate promoter of that movement for better industrial art in Sweden, out of which came the Swedish Exhibit which the Metropolitan showed. Our German Exhibit was in certain respects more important than is the Swedish one. It was for its time far more advanced than is the latter. Germany, through its Werkbund, set the pace of the new movement in Europe; and France, as the war opened, was about to hold an exhibit of the new art, being moved so to do by the discovery that Germany had far out-paced her. France's new art exhibit was deferred, on account of the war, until 1925, when it was set up in Paris.

I have not seen the Swedish Exhibit; but I am quite sure that it does not excel the one we showed from Germany in range, quality or value. The German one was shown in several other large cities after its display in the Newark Museum. . . .

I admit that I am a little sensitive in this matter of priority in advocating the advisability of the exploitation, by museums, of industrial art, products of machines and not merely old, rare and costly museum pieces; for I not only brought over that very valuable exhibit from Germany, when the Newark

Museum had an annual income of about $15,000; but I also preached then, and often since, in the public press, in magazines and in our own publications, to the effect that the art museum is in duty bound, by exhibits of varied kinds, to try to improve the public taste in the line of industrial art and thus make the improvement of designs therefor an obvious necessity.

Furthermore, as long ago as 1913, I raised the point that the Department Store was almost making the conventional Art Museum quite unessential.

Naturally I am rejoiced to see the world's richest museum, the Metropolitan,—a museum which by reason of its very wealth is grievously inhibited from venturing into new fields and new forms of activity—taking up modern industrial art and even joining hands with the Department store; and perhaps quite as naturally I am a little chagrined when I note that the art museum activities which I was almost the first to advocate, are being taken over with no word of congratulation to me for my foresight. . . .

I have written an outrageously long letter; but I wanted to assert myself a little, if only for the sake of our little museum and of the remote and rather unfriended city which maintains it; and also I wanted to put my plea in such a manner as to leave you assured of my good will and of my admiration for your great museum.[18]

DeForest responded to this tirade with a courteous but rather lame letter of apology and the incident was closed, at least on the surface. My point is simply that Dana, a civic-minded, genteel (but not gentle) amateur, made an incomparable museum director.

My fifth suggestion takes the form of a caveat: In responding to multiculturalism, watch out for the tendency to treat ethnic or racial groups as though they were monolithic. We know that Jews of German and Russian origin did not get along during the early twentieth century, and we tend to forget that just among Jewish immigrants from Russia there were some who aspired to assimilate while others deliberately ghettoized themselves. Similarly, during the Harlem Renaissance some African Americans were integrationist while others were separatists, and some were far more class-conscious than others. How many of us are aware that in 1918 Dr. Albert C. Barnes of Merion, Pennsylvania—that madcap art collector—organized a systematic survey designed to determine why so many in Philadelphia's sizable Polish community continued to resist assimilation by retaining their customs and language in a tightly knit community that resisted the goals of more "liberal" Polish leaders?[19]

My sixth and final suggestion: For a variety of reasons it would be desirable and appropriate for museums to mount more exhibits pertaining to aspects of the very recent past. (I am aware that *collecting* post-1945 objects is one of Common Agenda's high priorities.) It has become increasingly apparent that Americans have a penchant for historicizing modern events by means of popular as well as official culture (e.g., television docudramas of sensational episodes or heroic displays at such places as presidential libraries). Museums are rather more likely to be dispassionate and present these people and events in a judicious and sensitively contextualized way.[20]

Such exhibits could also serve as a healthy corrective to the hazards of selective memory. Nostalgia for the 1950s and '60s, for instance, manages to obliterate much that was unpleasant, merely banal, or even perverse about those decades. Nostalgia tends to be history without guilt, while this elusive thing called "heritage" is the past with two scoops of pride and no bitter aftertaste. I can think of very few ways that museums might contribute more significantly to our civic culture than by describing and seeking to explain contemporary history in a balanced and meaningful way.[21]

A prime example, for a starter, might involve the recent history of immigration and its implications for the ethnic composition of the United States. To undertake the entire story would surely stretch the resources of any single institution. But let me refer back to my remark about the complementarity of museums. Suppose a museum in Miami concentrated on immigration from the Caribbean, one in Houston on Hispanics, one in Los Angeles on Koreans, one in Chicago on refugees from eastern Europe, and so forth.

If we are truly concerned about understanding multiculturalism and wish to make its implications comprehensible to our fellow Americans, I can think of no more appropriate way to inaugurate a new epoch in museum development than by coordinating a network of shows that would examine the very core of this matter—a contemporary nation of nations—in a collegial mood of mutual support, creativity, and perhaps constructive criticism.

We all recall the Old Testament phrase from *Isaiah*: "Come now, and let us reason together." I propose a modest adaptation: Come now and let us brainstorm together; let us be resources for one another; and we shall accomplish our mission of enjoyment and enlightenment for all who seek it.

It remains trite, yet so true, that museums are simultaneously concerned with engaging people in the present while preserving objects and their meanings for posterity. If museums have an educational responsibility and a conservation mission, as we all know, they also need to be experimental, to take risks, and to be highly innovative within the responsible bounds of prudence. Were I the director of a museum, the compliment that I would cherish most might include the following nine words: "There's always something interesting going on at that place."

PART III

Changing

Perceptions

of the Past

Fig. 6.1 The Henry Grady Memorial, Atlanta, Georgia (1891) by Alexander Doyle. The figure of Memory is on the north (left) side of the memorial, and History is on the south (right) side. Courtesy of the Atlanta Journal/Constitution. Photograph by Louie Favorite.

6

Myth, Memory, and Amnesia in American Historical Art

It has long been commonplace for skillful historians to think of themselves as artists, or to achieve recognition as "artists" painting with words. That aspiration characterized such prominent mid-nineteenth-century romantic historians as William Hickling Prescott and Francis Parkman, as well as many of their contemporaries. Alternatively, this essay considers artists who aimed to record or to envision history. If they romanticized the past, so did the prestigious historians who were their peers. Examining the artists' careers may suggest to us that a tension existed between pursuit of the romantic and the authentic, though in reality the tension lies more in our perceptions than in their work. These artists did not regard authenticity and romanticism as incompatible or incongruous values. The former had to do with historical veracity as they understood it; the latter involved the spirit and emotional significance of what they depicted, not to mention its meaning for Americans in search of historically informed self-knowledge—as individuals and also collectively as a people.[1]

Although history presented as an art form has a venerable tradition—one that has been revisited with rhythmic regularity—we are less accustomed to thinking of art as a literal mode of historical memory and commentary. Doing so might seem nonaesthetic, or even anti-aesthetic. But the wistful laments that opened and closed the nineteenth century, when men and women contemplated the condition of historical art, remind us that a pantheon of history painting is precisely what some Americans sought to establish. "What appears yet wanting," warned the critic George Murray in 1812, is "a *national gallery* of the works of American artists consisting of subjects from our own history."[2]

Still, because influential artists of the antebellum period viewed the United States as Nature's Nation, they were inclined to privilege nature above history and regarded the former as our great feature, the latter as something from which we had been mercifully liberated. It was not unusual for history, especially Old World history, to be depicted as a story of regress rather than progress. Hence Thomas Cole's majestic pair titled *Past* and *Present*, both painted in 1838. The past renders a lively and glorious medieval tournament, with knights jousting in the foreground and a mighty castle behind them. The present offers a dismal castle lying in ruins, an intimation of mortality and a civilization in decline. Piles of stone heaped up by man—even the sites of heroic encounters—could not compete with the sublime spectacle of timeless and unsullied nature.

Nevertheless, some American artists *did* look to heroic encounters and achievements in their native land, and notably, though not entirely, from the more recent past. To appreciate the themes and subjects that most intrigued those artists, we might think in terms of a decahedron, a solid figure offering ten faces, or facets, of our early past. First, there are the "landings" of Columbus and other intrepid explorers, such as de Soto, La Salle, and Hudson. Second, there are highly dramatic episodes involving white contact with Indians, such as William Penn and his legendary treaty, or Pocahontas saving others and experiencing her own salvation at the hands of concerned Christians. Third, there are the patient Pilgrims: embarking from Holland, covenanting on the *Mayflower*, landing at Plymouth, and eventually giving thanks for a sustaining harvest. Fourth (and most detailed), there is the life of George Washington as an officer both young and mature, being domestic at Mount Vernon, presiding at the Constitutional Convention, retiring from civic life, and then returning to heed the call of duty. Fifth, there are strategic land battles followed by victorious surrender scenes from the War for Independence. Sixth, there are memorable naval battles that span the years from 1779 until 1862, featuring John Paul Jones and "Old Ironsides," or the USS *Constitution*. Seventh, there is the Mexican War, precipitated by President Polk in order to fulfill our continental destiny during the later

1840s. Eighth, there is the institution of slavery, but painted in such a way as to accentuate the positive—conducting the *last* slave auction held in New Orleans or promulgating the Emancipation Proclamation. (Ultimately, you see, we did the right thing.) Ninth, there are assorted episodes from the Civil War, military "moments" of haunting violence. And then, completing our decahedron, the life and death of Abraham Lincoln, steadfast statesman and Christian martyr.

There is more, much more, but it seems equally important to inventory those important aspects of our history that are conspicuously missing and to speculate why they went unpictured. The reasons are more complex than facile assumptions might suggest. For example, myths abound in our decahedron, but they are anecdotal myths that can be personified by a heroic individual, such as Princess Pocahontas, President Washington, or the prescient Lincoln. Some of our most consequential historical myths, however, are less susceptible to personification in a single canvas and do not appear: the genius of American politics for customarily escaping the kinds of ideological conflicts that so afflicted Europe; the United States as a place of opportunity, equality, and glorious individualism; the Virgin Land awaiting diligent newcomers who would make it forever fruitful on independent family farms and thereby feed the world.[3] We have personal myths and we have cosmic myths. Some of the latter, however, seem to have been too complex, or perhaps double-edged, for painters to daub in two dimensions and six colors. So they didn't.

History as *event* lends itself more readily to the painter's craft than history as *process*, as everyday life, or even as manifest in popular national slogans —such as "peace and plenty"—that appeared on pitchers and mugs, in speeches and banners, but seemed insufficiently iconic for the grandeur that proper historical art was expected to achieve.[4] How to envision the Bill of Rights, for instance, or passage of the great post-Civil War amendments (the Thirteenth, Fourteenth, and Fifteenth) is equally problematic. So, too, were civic events that involved criticism of cherished goals, or failures of nerve, or episodes that did not mobilize some sort of national consensus. Consequently we lack images of the Loyalists (Tories), the Anti-Federalists, Shays's Rebellion, the Hartford Convention (when New England contemplated secession in 1814), the women's rights convention at Seneca Falls, New York (1848), John Brown's dramatic raid at Harper's Ferry in 1859, or the hotly contested impeachment of President Andrew Johnson in 1868. We tend not to immortalize what is retrospectively embarrassing, inconclusive, or divisive.

Also missing are some occurrences deemed positive yet extremely difficult to depict, not because they are high ideals or abstractions (like the Bill of

Rights) but because their principal embodiment is a document such as a treaty, a bill of sale, or a statement of national policy (the Northwest Ordinance of 1787, the purchase of Louisiana and later Alaska, the Supreme Court's landmark opinion in *Marbury v. Madison*). The absence of the Alamo, the Battle of San Jacinto (facilitating independence for Texas in 1836), Custer's "Last Stand" (1876), or even the great gold rush to California in 1849 is only moderately hard to understand.[5] Imaginative artistic renderings of them do exist, but our sensibilities have subsequently been heightened where imperialism, greed, and the land rights of native Americans are concerned. Out of sight can sometimes mean out of mind—almost.

Ralph Ellison, one of our shrewdest authors, has written eloquently about the role of memory and amnesia in American culture. He has observed that by "seeking to move forward we find ourselves looking back and discovering with some surprise from whence we've come":

> Perhaps this is how it has to be. For given the circumstances of our national origins, given our vast geopolitical space and the improvised character of our society, and given the mind-boggling rapidity of our national growth—perhaps it is understandably difficult for Americans to keep in touch with what has happened to them. At any rate, in the two hundred years of our national existence a great deal has been overlooked or forgotten. Some developments become obscure because of the sheer rush and density of incidents which occur in any given period of time; others fade through conscious design, either because of an unwillingness to solve national dilemmas or because we possess such a short attention span and are given to a facile waning of our commitments. Then too, having had no adequate model to guide us in establishing what we told ourselves was to be a classless society, it has often been difficult for us to place people and events in a proper perspective of national importance. So it is well that we keep in mind the fact that not all of American history is recorded. And in some ways we are fortunate that it isn't, for if it were, we might become so chagrined by the discrepancies which exist between our democratic ideals and our social reality that we'd soon lose heart. Perhaps this is why we possess two basic versions of American history: one which is written and as neatly stylized as ancient myth, and the other unwritten and as chaotic and full of contradictions, changes of pace, and surprises as life itself. Perhaps this is to overstate a bit, but there's no denying the fact that Americans can be notoriously selective in the exercise of historical memory.[6]

When we give careful consideration to American historical art, we survey a fascinating but contested field that involves the politics of culture. Advocates of a national culture in nineteenth-century America expected it to be consistent with a democratic ethos, yet little of our historical art has been done in a vernacular style. Most of the paintings grandly glorify heroes rather than the common man or woman.[7] They celebrate the republic and some of its ideals, but not vox populi or popular sovereignty. (George Caleb Bingham's *County Election* (1851–52) is a notable exception.) They supply images of manifest destiny but rarely depict the environmental and human cost of achieving that destiny. Nor do they ordinarily notice the degradation of democracy when immigrants and working-class Americans were brutally repressed by government in cooperation with corporations during the later decades of the nineteenth century.

A distinguished historian of the Civil War era, David M. Potter, argued that for most of the nineteenth century the nature and meaning of American nationalism were not seriously contested in the United States. A remarkable consensus existed concerning our selection as a chosen people with a providential mission to spread our superior values and political system.[8] If Potter's assessment is correct about that consensus, then it helps to explain why there are so few "nay-sayers" or critics among the notable artists and their icons. In such paintings as *Libby Prison* (1863), David Gilmour Blythe consistently called attention to racism and political injustice, and *The Banishment of Roger Williams* by Peter F. Rothermel (ca. 1850) reminds us of Puritan intolerance toward dissent. But these iconoclastic statements have been handily overlooked, and their contextual meaning is not readily grasped.

It has been fashionable in recent years to refer to pictures as "texts" that can be read and understood. In order to do so, however, we require contextual information about the human agency that informs the pictorial panorama (along with social and political forces, ideological tendencies, military conflicts, religious impulses, aesthetic values and divisions) as well as about the artists and the circumstances in which their paintings were made—what once was called the "climate of opinion." Mark Twain pointed this out in a droll yet basic way in 1883 while discussing a (fanciful) historical painting that enjoyed great popularity in the former Confederacy. The picture by E. D. B. Julio was titled *The Last Meeting of Lee and Jackson* (1869; fig. 6.2). Twain happened to see it on display in Washington, D.C., and wrote in *Life on the Mississippi*:

> Both men are on horseback. Jackson has just ridden up, and is accosting Lee. The picture is very valuable, on account of the portraits, which are authentic. But, like many another historical picture, it means nothing without its label. And one label will fit it as well as another:
>
> > First Interview between Lee and Jackson.
> > Last Interview between Lee and Jackson.
> > Jackson Introducing Himself to Lee.
> > Jackson Accepting Lee's Invitation to Dinner.

Fig. 6.2 E. D. B. Julio, *The Last Meeting of Lee and Jackson* (1869). Courtesy of the Museum of the Confederacy, Richmond, Virginia. Photograph by Katherine Wetzel.

> Jackson Declining Lee's Invitation to Dinner—with Thanks.
> Jackson Apologizing for a Heavy Defeat.
> Jackson Reporting a Great Victory.
> Jackson Asking Lee for a Match.

It tells one story, and a sufficient one: for it says quite plainly and satisfactorily. "Here are Lee and Jackson together." The artist would have made it tell that this is Lee and Jackson's last interview if he could have done it. But he couldn't, for there wasn't any way to do it. A good legible label is usually worth, for information, a ton of significant attitude and expression in a historical picture.[9]

Despite his wry tone, Twain was serious, and well he should have been.

How often have we gone back to review an old favorite in some museum or gallery, only to learn that its title has been changed for some carefully researched reason. Sometimes the new and different title, or the reasons for its alteration, may actually affect our perception of the painting or of the artist's rationale for undertaking it. The same is true, oddly enough, of parodic versions of famous historical works. Who can ever again gaze with an innocent eye at Emanuel Leutze's *Washington Crossing the Delaware* (1851) after seeing Peter Saul's riotous spoof (1976) bearing a similar title. Our response to *Penn's Treaty with the Indians* by Benjamin West (1771) likewise changes after seeing Red Grooms's *William Penn Shaking Hands with the Indians* (1967) and listening to Grooms acknowledge that he chose the subject "more because of Mr. Benjamin West than Mr. Penn. . . . The atmosphere in his paintings is so thick it looks more like 20 thousand B.C. than just a few hundred years ago."[10]

Such parodies and resonances, along with the quips that accompany them, remind us that we must wear figurative bifocals when we view these paintings. We should do so, as it happens, for multiple reasons. How *does* one look at a pictorial cliché? As a text? As a document? As an artifact? The answer, quite clearly, is that we must see such paintings simultaneously as works of art (some of them good and some not so good) and as icons that reveal national or sectional values and assumptions. We also need bifocals in order to perceive the pictures both as contemporaries did *and* with our own more farsighted vision—critically yet with added complexity. The artist, for example, may have been responsible for innovations (such as vernacular clothing or human models of the correct nationality or ethnicity) that *we* take for granted but were actually quite bold a century and a half ago—and were done in order to achieve greater authenticity.[11]

We must also remain alert for distinctions *within* the genre that is so casually called history painting because the mode is not monolithic. Was the artist an actual witness to the events depicted on canvas? Or did the painter rely upon secondhand accounts, oral or written, that stimulated the iconic imagination? What was the artist's attitude toward history itself? Documentary or romantic? Authentic or mythic? Prior to the 1880s historians and artists shared common assumptions about presenting the past, especially the national past. It could legitimately be heroic, mythic, providential, and deliberately romanticized. After the 1880s, however, those aesthetic criteria were, if anything, nostalgically accentuated by the likes of Howard Pyle and N. C. Wyeth, whereas history as a professional discipline sought to become more scientific than mythic, more factual than visionary.

When we press the button that accelerates images to fast forward, however, we face dilemmas and perplexities that must be answered by each one of us individually. In our own time, for instance, enthusiasm for heroic moments and historical anecdotes is supposed to be infra dig, out of fashion. In reality, though, most of us enjoy anecdotes and yearn for heroes we can genuinely admire. We want to derive pleasure from the past even as we wish to learn from it. Robert Penn Warren put it well in his shrewd meditation upon the Civil War: "The asking and the answering which history provokes may help us to understand, even to frame, the logic of experience to which we shall submit.[12]

7

The Problem
of American
Exceptionalism:
A Reconsideration

National consciousness, which is not nationalism, is the only thing that will give us an
international dimension.
                              —Frantz Fanon, *The Wretched of the Earth* (1966)

Several new and important publications have appeared recently concerning a subject that has engaged many of us for decades—one that we discuss with colleagues and advanced students on a regular basis.* I am inclined to suspect that we continue to do so largely because the issue remains so intriguing. One striking feature of the latest contributions is that they differ so radically among themselves. The most visibly polarized are Ian Tyrrell's "American Exceptionalism in an Age of International History" (which repudiates American exceptionalism) and a collection of essays edited by Byron Shafer entitled *Is America Different? A New Look at American Exceptionalism* (which reaffirms the notion). Moreover, I have

---

* This essay was presented on April 3, 1992, at the annual meeting of the Organization of American Historians in Chicago.

noticed two other quite recent contributions that reinforce American exceptionalism as a historical phenomenon from diametrically opposite perspectives: management and labor, plus a third work that examines urban development in four "fragment" societies of Great Britain.[1]

Understandably, my initial response was to wonder about the dramatic discrepancy, particularly in view of the fact that Tyrrell is a historian while most of the rest are political scientists, sociologists, authorities on management, economics, religion, and education. An admittedly impressionistic pattern began to occur to me that is curious, indeed, because it seems the reverse of what one might expect. For about a quarter of a century following World War II, while tough-minded social scientists became increasingly wary of national character studies in general and American exceptionalism in particular, professional historians of diverse ideological persuasions (including Daniel J. Boorstin, David M. Potter, Frank Tannenbaum, Carl Degler, John Higham, and myself inter alia) continued to make inquiries and ventured generalizations about such slippery subjects. Subsequently, however, and for more than a decade now, such historians as Laurence Veysey, C. Vann Woodward, Eric Foner, Sean Wilentz, Akira Iriye, and Ian Tyrrell have expressed profound skepticism and have made American exceptionalism extremely unfashionable in their guild, whereas prominent social scientists such as Daniel Bell, Seymour Martin Lipset, Alex Inkeles, Sanford M. Jacoby, Samuel P. Huntington, Mona Harrington, John P. Roche, Peter Temin, Aaron Wildavsky, and Richard Rose have comfortably resuscitated and reaffirmed the whole gnarly matter and have done so largely on the basis of empirical studies.[2]

As a humanistic historian who has never been a card-carrying social scientist, my impulse would ordinarily be supportive of the currently skeptical historians. Yet in this instance, respecting this particular topic, I find the social scientists more persuasive—perhaps because they are, in fact, heavily reinforced by recent historical scholarship, as I hope to demonstrate below.

Before doing so, however, I want to address a few of the broader procedural and conceptual issues that have been raised in the most recent literature. The call for an internationalized historiography voiced by Tyrrell, Iriye, and others has been accompanied by a curious tendency to disparage or even discount the work of comparative history, especially if it happens to highlight differences rather than similarities. I find that tendency strange as well as sad because we waited so long for comparative history to really develop, and when it did, as it turned out, differences appeared to preponderate. Scholars such as Peter Kolchin and Alfred D. Chandler, whose work I regard as superb, had no problem with that outcome, yet the transnational enthusiasts seem to be morally or ideologically disposed to minimize all those irritating yet illuminating differences.

Surprisingly, few scholars have noted an inclination (less than a decade old) to believe that looking at subnational units of social organization might actually help us to get a better handle on the problem of American exceptionalism. I have in mind, for example, Richard Oestreicher's fine study of the working class in late nineteenth-century Detroit, which concedes that the dynamics of class formation and consciousness varied from one American city to another; or James McPherson's interesting suggestion that prior to the Civil War it was the North, rather than the South that was "exceptional," that is, a deviation from what the United States traditionally had been and valued; or Carl Becker's droll assertion that if the United States was exceptional, Kansas was distinctive within it![3]

What develops, then, from reading such studies end to end? Perhaps a realization that because of American heterogeneity we have not had a singular mode or pattern of exceptionalism. Rather, we have had a configuration of situations that are not static (see McPherson on regional exceptionalism), and consequently they reveal why it is both difficult and dangerous to conclude that the United States as a whole, over an extended period of time, is different from all other cultures with respect to some particular criterion.

Therefore, the next step in this necessarily intensive process may well be the internationalization of history *pari passu* the comparative history of American cities and regions, American unions and voluntary associations, American patterns of internal migration and mobility, American modes of advertising and expressions of taste, or even the geographic configuration (distribution) of syndicated columnists. That kind of domestic comparative history will have to be diachronic as well as synchronic in order to establish nuances of change over time.

I hope it will not seem banal if I suggest that international history ought to be accompanied by comparative "local history" that seeks to develop typologies; for Walt Whitman's words, "I am large, I contain multitudes," have become far more telling in the generations since he wrote those lines in *Song of Myself.*

The implications of local, national, and international history for our apprehension of American exceptionalism (not to mention their interconnectedness) become clearer when we notice that new societies in the nineteenth century looked to the United States as a prototype—though not necessarily a paragon—because they viewed it as the first, the largest, and the most advanced among freshly emerging yet diverse cultures. As one writer for *The Australian* phrased it in 1831, the United States was commonly considered "a model for all new countries and New South Wales (hereafter) in particular." Living in France during the 1950s prompted James Baldwin to wonder, "What does it mean to be an American?," and by the time he returned home the alienated Baldwin believed passionately in American exceptionalism and even used that now despised word "unique."[4]

When we pursue the interconnectedness of micro and macro scales of historical analysis, we achieve considerable illumination from two important comparative studies of management and labor. Starting with the latter, we find Gary Marks (a political scientist) wanting to explain the historical absence of a major labor party in the United States, noting the remarkable range of diversity in unionism *within* and *across* Western societies, and concluding that the absence of a European-style labor party resulted from the "unique character of American unionism." He insists upon the need for systematic understanding of the political orientations of particular unions, and quotes a tailor who spoke at the Denver convention of the American Federation of Labor late in 1894: "We have in this country conditions that do not exist in Great Britain. We have the 'spoil' system which is something almost unknown in Great Britain and on account of it we cannot afford to try at this time to start a political party as an adjunct with their unions."[5]

Marks observes that the United States was the only Western society in which workers could participate in politics prior to the institutionalization of unions and socialist political parties. He notices the persistent temptation to influence the two major political parties by participating in coalitions. He calls attention to the critical importance of closed unionism for understanding American exceptionalism. Nowhere else, Marks argues, was the "grip of craft unions on the union movement as strong or as durable" as it was in the United States from the 1890s onward. Following his in-depth case studies and systematic comparisons, Marks concludes that structural aspects of American politics posed much greater obstacles to a potential labor party than the British political system did. Marks also finds that while some American socialists may have been even more radical than their German counterparts, "the context in which American socialists acted made their strategies particularly sectarian. Whereas German socialists played a vital role in creating the Free Union movement, American socialists from the late 1880s had to respond to the establishment of an independent union movement along economistic craft lines."[6]

When we shift our attention from labor to management, the most current scholarship strongly supports an exceptionalist position also, and even contends that the comparative weakness of unionism in the United States must be attributed to the distinctive values and preferences of American managers, which caused them to be more hostile to unionism than managers in other nations. Sanford M. Jacoby, who teaches at UCLA's Graduate School of Management, argues that business in the United States has historically enjoyed an unusual degree of political power, and that in recent decades there has even been an increase in the extent of illegal employer resistance to unions. Jacoby insists that American employers "faced a different set of incentives and had more substantial resources to resist unionization than was true of employers elsewhere. These included economic and political factors not usually considered in either mainstream or Marxist analyses, such as the size and structure of firms and the state's role in the industrial relations system, which was more variable and complex than instrumental theories would have it."[7]

Jacoby demonstrates startling discrepancies between French, British, and American companies in terms of their respective approaches to long-range investment decisions. He attributes these differences to significant national variations in management education, in attitudes toward risk, in corporate career structures, and in tax laws. Not only did American managers have greater incentives to be hostile, according to Jacoby they also had available a wider range of political and ideological resources with which to implement that hostility. Labor in the United States had a more difficult time achieving employer recognition than labor elsewhere, because American employers had greater economic resources with which to carry out anti-union campaigns, both covert and overt. Finally, in Jacoby's view, what made the American situation highly unusual was not only the absence of a positive industrial relations policy, but also the government's willingness to stand aside during violent labor disputes, or even to mobilize the state's repressive means on behalf of employers.[8]

So, what I wish to offer is an impressionistic tally, a reckoning as it were, in which the impact of critical essays that have been appearing since the mid-1970s is weighed against the substantive scholarship that has emerged in the wake of those essays. Where do we actually stand? Is there a gap between the newly orthodox homilies that we assign our students and the unsettling implications of solid work recently produced by judicious and conscientious practitioners?

To answer those questions I shall proceed in four stages: first, a section devoted to the cultural and historical origins of American exceptionalism, included here, in part, because the full story is not familiar to everyone, and in part because the background of our problem is inseparable from its foreground—by which I mean the state of the art today. Second, I shall notice the critics of American exceptionalism and their resonance over time. It is noteworthy, I believe, that the critics are not necessarily un-American or even anti-American, just as the advocates of exceptionalist positions have not inevitably been spread-eagle nationalists. Third, I shall look at what has actually happened to the exceptionalist position in this age of careful, cosmopolitan comparisons. Has mindless self-deception merely given way to a sophisticated surfeit of national similarities? And fourth, what lessons can we learn by weighing the diagnostic against the intractably descriptive, the prescriptive against serious products of in-depth scholarship over the past dozen years?

The Historical and Cultural Origins of American Exceptionalism

When critics of American exceptionalism—the notion that the United States has had a unique destiny and history or, more modestly, a history with highly distinctive features or an unusual trajectory—identify those writers responsible for such objectionable myopia, their usual suspects date from the generation and circumstances directly following World War II: the Cold War, the consensus school of historians (exemplified by Daniel J. Boorstin and Louis Hartz), and ideological stimuli that shaped the American Studies enterprise. They commonly fail to recognize that American exceptionalism is as old as the nation itself and, equally important, has played an integral part in the society's sense of its own identity. Noah Webster provides a familiar case in point, but we should not overlook Samuel Latham Mitchill (1764–1831), a physician whose passion it became to promote a particular feeling of American identity that would be manifest in government and politics, literature and science, medicine and society. There were also people, such as William Findley of western Pennsylvania, who decided even before the eighteenth century ended that Americans had "formed a character peculiar to themselves, and in some respects distinct from that of other nations." [9]

Throughout the nineteenth century, imaginative writers and historians, popular orators and clergy joined a chorus that continually chanted an ode to the nation's special mission and readiness to fulfill it. Nick Salvatore has correctly argued that awareness of the republican tradition as a legacy of the American Revolution contributed significantly to a strong sense of exceptionalism, one that became pervasive in the popular culture. [10] However astute Tocqueville may have been in observing and explaining American distinctiveness, we should note that his "informants," such as Alexander Everett and Jared Sparks, insisted over and over again that the uniqueness of the United States could be understood only in terms of "our origins." A Bostonian reminded Tocqueville that "those who would like to imitate us should remember that there are no precedents for our history." Lest all of that be casually dismissed as predictable super-patriotism, we should keep in mind that Patrice Higonnet's recent study of *The Origins of French and American Republicanism* contrasts the individualistic character of American society with the persistence of corporatism in France.[11]

What is especially striking in the literature written about the United States by foreign observers is that the emphasis upon exceptionalism is so persistent and so powerfully felt. "The position of America is quite exceptional," Tocqueville wrote, and in 1851 Friedrich Engels warned Joseph Weydemeyer (his friend and Karl Marx's coworker) about "the special American conditions: the ease with which the surplus population is drained off to the farms, the necessarily rapid and rapidly growing prosperity of the country, which makes bourgeois conditions look like a beau ideal to them, and so forth." If it is noteworthy that most of Marx's coworkers who came to the United States after 1848 soon abandoned socialism, it is equally important that explanations that were offered for American exceptionalism by the likes of Francis Lieber, Hermann E. von Holst, James Bryce, H. G. Wells, G. K. Chesterton, and Hilaire Belloc tended to be complementary rather than redundant or contradictory.[12] The same is true of more scholarly writers since World War II whose concerns have ranged from the vision and venturesome nature of American businessmen to the comparative fluidity of our class structure.[13]

Curiously, although foreign observers have hardly been indifferent to scenery, environment, and natural resources in the United States, they have been less disposed than American writers to invoke those phenomena in attempting to account for major contrasts. The author of an 1818 essay on "National Poetry" found a literary imperative in "our country's being beautiful and sublime and picturesque," while a modern scholar (known for his iconoclastic revisionism) has asserted that American farmers were distinctively confident about their ability to conquer nature and adverse agricultural conditions, and that they were markedly successful in doing so.[14]

Environmental explanations for the special circumstances in North America date back to the colonial period, especially the eighteenth century, when it became virtually a cliché to call, for example, Virginia or Pennsylvania the "best poor man's Country in the World." Who could have imagined such a temperate climate, such fertile land, such fecund harvests? That mythos would eventually reinforce the early New England presumption that America was predestined to be a New Jerusalem, a site specially favored by God—perhaps the very place that he had chosen to initiate the millennial Kingdom of Christ. Jonathan Edwards firmly believed that America had a unique spiritual destiny and that the millennium would begin in New

England—all of which had unintended, secular implications for national self-confidence during the Revolutionary era and the young republic.[15] Other New Englanders would embroider vague yet earnest variations on that theme, even in times of crisis. Hence the assertion by James Russell Lowell in 1864 that "America is something without precedent," and hence the will to believe that artistic expression in the United States would be place-specific and therefore distinctive, not merely in its subject matter, but in its manner of expression.[16]

During the half-century following World War I, proponents of American exceptionalism who felt a particular affection or concern for the arts often explained their position in terms of economic organization, or a fluid social structure, or sometimes the sheer determination of creative people to differentiate their work from models of artistic expression produced elsewhere. Such statements, however vague and naive they may seem to us, were heartfelt and widely noticed. In 1936, for example, Bernard DeVoto supported Gilbert Seldes's assertion that "the mode of production of material life in the United States has been so different from what it has been anywhere else that the social and political life here is conditioned in a unique, characteristic form and function."[17] These kinds of sentiments came from cosmopolitan expatriates like Gertrude Stein (when she returned to the United States following a thirty-five-year absence), as well as from hopeful homebodies who extolled either native voices that already sounded distinctive (Thornton Wilder) or abstract expressionism that *would* be different by design (Clement Greenberg).[18]

There has been a curious tendency, by the way, to assume that prominent Americanists of the Progressive era were provincials whose limited perspectives can be explained accordingly. Frederick Jackson Turner, for example, was indeed a patriotic exceptionalist, yet he traveled through Europe in 1900, read a considerable amount about contemporary Europe, and discussed European history at great length with his colleague Charles Homer Haskins. Turner's exceptionalism did *not* result from intellectual narrowness or ignorance. Similarly, when Lewis Mumford spent almost a year in Great Britain in 1920 he developed a desire to preserve "the valuable part of the American heritage." Five years later, after he gave lectures in Geneva, Switzerland, his commitment to exceptionalism grew even stronger and he found in nineteenth-century American culture a fascinating wealth of native traditions in the arts. Charles and Mary Beard wrote *The Rise of American Civilization* during the mid-1920s following twenty-five years of extensive travel in Western Europe and Asia. When Mumford reviewed their book in *The New Republic*, he noted the Beards's penchant for making comparisons.[19]

Exceptionalism did not necessarily equate with chauvinism. Harsh critics of American culture liked to use hyperbole in order to highlight just how phenomenally mired in mediocrity the arts and intellectual life in the United States had become. H. L. Mencken is perhaps the most memorable example, but J. E. Spingarn comes to mind in literary criticism and Thomas Craven in the realm of art. "If the nations of Europe are agreed on any one thing," Craven complained in 1932, "it is that America is a pretty distinct place—peculiar, individual, unique, characterized by certain vile traits and low habits."[20]

Beginning in the 1930s, however, a symbolic quest for the "meaning of America" seemed to top the agenda of diverse writers: critics, historians of literature and culture, serious journalists, and even such watchdogs of the film industry as Will Hays. Gilbert Seldes began his *Mainland* in 1936 with a declaration that it was "an attempt to discover what America means; not so much what it means to me, as what it can mean in the world."[21] Jacques Barzun would echo those sentiments, virtually verbatim, in *God's Country and Mine* (1954). When Henry Luce wrote his widely noticed editorial about the "American Century" in *Life* magazine (February 1941), he also linked the "meaning of America" to "the meaning of our time." Later that same year the novelist James Boyd published a series of radio broadcasts that he had arranged for CBS under the title *The Free Company Presents . . . a Collection of Plays about the Meaning of America.*[22]

The notion that America had a palpable meaning persisted for more than two decades beyond 1941, and Luce publications played a major part in perpetuating the quest as a lofty goal. By the later 1960s, however, the war in Vietnam had become so bitterly divisive that the editor-in-chief of *Time* magazine proclaimed an unprecedented situation: The country had lost a working consensus "as to what we think America means." More than twenty years after that, moreover, when multiculturalism in secondary education became a subject of intense debate and partisanship, the editor of the *Journal of American History* observed that "the debate is really about the meaning of America."[23]

This spasmodic yet sustained discourse about the meaning of America, recurrent for more than sixty years now, may seem to ebb and flow; but from time to time it spills over into a pool that is still murkier; the meaning of Americanism. Two points are notable here. First, those who invoke that phrase have invariably been exceptionalists; and second, the invocation is intended to have ideological force, a point that I shall return to at the conclusion of this essay. "To analyze combinations of character that only our national life produces," a New Englander wrote in 1870, "to portray dramatic situations that belong to a clearer social atmosphere,—this is the higher Americanism." More than half a century later, in 1934, Leon Samson discussed the concept while explaining the peculiar potency of American exceptionalism: "When we examine the meaning of Americanism, we discover that Americanism is to the American not a tradition or a territory . . . but a doctrine—what socialism is to a socialist."[24]

Irving Howe, a committed socialist with an abiding concern about the persistent power of American exceptionalism, once remarked that it took "primarily an ideological or a mythic form, a devotion to the idea that this country could be exempt from the historical burdens that had overwhelmed Europe." Consequently, Howe did not reject the emotional reality of exceptionalism, and he explored its affective force as an ideological surrogate in a society not given to lucidly articulated ideological effusions. Howe's analysis is one of the most insightful that has appeared, yet it is incomplete in the sense that it is negative because it rationalizes exceptionalism as the celebration of an absence, namely, historical burdens. I am persuaded that the "meaning of America" and of "Americanism" have also had affirmative ideological content, exemplified by this representative extract from a speech given by Harry Overstreet, a philosopher, in 1937: "It is the high distinction of America to have been the first nation in civilized history to welcome different cultures and to give them free scope to participate in the building of a new nation."[25]

It is that kind of cosmic claim that has been featured so aggressively when Americans have attempted to explain the meaning of America. The historical narrative of nativism may suggest just how hollow such rhetoric can be. But we are not concerned here with authentic narratives. We are trying to catch hold of recurring rhetoric as a cultural reality and potent force.

Critics of American Exceptionalism and Their Resonances

Disdain for American exceptionalism first appeared in sustained fashion in 1975. It has not been monolithic, however, and at least five fairly discrete phases can be identified. One finds common ground and overlap, to be sure, but also disagreement and inconsistencies among the critics. Although space does not permit in-depth summaries, it is at least possible to identify some of the leading participants and indicate their points of departure.

First, essays appeared in the mid-1970s that clearly derived from circumstances involving the crisis of political morality: a national fall from grace in the wake of Watergate and, more important, humiliation in and about Vietnam. In "The End of American Exceptionalism," Daniel Bell acknowledged that the United States had had a unique history but that it was initially based upon a belief in moral superiority and subsequently upon sheer power. Now that illusions about the former had been shattered, and the latter had been rendered nugatory, all that remained of American exceptionalism, according to Bell, was the "constitutional system, with a comity that has been undergirded by history." He closed with the speculative hope that the United States would remain aware of the "moral complexity of history." Less than a year later Alexander E. Campbell, Professor of American History at Birmingham in England, argued that the United States had lost its claim to national purpose, that "most Americans are conscious of sharing problems which are world-wide rather than peculiar to themselves," and that the country had ceased to be a "great experiment" or the last best hope of earth.[26] The American Adam had lost his innocence and given way to a helpless, tarnished Gulliver.

The next move, which still seems to me the pivotal one, involved the appearance in 1979 of Laurence Veysey's compelling essay titled "The Autonomy of American History Reconsidered." Veysey was hardly insensitive to the same stimuli that had provoked Bell and Campbell, but his revisionism also arose from academic and scholarly concerns: namely, that excessive attention to contrasts flatly distorted historical realities; that industrialism and modernism had created some pervasive international patterns that historians had neglected at their peril; that the new social history mandated much more attention to transnational themes—such as mobility studies, which clearly demolished the customary claims for American distinctiveness in that regard. "The sobering demystification of America," Veysey wrote, "the new awareness that we are but one fractional (and internally fractionated) unit in a polyglot world, and that social history is composed of a vast number of separate and distinct pieces, like a mosaic that seldom stops at international boundary lines, has enabled students of American social evolution to view their subject with fewer blinders than before."[27]

Phase three of the emerging critique appeared in 1984 when Eric Foner and Sean Wilentz, swiftly joined by other historians of the working class, sought in various ways to address and redefine the persistent line of inquiry first introduced by Werner Sombart in 1906: "Why is there no socialism in the United States?" Because the responses of these historians are wide-ranging and probe deeply, there is considerable danger in compressing a brief summary, but their principal points include the following. Socialism failed to produce a successful political and class transformation in many other countries, not only in the United States; the absence of a powerful social democratic party here does not mean that American workers passively accepted the status quo; a vigorous tradition of radical protest has, in fact, existed in the United States ever since the later 1820s if not from Tom Paine's time in Philadelphia; the republican ideology provided meaning and direction for artisans and mechanics as well as the elite; and ethnicity has not been an insuperable barrier to working-class cooperation for political objectives.[28]

Phase four emerged as a familiar choir during the mid-and later 1980s, but the most strident soloist may well have been William C. Spengemann, whose *Mirror for Americanists* relentlessly argued against the distinctiveness of American literature and mocked the mindless assumptions, implicit or explicit, of those guilty of thoughtless chauvinism. "Although our feelings of cultural uniqueness persuade us that American literature is different," Spengemann observed, "our cultural paranoia forces us to prove that American literature is just as good as European literature, in exactly the same ways, and hence to concentrate our efforts upon the very works that, in measuring up to transnational standards, may well be our least distinctive productions." It is my impression, however, that Spengemann's position has met with proportionately less support from literary critics than the views of Veysey, Foner, and others have received from their colleagues in history.[29]

Phase five, which is the most diffuse and least cohesive of my groupings, concerns colonial as well as postcolonial societies and their systems of thought. Thus Jack P. Greene argued in 1988, following John M. Murrin and others, that "the central cultural impulse among the colonists was not to identify and find ways to express and to celebrate what was distinctively American about themselves and their societies but, insofar as possible, to eliminate these distinctions so that they might—with more credibility —think of themselves and their societies—and be thought of by the people in Britain—as demonstrably British." For apparently ideological reasons, resting mainly upon his conservative hostility to the "liberal-capitalist [critical] interpretation of the American founding," J. G. A. Pocock has condemned the Lockean emphasis that runs from Louis Hartz to John Diggins and Isaac Kramnick, and quips that Americans who prefer "the splendid misery of uniqueness" might be "happier if they shared their history with other people."[30]

I would be the first to confess that fault can be found with my five-phase evolution of the critique of American exceptionalism. Aside from the historian's penchant for imposing excessive order upon intractable materials, I wish to call attention to two awkward problems in particular. First, it must be recognized that some of the most prominent critics have placed themselves on record with categorical concessions of distinctiveness—not necessarily the whole works, America entire, but important components thereof. Let's look at four examples.

In 1974 I listened with rapt fascination as David D. Hall sandbagged a generation of exceptionalists, including Hartz, Handlin, Boorstin, Marvin Meyers, and Stanley Elkins, for overdramatizing a stark contrast between orderly societies in the Old World and disorderly ones in the New. Hall's recent innovative book on popular religion in colonial New England, however, acknowledges many determinative distinctions: The circumstances of New England in the seventeenth century, for example, were "not the circumstances to which Europeans were accustomed. The differences are great enough to force us to revise the very sense of 'popular religion.'" Hall contends that because space was much less consequential than in Europe, ordinary people could more readily ignore the obligations of organized religion, and church membership became a more voluntary matter than in Europe. When Hall turns to relationships between religious ritual and social order, he stresses the contrast between Old World hierarchies of rank and New World emphases upon collective godliness. Without minimizing the European origins of popular religion in the colonies, Hall leaves the reader with a clear sense of important deviations based upon variables that ranged from the environment to social values.[31]

Although Sean Wilentz is customarily regarded as a critic of American exceptionalism, his well-received *Chants Democratic* insists upon "distinctively American forms of class conflict" that arose from ideological differences over "fundamental American values" and led to "a distinctly American trade unionism." Similarly, an essay published by Eric Foner in 1988 demolishes some of the foolish reasoning that has been used to bolster American exceptionalism, yet acknowledges highly significant variations that occurred in different nations during the age of industrialization, accepts the "distinctive character of American trade unionism," and observes that the trajectory of socialist movements in the United States during the first half of the twentieth century varied significantly from their European counterparts.[32]

In the work of social historian Alan Dawley, adjustments have actually moved to and fro. In 1978 he observed that Gramsci's concept of hegemony had been misapplied to the United States because the prevalence here of industrial violence, racism, xenophobia, and reactive ethnic cultures did not, taken together for the later nineteenth and early twentieth century, conform to Gramsci's pattern of a dominant social group diffusing its notions of normative relations and realities throughout the culture. "If there is to be a school of cultural studies in the United States," Dawley wrote, following the lead of E. P. Thompson, "it will have to honor the 'peculiarities' principle and pay strict attention to special national characteristics." Ten years later Dawley developed this assertion but with a different spin in a short paper titled "Farewell to 'American Exceptionalism.'" There he took a position that I shall return to in my conclusion because it is judicious and has broad applicability. The United States is different but not exceptional, he remarked, not a curiosity in the political history of industrialization. Dawley urged that greater attention be given to variability in national patterns of capitalism, in the timing of capitalist development, in the disposition of social elites displaced by upwardly mobile industrialists, in the structure of state power, and in the diverse composition of various national working classes.[33]

I am *not* trying to imply that critics of American exceptionalism have been wildly inconsistent or mindlessly ambivalent. Rather, I do want to suggest that some of the most subtle among them have adjusted their views as fresh research and theoretical perspectives have emerged, that some have occasionally been misunderstood or misinterpreted, and above all that the best among them have tried very hard to be judicious, to look at all of the pertinent evidence, and to tally up accordingly. Thus Aristide A. Zolberg, who teaches political science at the New School for Social Research, is a comparativist who is quite partial to similarities. He nonetheless recognizes major contrasts between the development of capitalism (and its social consequences) in the United States and in Europe. He finds, for example, a greater degree of integration by American workers in *their* political and social system than occurred in Europe, particularly because of ideological tensions that were generated in Europe during and after World War I.[34]

An overview of the critics and revisionists, however brief, would not be complete without a look at the ideological Left because here, too, simplistic generalizations are not viable. The Old Left along with some progenitors of the New Left tended to believe quite passionately in American exceptionalism. I have in mind Dwight Macdonald, for instance, who wrote in 1959 of Nathanael West's *Miss Lonelyhearts* that it was a "marvelously pure expression of our special American sort of agony, the horror of aloneness, and of our kind of corruption, that of mass culture." In the same year C. Wright Mills declared that "in the United States there is no long-standing traditional establishment of culture on the European model." Mills also elaborated his belief that persons with white-collar vocations in the United States were decidedly different from their European counterparts.[35]

Connections between the New Left and American exceptionalism are more complicated. Giles Gunn has observed that critical assessments of exceptionalism within American Studies were by no means rooted exclusively in the New Left, yet they did arise during the later 1960s and early 1970s from a feeling of embarrassment with American chauvinism and parochialism, from a growing sense of international interdependence, and from antipathy to the consensus school of historiography.[36] A more scholarly and less ideological grounding for the critique then followed in the later 1970s; what transpired in the subsequent decade leaves one feeling fairly reluctant to generalize about the New Left. Fierce critics of exceptionalism remained vocal, to be sure, but advocates of American working-class distinctiveness, such as Mike Davis, could make a persuasive case for the potency of their belief in exceptionalism.[37]

Persistent Differentiations in the Age of Comparative Scholarship

Suppose we try to compile a tally, a rough and ready reckoning of major scholarship since 1980 in diverse fields and subdisciplines. The reason for choosing 1980 is not just to be recent and therefore up to date. Veysey's landmark essay appeared in 1979, and within five years, as we have noted, quite a few vigorous voices had spoken in ways that reinforced Veysey's critique. How far did the pendulum really swing after 1980? How much has our vocational vantage point been changed? The answer, based upon a survey of diverse books, is: not a whole lot.

Let's begin at the chronological beginning. *The Peopling of British North America*, by Bernard Bailyn, contends that the dynamics of land speculation "shaped a relationship between the owners and the workers of the land different from that which prevailed in Europe." Speculators had to offer very low rental fees in order to get land developed and enhance its value. Bailyn's emphasis upon the contrast between core and periphery, between the metropolis of empire and its marshlands, causes him to highlight the "distinctive" aspects of the colonial society and culture. That word, the "d" word, recurs frequently in Bailyn's recent work and represents a clear continuity with his earlier analyses of pre-Revolutionary politics.[38] Similarly, Jon Butler's reinterpretation of the first centuries of American Protestantism seeks to explain, among other things, why religious development in the New World differed so markedly from Britain's.[39]

Comparable conclusions emerge when we look to politics and public life. Leon D. Epstein is impressed by the limits that historical American circumstances have imposed upon the growth of political parties and their clout. "The distinctiveness of American parties is old and well established," he explains. "It is not mainly the product of the last few decades of widely perceived decline. As governing agencies, American parties have nearly always been less cohesive in national policymaking than parties in parliamentary regimes. And as extra-governmental organizations, their strength, where it existed, was traditionally state and local rather than national. Moreover, American parties have ordinarily been without the dues-paying mass memberships characteristic of European parties." Turning to public policy made manifest in historic pieces of legislation, Harold M. Hyman concludes that American exceptionalism "is not a busted superstition suitable only for the trash heap of history." He finds in certain key statutes a pattern of access to socioeconomic mobility and personal fulfillment that is "unique in the world."[40]

Recent historians of American literature, especially those whose orientation is more cultural and *con*textual than structural and textual, also tend to be exceptionalists. A notable example is David S. Reynolds's study of "subversive literature" during the early and mid-nineteenth century. While acknowledging its roots in earlier criminal and Gothic British fiction, Reynolds insists repeatedly, with multiple variations, that "it took on distinctly American characteristics when reinterpreted by authors who wished to find literary correlatives for the horrific or turbulent aspects of perceived reality in the new republic." He bolsters his case with numerous expressions by native writers that indicate just how earnestly they sought an American voice and vision. Not once but twice Reynolds quotes Ahab's eulogy for the sinking *Pequod*: "Its wood could only be American!" (8 and 549).[41]

In addition to numerous utterances of that sort by Herman Melville, Reynolds cites still others by Emerson, Whitman, Bushnell, obscure writers of sensational pulp fiction, and frontier humorists. The author also demonstrates just how many genres and subgenres lacked counterparts elsewhere: the dark adventure style, the irrational mode, and the confidence man as an ironic character type are a few of Reynolds's illustrations. Whether he is examining Crockett almanacs or George Lippard's grim urban melodramas, Reynolds insists that the blend of egalitarianism, frightful situations, and unorthodox literary strategies ("intentional disruptions of linear patterns and wholesale assaults on conventional literary rules," 198) is "at once totally American and totally bizarre" (452). Reynolds has added a considerable dimension and documentary depth to general themes long accessible to students of American literary history.[42]

There has been even greater unanimity among folklorists in assuming that American folk life reflected a distinctive national experience. Nevertheless the scope of what folklorists and historians of folk culture do has broadened during the past twenty-five years. In 1966 Alan Dundes complained that Americanists tended to neglect festivals, folk dance, art, cuisine, and related phenomena.[43]

In recent years, however, Mary Ryan has scrutinized the civic parade as a mirror of the nineteenth-century social order in the United States. She concludes that Americans devised a "distinctive and curious mode of public celebration" in which a sizable portion of the urban population organized into platoons, companies, regiments, ranks, and columns, and marched through public thoroughfares. "This particular type of celebratory perform- ance seems to have been an American invention." It was also more socially inclusive than its European counterparts. Similarly, David Glassberg's thorough study of American historical pageantry, which focuses on a period more than half a century after Ryan's, finds that civic pageantry provided a uniquely American form of "social ceremonial" even though it had obvious English models.[44]

If space permitted we could also look at the claims made recently for American distinctiveness in terms of middle-class values (rooted in "wide- spread economic opportunity"), in terms of the "uniquely American procliv- ity for joining voluntary groups," in terms of the functions of symbolic ethnicity and what Mary C. Waters has called "personally constructed American ethnic communities," and in the activities and assumptions of philanthropic organizations in relation to the responsibilities that govern- ment will and will not undertake.[45] Also, a meticulous study of Thomas A. Edison's reputation in American popular culture concludes that the aspect of American exceptionalism that appeared most often in conjunction with the Edison image "is that which glories in 'American inventive genius,' of which Edison is naturally seen as the 'incarnation.'" The literature is characterized by such phrases as "we are the most ingenious people in the world" and "America is the chosen home of invention."[46]

Other claims for American uniqueness that have appeared in the past decade, however, are less persuasive because little or no evidence is pre- sented to show whether any empirically comparative inquiry has been conducted. This is true of assertions on behalf of environmentalism, historic preservation, the situation of art and artists in the marketplace, and the overall configuration of governmental institutions in the United States.[47]

Marianne Debouzy has tactfully noted the tendency of some American historians to make unwarranted assumptions about working-class people in Europe.[48] I worry about colleagues who are insufficiently empirical and self-critical—who proceed, as Carl Becker once put it, without fear and without research.

∾

This brings me to the crux of this post-1980 reckoning: What happens to American exceptionalism when scholars take seriously the imperative to do comparative work? Laurence Veysey has been saying for twenty years that "careful comparison lies close to the heart of historical explanation." His distaste for the negative consequences of nationalism has caused Veysey (and more recently Akira Iriye) to call for transnational investigations and to assume that, in modern history especially, the quest for comparisons will more likely than not turn up similarities.[49]

Both C. Vann Woodward and Carl Degler, however, like to quote Marc Bloch, who pioneered in calling for comparative work and remarked in 1928 that "it is often supposed that the method has no other purpose than hunting out resemblances." Bloch contended that "correctly understood, the primary interest of the comparative method is, on the contrary, the observation of differences."[50] In my judgment, comparative scholarship produced in the past decade bears Bloch out—not because researchers *preferred* differences but simply because their investigations turned up a disproportionate imbalance favoring difference.

Based upon the survey of recent literature that I have made, it is my impression that researchers were not predisposed to find a preponderance of similarities *or* differences, and certainly that they had no stake in defending or propping up the precarious remains of American exceptionalism. In fact, most of the works that I am about to cite were *undertaken* during the later 1970s and early 1980s, when the very notion of American exceptionalism seemed to be least credible and most unfashionable. Although it may be excessively schematic, I am going to organize the overview that follows in terms of the three categories (or lines of inquiry) that have generated the greatest amount of comparative interest: race relations, class formation and attendant ideologies, and the role of the state in terms of active intervention versus degrees of restraint.[51]

With respect to the history of slavery, emancipation, and race relations, I call to your attention the consistent pattern that appears in four overtly comparative efforts. In *White Supremacy: A Comparative Study in American and South African History* (1981), George M. Fredrickson is ultimately more impressed by differences. Race relations in the United States acquired a highly particular character for several reasons: the geographical setting, the political origins and assumptions of the settlers, the overall population being constituted in a certain way, and because the indigenous peoples could not be readily recruited as a labor force. In Peter Kolchin's extraordinary book, *Unfree Labor: American Slavery and Russian Serfdom* (1987), the author is even more impressed by contrasts than by similarities. Whereas the latter are structural and to some extent causal, the differences are demographic, ethnic, or racial, and involve degrees of autonomy, more impersonal relations between masters and serfs in Russia (an absence of paternalism there), divergent modes of seeking redress and patterns of resistance, and differences in the ways the two systems of unfreedom were terminated, to mention only some of the contrasts. Ultimately, as Kolchin writes in his conclusion, "despite many similar features of Russian serfdom and southern slavery, there was a contrast in their viability. By the middle of the nineteenth century, as southern slavery was flourishing as never before, Russian serfdom constituted a bankrupt system widely recognized as on its last legs. . . . After the 1820s, when southerners were elaborating with increasing frequency and forcefulness their arguments in defense of the 'peculiar institution,' public defense of serfdom in Russia virtually disappeared."[52]

In 1969 C. Vann Woodward called the pattern of racial classification in the United States "unique"; twenty years later he rejected an exceptionalist interpretation of Reconstruction. Instead he urged historians to give "scrupulous attention to uniquely American conditions, but also to remember that the post-emancipation problem they attack was not unique to America." Rebecca Scott, effectively sustaining that point, highlights the particularity of geography and environmental patterns, contrasts the goals and political behavior of poor nonslaves in Brazil with the southern United States, and notes the absence of white violence aimed at former slaves in Brazil.[53]

When we turn to social structure, class formation, and attendant ideologies, the dynamics get somewhat more complex yet the outcome is essentially the same. A massive and nuanced study of Buffalo, New York, prior to 1860 demonstrates the development of what David A. Gerber considers a distinctively American situation. Bourgeois businessmen and their allies exercised social and moral authority in such a way that class differences among artisans and other occupational groups were muted. Moreover, temperance and related reform energies helped to integrate various strata into a common effort to create a bourgeois social order.[54]

Although Herbert G. Gutman always insisted that many Old World cultural traditions persisted in the New, he too believed that, in Ira Berlin's words, Protestantism and political access "clarified the special circumstances under which an American working class came into being. While religion might be central to the experience of workers on both sides of the Atlantic, there were still important differences of politics, class composition, and national domain." American workers had the vote and became active in partisan politics long before the Reform Act and Chartism began to effect slow changes in nineteenth-century Britain.[55] Gutman also believed that workers in the United States self-consciously sought to "assert their rights as Americans by distinguishing themselves from workers in other countries."

And he proclaimed the "unique history" of the American working class by calling attention to the "continued reinvigoration of preindustrial culture by wave upon wave of new preindustrial recruits." Gutman reached these conclusions precisely *because* he was familiar with European labor history and admired the work of E. P. Thompson, Raymond Williams, Sidney Pollard, and Eric Hobsbawm.[56]

Laurence Veysey suggested in 1979 that the onset of widespread industrialization during the later nineteenth century meant that nations undergoing the process, and their work forces, became more alike. But Aristide Zolberg, who is not sympathetic to conventional notions of exceptionalism, has recently concluded that the United States grew more distinctive rather than less as a consequence of undergoing the process. Why? According to Zolberg, the reason is that American industrial workers "constituted less of a critical mass in the United States than they did in Britain or Germany; and there is little doubt that the precocious development of a large segment of white-collar workers also contributed to the formation of a more diffuse sense of class among Americans more generally." Zolberg points to the development here of a form of capitalism organized around a segmented labor market, and in a variation of Gutman's view, Zolberg contends that the immigrants contributed to institutionalized segmentation as a "particularly pronounced feature of American industrial capitalism." He, too, believes that American workers consciously differentiated between their status as "labor" and their role as citizens more generally.[57]

Although Werner Sombart's famous query in 1906, "Why is there no socialism in the United States?" and his own response are no longer compelling, the issue will not disappear and elements of Sombart's answer still surface in scholarship stimulated by his question. Morris Hillquit once complained that the Socialist Party in the United States had to publish its literature in twenty different languages. For a union trying to organize a steel plant in Pittsburgh, where the work force was ethnically diverse, that could be a very serious problem. Hence Mike Davis observes that whereas the Western European class struggles of the 1880s and 1890s elicited a web of integrating proletarian institutions, the labor movement in the United States at that time was unable to generate a working-class culture that could overcome ethnic and religious bonds that remained powerful beyond the workplace. By 1910, Davis concludes, the American industrial city had developed a "strikingly different social physiognomy from that of European factory centers."[58]

Last though certainly not least, I find increasingly that when scholars function comparatively they are struck, in one way or another, with the state's *relatively* decentralized or noninterventionist nature, historically, in the United States. Aristide Zolberg makes a persuasive case that the most important "determinant of variation in the patterns of working-class politics" for the late nineteenth and early twentieth century seems to have been whether, "at the time this class was being brought into being by the development of capitalism, it faced an absolutist or a liberal state." In the Western world prior to World War I, "the relevant range of variation was defined by the United States as the democratic end of the continuum (at least for the white majority) and Imperial Germany at the other, which may be termed 'modernizing absolutism.'" Alfred D. Chandler's magisterial study of American business management finds that in Europe,

> the much larger military and governmental establishments were a source for the kind of administrative training that became so essential to the operation of modern industrial, urban, and technologically advanced economies. In Europe, too, the government played a much larger role than it did in the United States in financing, locating, and even operating the transportation and communication infrastructure. . . . In Europe, public enterprise helped to lay the base for the coming of modern mass production and mass distribution. In the United States this base was designed, constructed, and operated almost wholly by private enterprise.[59]

The role of the state also turns out to be a crucial variable in the comparative history of women, as Kathryn Kish Sklar and others have shown. The state has been a major factor in France, for example, by providing public assistance for migrating single women. In the United States, by contrast, the presumption in favor of limited government created major opportunities for activism and social service by women reformers. The situation in Great Britain fell in between these two "extremes": a fairly strong state policy implemented by means of voluntarism. Moreover, while prostitution tended to be regulated or licensed by the state in Europe, American morality could not countenance such flagrant tolerance, even in the interests of public health; so we substituted hypocrisy for "mere" regulation: payoffs to the police as a cover for free enterprise in sexual gratification.[60]

To summarize this section, then, a pronounced increase in comparative work since 1980 by historians of the United States has caused a very marked enhancement in our awareness of differences, but only a modest increase in the frequency and importance of similarities. Even among studies that do not attempt to be comparative in a systematic way, such as books about immigrant communities in the United States, sharp contrasts with group life in the Old World become compellingly noticeable.[61] And authors who choose explicitly to contest the idea of American exceptionalism are nonetheless obliged to acknowledge variations in racial attitudes, in the role of class in popular entertainments and their audiences, and in the uses of leisure.[62] If anything, the outcome today is very much at odds with the apparent agenda fifteen years ago and what that agenda caused me, for one, to anticipate in the historiographical trends that lay ahead.

What Have We Learned? Some Reconsiderations

What have we learned? What can be concluded? And where do we go from here? I believe we are obliged to acknowledge the swiftly spreading perception that "every country is different" and that each society or culture is exceptional in its own way(s). The most enlightened historians, irrespective of their national fields of inquiry or topical concerns, have recently begun making that point with some consistency.[63] This awareness warrants at least a minisurvey because Laurence Veysey insists upon the fundamental similarity of all claims to national distinctiveness—a point with which I cannot agree.[64]

E. P. Thompson inaugurated the "multipeculiarity" approach in 1965 when he published an essay critical of structuralist theorists, such as Perry Anderson, who sought to assess and explain the course of British history since the seventeenth century in terms of a Marxist model that regarded the pattern of modern French history as normative. Thompson insisted that "each national bourgeoisie has its own peculiar nastiness" and argued that the ruling class in eighteenth-century England constituted a "unique formation." Subsequently, Linda Colley has contended that class consciousness and national identity were *not* antithetical in Britain between 1750 and 1830, which historians had previously argued must inherently be the case. "Because British political, military, social and economic conditions were quite unique," Colley wrote, "national consciousness here assumed a peculiarly pervasive but also a peculiarly complex form."[65]

Manifestations of French exceptionalism with varied emphases and concerns—Tocqueville's proposition concerning the implications of a long history of governmental centralization, Jerrold Seigel's belief in the uniqueness of the French Revolution, the widely shared notion that for geographical and economic reasons France has a split personality—have been propounded by French, American, British, and other scholars of diverse nationalities. Advocates of Russian exceptionalism have emerged from academe as well as from activists and journalists in the political arena.[66]

Turning to a country where the issue of exceptionalism has aroused powerful passions during the past decade, in particular, Gordon Craig informs us that Germans have long been preoccupied with the question:

"What is truly German?" Distinguished historians in Germany, such as Karl Dietrich Bracher, have been committed to exceptionalism for reasons intensely critical of the Reich, and George L. Mosse, who left Germany as a young man, finds distinctiveness in the Enlightenment's failure to sink significant roots in German soil. Consequently, he believes, no German literature founded on revolutionary principles emerged, which provided the opportunity for a twisted national mystique to develop that would solidify national unity—a propensity that evoked a radically destructive response.[67]

The most provocative book in recent years about German exceptionalism, however, *The Peculiarities of German History* by David Blackbourn and Geoff Eley, actually argues just the opposite of what its title would seem to suggest—sort of. The revisionist authors are critical of the widely held belief that liberalism failed to take hold in nineteenth-century Germany, that consequently the bourgeoisie could not develop and play the positive role that it did elsewhere in the West, and that an autocratic, militaristic class of antidemocratic landowners put Germany on its disastrous path to the Third Reich. Without a successful bourgeois revolution in 1848, catastrophe became virtually inevitable: that has been the conventional wisdom.[68] (Here we have a fine illustration of why I disagree with Laurence Veysey. The notion of exceptionalism emerged in Germany to justify social and political failure, whereas it developed in the Untied States to explain moral and political success.)

If I may reduce a complex and controversial thesis to just a few of its most essential points, Blackbourn and Eley reject any attempt to assess nineteenth-century Germany by some external and abstract standards of liberal democracy. They acknowledge the singularity of British and French history, assert that each national case is different, and suggest that similar results may be produced by different modes of development or patterns of evolution. They believe that the basic characteristics and chronology of capitalist industrial development in Germany and the United States were comparable. They also detect parallel histories of trade union weakness and employer intransigence in the two countries, the latter manifest in ruthless forms of company paternalism.[69]

Blackbourn and Eley have managed, without any apparent attempt at irony, to produce an attack upon the historiography of German exceptionalism that tends, nonetheless, to leave the reader with a profound sense that German history has, indeed, been different if not "peculiar." Intentionally or not, their book suits the spirit of Johan Herder's relativism, a social philosophy that acknowledges the existence and importance of national differences while rejecting the assumption that one group's development or customs could be judged by the measure or achievement of another.[70] It is that outlook and set of assumptions, in my opinion, that underpins much that is best in comparative historical inquiry today.

Blackbourn and Eley also believe that the public and moral implications of historical writing have been felt with particular acuteness in Germany. They may very well be right, though similar implications (nuanced in different ways) have also emerged from New Left scholarship in the United States and Great Britain since the later 1960s. Prior to that time, at least in the United States, the quest for the "meaning of America" that I referred to earlier may have served to give historical writing about the United States an upbeat rather than a critical moral dimension. Surely, understanding the past in moral terms is considered desirable in many societies, yet I am not aware of any other that has been preoccupied with its own meaning, in a moral sense, for such a long time as ours. Given the persistence of American present-mindedness for several centuries, and given the Emersonian notion of the past as a burden to be shed, perhaps the "meaning of America," so rich with moralistic implications for the future, and for people not fortunate enough to be Americans, may have served as a surrogate for history.[71]

Because a few scholars who are interested in this whole issue (including Dorothy Ross and Ian Tyrrell) have begun to acknowledge that the fervent belief in national exceptionalism has a political and cultural history that is consequential, perhaps the time is now ripe for some sort of transnational team to undertake a comparative history of various national "exceptionalisms."[72] If and when that happens, I suspect that some surprises will emerge involving differences as well as similarities. Students of comparative urban development have noticed cultural, along with political, variables in attempting to explain why cities such as Chicago and Toronto developed in such divergent ways despite similar prospects and possibilities. I must say that I find the cultural explanations (an aggressive future-oriented elite in Chicago vs. a more cautious, conservative, genteel elite in Toronto) considerably more persuasive than the political and governmental ones.[73]

Unanticipated outcomes emerge when we look at recent work, for instance, by an astute younger Australian historian who insists upon an *absence* of exceptionalist thought in Australia during the first century of its existence—a very stark contrast to the situation in the United States at the same time. Richard White found:

> It was difficult in the nineteenth century to pin down what was distinctive about Australia, apart from its unique flora and fauna. On the one hand, the Australian colonists were busy identifying themselves with wider loyalties, considering themselves primarily as British, or as being one of the new societies, another America. On the other hand there were narrower loyalties competing with the sense of being distinctively Australian. Politically Austra-

lia had no formal existence until Federation: the colonies were separate political entities owing their allegiance directly to Britain.

White acknowledges that while "some sense of Australian identity" did develop during the nineteenth century, it occurred primarily in the 1890s and then during the Boer War. As late as 1887 the popular *Bulletin* perceived nothing distinctive about the Australian: its editors simply applied that label to a composite that it called "The Coming Man." National identity remained inchoate, perhaps a coming attraction.[74]

~

The writing of history is commonly affected, even driven, by a sense of moral mission or by ideology. Those kinds of connections are common if not universal. I am inclined to wonder, however, whether the sense of moral mission has not been peculiarly prominent in American culture in a rather perverse way. On the one hand, it usually is invoked with a vagueness that encourages misunderstanding, elasticity, distortion, and hypocrisy. Irving Howe, who believed in American exceptionalism as a cultural reality, insisted that "to recognize the power of the American myth of a covenant blessing the new land is simply to recognize a crucial fact in our history." Who could refuse to acknowledge the sheer force of that myth, despite its vagueness? Then Howe called our attention to the power of Americanism, and once again one wants to affirm his acuity, but Americanism is even vaguer than that covenant. So we begin to balk.[75]

But important new work, especially in the field of labor history, has provided us with abundant evidence that Americanization as a social construct, as well as political and governmental process, flourished as a result of diverse stimuli for more than half a century following the 1880s. Catherine Collomp, for instance, has observed that in the 1890s and beyond both the American Federation of Labor and the Knights of Labor responded to the menace of mass immigration by stressing their firm allegiance to an American sense of national identity rather than a transnational or even domestic working-class alliance. Organized labor deliberately emphasized "its American character," Collomp notes, "and becoming an agent in the regulation of the components of immigration. In this respect citizenship, as an incorporating value, was a more potent factor than—and directly in opposition to—working-class identity, an ideology that reinforced the political and national consensus." For Samuel Gompers, trade union membership became a surrogate form of American citizenship and, wherever appropriate, a prologue to it. Collomp concludes with a strong affirmation of American exceptionalism in the labor movement at the turn of the century, because the constricted scope of what Gompers perceived as a "legitimate working class" only reinforced a sense of union elitism, thereby creating, as she puts it, "a wider gap between skilled and unskilled workers than in other countries."[76]

In the decades that followed, government, visible intellectuals, unions, and large business firms all reinforced these powerful pressures for "Americanization," a quadripartite ideological phalanx that had no counterpart elsewhere in the world. Three examples will have to suffice. First, between 1902 and 1909 Woodrow Wilson used diverse occasions to articulate his favorite speech, "What It Means to Be an American," a theme that he continued to voice later throughout his presidency. Then, in her extraordinary book titled *Making a New Deal: Industrial Workers in Chicago, 1919–1939*, Lizabeth Cohen describes the Americanization programs privately developed and maintained by employers in Chicago during the 1920s.[77]

Finally, we have an illuminating recent book by Gary Gerstle called *Working-Class Americanism: The Politics of Labor in a Textile City, 1914–1960*. Its subject is the Independent Textile Union of Woonsocket, Rhode Island, arguably the most powerful textile workers' union in New England. Its *dramatis personae* are Franco-Belgian socialists and French-Canadian Catholics who came to Woonsocket to work in the woolen mills. Its dynamic emerges as leaders of both ethnic groups, but the Belgians especially are able to fashion a critique of capitalism by using the traditional political discourse that conservative Americanizers had devised at the turn of the century—the rhetoric of Americanism.[78]

Gerstle shrewdly observes that a national obsession with "Americanism" occurred during the 1920s and 1930s. Although he concedes that its meaning was vague, he looks at various texts, including transcripts of interviews, and finds four basic elements in the invocation of Americanism: nationalistic, democratic, progressive, and traditionalist. Consequently these elements of discourse could and did sustain various visions of politics. Among them, radicals and ethnics could present their socialist and communitarian ideals in the language favored by old-line Americans. They would thereby gain acceptability and achieve much of a difficult agenda. To Americanize did not necessarily mean to assimilate or accept the status quo. It did mean adapting Yankee discourse in ways that make "Americanism" seem even more vague on the surface, yet Gerstle describes particular people in particular situations using particular texts.[79] The role of ideology therefore becomes palpable in ways that it does not in Clifford Geertz's famous essay concerning "Ideology as a Cultural System."[80] And, *mirabile dictu*, because class and ethnicity are centrally involved, the links between ideology and American exceptionalism become considerably clearer than they once were.

Friedrich Engels turns out to have been remarkably prophetic. He forecast the tactics that American exceptionalism as a nativistic ideology would mandate. For success in politics, he pleaded, American socialists "will have to doff every remnant of foreign garb. They will have to become out and out American." [81] That is exactly what happened in Woonsocket, Rhode Island. When Marx and Engels actually examined particular cases, or situations, they too tended to sound like exceptionalists!

Curiously enough, however, leaders and members of the Independent Textile Union did not really disguise or fully shed their ethnic origins; rather, they simply *added* historical Americanism to their identities. Without entirely abandoning their traditional cultural life, they explicitly identified with George Washington and Abraham Lincoln. They emphasized the constitutional rights and political opportunities of American citizens. They frequently referred to "our forefathers." [82] Americanism mostly meant addition, but not much in the way of subtraction. The creation of compound identities has been a highly significant aspect of Americanization as a social process.

The value of books like *Working-Class Americanism* lies in the way that they serve notice: Cultural values and political discourse need not be vague or disembodied variables when we try to illuminate the particularities and peculiarities of life in the United States. They also connect with earlier studies that have been the objects of harsh criticism by skeptics of American exceptionalism. Henry Nash Smith's *Virgin Land*, for instance, needs to be reexamined and mined for material that demonstrates a greater degree of realism about political rhetoric in the United States than we ordinarily acknowledge. In 1860 Senator Louis T. Wigfall of Texas attacked Andrew Johnson's expansionism with these words: "The Senator from Tennessee supposes that we have a sort of blatherskiting Americanism that is going to spread over the whole continent, and cross the Pacific . . . and that, in the area of freedom, we are going to take in the whole world, and everybody is going to benefit us." [83] One of these days, someone will write a cultural history of Americanism, both the benign and the blatherskiting varieties. That will make a major contribution to our understanding of American exceptionalism because the author will want to ask what sorts of comparable discourse have occurred elsewhere. [84]

We are aware that the problem of American exceptionalism is a matter of considerable concern to sociologists (like Daniel Bell), to political scientists (like Seymour Martin Lipset), to lawyers, to literary historians and critics, and to students of public policy whose work I have not been able to explore here. [85] Although I see much that is valuable in what they have done, I also find most of it deficient in chronological specificity, lacking in sensitivity to change over time. I am persuaded that this is where historians can and should make a particular contribution. Gary Gerstle, for example, does an excellent job of showing the gradual process in Woonsocket whereby the French-Canadian workers shifted from extolling only their traditional heroes (early French explorers, generals who fought valiantly at Quebec, and *habitants*) to admiring the heroes of their adopted land as well. In 1937, none of the floats in an annual parade dramatized the familiar themes from French-Canadian history; by 1939 the dominant refrain was "Unionism is the spirit of Americanism."[86] These shifts occurred in increments—units of time and of a cultural process that the historian's vocation is best suited to analyze.

∿

Perhaps the schematization that follows, which is offered heuristically yet hesitantly, has at least three features that recommend its consideration. First, it takes change over time into account without seeking to be too chronologically precise when realism dictates only rough approximations. Second, it derives from cultural perceptions and from ideology, which have been emphasized as essential factors in the preceding pages. And third, it takes into account the inevitable presence of contradictory impulses, of yea-sayers and nay-sayers. It does not presume the existence of consensus about any system of belief, any situation, or any prospect as it appeared to historical participants. It offers a way of thinking about the elusive meaning of America as it was perceived at different times, yet acknowledges the existence of those who cried foul, sham, and hypocrisy.

During the century that followed 1775, the model of republicanism received adherence from people representing all classes of Americans and from newly arrived immigrants as well.[87] Nevertheless, democracy was not so widespread as its devotees believed, even though political participation may have been more accessible than anywhere else in all of human history. Free enterprise and capitalism flourished, but at a high cost in terms of human exploitation and wasted resources.

For three generations following 1875 the United States became a model, even an archetype, of democratic capitalism triumphant—to many—and yet the epitome of aggressive imperialism fueled by capitalist excess to many others.[88] The former may overestimate the accomplishments of the Progressive movement, the New Deal, and the Great Society legislation of the 1960s, but the latter unfairly demean those reformist impulses and the high standard of living achieved by large numbers of Americans.

In the decades following 1965 America entered a prolonged phase in which it resembled Gulliver: powerful yet incapable of achieving its basic objectives, willful yet indecisive, influential in an inconsistent and seemingly rudderless manner, undisciplined and increasingly plagued by gross materialism and consumerism. Others, however, would point to numerous innovations and achievements: in civil rights for minorities; new opportunities for women in the workplace; dramatic breakthroughs in science, health care, and applied technology; and, ultimately, an apparent vindication for free enterprise in the political and economic collapse of Communist states.[89]

If this national trajectory is distinctive, it is also burdened by dualistic tendencies and perceptions. If it is comparable in certain respects to what happened elsewhere—to Great Britain in phase two, for instance—it is quite different in phase one or three or both. It takes into account how Americans have perceived themselves, how foreigners and immigrants have perceived the United States, and how we have responded to their perceptions, admiring as well as unflattering.[90]

Where do we stand, then, in describing cultural developments and patterns in the United States? The words "unique" and "exceptional" must be used with extreme caution because both imply the existence of a norm that describes most or all other industrialized nations—a norm from which we alone deviate and to which, perhaps, we are somehow superior. The word "different" seems to me both acceptable and accurate because the United States *is* different. Such usage does not deny that other societies are different, too, but it follows the fundamental assumption, voiced by Carl Degler and others, that Americans "differ in some important ways from people of other nations."[91]

It seems reasonable to assert that while the United States has retained a great many differences, over time those differences have gradually become notably less exceptional. Some might even choose to argue that the "burden" of exceptionalism (i.e., profound difference) has perhaps passed to Japan. The rather lengthy historical period in which the concept of American exceptionalism carried a double meaning—one or both of which seemed compellingly persuasive—is now, I believe, over. The concept nonetheless retains its special importance for those of us who seek to understand the *historical* dynamics of American culture and values.

Finally, as for the "meaning" of America, I respond positively to Degler's suggestion that we pose the question: What has it meant, historically, to be an American or to have lived for an extended period of time in the United States? Answers to that kind of question, surely, will refresh our perennial interest in the meaning of America, particularly if we expand the question to read: What has it meant, historically, to be an American, and how have American perceptions of their experience compared with the process of self-recognition and self-deception in other societies?

The notion (or even notions) of exceptionalism is only one among various meanings that Americans can derive from and attach to their experiences as a nation—even when exceptionalism serves as a kind of compendium of other meanings, a summation that almost inevitably stimulates some sense of societal distinctiveness once the nation itself is identified as the primary locus and focus of national identity. Precisely because that same opportunity for summation is available to *other* self-reflexive cultures, some variant of exceptionalism has to be expected of all such collective introspection. Consequently, a crucial component in the comparative analysis of cultures becomes the comparative analysis of exceptionalism as a cultural phenomenon. Perhaps the next item on one or another agenda, therefore, will be the question: How exceptional *was* (past tense) American exceptionalism? I will venture a one-word hunch: very.

Coda, 1997

Because the notion of American exceptionalism has been (and continues to be) so controversial, I must acknowledge my satisfaction with work I have encountered since completing this essay that reinforces its basic stance. Eric Monkkonen insists that urban government in the United States is different from urban government in other former British colonies, and that the role of police has been different in the U.S. compared with Europe.[92] Similarly, Gene Bluestein believes that we need a totally different model for understanding folk culture in the United States in historical perspective as compared with folk culture elsewhere.[93] For emphasis upon "African-American exceptionalism" in the context of political culture in the United States, see Henry Louis Gates, Jr., and Hendrik Hertzberg, "The African-American Century," published in *The New Yorker*.[94] Many other examples could be cited. For stress upon the distinctiveness of contemporary American culture by a distinguished British journalist, see Martin Walker, *The Cold War: A History* (New York, 1994), 342–43.

8

Some Patterns
and Meanings of
Memory Distortion
in American History

W ithin less than a decade, beginning late in the 1980s, a distinctive body of writing began to appear that is concerned with aspects of collective memory in the history and culture of the United States. Comparable works have also been generated for France, Germany, Great Britain, Israel, and, to a lesser degree, Russia, Japan, and diverse developing nations or constituent social groups within those nations, such as tribes and sects.* Much of this literature emphasizes the socially constructed nature of memory and its political or cultural uses.

Although memory distortion per se has not commonly been a defining focus in this literature, it does emerge as an implicit theme, and sometimes rather prominently. Its appearance thus far more nearly resembles the highly visible vein patterns of a leaf rather than the exoskeleton of shellfish.

---

* This essay was presented on May 8, 1994, at the American Academy of Arts and Sciences in Cambridge, Massachusetts, as part of the first conference sponsored by the Harvard Center for the Study of Mind, Brain, and Behavior. The focus of that multidisciplinary conference was memory distortion.

That is, an interest in memory distortion has become noticeable without being a mobile, weight-bearing structure. It offers important patterns but rarely an architectural framework that gives explanatory shape to evidence or data. It suggests lines of interpretation rather than firm connecting links. Combined with material found in many older works, however, it enables us to speculate about a configuration of reasons why collective memory in the United States has been subject to distortion and alteration.

When the literature does touch upon distortions of collective memory, it routinely tends to do so in a cynical manner, ascribing manipulative motives or the maintenance of hegemonic control by dominant social groups. I find, however, that memory distortion, viewed in historical context, has occurred under diverse circumstances and for variable reasons. Some are quite properly regarded with a cynical eye, and may be considered, for convenience, negative (i.e., self-serving) instances of memory distortion. Others, however, might be regarded as positive, either because they have a democratizing outcome or else because they bring about a necessary readjustment of values or value systems that are out of sync— anomalous—in a particular time and place. If the adjustment helps to make the overall value system more coherent and functional, memory distortion may very well serve a benign purpose.

On still other occasions, memories are altered for reasons that are neither positive nor negative. Alteration may be a side effect of nationalism, or the desire for religious freedom, or the imperatives of domestic politics. In such instances, description and explanation serve us in more satisfactory ways than cynicism about bad faith or evil intent on the part of dominant elites.

In this chapter I examine three categories of memory distortion and alteration: first, social and cultural causes; second, nationalism and the *problematique* of American memory; and third, partisan politics and the uses (or misuses) of memory by leaders in public affairs, mainly American presidents. These categories are not watertight compartments, to be sure. There are elements of overlap and a blurring of highly permeable boundaries. Nevertheless, the range of illustrative situations that follows should at least indicate the very broad spectrum of circumstances under which collective memory undergoes distortion or alteration. If these situations supply less than a full-scale typology, they may at least serve to divert us from the reductive inferences that tend to be derived from such phrases, now virtually clichés, as "the invention of tradition" or "the heritage industry," the latter referring, most often, to commercialization (or even fabrication) of memories in a society whose thirst for nostalgia sometimes seems unquenchable.

The distortion of memories can, indeed, serve as a panacea for an age of anxiety. Yet I am persuaded that memory *and* amnesia have occurred in the American experience for a more complex array of reasons. What follows is designed to serve as an illustrative introduction to that complexity, at several levels and with assorted stimuli, motives, and consequences taken into account.

Social and Cultural Causes of Memory Distortion

Memory distortion has occurred in important instances because of a deep desire for social or religious autonomy; because the force of public opinion requires more logical coherence between disparate elements in a civic value system; or because of the desire for social accommodation or assimilation among newcomers in a nation of immigrants. Let's look at concrete instances of each situation.

During the 1620s and early 1630s, when Puritan dissenters in England suffered persecution at the hands of King Charles I and the Church of England, an anguished debate occurred among the Puritan dissenters: What was the most appropriate course of action for them? What did God expect of his saints? Should they emigrate to the New World, or did they have an obligation to stay, tough it out, and seek to reform a morally corrupt society from within? A majority actually chose the latter option and stayed, but a minority migrated to the Massachusetts Bay Colony with this rationale: Because the Church was hopelessly unreformed, they were obliged to leave in order to save their souls. But their mission would most likely not result in a permanent transplantation. The New Jerusalem that they expected to create would be so successful, such a model community in covenant with the Almighty, that they would eventually be recalled "in glory" to recreate their New Jerusalem at home.[1]

When the Civil War broke out in 1642 between the Royalists and the Calvinists (Cavaliers and Roundheads), the Puritans who had gone to New England should, in the name of consistency, have returned to the motherland to join their fellow dissenters in fighting the good fight. An opportunity to create the New Jerusalem at home was at hand. Nevertheless, very few returned because they now enjoyed considerable autonomy—not only from the Crown, but from sectarian Independents and Presbyterians whose theology and ecclesiastical politics they did not altogether share. After 1647 and the triumph of Oliver Cromwell's New Model Army and the creation of a Puritan Commonwealth, surely the self-exiled Puritans no longer had any excuse to remain overseas. According to their own explanations at the time of emigration, they should have returned to England to reinforce the new polity of Saints. The New Jerusalem was imminently at home.[2]

Once again, however, the Puritan leadership in New England, both secular and clerical, ever mindful of ecclesiastical differences that divided them from their brethren at home, chose to remain in the colonies of Massachusetts Bay, Connecticut, and ultra-dissident Rhode Island. They were not about to exchange their virtual autonomy in every sphere of life for Oliver Cromwell's iron-fisted control of a militant Commonwealth—or for the genuine risk of a royalist restoration. All of which required that memories of their own rhetoric during the 1620s and early 1630s be repressed or altered. Their mission to convert and Christianize heathen peoples in the New World suddenly seemed more imperative than ever. The need for a bulwark against Papist colonization in the Americas—France to the north and Spain to the south—also seemed greater than ever before.

So they stayed put and thereby provide us with an intriguing example, from the very onset of American history, that memories can readily, with scant embarrassment or challenge, be quietly repressed within a generation and replaced by alternative explanations, credible and defensible, for human impulses of the most elemental sort—such as relocating to a brave new world in quest of religious purity and autonomy.

For an illustration of memory distortion occurring because the sheer force of public opinion requires better coherence between the major components in a culture's value system, we need to "fast forward" two hundred years to the second quarter of the nineteenth century, when the political process and participation in public affairs began to be democratized during the so-called Age of Jackson. That new climate of opinion in American civic life required a major adjustment in the most fundamental assumptions about human nature and capacity for religious rebirth shared by most Americans ever since the early seventeenth century.

As Calvinists inspired by the Protestant Reformation, colonists had accepted the harsh doctrine of Predestination. God determined who would be saved and who would be damned even before an individual entered this world. Salvation and life everlasting derived from faith and faith alone. Good works kept the *social* covenant viable, but could not help an unregenerate soul become one of God's elect. It was an elitist system and, what was even more harsh, it was an inscrutably capricious system. The Almighty chose and disposed of souls for reasons that eluded human comprehension. Man's fate lay beyond his own control.[3]

The evangelical Protestantism that emerged from the Second Great Awakening during the early decades of the nineteenth century changed all of that, and consequently required theological and social acrobatics so that a value system that had endured for two centuries could be radically dismembered and disremembered. The concept of Predestination for a select few, derived from a long-standing interpretation of Original Sin, came to be supplanted by what is called the democratization of Christ's atonement. His death on the cross made possible the salvation of *all* rather than just a select group of pre-designated saints. Moreover, anyone could now make "a decision for Christ," undergo conversion, and be born again.[4]

Christianity, like the polity, became more inclusive and more participatory. An Old Testament God of justice, inscrutable and judgmental, gave way to a New Testament God of love, more forgiving and compassionate. Members of that culture redefined the very nature of Divinity and what He (prophetess Jemima Wilkinson said "She") expected or required of mortals. Memories of orthodox Calvinism, deeply ingrained after two centuries despite the Enlightenment, had to be repressed, rationalized away, and significantly reconfigured.[5] In this complicated transformation we tend to view the necessary distortion of collective memory as benign and beneficial, both because it served egalitarian ends and because it brought the dominant theological assumptions of American society into harmonic conjunction with emergent assumptions about political man and his capacities for civic participation and self-government.

Being a "nation of immigrants," as Franklin Delano Roosevelt described the United States to the assembled DAR in 1937, makes it more problematic for a genuinely collective memory to exist and function. A highly pluralistic society shares in common concerns about the present and aspirations for the future. There is a politically constructed past, to be sure, transmitted by the schools, and an ethnic past frequently regarded as marginally useful to the individual seeking acceptance and prosperity. In fact, one's "un-American" past could be a hindrance. A guidebook prepared for immigrant Jews during the 1890s offered advice heard by many other newcomers as well: "Hold fast, this is most necessary in America. Forget your past, your customs, and your ideals."[6]

Dramatic narratives have come to light in recent decades illustrating the astonishing lengths that immigrants would go to in order to conceal potentially embarrassing episodes and memories from their children and grandchildren. The purpose of such repression or distortion was simply to avoid impeding the Americanization and assimilation of second- and third-generation hyphenated Americans.[7] More often than not a revival of ethnic memory and culture had to wait until the third or even the fourth generation, when men and women, sufficiently secure about their American identity, could revive festivals, costumes, distinctive foods, and other Old World traditions. In doing so they frequently romanticized the past as a golden age of aspiration or courage—creating a mood of nostalgia that did not so much distort memories as fabricate them. Gazing at yellowed photographs and probing the recollections of ex-slaves and venerable forebears created myopic visions of the past —all the more deceptive because they seemed to be so empirically sound. Photographs and elderly relations surely don't lie. They are real windows on the past, albeit dim and dangerously opaque, at times, in their revelations. With such feelings we enter the realm of self-deception rather than distortion, more often than not, although self-deception is obviously a mode of distortion and may readily be transmitted from one generation to the next.[8]

Nationalism and Problematic Distortions of Memory

Although conflict commonly emerges as a significant factor in American society and politics, it is demonstrable that the dominant pattern has been one of conflict within consensus. All across the spectrum we find historically a profound loyalty to the U.S. Constitution and its legal parameters. There is a normative desire for political stability, and the combination of loyalty and stability under the oldest written national constitution in the world has, indeed, been impressive. But stability is achieved at a price: a tendency to depoliticize the civic past by distorting the nation's memories of it—all in the name of national unity, stability, and state-building.[9]

The most significant example of this phenomenon, and the best documented perhaps, concerns the astonishing distortions of collective memory, by both North and South, during the two generations following the American Civil War. Individuals on both sides did not forget their personal losses, of course, nor the massive disruption of their lives. Southerners long remained bitter, both about their crushing defeat and about their treatment by Northerners during Reconstruction. At that level, collective memories were vivid as well as reasonably veracious.[10]

Nevertheless, for about two decades there was an almost eerie silence in the press about the war and its causes. With some obvious exceptions, such as Walt Whitman, imaginative writers seemed to be too overwhelmed by the sheer enormity of the tragedy to compose significant works about it, despite the fact that a brothers' war ought to be the very stuff of great literature.[11] Healing the deep sectional scars and political wounds soon became imperative. Where had this impulse begun? In Abraham Lincoln's Gettysburg Address, no enemy is ever mentioned. Binding the nation together again—even redefining the nation as an imperishable federal state—swiftly became the order of the day. To achieve those goals, amnesia emerged as a bonding agent far preferable to memory. Picking at scabs on old wounds would not advance the paramount goal of reconciliation.

Beginning in the mid- and later 1880s, however, the twenty-fifth anniversary of various catastrophic battles elicited a spate of vastly popular books and articles. At the Blue–Gray reunions, veterans from both sides shook hands and even embraced. According to orations, sermons, editorials, and essays, each and every partisan had been brave, valiant, and courageous. Both sides had fought for causes they believed to be just. The history of racial issues in general and the institution of slavery in particular virtually disappeared from mainstream public discourse.

Perpetuating the actual provocations to battle would only prolong animosities and impede sectional reconciliation. Partial amnesia became the order of the day—just when the legal and social barriers to full citizenship for African Americans grew greater. This particular manifestation of memory distortion—repressing the racial issue as a major cause of the war—drew support from every section and social class. It persisted, moreover, for three-quarters of a century, reaching its apogee, perhaps, during the Golden Jubilee years of 1911 to 1915, but enjoying ongoing support from scholars as well as popular writers who explained the Civil War and Reconstruction to American students and the public at large. Not until the civil rights movement of the 1960s, and its aftermath, did the nation's greatest internal conflict begin to resemble in history what it had, in fact, been in reality.[12]

For a supplementary illustration of nationalism serving to alter collective memory, we might consider the immense influence of George Washington's farewell address, first published on September 17, 1796, as his second term moved toward closure. Writing during the chaos of Napoleonic upheaval overseas (with considerable assistance from Alexander Hamilton), Washington warned repeatedly against "foreign alliances, attachments, and intrigues":

> Why, by interweaving our destiny with that of any part of Europe, entangle our peace and prosperity in the toils of European ambition, rivalship, interest, humor, or caprice? It is our true policy to steer clear of permanent alliances with any portion of the foreign world.[13]

For more than a century that revered message provided a gyroscope for the conduct of American foreign policy, which remained more or less disentangled until the early twentieth century when presidents of both parties could not resist the temptation to intervene in politically unstable nations of Central America and the Caribbean. Despite broad support for such initiatives, Woodrow Wilson's opponents successfully defeated United States participation in the League of Nations during the post-World War I era by invoking memories of George Washington's wisdom and the enduring policy to which it gave rise.[14]

Intervention in Central America meant expansion and control but not alliances. After 1945, however, when the United States emerged as the world's dominant superpower, it became necessary either to ignore Washington's Farewell Address or else give it a radically different interpretation than Washington had intended: first, that if the United States acted with restraint during the 1790s it would enjoy freedom *from* restraint subsequently; and then the farewell address could, with some sophistry, be claimed as a powerful rationale for the necessity of American freedom of action.

Be that as it may, one wonders how George Washington would have viewed partisan "intrigues" by the Central Intelligence Agency, for example, in Indonesia during the 1950s or in Cuba during the 1960s. Or, for that matter, permanent alliances and commitments that ranged from NATO to SEATO to South Korea. The anti-Communist frenzy of the Cold War era made George Washington's advice anachronistic if not outright embarrassing. So the long-standing tradition of reading the entire Farewell Address out loud in both houses of Congress on Washington's birthday quietly vanished. A tradition had to be disremembered because a customary perception of the national interest had been turned upside-down.[15] Sometimes symbols have a way of outliving the concept they are supposed to represent. In this instance policy imperatives quashed a legendary memory. The legend came to be minimized in little-noticed texts, whereas the policy came to be maximized in initiatives with pretexts.

It does need to be added, however, that the United States is hardly peculiar, or alone, in allowing nationalism to distort collective memory. In recent years the Japanese have rewritten their history textbooks more than once under governmental supervision, first to erase their heinous behavior in East Asia during the 1930s and 1940s, and then to make concessions when the Korean, Chinese, and Philippine governments demonstrated that Japanese history books were guilty of whitewash and cover-up tactics. On May 6, 1994, for example, a humiliated Japanese Minister of Justice publicly retracted his assertion that Japanese troops "were not aggressors in World War II, committed no atrocities in the Chinese city of Nanking, and behaved no worse toward Korean and Chinese women than did U.S. and British soldiers."[16]

Domestic Politics, Partisanship, and the Uses of Memory

A plausible case could be made that the most successful (i.e., effective) American presidents have been the ones most likely to manipulate, "improve," or even distort their nation's collective memory. Take as an initial illustration the comparatively innocuous case of Thomas Jefferson as exemplified in his first inaugural address on March 4, 1801. The later 1790s had been absolutely tumultuous. Domestic politics have never been more virulent or venomous, and many citizens wondered whether a peaceful transition to a loyal opposition was even possible. It had not yet happened because only the Federalist Party had held power since the nation's inception in 1789.[17]

Understandably, then, Jefferson wanted to calm the fears of those who regarded him as a godless egalitarian, a Francophile and an Anglophobe, an advocate of state sovereignty, a wild-eyed civil libertarian with a mulatto mistress conceived from his father-in-law's loins. His first inaugural sought to minimize partisan differences, to draw a veil over the vicious hostilities of the 1790s. "Every difference of opinion," he declared, "is not a difference of principle. We have called by different names brethren of the same principle. We are all Republicans, we are all Federalists. If there be any among us who would wish to dissolve this Union or to change its republican form [such as Hamiltonian neo-monarchists], let them stand undisturbed as monuments of the safety with which error of opinion may be tolerated where reason is left free to combat it." To soothe those who feared that he might depart from George Washington's sage advice concerning foreign relations, Jefferson included language (little noticed ever since) that sounds more Washingtonian than the Father of His Country himself: "peace, commerce, and honest friendship with all nations, entangling alliances with none."[18] Thomas Jefferson created the presidential precedent of stealing a page from his opponents' gospel. As we shall see, Jefferson's heir in terms of party lineage, Franklin D. Roosevelt, perfected that precedent.[19]

In between, however, such presidents as Andrew Jackson and Abraham Lincoln, along with major politicians like Daniel Webster and Henry Clay, had to deal with threats of southern state secession in a nation that itself had emerged in 1776 by invoking the right to revolution. The Declaration of Independence, the most sacred and best known of all American texts, had announced unequivocally:

> That whenever any Form of Government becomes destructive of these ends [Life, Liberty and the Pursuit of Happiness, i.e., governmental protection of private property], it is the Right of the People to alter or abolish it, and to institute new Government, laying its foundation on such principles and organizing its powers in such form, as to them shall seem most likely to effect their Safety and Happiness.[20]

Both Andrew Jackson and especially Abraham Lincoln knew that text "cold" and fully understood that the United States had staked its own claim to independent nationhood upon Lockean principles of the right to revolution. How then could Jackson consistently deny South Carolina the right to secede in 1831, or Lincoln deny the Confederacy that right in 1861?[21] They did so by invoking a political fiction whose genesis is somewhat obscure: the notion of a "Perpetual Union." Exactly who invented that concept, and in what circumstances, is exceedingly hazy. What *is* clear is that for three decades following 1830 it became the ultimate line of defense for leaders who wished to deny a state (or states) the right to secede and be self-governing.[22]

The political fiction, moreover, required a monumental distortion of collective memory that seems to have troubled no one in the North and perplexed few people even in the South—perhaps because pro-Union sentiment there remained strong among many of those committed to the defense of slavery. In any event, the concept of "Perpetual Union" required an astonishing revision of historical reality in order to assert that the Union actually pre-existed the states. How could that possibly be? After all, the states declared their independence individually in 1776. Although most of them subscribed to a joint Declaration, that document did not create a government. Rather, eleven states composed brand-new constitutions that created autonomous governments, while Connecticut and Rhode Island simply converted their colonial charters into frames of government adequate for statehood. The Articles of Confederation defined a loose and weak Confederation that left most sovereignty in the hands of the states. The Constitutional Convention did not meet in Philadelphia until 1787. The document it created was not ratified until the summer of 1788, and the new national government did not begin until the spring of 1789 when Congress first gathered and George Washington was inaugurated.

The advocates of "Perpetual Union," however, highlighted an alternative sequence. The First Continental Congress, they observed, met on September 5, 1774, in Philadelphia, which is true, and little more than five weeks later, acting as a body, issued its Declaration and Resolves, a feisty assertion of grievances and rights. Then came the Second Continental Congress; then came the Confederation followed by the permanent federal government in 1789—all in a direct line of descent. Therefore the Union, being older than the states, was intended to be a perpetual union. Once a state joined, it did so irrevocably. The Union came first, the states second. The Union was superior, the states inferior. They simply could not legitimately secede.[23]

Although it may sound like a bizarre reconstruction of the political past, Abraham Lincoln relied upon that mystical, ahistorical formula during his remarkable pre-inaugural journey from Springfield to Washington, D.C., in February 1861, when he gave one speech after another conciliatory to the

South, all the while insisting upon the inviolable character of a "Perpetual Union."

Although we hear rather little about "Perpetual Union" after 1865, no one ever repudiated the fictive concept. It had served a highly utilitarian purpose, it received credence, and like many memories that outlast their immediate usefulness, it slowly dissipated to be replaced by a redefinition of the political nation that first appeared in Lincoln's Gettysburg Address but was capped expansively by the Supreme Court's decision in *Texas v. White* (1869), which legitimized "Perpetual Union" by contextualizing it more comprehensibly. According to the opinion written by Chief Justice Salmon P. Chase, when Texas joined the United States,

> she entered into an indissoluble relation. All the obligations of perpetual union, and all the guaranties of republican government in the Union, attached at once to the State. The act which consummated her admission into the Union was something more than a compact; it was the incorporation of a new member into the political body. And it was final. The union between Texas and the other States was as complete, as perpetual, and as indissoluble as the union between the original states.[24]

History had been supplanted by constitutional theory, while memory became a casualty of political expediency. Call it casuistry or sophistry, but not cynicism or hypocrisy. Those who rationalized the Union believed every word that they said and wrote.

Franklin D. Roosevelt provides us with a different kind of casuistry that was not merely expedient but cynical and manipulative as well. As a Democrat he fell heir to the party founded by Jefferson and Jackson. But as a superb coalition-builder and shrewd politician, he coveted the votes of African Americans and certain immigrant groups that had traditionally voted Republican—the party associated with Abraham Lincoln. Beginning in 1935–36, Roosevelt mentioned Lincoln at every possible opportunity in speeches and press conferences. Consequently, he succeeded in "reformulating" the memories of blacks and ethnic groups, who assumed that FDR must stand in a direct line of political descent from Lincoln! In 1936 they shifted their votes to FDR—partially for substantive reasons but partially because of image manipulation—and provided him with a hefty margin of victory in subsequent elections. Roosevelt clearly "stole" Lincoln from the Republican Party, and in the process successfully managed to maneuver the political memories of a great many people.[25]

More subtle and more complicated, of course, was FDR's need to honor Thomas Jefferson, the founder of his own party, while pursuing Hamiltonian policies that had defined the anti-Jeffersonian Federalist tradition, such as strong central government and management of the banking system to provide for economic growth.[26] Talk about a wolf in sheep's clothing! By the end of Roosevelt's second term, memories of America's contrapuntal political traditions had become conflated, blurred, and confused. Which statesmen had stood for what policies was anyone's guess. And no public forum, classroom, or journal provided much in the way of illumination on such matters.

More recently Ronald Reagan raised amnesia almost to the level of an art form with respect to "Irangate" and other policy initiatives that did not succeed. More to the point, however, even though they have all but vanished from memory in the civic culture, are the occasions when Reagan and his advisors deliberately (though not exactly deftly) attempted to distort public memory in order to advance an ideological agenda. Claiming that many New Deal administrators during the 1930s had been Socialists or Communists provides one example, and insisting that the United States fought the Vietnam War with "one hand tied behind our backs" supplies another.[27]

Even though news articles offering correctives appeared soon after each of these pronouncements, with formidable evidence from scholars and other authorities, the presidential "bully pulpit" exercised considerable and enduring influence upon collective memory. A fictive Rambo so favored by Reagan gradually became a blend of what some men did and many others might have done if only Gulliver hadn't been strapped down by small men of little brain and less courage.[28]

Conclusions and Comparisons

As I tried to suggest at the outset, the distortion or even the manipulation of collective memory does not always, or inevitably, occur for cynical or hypocritical reasons. That has certainly been the case on occasion, as we have seen, but memory distortion also occurs commonly in postcolonial situations where the creation of national identity is necessary for functional reasons of political and cultural cohesion. The United States alone provides abundant documentation on this point.[29]

Moreover, even when leaders (political and spiritual) do engage in memory distortion or "practice" historical amnesia, we must recognize that members of the public at large are often likely to believe and internalize the rationalizations they receive. Frequently, as we have seen, the willful alteration of collective memory becomes a necessity for a viable, progressive society. How else can it coherently adapt to change, often desirable change, without being plagued by a sense of inconsistency or sham?

When our scope becomes more international, moreover, we find that the

United States is not alone in presenting us with instances of memory distortion on account of diverse stimuli with variable consequences. Constructive, "positive," or harmless examples of memory reconstruction, as described at the end of the preceding paragraph, can be found in Mexico, Scandinavia, and France.[30] A greater degree of distortion—yet still neither cynical nor harshly hegemonic—resulting from a sense of shame or the need to define national identity in more particular ways, can be found in Brazil, England, Germany, France, and Israel.[31]

And then, undeniably, there are also egregious instances of memory distortion whose sole or primary purpose is to legitimize a regime, empower a rising social class, or else reduce (or even eliminate) the stigma of war crimes or inhumane atrocities.[32]

Although space does not permit systematic consideration of memory distortion on the part of individuals, I want to conclude with the observation that here, too, motives range from benign to moralistic or didactic (the autobiographies of Benjamin Franklin and Henry Adams) to self-serving (the political memoirs of such presidents as Truman, Nixon, and Reagan) to utterly malicious (Ernest Hemingway's posthumous memoir, *A Moveable Feast*, 1964).

None of these instances or categories comes as any sort of revelation. More difficult to evaluate, however, are literary works derived from memory that nonetheless are more concerned with artistry than veracity, works such as Mark Twain's *Life on the Mississippi* (1883) or Anaïs Nin's *Diary* (7 vols., 1966–80) or James Baldwin's *Notes of a Native Son* (1957), books that embroider autobiographical memories in varying degrees with diverse motives. Unlike the political memoirists, who would vigorously deny any deliberate act of memory distortion, creative writers have other objectives that, in their view, validate sins of omission or commission, inhibition or exhibition. As Anaïs Nin said, "the only person I do not lie to is my journal. Yet out of affection even for my journal I sometimes lie by omissions. There are still so many omissions!"[33]

Most intriguing of all, however, at least in my view, are the would-be memoirists who set their projects aside because they recognize that their memories have been sieve-like and integrity compels them to avoid even inadvertent distortion—like the cultural critic Gilbert Seldes (1893–1970),[34] or like the writer Allen Tate, who abandoned a projected memoir in the 1970s, some years after he had started it, for a cluster of reasons that illuminate the highly complex and subjective nature of remembrance in the face of fear—fear that the synapses may fail to connect, but even worse, fear that they might connect all too well, resulting in unwanted revelations about oneself and others. Tate explained this dilemma with immense charm in his

Preface to *Memoirs and Opinions*:

> In 1966 I decided to write an entire book of memories, and I was persuaded by
> certain friends that my "prodigious memory" would make the task an easy
> one. After I had written, with considerable difficulty, "A Lost Traveller's
> Dream" and "Miss Toklas' American Cake," I decided to try something else
> —what, I couldn't then be sure. My memory became less and less prodigious:
> my account of my first year in Paris had to be "checked" twice for the
> exposure of seventeen errors of simple fact. But this is not the principal reason
> why I decided to halt the memoir.
>
> The "real" reason was that, unlike Ernest Hemingway in *A Moveable Feast*,
> I couldn't bring myself to tell what was wrong with my friends—or even mere
> acquaintances—without trying to tell what was wrong with myself. I am not
> sure even now, what was, or is, wrong with me, and I was unwilling to give
> the reader the chance to make up his own mind on this slippery matter. Then,
> too, I fell back on authority: I couldn't let myself indulge in the terrible
> fluidity of self-revelation.[35]

The immense irony, however, is that the circumstances of Tate's youth,
early manhood, and family background were (and are) so deeply veiled in
mystery, even to him, that he (and we) do not know where veracity ends and
distortion begins. The first third of his life remains an enigma.[36] So much
for those who claim that compared to the empirical verifiability of personal
memory, collective memory is a will-o'-the-wisp. I have found them equally
elusive.

Perhaps it might be appropriate to close with some queries—I suppose we
should call them rhetorical—jotted down by Bronson Alcott, the Massachusetts transcendentalist, mystic, and sometime seer, a self-educated contemporary of Ralph Waldo Emerson. Four of his provocative queries give us
pause.

> Which is the older, the memory, the thing remembered, or the person
> remembering?
>
> Can you remember when you did not remember?
>
> Which is predecessor, Time or the memory?
>
> Are moments born of the memory, or memory of the moments?[37]

Giving pause gave meaning, if not memory, to Bronson Alcott's life. It could
very well do the same for ours.

9

History Is Our Heritage: The Past in Contemporary American Culture

One of the most curious anomalies in contemporary American culture ought to be a matter of considerable concern to historians and other educators. New museums and historic sites open to the public at regular and frequent intervals. After a decline in the late 1970s and early 1980s, attendance at many historical museums, villages, and other sites is on the rise. Their educational outreach programs have been redefined and the quality of interpretive activities is more thoughtful than it was fifteen or twenty years ago. The bicentennial of the U.S. Constitution provided an occasion for new curricula to be developed for the teaching of civics, history, and the genesis of American government. Consequently, many more students have been asked to think carefully about the evolution of the present state of our political system.

Looked at more closely, however, the place of history in modern American life is both superficial and precarious. Recent studies have revealed an alarming degree of ignorance and apathy. Our students know only a fraction of the history that we would like them to know, and much less than they would need to know as informed voters, decision makers, or simply as persons able to comprehend the complexities of daily news, both national and international.

The problem is not confined, however, to our young people. Abundant evidence indicates that amnesia concerning the American past afflicts those who are responsible for policy at all levels. Public polls and extensive interviews confirm the realization that we are moving forward at an accelerated pace without having the advantage of a first-rate rearview mirror. The variety of topics affected by this amnesia, moreover, is alarmingly broad. It ranges from the origins and nature of New Deal measures designed to combat the Great Depression, to the changing historical circumstances of Native Americans, the civil rights of African Americans, and the prolonged series of national anxieties concerning potentially "conspiratorial" threats to overthrow our government. The "Big Red Scare" that followed World War I, and then McCarthyism in the wake of World War II, do not linger as meaningful object lessons for a society so long prone to periodic spasms of nervous apprehension about threats of ideological subversion.

How can we best comprehend and come to grips with this anomalous pattern of historical indifference and ignorance in an age of escapist nostalgia? Have we perpetuated upon ourselves a form of self-deception? I believe that we have, in fact, and that highly selective, sentimental, and sanitized versions of American history have produced a severely simplified vision of how we came to be the society we now are.

Underlying this pattern is a trend that I call the "heritage phenomenon." If we can understand the distinction between history and heritage, we may be able to explain the anomaly of historical ignorance on the part of a people that appear to share a widespread enthusiasm for the past. The dynamics of that "heritage phenomenon" can supply us with a context for coming to terms with the peculiar status of history in our society as well as in our schools today.

For more than a full generation now, beginning in the mid-1950s, "heritage" has been one of the key words in American culture. The frequency of its usage has also increased markedly in Great Britain and the Commonwealth, to be sure, and in some of the same ways,[1] but the popularity and pervasiveness of this "buzzword" in the United States is becoming utterly astounding. Therefore the phenomenon requires our attention for various reasons but particularly because it can illuminate the complex (and often self-contradictory) transformation of historical consciousness among Americans who come from diverse backgrounds: diverse in terms of region, ethnicity, class, and level of education. Notions of "heritage" in American popular culture are richly revealing for anyone interested in the status of history and historical understanding in contemporary society.

Before getting to the "how" and the "why" of this trend, however, we must start with the seemingly simple, basically descriptive "what." Ultimately we want to specify the implications of a cultural trend, but first we must describe it, exemplify it, and, precisely because it is so ubiquitous, try to break it down into comprehensible categories.

At the national level, for instance, one immediately thinks of the National Trust for Historic Preservation, established at the end of the 1940s. Its introductory brochure, which makes an attractive appeal for membership, has three carefully chosen words placed on the cover: "Guarding America's Heritage." A major report, cosponsored by the National Trust and Colonial Williamsburg in 1965, carried the title "With Heritage So Rich." One also thinks of the Museum of Our National Heritage, which opened in Lexington, Massachusetts, on April 20, 1975, under the auspices of the Scottish Rite Masonic organization.

At the state level we find that "heritage" has gradually broadened its meaning. In 1957, for example, five organizations jointly sponsored an elegant Virginia Heritage Dinner in order to celebrate "the 350th Anniversary of the Founding of Our Country." That really meant the first permanent English colony, established at Jamestown. The occasion also seemed to use heritage as a near synonym for history.

In 1974, after eight years of developmental planning, the Wisconsin Department of Natural Resources established an outdoor historical park on forty-three acres of land at the edge of Green Bay on the Fox River. It is called Heritage Hill State Park, and the cover of its big brochure defines its mission as "preserving our heritage through 'Living History.'" The four illustrative sections of that brochure are designated as Pioneer Heritage, Heritage of Growth, Military Heritage, and Religious and Small Town Heritage.

The increasingly ecumenical nature of "heritage" is exemplified by New York, which observed an Architectural Heritage Year in 1986 (promoted by the Preservation League of New York State), and had 1988 designated (by Governor Mario Cuomo) as Community Heritage Year. The latter is occasioned by the bicentennial of the 1788 Town Laws, which brought new towns into being and defined the responsibilities of all existing communities in the Empire State.[2]

At the local level, "heritage" is most notably hooked up with historic preservation, although the chosen sites may vary considerably in character. In northeastern Massachusetts, for instance, Heritage Park in downtown

Lowell, run by the National Park Service, is a nineteenth- and early twentieth-century industrial restoration. It offers quite a sharp contrast to rustic Historic Deerfield, Inc., located near the Berkshires and founded in 1952 as Heritage Foundation by Mr. and Mrs. Henry Flynt in order "to promote the cause of education in and appreciation of the rich heritage of the early colonies."

Architectural preservation is the primary mission of the Heritage Foundation of Oswego, New York; the Naperville Heritage Society in Illinois, which received its impetus in 1968 when a venerable mansion was on the verge of destruction; the Athens-Clarke Heritage Foundation, which has maintained the Church-Waddel-Brumby House (1820) as a Welcome Center for Athens, Georgia, since 1971; and Texas Heritage, a private organization that is restoring the home built by a Fort Worth cattle baron back in 1912.

The Dallas County Heritage Society was formed in 1966 to prevent the destruction of Millermore, the largest surviving antebellum home in Dallas (built 1855–62). Most of the structures in Old City Park are Victorian, however, and the Society's leaflet makes the following claim: "Walking across their floors, peeking into their rooms, using their tools and toys and trivia . . . [*sic*] People are history. How people have lived is the basis for how we see life."

Houston's counterpart is called the Harris County Heritage Society, a private, nonprofit organization that also maintains a cluster of nineteenth-century buildings "Where Houston Remembers." Members of the society serve as docents in Sam Houston Park, "work in the Yesteryear Shop and Tea Room, organize and host lectures and workshops, and stage the annual Heritage Ball, Candlelight Tour and other special events."

Various structures located at Heritage Square in Los Angeles began to undergo restoration in 1968 owing to the joint auspices of the Cultural Heritage Foundation and the city's new Cultural Heritage Board. The endeavor has proceeded at a snail's pace, however, because the city contributes *no* money to the project and volunteers come and go, but mostly go. As the *Los Angeles Times* remarked in 1976, this reflects "the sluggish historical consciousness for which the region is noted."[3]

Pasadena, on the other hand, which has a Cultural Heritage Commission, adopted a cultural heritage ordinance in 1976 that requires permission in order to demolish buildings that are more than fifty years old. The commission is then allowed thirty days to determine whether the building in question has historical or cultural significance and whether it can be saved.[4]

Heritage is not inevitably used as a codeword for the salvation of old structures. Sometimes it signifies the struggles for survival that various groups and subcultures have undergone. In 1982, for example, the Indiana Committee for the Humanities, the Indiana Historical Society Library, and the Muncie Public Library produced a striking photographic exhibit entitled "This Far by Faith: Black Hoosier Heritage." The display was accompanied by a booklet with the same title, and a brochure that began: "Our heritage stares out at us from each photograph in this exhibit." It ended with a passage from Langston Hughes's poem, "History":

> The past has been a mint
> Of blood and sorrow.
> That must not be
> True of tomorrow.

A long-neglected Georgian mansion in Philadelphia became the subject of considerable controversy in 1987–88 after the American Women's Heritage Society (a predominantly black organization) spent more than $50,000 on repairs, fitting out period rooms that range from early American to contemporary, and sponsoring frequent exhibits "that emphasize Black history and achievement." Several civic groups strenuously disapprove of what has been done with the Belmont Mansion (overlooking the Schuylkill River and Fairmount Park), however. A report prepared by a charitable foundation declared in 1987 that "this current use may not be the best use. This house may be a property of such consummate value to the city that it should be more open to the city, possibly as a reception center for dignitaries." Philadelphians are presently fighting over the most appropriate use and presentation of their urban heritage.[5]

For certain groups, "heritage" has become an ideologically useful or meaningful label. The Heritage Foundation headquartered in Washington, D.C., serves as a conservative think tank and political action group. It also publishes a fair amount of literature to promote and explain its causes, which include a vigorous defense of the free enterprise system. Yet another Heritage Foundation, based in Trumbull, Connecticut, displays on its letterhead a screaming eagle perched upon an open Bible, below which a dozen words from Psalm 61 appear: "Thou hast given us the heritage of those that fear thy name." Nationalism and fundamentalism can comfortably complement one another.

The heritage emphasis has also become valuable, however, to entrepreneurs offering safe havens in a world that is commercial as well as secular, self-indulgent, and intensely concerned with social status. Heritage Hills of Westchester, New York, offers condominiums in a thousand-acre "country setting of beauty, woods, ponds and streams." Where is the heritage?

The recreational opportunities are the best. Heritage Hills offers a private golf course and health club with gym, saunas and whirlpool. There are swimming pools, tennis courts and a jogging path. The homes are the best. Fine craftsmanship and quality are evident throughout these beautifully designed homes. . . . There's even a private shuttle service to the nearby commuter train station.

A much more lavish set of homes, located near Morristown, New Jersey, is offered by New Vernon Heritage at prices starting at $1.2 million. Where is the heritage? According to one advertisement, "the architecture, reflecting a return to the classic, will include English manors, French chateaus, and Irish country houses." A rather eclectic heritage, if you will, and if you are willing to live with mixed manors.

In the world of business, "heritage" seems to connote integrity, authenticity, venerability, and stability. Hence the Heritage Federal Bank in Franklin, Tennessee; World-Heritage Realty for vacation sites in Maggie Valley, North Carolina, snuggled along the edge of the Great Smoky Mountains; the Heritage Building, a large office complex in downtown Dallas, Texas; and Heritage Hall Gallery in Lansdale, Pennsylvania, the home of Heritage Collectors' Society, which specializes in restoring, framing, and selling historic documents for "interior accent." A decorator's delight: cover your walls with "original documents signed by those who shaped our nation's destiny."

As for achievement recognition, in 1982 the National Endowment for the Arts created a program of National Heritage Fellowships, "the country's highest award for accomplishment in a traditional arts field." Three years later the recipients included a Hawaiian quiltmaker from Honolulu who has hand-stitched more than one hundred quilts and designed more than four hundred quilt patterns; a Lakota Sioux from Grass Creek, South Dakota, who worked to preserve the Indian craft of porcupine quill decoration; and a working cowboy who "has told more tall tales and sung more cowboy songs than anyone in Mountain View, Arkansas, can count."[6]

These $5000 fellowships were awarded on a one-time-only basis by the Folk Arts Program at NEA. For our purposes they fill out the heritage spectrum, ranging from institutions to individuals, from the public sector to the private, from statements of purpose to advertisements, and from identity to destiny. The question yet remains, however, what does heritage actually have to do with history and social memory?

∼

Basically, I suppose, the essential answer must be "everything and nothing." In some situations, such as Heritage Hills condominiums, the word concept bears absolutely no relationship to the past. It is simply a euphonious phrase that portends a sheltered if not sybaritic life-style.

In other situations, heritage seems to be very nearly a euphemism for selective memory because it means, in functional terms, what history has customarily meant: namely, that portion of the past perceived by a segment of society as significant or meaningful at any given moment in time.[7]

In still other situations, heritage is virtually intended as an antonym for history, or else it passes as sugar-coated history. But that really means more than mere palatability. It involves an explicit element of anti-intellectualism—the presumption, for example, that history experienced through sites and material culture must be more memorable than history presented on the printed page. An advertisement for New Jersey's *Heritage Guide* shows a winsome modern lass seated at a Chippendale game table from the Revolutionary era. Above her flaxen hair are two lines with a didactic imperative: Let Your Children Experience American History Instead of Just Reading About It.[8]

Many of those who run outdoor museums and similar sites make strident claims about the authenticity of what they have to offer. They also tend to make pejorative statements about the perils of historical imagination—as though that were an *undesirable* quality to encourage in adolescents. And the promotional materials of such administrators are likely to claim that hands-on heritage-as-history guarantees enjoyment, unlike the deadly dull sort of history that is dispensed in the classroom, the library, and via the medium of print. Take, as one representative illustration, these exuberant assertions from the initial page of a booklet produced by Heritage Hill State Park in Green Bay, Wisconsin:

> You don't have to imagine how life was in northeast Wisconsin 100 years ago! When you leave Heritage Hill's Visitor Center, you will actually experience the past through living history. . . . The people who "live" in Heritage Hills' historical structures eat, work, dress and talk exactly as though they were living in bygone days. To them, modern conveniences and language patterns do not exist. . . . Living history brings an added dimension to the historical museum which allows you to learn about your "roots" and enjoy it![9]

When we ask why the heritage rubric has sustained such remarkable appeal, we must start with nostalgia. The nation has been hankering after various imagined golden ages—for more innocent and carefree days—ever since the early 1970s. There is nothing necessarily wrong with nostalgia per se, but more often than not the phenomenon does mean a pattern of selective memory. Recall the good, but forget the unpleasant. And that is just what has happened. The 1965 report published by the National Trust, "With

Heritage So Rich," articulated the problem succinctly: "A nation can be a victim of amnesia."[10] The spate of reports that appeared in 1987 indicate that cultural amnesia has overwhelmed the American populace with unusual force.[11]

The heritage syndrome, if I may call it that, almost seems to be a predictable but certainly nonconspiratorial response—an impulse to remember what is attractive or flattering and to ignore all the rest. Heritage is comprised of those aspects of history that we cherish and affirm. As an alternative to history, heritage accentuates the positive but sifts away what is problematic. One consequence is that the very pervasiveness of heritage as a phenomenon produces a beguiling sense of serenity about the well-being of history—that is, a false consciousness that historical knowledge and understanding are alive and well in the United States.

Although American knowledge and understanding of history are *not* altogether healthy, neither is the outlook quite so grim as it may sound. An upbeat emphasis upon heritage can serve as a stimulus to prudent public policy and enhanced concern for a more meaningful relationship between past and present. As a *New York Times* editorial phrased the matter in 1975, referring to New York City's landmark legislation and the campaign to "save" Grand Central Terminal, repercussions of that legislation "are already being felt in other places where the problem of the preservation of a city's and a nation's heritage meet the problem of economic hardship and the rights of property."[12]

One of the more welcome features of the heritage surge involves the development of contacts, even enduring relationships, between popular and academic history. Scholars have been writing for *American Heritage* ever since it began to appear in its present guise during the mid-1950s. Energetic and creative teachers of history and social studies in our secondary and primary schools are presently publishing essays with such titles as "Planning for Local Heritage Projects." Staff members at the Smithsonian Institution, assessing the quincentennial of Columbus's arrival in the Western Hemisphere (1992), observed that "historic anniversaries are even more important to us as a time to focus on our civic heritage and in the case of Columbus, on our world heritage."[13]

Precisely because the heritage phenomenon has become so strong, and because some of its features may seem superficial or self-serving for assorted groups or individuals, there is a genuine risk that critical observers may conclude that "real" history must be 180 degrees removed from the tainted stuff that parades as heritage. What nonsense! Hasn't serious history *always* contained elements of national mythology? Bernard DeVoto once reassured Catherine Drinker Bowen (with a touch of irony) that it was okay to be "romantic about American history. . . . It is the most romantic of histories. It began in myth and has developed through three centuries of fairy stories." [14]

It can be too easily overlooked that, for generations, scholarly students of American history have been motivated by a passion to describe and explain the national heritage. In 1953, Samuel Flagg Bemis wrote Van Wyck Brooks a paean of praise for "all of those high-minded things of our heritage and the goodly currents of our life which you have done so much to hold up before the American people." [15]

Moreover, high-minded creative writers and artists who were neither professional historians nor conservative white males like Bemis, and whose past presented a saga of punishment rather than praise, nonetheless felt compelled to contemplate their heritage and communicate their apprehensions and ruminations. Hence Countee Cullen's long poem, called "Heritage," written in the 1920s: [16]

> One three centuries removed
> From the scenes his father loved,
> Spicy grove, cinnamon tree,
> What is Africa to me?

Cullen's wistful lines, along with comparable works by members of many other ethnic groups and subcultures, remind us to acknowledge the presence of multiple heritages—surely no shock in a nation of immigrants. Cullen's poignant poem also reminds us that heritage need not be a mindless affirmation of congenial memories. It has become commonplace to say that one sound reason for studying history is to enrich the understanding of identity—my own along with those of the several groups with which I identify. That, too, is a legitimate preoccupation of those intrigued by heritage. [17]

There are, in addition, events and anniversaries that inevitably remind us that history as heritage has not been free from tension, conflicting value systems, or even violence. In 1983, for example, the Gettysburg National Military Park, Gettysburg Travel Council, Gettysburg College, and the Mason-Dixon Civil War Collectors Association began to sponsor Civil War Heritage Days—more than a week of living history encampments, a reenactment of part of the Battle of Gettysburg (July 1–3, 1863), and a Civil War Collector's show. In 1986 the fourth annual Civil War Heritage Days were attended by more than 50,000 people. [18]

The unfortunate thing about this heritage boom is that it can lead, and has led, to commercialization, vulgarization, oversimplification, and tendentiously selective memories—which means both warping and whitewashing a fenced-off past. Any or all of these processes provide a disservice to the groups affected. We are better off without heritage than with it when it causes self-deception.[19]

The redeeming virtue of heritage, however, is that it can also serve as a powerful stimulus to the popularization, and hence to the democratization, of history. Heritage that heightens human interest may lead people to history for purposes of informed citizenship, or the meaningful deepening of identity, or enhanced appreciation of the dynamic process of change over time. American responses to "progress," for instance, have frequently followed patterns of ambivalence or rejection rather than mindless approval[20]—a lesson that history can teach whereas "heritage" is less likely to do so.

~

What specific implications does the heritage phenomenon have for classroom teachers and their work? The good news, obviously, is that opportunities for extramural enrichment are rapidly expanding. Class trips to historic sites, farms, factories, and villages are increasingly accessible, and such visits can bring the past alive and make it fascinating in ways that are difficult to achieve in the classroom or library alone.

The more challenging news, however, is that such trips require careful preparation and thoughtful follow-up. I have accompanied interpretive tours where I happened to join a high school class. The guides (from the National Park Service, for instance) did an excellent job of explaining their particular site, but I learned from conversations with the students that they had been given scanty prior background reading to help them understand the context of, in one instance, the onset of American industrialization and development of the factory system. At this particular site, fortunately, the tour began with a very fine twenty-minute film. But most sites are not so well set up, and at many the docents are experts on the particulars of their place—the genealogy of a structure and its inhabitants, for instance—but not on the larger pattern or trend of which it is a part. Consequently, it is essential that those patterns or trends be adequately included in the formal learning process. The best history teaching takes into account "how" and "why" along with "what," "when," and context.

Heritage can be used to explain the importance of ethnicity and religion in shaping American pluralism, for example, but in order to do so successfully the teacher must transcend the chauvinism that characterizes associations formed by hyphenated Americans or the particularism of denominational or sectarian pride. Heritage can also be used to teach the history of work, professionalization, and economic change in the United States, but in the process teachers must make clear just how different eighteenth-century agriculture and nineteenth-century medical practice were from their late twentieth-century descendants. The heritage phenomenon sometimes has a tendency to overemphasize continuity at the expense of transformation. Teachers need to be as knowledgeable about the interpretive biases of the sites they visit as they are familiar with the orientation of the textbook they assign.

We must also recognize that the heritage phenomenon tends to be upbeat and affirmative in an unqualified way about the American past. Without minimizing what has truly been a remarkable saga of achievements, teachers should be sure to take into account the human and environmental "costs" of many of those achievements. We will not adequately prepare our students for the future if we do not communicate the history of failure as well as the history of success: the failure of rebels with and without a cause, the failure of the framers to resolve all the vexing political problems they faced in 1787, the failure of subsequent reform movements to solve entirely the social ills they responded to, and so forth.

Our heritage phenomenon has the great virtue of accentuating the common core of values, institutions, and experiences that Americans have shared, and to which newcomers have accommodated in the process of becoming Americans. Undeniably, many aspects of the heritage phenomenon provide the glue that holds us all together.

Appropriate attention to those aspects, however, should not cause us to neglect those wonderfully symbolic nay-sayers who seemed out of tune with their times yet may have been prophetic of changes in the American value system. Such figures as Roger Williams, John Woolman, Sojourner Truth, Elizabeth Cady Stanton, Henry David Thoreau, and Frederick Douglass come quickly to mind as examples. One of the marvels of American history is the way certain deviant visionaries subsequently came to be regarded as prophetic leaders, and conversely, the way some popular figures subsequently seem to have been demagogues, do-nothings, or just plain disappointments.[21]

The heritage phenomenon *can* be a potent pedagogical device. It may be used to transmit with memorable force the most attractive and altruistic American values, such as equal justice, full participation in public affairs, broadened economic opportunities for all segments of society, religious toleration, regionalism and the significance of a sense of place, the value of intergenerational connectedness, and so forth.

This highly visible heritage phenomenon is less likely, however, to inform our students about those forces that have undermined our ideals, such as excessive physical mobility, or present-minded hedonism, or commercial opportunism, that may be destructive to the environment and our natural resources.

Nor is the heritage phenomenon as I have described it likely to inculcate the need for a discriminating memory—the inescapable fact that not all sites and structures, heroes and heroines, events and objects are equally important. Nor does the heritage phenomenon lend itself very well to the integrative habit of mind that we call synthesis: understanding how discrete but contemporaneous or sequential occurrences are connected to one another.

Nor does it ordinarily help us to recognize and account for differential rates of social and political change, or the ways in which patterns of intergroup conflict emerge and later are reconciled over extended periods of time. Precisely because these are all fundamental aspects of historical experience, it is essential that we teach historical habits of the mind that will enable young people to cope with such matters as component parts of the civic culture.

Although history is surely heritage simply because all of the known past is our legacy, there is more to history than heritage alone. In fact, the heritage phenomenon provides us with vivid reminders that teachers, texts, and classrooms remain indispensable. At the end of June 1988, for example, more than 70,000 people converged on Gettysburg, Pennsylvania, to spectate and participate in a seventeen-day observance of the 125th anniversary of the Battle of Gettysburg. Presumably this was a self-selecting audience. Why go to Gettysburg if you aren't *some* sort of history buff? Nevertheless, one of the participants in the elaborate reenactment of the battle, a blue-clad man from Michigan, remarked that "I can go into McDonald's wearing my uniform, and people will ask me which side I'm on." [22]

In the last analysis, it seems to me that two conclusions are inescapable. First, that schools and museums, historical organizations and textbooks have a responsibility to package and present "heritage" contextualized rather than in vacuo. They must acknowledge that heritages (plural) sometimes compete with one another (as the Italian Americans and Scandinavian Americans did a century ago when the four hundredth anniversary of Columbus's voyages approached), and that tensions among ethnic groups or communities have sometimes been creative, sometimes corrosive, sometimes benign, at other times scarring. [23]

My second conclusion should by now be quite clear. "Heritage" as we have known it is not necessarily history, but the *whole* of history, whether we like it or not, is heritage. The great imperative, therefore, for schools and teachers, textbook writers and curriculum developers, docents and educators at museums and historic sites, is to remember that heritage—this remarkably pervasive notion in American culture during the past three decades—really isn't an alternative to history, or a surrogate for it, but a prologue and a preparation for the pasts (wars and all) that produced the present (warts and all).

Stephen Dedalus once stated, courtesy of James Joyce, that "history is a nightmare from which I am trying to awake." Perhaps; but heritage in its many guises can be a beguiling daydream. We must elude the soothing self-satisfaction that it induces. Heritage as an enticement, however, could conceivably bring us to history as enchantment, as mental exercise, and as a source of self-knowledge that points toward enlightenment if not wisdom.

Notes

Introduction

1. See Peter Novick, *That Noble Dream: The "Objectivity Question" and the American Historical Profession* (New York, 1988).

2. See Kammen, essay-review concerning collective memory, *History and Theory* 34, no. 3 (1995): 245–61.

3. Quoted in Robert Coles, *Erik H. Erikson: The Growth of His Work* (Boston, 1970), 181.

4. Thompson, *Customs in Common: Studies in Traditional Popular Culture* (New York, 1990), 13; James Hoopes, *Van Wyck Brooks: In Search of American Culture* (Amherst, Mass., 1977), 39.

5. See Daniel Walker Howe, ed., *Victorian America* (Philadelphia, 1976), 5; Alan Trachtenberg, *The Incorporation of America: Culture and Society in the Gilded Age* (New York, 1982), 9, 143.

6. Williams, *Culture and Society, 1780-1950* (London, 1958); Williams, "Culture Is Ordinary," in Williams, *Resources of Hope: Culture, Democracy, and Socialism* (London, 1989), 41–55.

7. Emerson, "The American Scholar," in Robert E. Spiller, ed., *Nature, Addresses, and Lectures* (Cambridge, Mass., 1979), 65; Jacques Barzun is quoted in David Brion Davis, "Some Recent Directions in American Cultural History," *American Historical Review* 73 (Feb. 1968): 697.

8. Huizinga, "The Task of Cultural History" (1929) in Huizinga, *Men and Ideas: Essays* (New York, 1959), 64.

9. See Kuno Francke, "The Study of National Culture," *Atlantic Monthly* 99 (March 1907): 409–16; Benedict, *Patterns of Culture* (Boston, 1934); Fairbank, "Probing the Chinese Mind—Reports from Two U.S. Experts," *U.S. News and World Report* 71 (Sept. 6, 1971): 80.

10. See also Kammen, *Mystic Chords of Memory: The Transformation of Tradition in American Culture* (New York, 1991); Kammen, *Meadows of Memory: Images of Time and Tradition in American Art and Culture* (Austin, Tex., 1992); Kammen, essay-review in *History and Theory* 34, no. 3 (1995): 245–61; and Kammen, "Public History and the Uses of Memory," in *Public Historian* 19 (Spring 1997): 53–56.

11. Pierre Bourdieu and Alain Darbel, *L'Amour de l'art: Les Musées et leur public* (Paris, 1966), esp. 114, 147; and see Kammen, "Charles Burchfield and 'the Procession of the Seasons,'" in Nannette V. Maciejunes, ed., *On the Middle Border: The Art of Charles E. Burchfield* (New York, 1997), 38–49.

12. Barzun, "Distrust of Brains," *The Nation* 160 (Jan. 6, 1945): 18-19; Beard to Barzun, Jan. 6, 1945, Barzun papers, Manuscripts and Special Collections, Butler Library, Columbia University, New York.

13. Ernest Samuels, ed., *The Education of Henry Adams* (Cambridge, Mass., 1973), 319; Powell's review of Beard, *The Republic* (1943), in *Harvard Law Review* 57 (April 1944): 580.

14. See Smith, *The History of the Province of New-York*, ed. by Michael Kammen (Cambridge, Mass., 1972), I: xxx–xxxii.

15. See Bryce Lyon, Henri Pirenne: *A Biographical and Intellectual Study* (Atlantic Highlands, N.J., 1974), 233–76; Norman F. Cantor, *Inventing the Middle Ages* (New York, 1991), 132; J. H. Hexter, *On Historians* (Cambridge, Mass., 1979), 104–5, 139; Braudel, "Personal Testimony," *Journal of Modern History*, 44 (Dec. 1972): 453–54.

16. See "Michael Kammen," *Contemporary Authors: Autobiography Series*, vol. 23 (Detroit, 1996), 133–63.

Chapter 1
Personal Identity and the Historian's Vocation

1. Hughes is quoted by Woodward in *Thinking Back: The Perils of Writing History* (Baton Rouge, 1986), 30. For Hughes's autobiography see *Gentleman Rebel: The Memoirs of H. Stuart Hughes* (New York, 1990).

2. See Joan Shelley Rubin, *The Making of Middlebrow Culture* (Chapel Hill, 1992), ch. 1, "Self, Culture, and "Self-Culture in America"; Wilfred M. McClay, *The Masterless: Self & Society in Modern America* (Chapel Hill, 1994). When Daniel Walker Howe delivered the Carl Becker Lectures in History at Cornell in October 1994, he titled the series "The Construction of the Self in Antebellum America." See also Sacvan Bercovitch, *The Puritan Origins of the American Self* (New Haven, 1975).

3. Novick, *That Noble Dream: The "Objectivity Question" and the American Historical Profession* (New York, 1988), 11.

4. Sacvan Bercovitch, *The Rites of Assent: Transformations in the Symbolic Construction of America* (New York, 1993), 1-28, quotation at 1. An exhibition titled "Picasso and the Weeping Women" began at the Los Angeles County Museum of Art, Feb. 13 to May 1, 1994, and then traveled to other museums across the United States. On the feminist perspective, see Andrew Ross, *No Respect: Intellectuals & Popular Culture* (New York, 1989), 176; and Roger Adelson, "Interview with Joan Jensen," *Historian* 56 (Winter 1994): 252: "the feminist movement galvanized my interest in the 1970s. Those of us in that first generation of women historians saw a connection between our personal life and our professional life."

5. See Nancy F. Cott, ed., *A Woman Making History: Mary Ritter Beard Through Her Letters* (New Haven, 1991), 3, 18; but see Charles Beard to Merle Curti, June 13, 1943, Curti papers, box 4, State Historical Society of Wisconsin, Madison: "When I finish up a job on hand, I am going to try to think about historiography. In other words, now that I am damned near dead, I am beginning to wonder what I have been doing all my life."

6. L. P. Curtis, Jr., ed., *The Historian's Workshop: Original Essays by Sixteen Historians* (New York, 1970); Potter to L. P. Curtis, Jr., Jan. 26, 1967, Potter papers, box 1, Special Collections, Stanford University Libraries. Potter went on to add the following: "I was involved in a similar inquiry for the SSRC once, and I discovered, for instance, that Robert R. Palmer seemed to have almost no conscious awareness of how he constructs and writes his histories." Palmer's contribution to *The Historian's Workshop* is titled "The Age of the Democratic Revolution."

7. H. Lark Hall, *V. L. Parrington: Through the Avenue of Art* (Kent, Ohio, 1994), 72, 121, 200, 210, quotation at 200.

8. Dale Morgan to Juanita Brooks, May 23, 1946, in John Phillip Walker, ed., *Dale Morgan on Early Mormonism: Correspondence & a New History* (Salt Lake City, 1986), 120–21; and see Brodie, *No Man Knows My History: The Life of Joseph Smith, the Mormon Prophet* (New York, 1945).

9. Wilbur R. Jacobs, "The West Is Best as a State of Mind," unpubl. paper presented at the annual meeting of the Western Historical Association, Oct. 1993; Roger Adelson, "Interview with John Demos," *Historian* 55 (Spring 1993): 445–46. See also Rudolph J. Vecoli, "Italian Immigrants with Working-Class Movements in the U.S.: A Personal Reflection on Class and Ethnicity," *Journal of the Canadian Historical Association* 4 (1993): 304.

10. Catton (1899-1978) to Oliver Jensen, Sept. 26, [1968], Catton papers, folder B-C297-B, American Heritage Center, University of Wyoming, Laramie. For Catton's autobiography, see *Waiting for the Morning Train* (Garden City, N.Y., 1972).

11. Athearn, "A View from the High Country," *Western Historical Quarterly* 2 (April 1971): 127.

12. Duberman, "On Becoming an Historian," in Duberman, *The Uncompleted Past* (New York, 1971), 339.

13. Casey Blake and Christopher Phelps, "History as Social Criticism: Conversations with Christopher Lasch," *Journal of American History* 80 (March 1994): 1315–16; Richard Wightman Fox, "An Interview with Christopher Lasch," *Intellectual History Newsletter* 16 (1994): 6–7; D'Emilio, "Not a Simple Matter: Gay History and Gay Historians," *Journal of American History* 76 (Sept. 1989): 436, 439.

14. Robert Padgug and Jon Wiener, "From the Abolitionists to Gay History: An Interview with Martin Bauml Duberman," *Radical History Review*, no. 42 (Fall 1988): 65-86; Duberman, *Cures: A Gay Man's Odyssey* (New York 1991), 56, 60, 63, 116–17, 223–24, 257–58; Duberman, "On Becoming an Historian," 335–56.

15. D'Emilio, "Not a Simple Matter," 436, 439–40; D'Emilio, *Making Trouble: Essays on Gay History, Politics and the University* (New York, 1992), xiii–xli, 142-43; Duberman, "The Limitations of History," *Antioch Review* 25 (Summer 1965): 283–96; Duberman, *Black Mountain: An Exploration in Community* (New York, 1972); D'Emilio, *Sexual Politics, Sexual Communities: The Making of a Homosexual Minority in the United States, 1940–1970* (Chicago, 1983).

16. May, *The Enlightenment in America* (New York, 1976), xvii. May supplied the very same kind of prefatory candor when he published *The Divided Heart: Essays on Protestantism and the Enlightenment in America* (New York, 1991), 6–14. For an explicit echo from a very different perspective, see Warren I. Susman, *Culture as History: The Transformation of American Society in the Twentieth Century* (New York, 1984), 270.

17. Roger Adelson, "Interview with Joan Jensen," *Historian* 56 (Winter 1994): 246. See also Novick, *That Noble Dream*, 6; Lois W. Banner, "The Irony of Memory: Finding a Los(t) Angeles," *Pacific Historical Review* 63 (Feb. 1994): 1–18.

18. Cronon's autobiographical reflections are particularly impressive because he uses them to show how ignorant we are of the historical determinants that shaped the world we take for granted as "given." Although his childhood impressions of Chicago and its environs were utterly uninformed, they obviously piqued his curiosity since he chose Chicago and its hinterlands as the subject of his Ph.D. dissertation. Cronon, *Nature's Metropolis: Chicago and the Great West* (New York, 1991), 5–8, 371–74, 379–85; Scott, *Making the Invisible Woman Visible* (Urbana, Ill., 1995), xi–xxvii; Lasch, *The True and Only Heaven: Progress and Its Critics* (New York, 1991), 25-37; Meier, *A White Scholar and the Black Community, 1945–1965: Essays and Reflections* (Amherst, Mass., 1992), 3–38; Tuttle, *"Daddy's Gone to War": The Second World War in the Lives of America's Children* (New York, 1993), vii–xii; Bercovitch, *The Rites of Assent*, 1-28; Hutton, *History as an Art of Memory* (Hanover, N.H. 1993), xi–xxv; Zuckerman, *Almost Chosen People: Oblique Biographies in the American Grain* (Berkeley, 1993), 1–20. For the personalizing trend overall, especially among literary historians and critics, see Adam Begley, "The I's Have It," *Lingua Franca* 4 (April 1994): 54–59.

19. Cott, ed., *A Woman Making History: Mary Ritter Beard Through Her Letters*, 44–45; Fox to Boyd, Sept. 23, 1943, Fox papers, Schaffer Library, Union College, Schenectady, N.Y.; Lifton,

"On Becoming a Psychohistorian," in Lifton, *History and Human Survival* (New York, 1970), 5; Barzun, *Clio and the Doctors: Psycho-History, Quanto-History and History* (Chicago, 1974). See also Novick, *That Noble Dream*, 221.

20. Becker, review of L. Cecil Jones, *The Interpretation of History*, in *The Dial*, 59 (Sept. 2, 1915), 148; Du Bois, *Black Reconstruction in America, 1860–1880* (New York, 1935), 714. Du Bois responded subtly regarding this issue. On Sept. 28, 1938, he told Augustus M. Kelley that "I have sympathy for the ideal of cold, impartial history; but that must not be allowed to degenerate as it so often has into insensibility to human suffering and injustice. The scientific treatment of human ills has got to give evil full weight and vividly realize what it means to be among the world's oppressed." (Herbert Aptheker, ed., *The Correspondence of W. E. B. Du Bois* (Amherst, 1976), II: 174.) For the diversity of views early in the twentieth century, see especially Novick, *That Noble Dream*, 101–2.

21. For Pierce and Sydnor, see below. Susan Stout Baker, *Radical Beginnings: Richard Hofstadter and the 1930s* (Westport, Conn., 1985), 239–40; Louis Hyde, ed., *Rat & the Devil: Journal Letters of F. O. Matthiessen and Russell Cheney* (Hamden, Conn., 1978), 12, 17, 26–27, 47–48, 52, 91, 104, 197, 200. See also Novick, *That Noble Dream*, 46.

22. Schlesinger, Jr., to Hofstadter, May 30, 1944, Hofstadter papers, Rare Book and Manuscript Library, Columbia University, New York. See Hofstadter, "U. B. Phillips and the Plantation Legend," *Journal of Negro History* 29 (April 1944): 109–24. Curti to the author, June 20, 1993.

23. Arthur M. Schlesinger, *In Retrospect: The History of a Historian* (New York, 1963); John D. Hicks, *My Life with History: An Autobiography* (Lincoln, Nebr., 1968); Roy F. Nichols, *A Historian's Progress* (New York, 1968); Dexter Perkins, *Yield of the Years: An Autobiography* (Boston, 1969); Thomas A. Bailey, *The American Pageant Revisited: Recollections of a Stanford Historian* (Palo Alto, 1982).

24. Roger Adelson, "Interview with Gilbert C. Fite," *Historian* 56 (Autumn 1993): 2, 12, 14–15. For a similar configuration of the personal and the professional more recently, however, see Thomas C. Holt, "Marking: Race, Race-Making, and the Writing of History," *American Historical Review* 100 (Feb. 1995): 20.

25. Nevins to Arthur M. Schlesinger, Sr., May 24, 1928, Schlesinger papers, box 3, Harvard University Archives, Cambridge, Mass.

26. Hofstadter, *The Progressive Historians: Turner, Beard, Parrington* (New York, 1968), 442.

27. Miller to Percy Holmes Boynton (his Ph.D. supervisor), April 15, 1935, Boynton papers, box 1, Regenstein Library, University of Chicago. In fact, Miller would publish *The New England Mind: The Seventeenth Century* in 1939. For the anxieties of Henry Nash Smith, see Richard Bridgman, "The American Studies of Henry Nash Smith," *American Scholar*, 56 (Spring 1987): 261–63, 268.

28. Hofstadter to Merle Curti, Oct. 10, 1950, Curti papers, box 19. Hofstadter had published his second book, *The American Political Tradition* in 1948, and his third appeared in 1952, *The Development and Scope of Higher Education in the United States*, co-authored with C. DeWitt Hardy. In 1950, the year he wrote to Curti, Hofstadter published five articles.

29. Kahn is quoted in the *New York Times*, Oct. 23, 1972, p. 40. For engaging comments on the futility of being a writer, see Dr. Samuel Johnson, "The Rambler," no. 146 (Aug. 10, 1751), reprinted in Johnson, *Works* (1825), III: 192–96.

30. Interview with Jonathan Spence in Gail Porter Mandell, *Life into Art: Conversations with Seven Contemporary Biographers* (Fayetteville, Ark., 1991), 167. Among Spence's best known books are *Emperor of China* (1974), *The Death of Woman Wang* (1978), *The Gate of Heavenly Peace* (1981), *The Memory Palace of Matteo Ricci* (1984), and *The Search for Modern China* (New York, 1990).

31. Eliot, *Notes Towards the Definition of Culture* (London, 1948), 86.

32. R.W. Southern, "Aspects of the European Tradition of Historical Writing: The Sense of the Past," *Transactions of the Royal Historical Society*, 5th series, 23 (1973): 263. For current perspectives on the "unstable past," see Peter Stansky's review in *Journal of Interdisciplinary History* 25 (Spring 1995): 687, and various essays by Joan W. Scott.

33. Albee, *Who's Afraid of Virginia Woolf?* (New York, 1962), 68.

34. Southern, *The Shape and Substance of Academic History: An Inaugural Lecture Delivered before the University of Oxford on 2 November 1961* (Oxford, 1961), 11.

35. Hall, *V. L. Parrington*, 89–92, 94–96; Hicks, *My Life with History*, 63, 83; Bailey, *American Pageant Revisited*, 28–29, 49–50, 72. For an interesting contrast, see Vincent Harding's description of his dual experience as a graduate student in history at the University of Chicago and, simultaneously, his independent existence as a lay pastor in a small Seventh Day Christian Church on the South Side of Chicago. What he calls "the integration of my personal quest with the academic environment" mattered greatly to him. Interview by Hazel Carby and Don Edwards, "Vincent Harding," in Henry Abelove et al., eds., *Visions of History* (New York, 1983), 221–22.

36. H. R. Trevor-Roper, "The Past and the Present: History and Sociology," *Past and Present*, no. 42 (Feb. 1969): 16; Leonard Krieger, *Ranke: The Meaning of History* (Chicago, 1977), 7, 13; Glenn C. Altschuler, *Andrew D. White: Educator, Historian, Diplomat* (Ithaca, 1979), ch. 12.

37. Jameson to Henry Morse Stephens, Feb. 24, 1919, Stephens papers, box 4, Bancroft Library, University of California, Berkeley. For an exemplary echo of this viewpoint, see Robert H. McNeal (who calls himself a "confused deist agnostic"), "History vs. Theology," *Columbia University Forum* 6 (Fall 1963): 45–48. For a historical overview of the whole problem, see George M. Marsden, *The Soul of the American University: From Protestant Establishment to Established Nonbelief* (New York, 1994), and Peter Steinfels, "Scholar Calls Colleges Biased Against Religion," *New York Times*, Nov. 26, 1993, p. A14.

38. Mack Thompson to the Standing Committee, March 21, 1979, and attachments, in the possession of the author; Tonsor, "Myth, History, and the Problem of Desacralized Time," *Continuity: A Journal of History*, no. 4/5 (Spring/Fall 1982): 21–22. I believe that Tonsor's views would have been shared by such diverse scholars as Lewis W. Spitz, Martin E. Marty, Charles B. Hosmer, and Timothy L. Smith.

39. William H. B. Court, "Growing Up in an Age of Anxiety," in Court, *Scarcity and Choice in History* (London, 1970), 17, 56; Douglas Greenberg and Stanley N. Katz, eds., *The Life of Learning* (New York, 1994), 21; Ross Terrill, *R. H. Tawney and His Times: Socialism as Fellowship* (Cambridge, Mass., 1973), 164, 191, 263–70.

40. M. D. Knowles, "Christopher Dawson," *Proceedings of the British Academy* 57 (1973): 439–52; C. N. L. Brooke, "David Knowles," ibid. 61 (1976): 439–77; Maurice Cowling, "Herbert Butterfield," ibid. 65 (1981): 595–609, esp. 597, 605; John Clive, "The Prying Yorkshireman: Herbert Butterfield and the Historian's Task," in Clive, *Not by Fact Alone: Essays on the Writing and Reading of History* (New York, 1989), esp. 288–92. For a quirky yet intensely interesting close-up of Knowles (especially) and Dawson, see Norman F. Cantor, *Inventing the Middle Ages: The Lives, Works, and Ideas of the Great Medievalists of the Twentieth Century* (New York, 1991), 296–326, 330–31, but esp. 316–17.

41. Toynbee, "I Owe My Thanks," *Saturday Review of Literature* 37 (Oct. 1954): 54; Toynbee, *Experiences* (New York, 1969), 88–91; C. T. McIntire and Marvin Perry, eds., *Toynbee: Reappraisals* (Toronto, 1989), 63–92, 195–226. See also Michael Gauvreau, "Baptist Religion and the Social Science of Harold Innis," *Canadian Historical Review*, 76 (June 1995): 161–204.

42. Davis, "An Appreciation of Roger Anstey," in Christine Bolt and Seymour Drescher, eds., *Anti-Slavery, Religion, and Reform: Essays in Memory of Roger Anstey* (Hamden, Conn., 1980), 12, 14–15. See also Anstey, *The Atlantic Slave Trade and British Abolition, 1760–1810* (Atlantic Highlands, N.J., 1975), esp. 405–6.

43. Link, "The Historian's Vocation," *Theology Today* 19 (April 1962): 75-89, esp. 81, 88; John Milton Cooper, Jr., "The Papers of Woodrow Wilson," OAH *Newsletter* (Nov. 1993): 5. See also George B. Tindall, "The Formative Years," in John Milton Cooper, Jr., and Charles E. Neu, eds., *The Wilson Era: Essays in Honor of Arthur S. Link* (Arlington Heights, Ill., 1991), 7–29, and more generally, Novick, *That Noble Dream*, 408.

44. See, e.g., his five-volume biography of Woodrow Wilson (Princeton, 1947-65), and for the barest traces of Link's own empathetic commitments, vols. I: 94, 321; II: 64–67, 280; III: 45, 420. Link, *The Impact of World War I* (New York, 1969), *The Progressive Era and the Great War, 1896–1920* (New York, 1969), and *Woodrow Wilson and the Progressive Era, 1910–1917* (New York, 1954).

45. See Sydnor, *Slavery in Mississippi* (New York, 1933); *A Gentleman of the Old Natchez Region: Benjamin L.C. Wailes* (Durham, 1938); *The Development of Southern Sectionalism, 1819–1848* (Baton Rouge, 1948); *Gentlemen Freeholders: Political Practices in Washington's Virginia* (Chapel Hill, 1952). For slight traces of Sydnor's Christian concerns in his scholarship, see *Slavery in Mississippi*, 56, 61; *Development of Southern Sectionalism, 1819–1848*, 89, 294, 299–300.

46. Sydnor papers, box 6, Dalton-Brand Research Room, Perkins Library, Duke University, Durham, N.C. The folder containing these sketchy notes is located at the end of Sydnor's correspondence. The notes may have been used for a talk that Sydnor gave in May 1953 to the Men's Club of the First Presbyterian Church of Norfolk, Virginia. One month later he was involved in a serious automobile accident, and he died early in 1954 of a coronary thrombosis.

47. Sydnor, "The Christian as an Interpreter of History," Sydnor papers, box 6.

48. See Kenneth Scott Latourette, "The Christian Understanding of History," *American Historical Review* 54 (Jan. 1949): 259–76; Ronald H. Nash, ed., *Ideas of History* (New York, 1969), I: ch. 9, "The Christian Understanding of History." For a somewhat different sensibility and degree of openness, however, see the work of Frederick B. Tolles (1915–75), once referred to as the "Pope" of Quaker history. His books included *Meeting House and Counting House: The Quaker Merchants of Colonial Philadelphia* (Williamsburg, 1948) and *Quakers and the Atlantic Culture* (New York, 1960), and he edited *The Witness of William Penn* (New York, 1957).

49. May, *Coming to Terms: A Study in Memory and History* (Berkeley, 1987), 304–5; Woodward, *Thinking Back: The Perils of Writing History*, 105-6, 137; Schlesinger, Jr., *The Politics of Hope* (Boston, 1962), 97–125; Greenberg and Katz, eds., *The Life of Learning*, 63.

50. Less frequently mentioned yet expansive and notably influential is the second volume of Niebuhr's *The Nature and Destiny of Man: A Christian Interpretation* (New York, 1943), esp. chs. 1–4 and 10, concerning human destiny and history, the possibilities and limits of history, the fulfillment of history, and "the end of history."

51. See Eric Cochrane, "What Is Catholic Historiography?," *Catholic Historical Review* 61 (April 1975): 169–90; John Lukacs, "The Historiographical Problem of Belief and of Believers: Religious History in the Democratic Age," ibid., 64 (April 1978): 153–67. See also Andrew C. McLaughlin to George Lincoln Burr, Feb. 24, 1909, McLaughlin papers, box 1, Regenstein Library, University of Chicago; and cf. Paul Archambault, "An Interview with Jacques Le Goff," *Historical Reflections* 21 (Winter 1995): 177–80.

52. See May, *Coming to Terms*, passim; May, *The Divided Heart: Essays on Protestantism and the Enlightenment in America* (New York, 1991), 3–32, and, *Ideas, Faiths, and Feelings: Essays on American Intellectual and Religious History, 1952-1982* (New York, 1983), chs. 4, 7–9.

53. Bushman, *Joseph Smith and the Beginnings of Mormonism* (Urbana, 1984), 3.

54. Juanita Brooks, *Quicksand and Cactus: A Memoir of the Southern Mormon Frontier* (Salt Lake City, 1982), xxviii–xxix, xxxii; Walker, ed., *Dale Morgan on Early Mormonism*, 87-88.

55. Levi S. Peterson, "Juanita Brooks: The Mormon Historian as Tragedian," *Journal of Mormon History* 3 (1976): 47, 54. See also Dale Morgan to Fawn M. Brodie, Sept. 10, 1943, and Dec. 22, 1945, Brodie papers, box 7, Marriott Library, Special Collections, University of Utah,

Salt Lake City. In the first of these letters, Morgan commented that Brooks "has a keen mind, extraordinary energy, and great independence of outlook. In fact she is the only professing Mormon for whom I have any respect as a historian and Juanita has her fears about just how orthodox she really is."

56. William Mulder, "Discovering Our Past, Creating Our Future: The Example of Fawn McKay Brodie," remarks read at the University of Utah's Women's Resource Center Conference: "Women of the West," March 8, 1986, six-page TS, Brodie papers, box 4.

57. Fawn Brodie to her parents, May 18 and 24, 1943, Brodie papers, box 2. On November 11, 1945, Dale Morgan empathized with Brodie's fear of hurting her grandmother: "You and I don't really want to upset the beliefs of people who have lived by those beliefs and which give value and meaning to their lives"(Brodie papers, box 7).

58. Morgan to Brodie, Sept. 10, 1943, Brodie papers, box 7; Dean Brimhall to Brodie, March 24, 1946, ibid., box 2.

59. Morgan to Brodie, Jan. 6 and May 15, 1946, Brodie papers, box 7. More than 25 years later, some devout Mormons continued to believe that Fawn's Jewish husband had actually written *No Man Knows My History*. In 1979 Fawn set the record straight in a letter to an LDS high priest living in Ogden. "My book on Joseph Smith," she wrote, "was entirely researched by me, not my late husband. . . . Many people have misunderstood my thanks to him in the preface of my book. The volume would have been a harsher indictment of Joseph Smith had it not been for his influence. I was angered by the obvious nature of the fraud in his writing of the *Book of Mormon*; I felt that his revelations all came out of needs of the moment and had nothing to do with God, and I thought the frantic search for wives in the last four years of his life betrayed a libertine nature that was to me at the time quite shocking. My husband kept urging me to look at the man's genius, to explain his successes, and to make sure that the reader understood why so many people loved him and believed in him. If there is real compassion for Joseph Smith in the book, and I believe there is, it is more a result of the influence of my husband than anyone else." See Revere Hansen to Kenneth W. Godfrey, March 2, 1973, Brodie papers, box 9; Hansen to Brodie, Jan. 20, 1979, ibid.; Brodie to Hansen, Jan. 29, 1979, ibid.

60. Dale Morgan to Brodie, June 15, 1948, ibid., box 7; Alfred L. Bush to Brodie, Aug. 24, 1972, ibid., box 4; Sandra Tanner to Brodie, June 29, 1977, ibid., box 10.

61. Brodie to Jerome Stoffel, Nov. 3, 1967, ibid., box 9. See also same to same, Oct. 18, 1967, ibid.

62. Brodie to Stoffel, May 3, 1968, ibid., box 9. See also a lecture that Brodie gave at the University of Utah in 1970 titled "Can We Manipulate the Past?" Her 17-page typescript is in the Brodie papers, box 69, esp. 3, 7–8. This became the first in a series known as the American West Lectures.

63. Brodie to Everett L. Cooley, Nov. 16, 1970, ibid., box 4; C. M. V. Dobay to Brodie, Feb. 29, 1980, ibid., box 5.

64. Brodie to C. M. V. Dobay, March 4, 1980, ibid.

65. Hexter, "The Historian and His Day"(1954) in Hexter, *Reappraisals in History* (Evanston, Ill., 1961), 7–8; Elton, "The Historian's Social Function," *Transactions of the Royal Historical Society*, 5th series, vol. 27 (1977): 210. Both pieces, of course, follow directly in the footsteps of Herbert Butterfield, *The Whig Interpretation of History* (London, 1931). See also G. R. Elton, "Herbert Butterfield and the Study of History," *Historical Journal* 27 (Sept. 1984): 729–43. For the finest and most succinct statement on the need to strike a balance between detachment and engagement, between respecting the pastness of the past and using history as a weapon in the service of social activism, see Richard Hofstadter, *The Progressive Historians: Turner, Beard, Parrington* (New York, 1968), 464–65.

66. Higham, "Beyond Consensus: The Historian as Moral Critic," *American Historical Review* 67 (April 1962): 619, 621; Henry Glassie, "Meaningful Things and Appropriate Myths:

The Artifact's Place in American Studies," *Prospects* 3 (1977): 29. See also Lifton, *History and Human Survival*, 16. For a rejection of "the kind of monolithic moralism which seems to me the negation of history," see David Donald to David M. Potter, Feb. 12, 1965, Potter papers, box 1, Stanford University Libraries, Special Collections, Stanford, Calif. See also Bernard W. Shee-han, "The Problem of Moral Judgments in History," *South Atlantic Quarterly* 84 (Winter 1985): 37–50.

67. See Merle Curti to Harry Elmer Barnes, April 27, 1952, Barnes papers, box 38, American Heritage Center, University of Wyoming, Laramie; Curti to Barnes, Jan. 7, 1955, ibid., box 43; Stefan F. Blaschke to Allan Nevins, Nov. 1, 1955, with Nevins's undated reply handwritten on p. 2, Nevins papers, box 2, Huntington Library, San Marino, Calif. For the Cold War context of this celebration of objectivity as a hallmark of thought in the free world, see Novick, *That Noble Dream*, 299–300, 374–75.

68. Cochran to Curti, Oct. 10, 1948, Curti papers, box 9.

69. Hofstadter to Curti, [Dec. 1953?], Curti papers, box 19. See also Irving Howe, *A Margin of Hope: An Intellectual Autobiography* (San Diego, 1982), 322. Late in his life Hofstadter explained to a colleague that as an undergraduate, "and at the beginning of my graduate studies I still thought of myself as being basically a Marxist. . . . I am grateful to you for perceiving the radical emphasis in my approach to consensus and doubly grateful for differentiating me from Boorstin, whose work I am not very fond of." Hofstadter to Arthur M. Schlesinger, Jr., March 1, 1968, Hofstadter papers, Rare Book and Manuscript Library, Columbia University, New York. Hofstadter was writing in response to Schlesinger's essay about his work in Marcus Cunliffe and Robin W. Winks, eds., *Pastmasters: Some Essays on American Historians* (New York, 1969), 278–315.

70. Higham to Curti, Feb. 26, 1954, Curti papers, box 19; Curti, "Human Nature in American Thought: Retreat from Reason in the Age of Science," *Political Science Quarterly* 68 (Dec. 1953): 492–510.

71. Blake and Phelps, "History as Social Criticism: Conversations with Lasch," 1311, 1320, 1322. For the ideological diversity of left and radical historians, see Howe, *A Margin of Hope*, 322, and Maurice Isserman, *If I Had a Hammer: The Death of the Old Left and the Birth of the New Left* (New York, 1987).

72. Blake and Phelps, "History as Social Criticism: Conversations with Lasch," 1322, 1329; Fox, "An Interview with Lasch," 4–5, 8–13.

73. Blake and Phelps, "History as Social Criticism: Conversations with Lasch," 1326; Gut-man, *Power & Culture: Essays on the American Working Class* (New York, 1987), 46–47.

74. See Gabriel Kolko to Merle Curti, July 14, 1962, Curti papers, box 23; Eugene D. Genovese, "On Being a Socialist and a Historian," in Genovese, *In Red and Black: Marxian Explorations in Southern and Afro-American History* (New York, 1973), 3–22; Paul Buhle, ed., *History and the New Left: Madison, Wisconsin, 1950-1970* (Philadelphia, 1990), esp. chs. 8, 11, 20, and 24; Elizabeth Fox-Genovese, "Socialist-Feminist American Women's History," *Journal of Women's History* 1 (Winter 1990): 181–210.

75. Mark Naison and Paul Buhle, "David Montgomery," in Abelove et al., *Visions of History*, 174. See also Jonathan M. Wiener, "Radical Historians and the Crisis in American History, 1959–1980," *Journal of American History* 76 (Sept. 1989): 399–434; Howard Zinn, *You Can't Be Neutral on a Moving Train: A Personal History of Our Times* (Boston, 1994). And see Hofstadter's unexpected and warm assessment of C. Wright Mills, written in 1963: "His work was under-taken as a kind of devotional exercise, a personal discipline. . . ." Quoted in Richard Gillam, "Richard Hofstadter, C. Wright Mills, and 'the Critical Ideal,'" *American Scholar* 47 (Winter 1977–78): 85.

76. See Tansill, *Documents Illustrative of the Formation of the Union of the American States* (Washington, D.C., 1927); *America Goes to War* (Boston, 1938); *Back Door to War: The Roosevelt*

Foreign Policy, 1933–1941 (Chicago, 1952); *America and the Fight for Irish Freedom, 1866–1922* (New York, 1957). Arthur Link remembers being assigned *America Goes to War* as an undergraduate at Chapel Hill in 1939.

77. Tansill to Barnes, April 4, 1947, Barnes papers, box 33, American Heritage Center, University of Wyoming, Laramie.

78. Tansill to Barnes, Jan. 23, 1953, ibid., box 40. Two years later Tansill declared that "Leopold is a cheap son-of-a bitch with little scholarship but with enough brass to supply large knockers for every door in America. I have deep contempt for him." Tansill to Barnes, Aug. 31, 1955, ibid., box 43.

79. Tansill to Barnes, April 1, 1956, ibid., box 44. The Georgetown University Archives, Lauinger Library, Washington, D.C., has voluminous material pertaining to Tansill, including correspondence and newspaper clippings concerning controversies.

80. See, but with caution, Marian J. Morton, *The Terrors of Ideological Politics: Liberal Historians in a Conservative Mood* (Cleveland, 1972).

81. Potter to Charles Madison, May 5, 1953, Potter papers, box 22, Department of Special Collections, Stanford University Libraries. Madison (1895–?) had been born in Russia, was Jewish, considered himself a historian and belonged to the American Historical Association.

82. Ibid.

83. Madison to Potter, May 6, 1953, ibid.; Potter to Madison, June 4, 1953, ibid. See also Potter to Madison, June 11 and Sept. 14, 1953, ibid.

84. Potter to Madison, Sept. 14 and Dec. 2, 1953, ibid.; Charles A. Madison, *Leaders and Liberals in 20th Century America* (New York, 1961), esp. 363–411. For another example of Potter's astonishing moderation and judiciousness, see Hugh Davis Graham to Potter, July 13, 1967, Potter papers, box 1.

85. Potter to John [Rosenberg?], May 1965, Potter papers, box 1; Potter, "Interpreting American History," in John A. Garraty, ed., *Interpreting American History: Conversations with Historians* (New York, 1970), II: 325. Potter had reviewed Hartz's book fifteen years earlier in the *Yale Review* 44 (June 1955): 620–22.

86. David Donald to Potter, Dec. 28, 1959, Potter papers, box 3; Woodward to Potter, April 25, 1960, ibid.; Potter to Curti, Jan. 10, 1962, Curti papers, box 34. For Potter's subtle brilliance on Woodward's racial liberalism in relation to his historical writing, see Potter, "C. Vann Woodward," in Cunliffe and Winks, eds., *Pastmasters*, 397–98, 401–2, 406–7.

87. Rayford W. Logan diaries, June 19, 1941, Logan papers, box 3, Manuscript Division, Library of Congress.

88. Pierce to Leslie Decker (*Wisconsin Magazine of History*), March 21, 1957, Pierce papers, box 16, Regenstein Library, University of Chicago. In 1928 Pierce wrote the following to Merle Curti, then teaching at Smith College: "You asked whether I think a woman should have her cake and eat it too. Of course as a professional woman I feel that she should have, but I suppose that in many cases circumstances make it necessary for one to put on a different kind of frosting than she has at first planned" (March 12, 1928, Curti papers, box 33).

89. Schlesinger to Curti, Aug. 14, 1927, Curti papers, box 36; Schlesinger to Pierce, Nov. 5, 1936, Pierce papers, box 15. On May 22, 1940, Carl Wittke sent Pierce a strong recommendation for a recent Oberlin graduate to be a research assistant on Pierce's multivolume history of Chicago. After citing the young woman's many skills, Wittke observed that "she will not disrupt your male staff, although they will find her attractive" (Pierce papers, box 16).

90. Adair to John Monro, May 11, 1967, Adair papers, box 3, Huntington Library, San Marino, Calif. Like Paul Wallace Gates of Cornell, and most of Adair's male contemporaries, aspiring young historians were designated by gender as "men" and "girls". On the problematic issue of women Ph.D.s pursuing a professional career and marriage, see Alma P. Foerster to Charles S. Sydnor, Aug. 29, 1939, and Sydnor to Foerster, Sept. 13, 1939, Sydnor papers, box 3.

91. Kenneth Robert Janken, *Rayford W. Logan and the Dilemma of the African-American Intellectual* (Amherst, 1993), esp. 17, 70–71, 74, 80, 84, 104.

92. Logan diaries, March 16, 1940 [the entry seems to have been remembered and written on Jan. 3, 1943], Jan. 13, 1941, Logan papers, box 3; Janken, *Logan*, 208–9.

93. Logan diaries, Feb. 9, March 20 and 22, 1941, Logan papers, box 3; Janken, *Logan*, 178–79, 194, 218–19. See also the autobiographical memoir by W. Sherman Savage (1890–1980), ten chapters in typescript that stop in 1964, at Huntington Library, San Marino, Calif.

94. John Herbert Roper, *C. Vann Woodward: Southerner* (Athens, Ga., 1987), 165–67; Adair to Howard K. Beale, March 7, 1958, Adair papers, box 3, Huntington Library.

95. Stephenson to Green, Oct. 7, 1956, Stephenson papers., box 13, Perkins Library, Duke University; also Stephenson to Boyd C. Shafer, Oct. 10, 1956, ibid., box 28; Shafer to Stephenson, Oct. 16, 1956, ibid.

96. Green to Stephenson, Oct. 24, 1956, ibid., box 13. See also James G. Randall to Stephenson, July 16, 1948, ibid., box 26; and Franklin, *Race and History: Selected Essays, 1938–1988* (Baton Rouge, 1989), esp. 277–320.

97. Gates to Fred C. Cole, May 8, 1951, Stephenson papers, box 12.

98. Stephenson to Carl Wittke, May 3, 1951, ibid., box 36; Owsley to Stephenson, Oct. 6, 1952, ibid., box 23. Owsley wrote *State Rights in the Confederacy* (Chicago, 1925), *King Cotton Diplomacy: Foreign Relations of the Confederate States of America* (Chicago, 1931), and *Plain Folk of the Old South* (Baton Rouge, 1949).

99. Joseph Mathews to David M. Potter, Jan. 30, 1960, Potter papers, box 3.

100. Ibid.

101. Genovese, "Race and Class in Southern History: An Appraisal of the Work of Ulrich Bonnell Phillips," *Agricultural History* 41 (Oct. 1967): 345–58, followed by the comments of Potter, Stampp, and Elkins, 359–72; Phillips, "The Central Theme of Southern History," *American Historical Review* 34 (Oct. 1928): 30–43; Merton L. Dillon, *Ulrich Bonnell Phillips: Historian of the Old South* (Baton Rouge, 1985).

102. Avery O. Craven to David M. Potter, April 1968, Potter papers, box 1. See also Craven's follow-up, expanding upon his grievance, Aug. 1, 1968, ibid.

103. Joan J. Brumberg and Nancy Tomes, "Women in the Professions: A Research Agenda for American Historians," *Reviews in American History* 10 (June 1982): 276; Jill Ker Conway, *True North: A Memoir* (New York, 1994), 34. See also Gerhard L. Weinberg, "Changes in the Place of Women in the Historical Profession: A Personal Perspective," *History Teacher* 29 (May 1996), 323–27, and Gerda Lerner, "A View from the Women's Side," *Journal of American History*, 76 (Sept. 1989): 446–56.

104. Stephenson to Coulter, Jan. 9, 1946, Stephenson papers, box 7; Coulter to Stephenson, Jan. 12, 1946, ibid. Woodfin edited *Another Secret Diary of William Byrd of Westover, 1739–1741, with Letters & Literary Exercises, 1696–1726* (Richmond, 1942) and published *Nathaniel Beverly Tucker: His Writings and Political Theories, with a Sketch of His Life* (Richmond, 1917).

105. Edward P. Alexander to Nevins, Nevins papers, box 2, Huntington Library. See, in general, Joan W. Scott, "American Women Historians, 1884–1984," in Scott, *Gender and the Politics of History* (New York, 1988), 178–98.

106. Scott does not mention Pierce at all, and there are just two very brief allusions in Jacqueline Goggin, "Challenging Sexual Discrimination in the Historical Profession: Women Historians and the American Historical Association, 1890–1940," *American Historical Review* 97 (June 1992): 793, 800. The most useful biographical information will be found in the "Comments" given at her memorial service at the University of Chicago on November 1, 1974. I am indebted to Professor Emmet Larkin of Chicago for sending me these 30 pages, along with the Department's *Newsletter* for 1976, which contains a substantial obituary.

107. Pierce, *Public Opinion and the Teaching of History in the United States* (New York, 1926),

Pierce, *Civic Attitudes in American School Textbooks* (Chicago, 1930), *Citizens' Organizations and the Civic Training of Youth* (New York, 1933), and *A History of Chicago* (New York, 1937–57), 3 vols. For the circumstances of women, see esp. I: 187–90, II: 295–97, 455–59, 487–89, III: 238, 324, 382. Similarly, according to Barbara Melosh, women artists of the 1930s "left few traces of a recognizably female vision." She also observes that "women operated successfully . . . by adapting male standards of public and artistic discourse." See *Engendering Culture: Manhood and Womanhood in New Deal Public Art and Theater* (Washington, D.C., 1991), 219–20, 227.

108. Pierce to Schlesinger, Aug. 9, 1932, Pierce papers, box 15, Regenstein Library, University of Chicago; Schlesinger to Pierce, Aug. 15, 1932, ibid.

109. Pierce to Schlesinger, Aug. 9, 1932, ibid.

110. Curti to Pierce, Nov. 15, 1940, ibid., box 9; Pierce to Curti, Nov. 26, 1940, ibid. But see Pierce, *History of Chicago*, III: 469, where Pierce takes pride in the fact that in Victorian Chicago, distinctively, women were customarily included in the after-dinner conversation rather than being banished while the men enjoyed their cigars and brandy.

111. Pierce to Schlesinger, Aug. 5, 1941, Pierce papers, box 15; Curti to Pierce, July 15, 1941, ibid., box 9; Pierce to Curti, July 24, 1941, ibid. It should be remembered, however, that movement up the ladder in those days could also be capricious and frustrating for males as well. Leonard W. Labaree (a contemporary of Bessie Pierce), the prominent successor to Charles M. Andrews, remained an untenured assistant professor at Yale for fourteen years. See Benjamin W. Labaree, "Classrooms," *William and Mary Quarterly* 52 (July 1995): 488.

112. Curti to Pierce, May 27, 1949, Pierce papers, box 7. For examples of the kinds of slights that Pierce put up with, see Curti to Pierce, Jan. 18, 1942, ibid., box 9. Curti lamented that Pierce had been ignored by an SSRC committee on local history, sad "in view of the outstanding work you have done in the field." And see Pierce to Curti, July 28, 1944, ibid., box 6, and Curti to Pierce, July 31, 1944, ibid.

113. Pierce to Curti, June 14, 1949, ibid., box 7.

114. Pierce to Bayrd Still, March 21, 1949, Pierce papers, box 16.

115. Pierce to Wendell H. Stephenson, May 27, 1949, Stephenson papers, box 24; Stephenson to George E. Mowry, July 7, 1949, ibid.; Mowry to Stephenson, July 15, 1949, ibid.; Stephenson to Pierce, Aug. 15, 1949, ibid.

116. Pierce to Stephenson, Sept. 15, 1949, ibid., box 8; Billington to Stephenson, July 13, 1950, ibid.; Stephenson to Billington, July 21, 1950, ibid.; Stephenson to Pierce, Aug. 16, 1950, Pierce papers, box 13.

117. Mrs. Clarence S. Paine to Pierce, Nov. 6, 1950, Pierce papers, box 13.

118. Pierce to Barnes, Jan. 21, 1950, ibid., box 6; Barnes to Pierce, Jan. 29, 1950, ibid.; Pierce to Barnes, Feb. 16, 1950, ibid. Barnes recommended Caroline Robbins of Bryn Mawr for a position in early modern English and American history at Chicago, describing her as "a very vital, dynamic sort of person, an Englishwoman but nevertheless very Bryn Mawr. . . . She is a real scholar. . . . She has the encumbrance of a husband who also teaches. . . . She probably would not move without him."

119. Jeannette P. Nichols, who taught political, diplomatic, and economic history at the University of Pennsylvania, not only enjoyed the company of men, she somehow managed simultaneously to be a flirt, a tease, and yet "one of the guys." In 1956 the Mississipi Valley Historical Association (MVHA) held a dinner when the AHA met in St. Louis. Wendell Holmes Stephenson, then president-elect of the MVHA, invited Nichols to speak following the dinner. For her subject she chose "A Half Century of Evolution in American Diplomacy." On December 28, 1956, she sent Stephenson this note: "Set your dear heart at rest, the speaker's dress is *not* new, long, decolléte. But reliable opinion reports that it is not unbecoming. So, it can well dine in the company of one of the handsomest presiding officers the historical guild affords, and he can wear whatever garb pleases him" (Stephenson papers, box 23). Like Pierce, Nichols

managed to walk a tightrope between pleasing femininity and no-nonsense professional assertiveness. Born in 1890, she was Pierce's exact contemporary.

120. Author's conversations with John Hope Franklin, Emmet Larkin, and Karl F. Morrison; quotation from Hutchinson's "Comments" on Nov. 1, 1974, pp. 17, 25 of TS provided the author by Larkin.

121. Peter Loewenberg to Robert Wohl, March 30, 1971, Brodie papers, box 55; Fawn Brodie to Chancellor Charles E. Young, July 16, 1971, ibid. The records of Brodie's employment and her promotion controversy at UCLA are all in ibid. She retired in July 1977 after teaching her last class in the fall quarter of 1976.

122. Erikson to Brodie, Aug. 9, 1972, Brodie papers, box 4; Brodie to Erikson, Aug. 24, 1972, ibid. See also Brodie, *Thomas Jefferson: An Intimate History* (New York, 1974); Erikson, *Dimensions of a New Identity* (New York, 1974), esp. part 1.

123. Quoted in Hyde, ed., *Rat & the Devil: Journal Letters of Matthiessen and Cheney*, 12.

124. John D'Emilio, *Making Trouble: Essays on Gay History, Politics, and the University*, xl–xli, 142–43. See also Henry Abelove, "The Queering of Lesbian/Gay History," *Radical History Review*, no. 62 (Spring 1995): 44–57; Padgug and Wiener, "An Interview with Martin Bauml Duberman," 65–86.

125. Robert Dawidoff, "History . . . But," *New Literary History* 21 (Winter 1990): 403.

126. Ibid., 404.

127. Ibid., 404–406.

128. See Beard to William B. Munro, May 12, [1946?], Munro papers, box 1, Huntington Library, San Marino, Calif.

129. For Koch, *American Historical Review* 77 (Feb. 1972): 246–47; Charles McLaughlin to David M. Potter, May 5, 1959, Potter papers, box 3. *The Papers of Frederick Law Olmsted*, edited by McLaughlin, began to appear in 1977 and the volumes (six so far) continue with McLaughlin now living in semiretirement.

130. William Quentin Maxwell to Nevins, Oct. 7, 1954, and Jan. 10, 1955, Nevins papers (addenda), boxes 1 and 2, Huntington Library; Maxwell, *Lincoln's Fifth Wheel: The Political History of the United States Sanitary Commission* (New York, 1956), v. In 1970 Nevins donated $40,000 to Columbia University to establish a fund "for the assistance of crippled or disabled students," a fund that would bear Maxwell's name. Nevins to the Bursar of Columbia, March 20, 1970, Nevins papers, box 45, Huntington Library. On Jan. 10, 1955, Maxwell told Nevins: "I feel no 'despair'; but isolated. . . ."

131. Longmore, *The Invention of George Washington* (Berkeley, 1988), 4. For an autobiography written by a historian in an earlier generation who remained astonishingly active and productive, despite cerebral palsy, see Earl Schenck Miers (1910–72), *The Trouble Bush* (Chicago, 1966), esp. 85, 152, 156, 208, 242–60, 301, 304.

132. Longmore, *Invention of George Washington*, 34, 63. See also Longmore, "A Note on Language and the Social Identity of Disabled People," *American Behavioral Scientist* 28 (Jan. 1985): 419–23.

133. Longmore, *Invention of George Washington*, 11, 51, 52, 138, 181–82. I am deeply grateful to Longmore for his thoughtful and lengthy letter of Nov. 26, 1995.

134. Longmore, "Uncovering the Hidden History of People with Disabilities," *Reviews in American History* 15 (Sept. 1987): 355–64; Longmore, "Screening Stereotypes: Images of Disabled People in Television and Motion Pictures," *Social Policy* 16 (Summer 1985): 31–37; Longmore, "The Life of Randolph Bourne and the Need for a History of Disabled People," *Reviews in American History* 13 (Dec. 1985): 581–83.

135. Longmore, "The Life of Randolph Bourne," 585–86.

136. Miles, *To All Appearances: Poems New and Selected* (Urbana, 1974), 39.

137. Bridenbaugh to Fred C. Cole, April 7, 1947, Stephenson papers, box 4. David Potter wrote

the following to Lillian Schlissel on April 12, 1965, when she sent him a copy of *The World of Randolph Bourne*: "I am sorry it has taken a book to jar me into writing. I am somewhat pathological about writing letters, or, in lay language, a mess. Like many other delinquent letter-writers, or non-letter writers, I value my friends and am my own worst enemy because I fail to keep in touch with them" (Potter papers, box 1).

138. Curti to the author, June 20, 1993.

139. Adelson, "Interview with Gilbert C. Fite," 3; Winther, "Strictly Personal," *Western Historical Quarterly* 1 (April 1970): 127–28; Stone, autobiographical essay in Greenberg and Katz, eds., *The Life of Learning*, 19; Court, "Growing Up in an Age of Anxiety," 12–13; Toynbee, *Experiences* (New York, 1969), 91; Braudel, "Personal Testimony," *Journal of Modern History* 44 (Dec. 1972): 449. See also Paul Archambault, "An Interview with Jacques Le Goff," *Historical Reflections* 21 (Winter 1995): 167.

140. Becker, "Frederick Jackson Turner," in *Everyman His Own Historian: Essays on History and Politics* (New York, 1935), 191–232; Curti to the author, June 20, 1993. See also Guy Stanton Ford, *On and Off the Campus* (Minneapolis, 1938), 9–11.

141. Athearn, "A View from the High Country," 127–28; Franklin, "A Life of Learning," in Greenberg and Katz, eds., *A Life of Learning*, 76; Ellen Fitzpatrick, "Caroline F. Ware and the Cultural Approach to History," *American Quarterly* 43 (June 1991): 179–80; Hughes, *Gentleman Rebel: The Memoirs of H. Stuart Hughes*, 96, 108.

142. Fox, "An Interview with Lasch," 7; Adelson, "Interview with John Demos," 435; Zuckerman, *Almost Chosen People: Oblique Biographies in the American Grain*, 5–6; Carol Lasser, "Linda Gordon," in Abelove, ed., *Visions of History*, 74. I am fascinated by the number of books dedicated to Warren Susman by scholars who had been his undergraduate students at Rutgers College.

143. Baker, *Radical Beginnings: Richard Hofstadter and the 1930s* (Westport, Conn., 1985), ch. 4 and 115–18, 122–23; Curti to the author, June 20, 1993.

144. For Dwight L. Dumond's repudiation of the work of Ulrich B. Phillips, whom he succeeded at the University of Michigan, see Merton L. Dillon, "Gilbert H. Barnes and Dwight L. Dumond: An Appraisal," *Reviews in American History* 21 (Sept. 1993): 542–51. For Christopher Lasch's establishment of an independent trajectory in relation to Richard Hofstadter, see Fox, "An Interview with Lasch," 9. And see Michael Zuckerman, "Fiction and Fission: Twentieth-Century Writing on the Founding Fathers," in M. Zimmermann, ed., *Religion, Ideology, and Nationalism in Europe and America: Essays Presented in Honor of Yehoshua Arieli* (Jerusalem, 1986), 227–42.

145. Higham to Curti, March 10, 1953, Curti papers, box 19. Higham's essay, "Intellectual History and Its Neighbors," appeared in *Journal of the History of Ideas* 15 (June 1954): 339–47. May served as a discussant at that session.

146. Higham to Curti, March 10, 1953, Curti papers, box 19. Twenty-five years later Higham would be the co-organizer of a conference held in honor of Curti's eightieth birthday. The proceedings were published as John Higham and Paul K. Conkin, eds., *New Directions in American Intellectual History* (Baltimore, 1979).

147. Bailyn's review appeared in the *New England Quarterly* 27 (March 1954): 112–18, the quotations at 115 and 117.

148. Miller, Preface to the Beacon Press edition (Boston, 1961), no pagination.

149. Leonard W. Labaree to Potter, March 3, 1938, Potter papers, box 2.

150. Potter to Ralph H. Gabriel, April 3, 1939, ibid.; Labaree to Potter, April 15, 1939, ibid.

151. Erwin R. Goodenough to Potter, April 27, 1939, ibid. In 1943 Douglass Adair also received a much needed extension of the terminal date for submitting his dissertation, which became an unpublished classic. See Hartley Simpson to Adair, June 22, 1943, Adair papers, box 2, Huntington Library; and Adair, "The Intellectual Origins of Jeffersonian Democracy:

Republicanism, the Class Struggle, and the Virtuous Farmer" (Ph.D. diss., Yale University, 1943).

152. Adair to Thad Tate, Sept. 13, 1965, Adair papers, box 3.

153. For prime examples, see David Riesman to Hofstadter, July 9, 1963, and Daniel Bell to Hofstadter, Feb. 19, 1968, Hofstadter papers, Rare Book and Manuscript Collection, Butler Library, Columbia University, New York. Riesman responded to the manuscript of *Anti-intellectualism in American Life* and Bell responded to *The Progressive Historians*.

154. Woodward to Hofstadter, Aug. 9, 1967, Hofstadter papers. An affectionate postscript to Beatrice Hofstadter is signed "Rabbi C. Vann Finkelstein."

155. Hofstadter, "The Pseudo-Conservative Revolt" in Bell, ed., *The Radical Right* (Garden City, N.Y., 1963); Potter's review appeared in *The New Leader*, June 24, 1963, pp. 26–27.

156. The three extracts that follow are from Hofstadter to Potter, July 2 and 12, 1963, Hofstadter papers; Potter to Hofstadter, July 8, 1963, ibid.

157. See the double necrology in the *Journal of American History* 58 (Sept. 1971): 307–15; Hofstadter, *The Paranoid Style in American Politics and Other Essays* (New York, 1965) and *The Progressive Historians: Turner, Beard, Parrington* (New York, 1968); Don E. Fehrenbacher, ed., *History and American Society: Essays of David M. Potter* (New York, 1973).

158. See Nicholas Lemann, "History Solo: Non-Academic Historians," *American Historical Review* 100 (June 1995): esp. 788–91, 797–98. For the enduring hostility to academic historians felt by James Flexner (Catherine Drinker Bowen's cousin), see Flexner, *Maverick's Progress: An Autobiography* (New York, 1996), 5, 13, 101, 298, 334–36, 424–26, 428–30.

159. Bowen to Powell, April 4, 1965, Bowen papers, box 37, Manuscript Division, Library of Congress. See also Powell to Bowen, June 15 and Aug. 18, 1963, ibid., and Bowen to Powell, Dec. 21, 1965, and one undated but presumably 1965, ibid. In the December 21 letter, when she was beginning her final revisions, Bowen felt especially anguished: "I cant go into the states and their particularites [*sic*] and laws; I havent room, not to mention knowledge. Its horrible. And a popular book on this subject is perhaps an impossibility, a contradiction in terms."

160. Bowen to Edward Weeks, April 20, 1966, ibid. For her summary statement of what she sought to do in this book and its relationship to previous scholarly works on the subject, see Bowen to Weeks, Jan. 22, 1966, ibid.

161. Mumford to Brooks, July 22, 1925, in Robert E. Spiller, ed., *The Van Wyck Brooks–Lewis Mumford Letters: The Record of a Literary Friendship, 1921–1963* (New York, 1970), 31; for an illustration of Brooks's warm encouragement for such a project, combined with a snide critique of Parrington's work, see Brooks to Mumford, Oct. 25, 1931, in ibid., 70–71.

162. Mumford to Brooks, Dec. 27, 1932, ibid., 84, and Brooks's agreement, Dec. 30, 1932, ibid., 85.

163. Powell to the Committee on Admissions, the Century Association, Nov. 15, 1936, Powell papers, box A, Harvard Law School Library, Cambridge, Mass.

164. In addition to the Brooks–Mumford letters, see Wallace Stegner, ed., *The Letters of Bernard DeVoto* (Garden City, N.Y., 1975); George F. Kennan, "Catherine Drinker Bowen (1897–1973)," *Proceedings of the American Academy of Arts and Letters*, 2nd ser., no. 24 (1974): 134–36; and James Thomas Flexner, *Maverick's Progress* (New York, 1996).

165. See Paul Boyer and Stephen Nissenbaum, *Salem Possessed: The Social Origins of Witchcraft* (Cambridge, Mass., 1974); Jacquelyn Dowd Hall et al., *Like a Family: The Making of a Southern Cotton Mill World* (Chapel Hill, 1987); Stanley Elkins and Eric McKitrick, *The Age of Federalism* (New York, 1993).

166. See Morison, "History Through a Beard," in Morison, *By Land and by Sea: Essays and Addresses* (New York, 1953), 328–45; Handlin's review of Williams, *The Contours of American History* in *Mississippi Valley Historical Review* 48 (March 1962): 743–45; Handlin, *Truth in History* (Cambridge, Mass., 1979), 145–48, 156, 161; Lloyd C. Gardner, ed., *Redefining the Past: Essays in*

Diplomatic History in Honor of William Appleman Williams (Corvallis, Ore., 1986), 12–13; Williams, *Contours of American History*, 2nd ed. (New York, 1988), 4–5.

167. Novick, *That Noble Dream*, 475–76. For Ward, see *New York Times*, Aug. 6, 1985, sec. 2, p. 10; and *Proceedings of the American Antiquarian Society* 96 (1986): 21–23. For Gene Wise, see *American Quarterly* 35 (Winter 1983): 457–58.

168. Adair to Morgan, April 6, 1966, Adair papers, box 3. See Adair, "Fame and the Founding Fathers," in Trevor Colbourn, ed., *Fame and the Founding Fathers: Essays by Douglass Adair* (New York, 1974), 3–26.

169. For writings by and about the two scholars that do not mention the episode at all, see William H. McNeill, *Arnold J. Toynbee: A Life* (New York, 1989); Roland N. Stromberg, *Arnold J. Toynbee: Historian for an Age in Crisis* (Carbondale, 1972), 104; *Allan Nevins on History* (New York, 1975), 137–38, 170.

170. See Mort Reis Lewis, "A Country Boy at the Huntington: The Many Lives of Allan Nevins," Lewis papers, box 2, Huntington Library. Lewis was a writer and producer of television programs who had an absorbing interest in history. He also greatly admired Nevins.

171. William H. McNeill, *Arnold J. Toynbee: A Life* (New York, 1989), 244–45; "Interview: Arnold Toynbee," *Playboy* 14 (April 1967): 57–76, 166–69.

172. Toynbee, *Experiences* (New York, 1969), 88–89.

173. Nevins to Lillian K. Bean, Oct. 1, 1964, Nevins papers, box 45, Huntington Library; interview with Lillian K. Bean by Mort Reis Lewis (Nov. 1970), 47-page TS, p. 2, ibid.

174. Nevins to Bean, May 19, 1970, Nevins papers, box 45. See also Nevins's journal for Feb. 26, 1966, Nevins papers, box 32, Butler Library, Columbia University, New York.

175. Toynbee to Nevins, April 23, 1967, Nevins papers, box 44, Huntington Library.

176. See Meyer Levin, "Abraham Lincoln Through the Picture Tube," *Reporter* 8 (April 14, 1953): 31–33; Laurence Bergreen, *James Agee: A Life* (New York, 1984), 368–74, esp. 373–74.

177. Nevins's journals are with his papers at the Rare Book and Manuscript Collection, Butler Library, Columbia University. Because he typed them himself, there are a fair number of typographical errors. It would serve no useful purpose to retain them, so I have silently corrected them. A scattering of *sic*s would only distract the reader.

178. Letter dated May 2, 1967, in Christian B. Peper, ed., *An Historian's Conscience: The Correspondence of Arnold J. Toynbee and Columba Cary-Elwes, Monk of Ampleforth* (Boston, 1986), 477–78.

179. *Los Angeles Times*, April 30, 1967, pp. 3, 24.

180. Ibid.

181. Interview with Lillian K. Bean, Oct. 1971, p. 33, Nevins papers, Huntington Library; interview with John Loftis and John Niven by the author, March 15, 1994, at the Huntington Library.

182. Toynbee to Nevins, Aug. 2, 1967, Nevins papers, box 44, Huntington Library; Nevins to Toynbee, March 3, 1969, ibid., box 45; *New York Times*, March 6, 1971, p. 1.

183. Eric Goldman, *John Bach McMaster: American Historian* (Philadelphia, 1943), 12–13; Miller, *Errand into the Wilderness* (Cambridge, Mass., 1956), vii.

184. See Ray Allen Billington, *Frederick Jackson Turner: Historian, Scholar, Teacher* (New York, 1973), 37, 41, 153, 236–37, 322–23, 325–26, 376–77, 433–35.

185. Robert V. Hine, *Second Sight* (Berkeley, 1993).

186. Williams, "Culture Is Ordinary" (1958), in Williams, *Resources of Hope: Culture, Democracy, Socialism* (London, 1989), 3–18.

187. Einstein, "Autobiographical Note," in Paul A. Schilpp, ed., *Albert Einstein: Philosopher-Scientist* (Evanston, Ill., 1949), 2–95, quotation at 5–7. I kept this shrewd observation very much in mind when writing my own autobiographical essay in 1995. See "Michael Kammen," *Contemporary Authors: Autobiography Series* 23 (Detroit, 1996): 133–63.

188. Polanyi, *Personal Knowledge: Towards a Post-Critical Philosophy* (Chicago, 1958).

189. Watson, *The Double Helix: A Personal Account of the Discovery of the Structure of DNA* (New York, 1968). See also Alberta Arthurs, "The Humanities in the 1990s," in Arthur Levine, ed., *Higher Learning in America, 1980–2000* (Baltimore, 1993), 262–63.

190. John Updike, *Self-Consciousness: Memoirs* (New York, 1989), 209.

Chapter 2
Culture and the State in America

1. Gingrich, "Cutting Cultural Funding: A Reply," *Time*, Aug. 21, 1995, pp. 70–71.

2. A. Hunter Dupree, *Science in the Federal Government: A History of Policies and Activities* (1957; rpt., Baltimore, 1986), 215–20, 293; Richard McKinzie, *The New Deal for Artists* (Princeton, 1973), 151–54, 185; Gary O. Larson, *The Reluctant Patron: The United States Government and the Arts, 1943–1965* (Philadelphia, 1983), 42, 221.

3. J. Mark Davidson Schuster, *Supporting the Arts: An International Comparative Study* (Washington, D.C., 1985); Richard M. Merelman, *Partial Visions: Culture and Politics in Britain, Canada, and the United States* (Madison, Wisc., 1991).

4. See Marlise Simons, "France to Form New Body to Further Protect Culture," *New York Times*, Feb. 25, 1996, p. 12.

5. Horace Kallen, *Culture and Democracy in the United States: Studies in the Group Psychology of the American Peoples* (New York, 1924), 123.

6. Cited in Stephen Miller, *Excellence & Equity: The National Endowment for the Humanities* (Lexington, Ky., 1984), 21–22.

7. Congressional Record, 89th Cong., 2 sess., Sept. 19, 1966, p. 22957.

8. See Gail Levin, *Edward Hopper: An Intimate Biography* (New York, 1995), 277; McKinzie, New Deal for Artists, 58; Jerre Mangione, *The Dream and the Deal: The Federal Writers' Project, 1935–1943* (Boston, 1972), 102–3; Michael Kammen, *The Lively Arts: Gilbert Seldes and the Transformation of Cultural Criticism in the United States* (New York, 1996), 11–12, 200, 319, 371.

9. Russell Lynes, Confessions of a Dilettante (New York, 1966), 22–23. As late as 1953 symphony orchestra directors were almost unanimously opposed to any government subvention for orchestras. They preferred to rely upon socially elite patrons and foundations. See Alice Goldfarb Marquis, *Art Lessons: Learning from the Rise and Fall of Public Arts Funding* (New York, 1995), 30, 242–43.

10. Alfred Runte, *National Parks: The American Experience* (Lincoln, Nebr., 1979), esp. chs. 2 and 3; Hal Rothman, *Preserving Different Pasts: The American National Monuments* (Urbana, Ill., 1989).

11. Marquis, *Art Lessons*, 170–71; Schuster, *Supporting the Arts*. In 1991 private individuals contributed $8.8 billion to the arts and humanities in tax deductible donations, a figure widely noticed and deeply envied abroad.

12. Charles C. Mark, *A Study of Cultural Policy in the United States* (Paris, 1969), 11. For astute historical background, see Stanley N. Katz, "Influences on Public Policies in the United States," in *The Arts and Public Policy in the United States*, ed. W. McNeil Lowry (Englewood Cliffs, N.J., 1984), 23–37. Cf. Margaret Jane Wyszomirski, "The Politics of Art: Nancy Hanks and the National Endowment for the Arts," in *Leadership and Innovation: A Biographical Perspective on Entrepreneurs in Government*, eds. Jameson W. Doig and Erwin C. Hargrove (Baltimore, 1987), 207–45, esp. 219–20.

13. Marquis, *Art Lessons*, 88; Michael Straight, *Twigs for an Eagle's Nest: Government and the Arts, 1965-1978* (New York, 1979), 96; Michael Macdonald Mooney, *The Ministry of Culture: Connections Among Art, Money, and Politics* (New York, 1980), 49, 250–51. More than one scholar considers it a functional "myth" that the U.S. has no national arts policy. See Margaret Jane

Wyszomirski, "Federal Cultural Support: Toward a New Paradigm?," *Journal of Arts Management, Law and Society* 25 (Spring 1995): 76–77.

14. Marquis, *Art Lessons*, 157; Livingston Biddle, *Our Government and the Arts: A Perspective from the Inside* (New York, 1988), ch. 55, esp. 398–99; Thomas J. Downey interview by Michael Kammen, Jan. 11, 1996. Cf. Samuel Lipman, "The State of National Cultural Policy," in Andrew Buchwalter, ed., *Culture and Democracy: Social and Ethical Issues in Public Support for the Arts and Humanities* (Boulder, 1992), 47–57.

15. Miller, *Excellence & Equity*, 54; Terri Lynn Cornwell, "Party Platforms and the Arts," in *Art, Ideology, and Politics*, eds. Judith H. Balfe and Margaret Jane Wyszomirski (New York, 1985), 252–53.

16. Marquis, *Art Lessons*, 42, 96–97.

17. Ibid., 93; H. R. Haldeman, *The Haldeman Diaries: Inside the Nixon White House* (CD-ROM) (Santa Monica, Sony ImageSoft, 1994), Nov. 11 and 20, 1972.

18. August Heckscher interview by Michael Kammen, Dec. 19, 1995; for Kennedy's vagueness on what the government might actually do in support of culture, see his "Remarks at Amherst College upon Receiving an Honorary Degree, October 26, 1963," in *Public Papers of the Presidents of the United States: John F. Kennedy, Containing the Public Messages, Speeches, and Statements of the President, Jan. 1 to Nov. 22, 1963*, 3 vols. (Washington, 1962–64), III: ch. 16, esp. 427, 448, 450.

19. Rhodri Windsor Liscombe, *Altogether American: Robert Mills, Architect and Engineer, 1781–1855* (New York, 1994).

20. For raised eyebrows by art critics in response to this innovation, especially its emphasis on modern art, see Edward Alden Jewell, "Eyes to the Left," *New York Times*, Oct. 6, 1946, sec. 2, p. 8. For congressional resistance and actual curtailment in 1947, see *New York Times*, May 6, 1947, pp. 1, 5.

21. Gilbert Seldes, "MacLeish: Minister of Culture," *Esquire* 23 (June 1945): 103; Taylor D. Littleton and Maltby Sykes, *Advancing American Art: Painting, Politics, and Cultural Confrontation at Mid-Century* (Tuscaloosa, 1989); Jane De Hart Mathews, "Art and Politics in Cold War America," *American Historical Review* 81 (Oct. 1976): 762–87; obituary of Willis Conover, *New York Times*, May 19, 1996, p. 35.

22. Peter Coleman, *The Liberal Conspiracy: The Congress for Cultural Freedom and the Struggle for the Mind of Postwar Europe* (New York, 1989); Christopher Lasch, "The Cultural Cold War: A Short History of the Congress for Cultural Freedom," in *Towards a New Past: Dissenting Essays in American History*, ed. Barton J. Bernstein (New York, 1968), 348–49.

23. Quoted in Coleman, *Liberal Conspiracy*, 234. For the CIA's public defense of its policy, see Thomas W. Braden, "I'm Glad the CIA Is 'Immoral'," *Saturday Evening Post* 240 (May 20, 1967): 12, 14.

24. Mary W. M. Hargreaves, *The Presidency of John Quincy Adams* (Lawrence, 1985), 165-72; Adams's first annual message to Congress, Dec. 6, 1825, in James D. Richardson, comp., *Messages and Papers of the Presidents, 1789-1897* (Washington, D.C., 1899), II: 311–17.

25. See William Stanton, *The Great United States Exploring Expedition of 1838–1842* (Berkeley, 1975); William H. Goetzmann, *Exploration and Empire: The Explorer and the Scientist in the Winning of the American West* (New York, 1966); Wallace Stegner, *Beyond the Hundredth Meridian: John Wesley Powell and the Second Opening of the West* (Boston, 1954).

26. Wilcomb E. Washburn, "Joseph Henry's Conception of the Purpose of the Smithsonian Institution," in *A Cabinet of Curiosities: Five Episodes in the Evolution of American Museums*, ed. Walter Muir Whitehill (Charlottesville, Va., 1967), 113.

27. Ibid., 145–46.

28. *Annual Report of the Board of Regents of the Smithsonian Institution . . . for the Year Ending June 30, 1904* (Washington, D.C., 1905), 5–6.

244 | *Notes to Pages 84–88*

29. Victoria de Grazia, "Mass Culture and Sovereignty: The American Challenge to European Cinemas, 1920–1960," *Journal of Modern History* 61 (March 1989): 59; Ariel Dorfman and Armand Mattelart, *How to Read Donald Duck: Imperialist Ideology in the Disney Comic* (New York, 1975), 18–19.

30. See, among others, Mangione, *The Dream and the Deal: The Federal Writers' Project, 1935–1943*; Karal Ann Marling, *Wall-to-Wall America: A Cultural History of Post-Office Murals in the Great Depression* (Minneapolis, 1982); Barbara Melosh, *Engendering Culture: Manhood and Womanhood in New Deal Public Art and Theater* (Washington, D.C., 1991); and Michael Kammen, *Mystic Chords of Memory: The Transformation of Tradition in American Culture* (New York, 1991), ch. 14.

31. Quoted in Mangione, *The Dream and the Deal*, 321–22. See also Melosh, *Engendering Culture*; Jane De Hart Mathews, *The Federal Theatre, 1935–1939: Plays, Relief, and Politics* (Princeton, 1967); and Carol Brightman, *Writing Dangerously: Mary McCarthy and Her World* (New York, 1992), 258.

32. Marcia Pointon, "Imaging Nationalism in the Cold War: The Foundation of the American National Portrait Gallery," *Journal of American Studies* 26 (Dec. 1992): 368; Joe Klein, *Woody Guthrie: A Life* (New York, 1980), 363.

33. *New York Times*, Sept. 29, 1954, p. A25. See also Karal Ann Marling, *As Seen on TV: The Visual Culture of Everyday Life in the 1950s* (Cambridge, Mass., 1994), 270.

34. *New York Times*, Sept. 29, 1954, p. A25.

35. "The New Role for Culture," *Life*, Dec. 26, 1960, pp. 44–45. See also William Attwood, "A New Look at America," *Look*, July 12, 1955, pp. 48–54.

36. Heckscher, "The Quality of American Culture," in *Goals for Americans: Programs for Action in the Sixties* (New York, 1960), 141. See also Heckscher, *The Public Happiness* (New York, 1962) and *The Arts and the National Government: A Report to the President* (Washington, 1963).

37. On the morning of November 22, 1963, the *New York Times* announced that Richard N. Goodwin, not yet 32 years of age, would succeed Heckscher, who had left the position in June. The article noted that many in Washington were puzzled by the delay in naming a successor. One observer said: "You hear a lot of talk about culture in this town, but there's not much action." (p. 34). See Richard N. Goodwin, *Remembering America: A Voice from the Sixties* (Boston, 1988), 222–25.

38. Arthur M. Schlesinger, Jr., *The Politics of Hope* (Boston, 1962), 254–61, esp. 255; James L. Baughman, *The Republic of Mass Culture: Journalism, Filmmaking, and Broadcasting in America since 1941* (Baltimore, 1992), 95.

39. Schlesinger, *Politics of Hope*, 259–60.

40. See Milton C. Cummings, "To Change a Nation's Cultural Policy: The Kennedy Administration and the Arts in the United States, 1961–1963," in *Public Policy and the Arts*, ed. K. V. Mulcahy and C. R. Swaim (Boulder, 1982), 141–68; Milton C. Cummings, "Government and the Arts: An Overview," in *Public Money and the Muse*, ed. Stephen Benedict (New York, 1991), 31–79.

41. Ronald Berman, *Culture and Politics* (Lanham, Md., 1984), ch. 8; Mondale is quoted in Mooney, *Ministry of Culture*, 21. Whether or not the humanities can "provide a level of excellence toward which all should strive and through which all can derive pleasure" was the essential focus of a major conference concerning "Government and the Humanities" held in December 1978 at the Lyndon B. Johnson School of Public Affairs at the University of Texas at Austin. See *Government and the Humanities: Toward a National Cultural Policy*, ed. Kenneth W. Tolo (Austin, Texas, 1979), 1–2, 7–8, 28, 33–34, 38, 70–71, 74, 131. For a comment by Mrs. Mondale similar to the one quoted above, see ibid., 7–8.

42. See Tolo, ed., *Government and the Humanities*, 134 and passim; letter to the editor from Judith Huggins Balfe, *New York Times*, March 22, 1995, p. A18; Joseph Duffey to the author,

Jan. 18, 1996.

43. Straight, *Twigs for an Eagle's Nest*, 175; Marquis, *Art Lessons*, 165, quoting Frank Hodsoll in 1981 when he was sworn in as the chairman of NEA; Livingston Biddle interview by Michael Kammen, Jan. 11, 1996.

44. See Marquis, *Art Lessons*, 180; interview with Livingston Biddle, Jan. 11, 1996.

45. Biddle, *Our Government and the Arts*, 319–20, 330–31; Berman, *Culture and Politics*, 47, 148, 151-58; Marquis, *Art Lessons*, 106–8, 110, 112, 139, 229; Margaret Jane Wyszomirski, "The Politics of Arts Policy: Subgovernment to Issue Network," in *America's Commitment to Culture: Government and the Arts*, eds. Kevin J. Mulcahy and Wyszomirski (Boulder, 1995), 58.

46. Jeffrey Love, "Sorting Out Our Roles: The State Arts Agencies and the NEA," *Journal of Arts Management and the Law* 21 (Fall 1991): 215–26; Jonathan Katz interview (director of the National Assembly of State Arts Agencies) by Michael Kammen, Jan. 10, 1996, and pamphlets received from Mr. Katz; seminar led by Robert L. Lynch (president of the National Assembly of Local Arts Agencies), Feb. 13, 1996, at the American Council of Learned Societies in New York City.

47. For Charles Frankel's version of this phrasing in 1978, see Tolo, ed., *Government and the Humanities*, 124. Letters from Jamil Zainaldin (president of the Federation of State Humanities Councils, to Michael Kammen, Dec. 4 and 12, 1995 (in author's possession), accompanied by brochures and pamphlets.

48. See Monty Noam Penkower, *The Federal Writers' Project: A Study in Government Patronage of the Arts* (Urbana, 1977), 26–27, 29, 31–33, 39, 48, 50, 98.

49. For illustrations of grass-roots support for retaining the national endowments and the state-based councils, see *New Orleans Times-Picayune*, Jan. 15, 1995; *Maine Sunday Telegram*, Jan. 22, 1995, p. 4c; *Wichita Eagle*, Jan. 30, 1995, p. 11A; *Hartford Courant*, Feb. 8, 1995, pp. A1, A8; *Boston Sunday Globe*, April 23, 1995, p. 2NH; *Albuquerque Journal*, June 19, 1995, p. A7; *Box Elder News Journal* (Brigham City, Utah), Aug. 9, 1995, p. 2. On Aug. 21, 1995, radio station KPBS of northern California did a program on the impact of humanities funding in northern California. Similar programs aired in other states. On April 7, 1995, the CBS Evening News "Eye on America" did a close-up of "The Piney Woods Opry" in Abita Springs, La. Similar close-ups appeared on the other major networks.

50. See McKinzie, *New Deal for Artists*; Marling, *Wall-to-Wall America*; Melosh, *Engendering Culture*.

51. See Fannie Taylor and Anthony L. Barresi, *The Arts at a New Frontier: The National Endowment for the Arts* (New York, 1984); Mulcahy and Wyszomirski, eds., *America's Commitment to Culture: Government and the Arts*.

52. There were 160 local arts agencies in 1965; there are 3800 in 1996. In 1983 state support for the NEH state humanities councils was $150,000. By 1995 it was close to $3 million.

53. See Nina Kressner Cobb, *Looking Ahead: Private Sector Giving to the Arts and the Humanities* (Washington, 1995); Commission on the Humanities, *The Humanities in American Life* (Berkeley, 1980); and Merrill D. Peterson, *The Humanities and the American Promise: Report of the Colloquium on the Humanities and the American People* (Chicago, 1987).

54. *Annals of the American Academy of Political and Social Science* 471 (Jan. 1984), an issue devoted to "Paying for Culture," esp. 117–31. For Spain see *New York Times Sunday Magazine*, Oct. 4, 1992, p. 27; *New York Times*, June 19, 1993, p. 1.

55. See Robert Wangermée, *Cultural Policy in France* (Strasbourg, 1991); Antoine Bernard, *Le Ministère des affaires culturelles et la mission culturelle de la collectivité* (Paris, 1968).

56. See John Rockwell, "French Culture Under Socialism," *New York Times*, March 24, 1993, p. C15; *Ministère de la culture, de la communication et des grands travaux* (Paris, 1990), an elegant promotional booklet.

57. Schuster, *Supporting the Arts*, 18.

58. Janet Minihan, *The Nationalization of Culture: The Development of State Subsidies to the Arts in Great Britain* (New York, 1977); Raymond Williams, "The Arts Council," in Williams, *Resources of Hope: Culture, Democracy, Socialism* (London, 1989), 41–55. The essay dates from 1979.

59. For helpful information and insights supporting the four paragraphs that follow, see Frederick Dorian, *Commitment to Culture: Art Patronage in Europe, Its Significance for America* (Pittsburgh, 1964); Milton C. Cummings, Jr., and Richard S. Katz, "Government and the Arts: An Overview," in *The Patron State*, eds. Cummings and Katz (New York, 1987), 5–7; John Pick, *The Arts in a State: A Study of Government Arts Policies from Ancient Greece to the Present* (Bristol, Eng., 1988).

60. See Martin Warnke, *The Court Artist: On the Ancestry of the Modern Artist*, 2nd edition (Cambridge, Eng., 1993); Andrew McClellan, *Inventing the Louvre: Art, Politics, and the Origins of the Modern Museum in Eighteenth-Century Paris* (Cambridge, Eng., 1994); Cecil Gould, *Trophy of Conquest: The Musée Napoléon and the Creation of the Louvre* (London, 1965).

61. Minihan, *The Nationalization of Culture: The Development of State Subsidies to the Arts in Great Britain*, esp. 9, 12, 18; Shannon Hunter Hurtado, "The Promotion of the Visual Arts in Britain, 1835–1860," *Canadian Journal of History* 28 (April 1993): 59–80.

62. John S. Harris, *Government Patronage of the Arts in Great Britain* (Chicago, 1970).

63. There is an unnoticed lesser irony. In 1989, the very year of the Mapplethorpe brouhaha, Beijing's Museum of Fine Arts in the puritanical Peoples Republic of China mounted an exhibition of nude paintings in an effort to stimulate ticket sales. The show set a new attendance record for the museum! See also Jianying Zha, *China Pop* (New York, 1995), 105.

64. See Schuster, *Supporting the Arts*, 1, 41, 48; Dorian, *Commitment to Culture*, 446–47; Christopher Price, "Culture in a Cold Climate" and Hans F. Dahl, "In the Market's Place: Cultural Policy in Norway," both in *Annals of the American Academy of Political and Social Science* 471 (Jan. 1984): 122, 123, 127; "Canada Council Wants Writers' Money," *Toronto Globe and Mail*, May 10, 1995, p. A21; "A Czech Wields Hatchet on Arts," *New York Times*, Nov. 14, 1995, p. C13.

65. Gustave Flaubert to Louise Colet, [Dec. 28, 1853], in *The Letters of Gustave Flaubert, 1830–1857*, ed. and trans. Francis Steegmuller, 2 vols. (Cambridge, Mass., 1980), I, 206.

66. See Albert Jay Nock, *Our Enemy, the State* (New York, 1935); Wilfred M. McClay, *The Masterless: Self and Society in Modern America* (Chapel Hill, 1994), 222–23.

67. William J. Keens, "The Arts Caucus: Coming of Age in Washington," *American Arts* 14 (March 1983): 16–21; Thomas J. Downey interview by Michael Kammen, Jan. 11, 1996.

68. For the view that absolute partnership between state and national entities is unattainable because achieving a consensus among all of the diverse sectors and policy-makers, public and private, is simply impossible, see Paul J. DiMaggio, "Can Culture Survive the Marketplace?," in *Nonprofit Enterprise in the Arts: Studies in Mission and Constraint*, ed. Paul J. DiMaggio (New York, 1986), 73.

69. Jamil Zainaldin interview by Michael Kammen, Jan. 11, 1996.

70. Merrill D. Peterson, "The Case for the Public Humanities," in *The Humanities and the American Promise* (Report of the Colloquium on the Humanities and the American People), (Austin, Tex., Oct. 1987), 5–19; *National Task Force on Scholarship and the Public Humanities* (American Council of Learned Societies Occasional Paper, No. 11, New York, 1990); Frankel is quoted in Miller, *Excellence and Equity*, 130.

71. *Art Journal* 48 (Winter 1989) devoted a special issue to "Critical Issues in Public Art"; Margaret Jane Wyszomirski, "Public Art Issues," in *Arts and the States: Current Legislation*, ed. Catherine Underhill (Denver, 1988), 3; Casey Nelson Blake, "An Atmosphere of Effrontery: Richard Serra, *Tilted Arc*, and the Crisis of Public Art," in *The Power of Culture: Critical Essays in American History*, eds. Richard Wightman Fox and T. J. Jackson Lears (Chicago, 1993), 270–71.

72. See James J. Sheehan, *German History, 1770–1866* (New York, 1989), chs. 3, 6, 9, 13.

73. Adams, "The Tendency of History" (Dec. 12, 1894), in Henry Adams, *The Degradation of the Democratic Dogma*, intro. by Brooks Adams (1919; rpr., New York, 1969), 125.

74. See Hofstadter, *Anti-Intellectualism in American Life* (New York, 1963).

Chapter 3
Temples of Justice: The Iconography of Judgment and American Culture

1. *New York Times*, September 24, 1889, p. 8; December 8, 1889, p. 11; December 15, 1889, p. 3.

2. Fred Lewis Pattee, ed., *The Poems of Phillip Freneau: Poet of the American Revolution* (Princeton 1902–7), III: 191–92. Late in the nineteenth century, however, Henry Adams chided his younger brother, Brooks Adams, "that you, with your lawyer's method, only state sequences of fact, and explain no causes." B. Adams, *The Emancipation of Massachusetts: The Dream and the Reality*, with an Introduction by Perry Miller (Boston, 1962), xxxv.

3. James Bryce, *The American Commonwealth*, 2nd edition (New York, 1891), I: 248.

4. Drawn from a document prepared by John H. Powell for Catherine Drinker Bowen around 1965. Bowen Papers, Box 37, Manuscript Division, Library of Congress, Washington, D.C. For a different emphasis, see Richard E. Ellis, *The Jeffersonian Crisis: Courts and Politics in the Young Republic* (New York, 1971), esp. ch. 11.

5. James Madison, *The Federalist*, Number 51, in Jacob E. Cooke, ed., *The Federalist* (Middletown, Conn., 1961), 352. See also Michael Kammen, " 'The Rights of Property and the Property in Rights': The Problematic Nature of 'Property' in the Political Thought of the Founders and the Early Republic," in Ellen F. Paul and Howard Dickman, eds., *Liberty, Property, and the Foundations of the American Constitution* (Albany, 1989), 1–22.

6. George Washington to Theodorick Bland, April 4, 1783, in John W. Fitzpatrick, ed., *The Writings of George Washington* (Washington, D.C., 1938), XXVII: 294; George Washington to John Jay, May 18, 1786, in ibid., XXVIII:431–32.

7. See Edward Muir, *Civic Ritual in Renaissance Venice* (Princeton, 1981), 288; John Locke, *First Treatise of Civil Government*, in Peter Laslett, ed., *Two Treatises of Government* (New York, 1970), ch. 4, sec. 42.

8. Charles S. Hyneman, and Donald S. Lutz, eds., *American Political Writing During the Founding Era, 1760–1805* (Indianapolis, 1983), 704; Sandra F. VanBurkleo, " 'Honor, Justice, and Interest': John Jay's Republican Politics and Statesmanship on the Federal Bench," *Journal of the Early Republic* 4 (Fall 1984): 239–74; Richard Polenberg, *Fighting Faiths: The Abrams Case, the Supreme Court, and Free Speech* (New York, 1987), 77–78; Langdon Mitchell, *Understanding America* (New York, 1927), 195; George H. Nash, *The Conservative Intellectual Movement in America since 1945* (New York, 1976), 236, 241.

9. Located in Old Sturbridge Village, Massachusetts (acc. no. 57.1.9).

10. See *Philadelphia: Three Centuries of American Art, Bicentennial Exhibition, April 11–October 10, 1976* (Philadelphia, 1976), 260–61; Stanley Idzerda, A. C. Loveland, and M. H. Miller, *Lafayette, Hero of Two Worlds: The Art and Pageantry of His Farewell Tour of America, 1824–1825* (Flushing, N.Y., 1989), 127; and W. H. Faude, "Old State House, Hartford, Connecticut," *Antiques* 117 (March 1980): 626–33, esp. 629.

11. Muir, *Civic Ritual in Renaissance Venice*, 114; Baldassare Peruzzi (Siena 1481–1536), *Allegory of Justice* (High Museum of Art, Atlanta, Georgia (acc. no. 71.9)). In Trogir, Yugoslavia, near Split, the city loggia, located in the town square, has a relief of Justice carved in marble by Nicholas of Florence in 1471.

12. For a subsequent example and perpetuation of the tradition, see Duncan Ferguson, *Justice* (1935), a plaster figure created for the federal courthouse in Newark, New Jersey. *American Art*

in the Newark Museum: Paintings, Drawings and Sculpture (Newark, N.J., 1981), 406.

13. James Wilson, "Of the Nature of Courts," in Robert G. McCloskey, ed., *The Works of James Wilson* (Cambridge, Mass., 1967), II: 495.

14. See Katharine Fremantle, "The Open *Vierschaar* of Amsterdam's Seventeenth-Century Town Hall as a Setting for the City's Justice," *Oud Holland* 77, no. 3 (1962): 205–34; Marian M. Ohman, "Diffusion of Foursquare Courthouses to the Midwest, 1785–1885," *Geographical Review* 72 (April 1982): 171–89, is useful but does not pursue iconographic or symbolic aspects.

15. In seventeeth-century America, a great many congregations initially met in secular town houses or meetinghouses. That did not mean that churches were socially unimportant. It simply meant that separate public structures used only as churches were a luxury that most communities could not initially afford. The same was true of courthouses, but that phenomenon endured much longer. For "rude taverns" serving as courthouses in the 1840s and 1850s, see C. Peter Magrath, *Morrison R. Waite: The Triumph of Character* (New York, 1963), 43–44. A. Wighe's *Rural Court Scene* (1849) depicts a trial being held in a barn, but with the principals rather nattily dressed. See H. W. Williams, Jr., *Mirror to the American Past: A Survey of American Genre Painting, 1750–1900* (Greenwich, Conn., 1973), fig. 93.

16. See Russell Smith, *Old Courthouse* (1835), which depicts a structure once located in Philadelphia at Second and Market streets that was built in 1708 and demolished in 1837 (painting in the Historical Society of Pennsylvania, Philadelphia). See also *Court or Town House Square, Salem [Massachusetts] 1830*, which shows the courthouse designed by Samuel McIntire in 1785 and demolished in 1839 (oil-on-panel painting in Essex Institute, Salem, Massachusetts). The Baltimore Museum of Art has a blue ceramic plate that shows the Baltimore County Courthouse erected in 1808 and 1809, and destroyed by fire in 1835 (acc. no. 30.65.76).

17. See Robert Bishop, *American Folk Sculpture* (New York, 1974), 22. *Felon* is now incarcerated in the Rhode Island Historical Society, Providence.

18. Idzerda et al., *Lafayette, Hero of Two Worlds*, 114–15; Morton Keller, *The Art and Politics of Thomas Nast* (New York, 1968), fig. 145.

19. Polenberg, *Fighting Faiths*, 258; Michael Kammen, *A Machine That Would Go of Itself: The Constitution in American Culture* (New York, 1986), 266–69.

20. There is an elegant view of Richmond (ca. 1796) by Benjamin Henry Latrobe, featuring the temple-like statehouse (Maryland Historical Society, Baltimore).

21. Eudora Welty, *One Writer's Beginnings* (Cambridge, Mass., 1984), 47.

22. For an admirable survey, see Herbert A. Johnson and Ralph K. Andrist, *Historic Courthouses of New York State: 18th and 19th Century Halls of Justice across the Empire State* (New York, 1977).

23. See Edmund S. Morgan, *Inventing the People: The Rise of Popular Sovereignty in England and America* (New York, 1988), 183, 185–86.

24. Bernard Bailyn, *The Origins of American Politics* (New York, 1968), 68–69; Lois G. Carr, "Extension of Empire: English Law in Colonial Maryland" (unpubl. ms., 1987), 28.

25. J. P. Whittenburg, "Planters, Merchants, and Lawyers: Social Change and the Origins of the North Carolina Regulation," *William and Mary Quarterly*, 3rd ser., 34 (April 1977): 225–28, 237; Michael Kammen, *Sovereignty and Liberty: Constitutional Discourse in American Culture* (Madison, Wisc., 1988), 49; M.A. Bellesiles, "The Establishment of Legal Structures on the Frontier: The Case of Revolutionary Vermont," *Journal of American History* 73 (Dec. 1987): esp. 897, 901–3, 906–11. For a reverse twist, see Edmund S. Morgan and Helen M. Morgan, *The Stamp Act Crisis: Prologue to Revolution* (Chapel Hill, 1953), 139–43, 168–79.

26. See John L. Brooke, "To the Quiet of the People: Revolutionary Settlements and Civil Unrest in Western Massachusetts, 1774–1789," *William and Mary Quarterly*, 3rd ser., 46 (July 1989): 425–28, 431, 438, 442; Richard B. Morris, *The Forging of the Union, 1781–1789* (New York, 1987), 258–66; James McClurg to James Madison, Aug. 22, 1787, and James Madison to Thomas

Jefferson, Sept. 6, 1787, in Robert A. Rutland et al., eds., *The Papers of James Madison* (Chicago, 1977), X: 155, 164.

27. See Ron Powers, *White Town Drowsing* (Boston, 1986), 129; *New York Times*, Sept. 10, 1989, p. H37; Laurie Lisle, *Portrait of an Artist: A Biography of Georgia O'Keeffe* (New York, 1980), 394. And for the phenomenon in American fiction, see Larry McMurtry, *Cadillac Jack* (New York, 1982), 267.

28. S. Y. Edgerton, Jr., "Icons of Justice," *Past & Present*, no. 89 (Nov. 1980): 29.

29. For a lovely watercolor by Theodore Sandford Doolittle of the courthouse square in the village of Ovid, New York (ca. 1840), see Richard J. Koke, comp., *American Landscape and Genre Paintings in the New-York Historical Society* (Boston, 1982), I: 279–80.

30. *Evening Sun* (Norwich, New York), July 23, 1976; Richard M. Dorson, *Bloodstoppers & Bearwalkers: Folk Traditions of the Upper Peninsula* (Cambridge, Mass., 1952), 176–80.

31. See Jean H. Baker, "The Ceremonies of Politics: Nineteenth-Century Rituals of National Affirmation," in William J. Cooper et al., eds., *A Master's Due: Essays in Honor of David Herbert Donald* (Baton Rouge, 1985), 165, 170.

32. See Thomas Hart Benton, *Courthouse Oratory* (ca. 1940–42) (oil on canvas), in Matthew Baigell, *Thomas Hart Benton* (New York, 1973), fig. 144.

33. For a superb pictorial survey, see Richard Pare, ed., *Court House: A Photographic Document* (New York, 1978), a volume that really is a visual treat.

34. See Constance M. Greiff, *Lost America, from the Mississippi to the Pacific* (Princeton, 1972), which includes photographs of various courthouses that have not survived. Only one, the Marion County Courthouse in Salem, Oregon (1873–94), is surmounted by a figure of Justice. See pp. 40–41.

35. After the United States Supreme Court moved to its new home in 1935, novelist Kenneth Roberts managed to obtain for $30 a carved eagle with an eight-foot wingspread that had graced the Court's former quarters in the Capitol. See John Tebbel, *George Horace Lorimer and the Saturday Evening Post* (Garden City, N.Y., 1948), 278.

36. New York Times, Oct. 8, 1888. p. 1.

37. Ibid., Oct. 24, 1889, p. 5. For a modern instance of a similar, successful effort, see Arnold M. Berke, "Taking the Initiative," *Preservation News* (Jan. 1989): 1.

38. For Pippin's *West Chester [Pennsylvania] Courthouse* (1940), see *Hicks, Kane, Pippin: Three Self-Taught Pennsylvania Artists* (exhibition catalogue) (Pittsburg, 1966), 93. For Seymour's paintings of courthouses, including the Chowan County Courthouse in Edenton, North Carolina, the second oldest one in continuous use in the United States, see Theodore E. Stebbins, Jr., and Galina Gorokhoff, comps., *A Checklist of American Paintings at Yale University* (New Haven, 1982), 124.

39. Joseph Leach, *The Typical Texan: Biography of an American Myth* (Dallas, 1952), 32.

40. The Brickey painting is located in the National Portrait Gallery, Washington, D.C. The Schussele is in the Gilcrease Museum, Tulsa, Oklahoma. For context, see *In This Academy: The Pennsylvania Academy of the Fine Arts, 1805–1976: A Special Bicentennial Exhibition* (Washington, 1976), 115–16.

41. Carolyn Taitt, "Mural Paintings of the Illinois Supreme Court," *Journal of the Illinois State Historical Society* 77 (Spring 1984): 13; C. B. Galbreath, "Ezra Meeker: Ohio's Illustrious Pioneer," *Ohio Archaeological and Historical Publications* 36 (1927): 13–14.

42. Charles J. Maland, *American Visions: The Films of Chaplin, Ford, Capra, and Welles, 1936–1941* (New York, 1977), ch. 3.

43. Quoted in E. Maurice Bloch, *George Caleb Bingham: The Evolution of an Artist* (Berkeley, 1967), 239–40, pl. 184.

44. For Glackens's *Courtroom* (n.d.), done for the *Saturday Evening Post*, see *American Watercolors, Drawings, Paintings and Sculpture of the 19th and 20th Centuries* (Christie's catalogue)

(1988), fig. 80A. For Benton's *Trial by Jury*, see Baigell, *Thomas Hart Benton*, fig. 206. And see T. H. Benton, *An Artist in America*, 4th ed. (New York, 1983), 52–53.

45. Quoted in Leon F. Litwack, "Trouble in Mind: The Bicentennial and the Afro-American Experience," *Journal of American History* 74 (Sept. 1987): 328.

46. Kammen, *Sovereignty and Liberty*, 133, fig. 17; Bruce W. Chambers, *The World of David Gilmour Blythe (1815–1865)* (Washington, 1980), 63, 70, figs. 40, 46.

47. Located at the Art Institute of Chicago (acc. no. 1954.438).

48. See Learned Hand, *The Spirit of Liberty*, 3rd ed. (New York, 1960), 306-7. For a different version, see Edward J. Bander, comp., *Justice Holmes Ex Cathedra* (Charlottesville, 1966), 213.

49. See Laurence M. Friedman, "Total Justice: Law, Culture, and Society," *Bulletin of the American Academy of Arts and Sciences* 40 (1986): 24–39.

50. John T. Noonan, Jr., *Persons and Masks of the Law: Cardozo, Holmes, Jefferson, and Wythe as Makers of the Masks* (New York, 1976).

51. For context, see Carol J. Greenhouse, "Just in Time: Temporality and the Cultural Legitimation of Law," *Yale Law Journal* 98 (1989): esp. 1645–49; John L. Comaroff and Simon Roberts, *Rules and Processes: The Cultural Logic of Dispute in an African Context* (Chicago, 1981); Max Gluckman, *The Judicial Process among the Barotse of Northern Rhodesia* (Glencoe, Ill., 1955).

52. For a superb example of a similar three-foot "nail-fetish" that Mary Kingsley brought back from West Africa in 1893, see *History Today* 37 (May 1987): 15. The one shown in fig. 3.18 was collected in 1903 by a specialist in Belgian Congo culture and artifacts. See also William N. Fenton, *The False Faces of the Iroquois* (Norman, Okla., 1987).

53. Non–Western and preindustrial societies have their temples of justice, too. At the Philbrook Art Center in Tulsa, Oklahoma, for example, there is a pair of "houseposts" from a nineteenth-century Yoruba "Palace of Justice" (Zaire), made of carved and painted wood (acc. no. 75.28.6).

54. See Francis N. Stites, *John Marshall: Defender of the Constitution* (Boston, 1981), 88; G. Edward White, *Earl Warren: A Public Life* (New York, 1982), 163-64, 166-68.

55. Gerald Gunther, ed., *John Marshall's Defense of McCulloch v. Maryland* (Stanford, 1969), 78–105, 155–214.

56. See, especially, George L. Haskins and Herbert A. Johnson, *Foundations of Power: John Marshall, 1801–1815*, vol. 2 of *The Oliver Wendell Holmes Devise History of the Supreme Court of the United States* (New York, 1988), and G. Edward White, *The Marshall Court and Cultural Change, 1815–1835*, vols. 3 and 4 of *The Oliver Wendell Holmes Devise History of the Supreme Court of the United States* (New York, 1988).

Chapter 4
"Our Idealism Is Practical": Emerging Uses of Tradition in American Commercial Culture, 1889–1936

1. *New York Times*, Feb. 23, 1887, p. 3.

2. Ibid., Feb. 23, 1888, p. 8.

3. See Robert Bishop, ed., *Selected Treasures of the Greenfield Village and Henry Ford Museum* (Dearborn, Mich., 1969), 24–33, 56; *New York Times*, April 7, 1937, p. 31.

4. T. J. Jackson Lears, "Some Versions of Fantasy: Toward a Cultural History of American Advertising, 1880–1930," in *Prospects: the Annual of American Cultural Studies*, vol. 9 (New York, 1984), 388.

5. *New York Times*, April 29, 1889, p. 8; Charles H. Carpenter, Jr., "The Tradition of the Old: Colonial Revival Silver for the American Home," in Alan Axelrod, ed., *The Colonial Revival in America* (New York, 1985), 139–58; Alvin Moscow, *The Rockefeller Inheritance* (Garden City, N.Y., 1977), 119–20.

6. *New York Times,* Aug. 9, 1887, p. 8; Sept. 7, 1887, p. 5; Sept. 11, 1887, p. 9.

7. Ibid.: Sept. 14, 1887, p. 8; Sept. 25, 1887, p. 5; Nov. 13, 1887, p. 9; April 15, 1888, p. 2.

8. See Michael Kammen, *A Machine That Would Go of Itself: The Constitution in American Culture* (New York, 1986), 145–151.

9. *New York Times,* Feb. 18, 1889, p. 4.

10. Ibid.: Aug. 11, 1889, p. 4; Aug. 17, 1889, pp. 4, 8.

11. See R. Reid Badger, *The Great American Fair: The World's Columbian Exposition and American Culture* (Chicago, 1979), ch. 6.

12. See *Report of the Board of General Managers of the Exhibit of the State of New York at the Pan-American Exposition* (Albany, 1902), 11.

13. David Glassberg, *History into Ritual: Community Pageantry and Historical Consciousness in the Early Twentieth Century* (Chapel Hill, 1987), ch. 5.

14. Albert Steves, Jr., to Mrs. Maurice Moore, Jr., Dec. 10, 1923, Lee Chapel Papers (2373), Alderman Library, University of Virginia, Charlottesville.

15. Francis Henry Taylor, *Pierpont Morgan as Collector and Patron, 1837–1913* (New York, 1970), 28, 32.

16. Wendy Kaplan, "R. T. H. Halsey: An Ideology of Collecting American Decorative Arts," *Winterthur Portfolio* 17 (Spring 1982): 43–44.

17. See Albro Martin, *James J. Hill and the Opening of the Northwest* (New York, 1976), 578, 600.

18. C. B. Hanna to Ralph Budd, Oct. 23, 1924, in Great Northern Papers, file PSF 11619, box 371, Minnesota Historical Society, Manuscripts Division, St. Paul, Minnesota (referred to hereafter as GNP1).

19. See the memorandum prepared for Budd by W. R. Mills, June 30, 1925, GNP1.

20. Budd to Mills, July 5, 1925, GNP1.

21. Budd to Lord Byng of Vimy, May 25, 1925; Mrs. C. M. Russell to Budd, May 27, 1925; Doane Robinson to Budd, June 5, 1925; GNP1.

22. David Hilger to Budd, July 6, 1925, GNP1.

23. *The Upper Missouri Historical Expedition,* 8 pp., GNP1.

24. Ibid., 7.

25. *Program of Events, Upper Missouri Historical Expedition: Itinerary of Upper Missouri Special Via Great Northern Railway, July 16–21, 1925,* GNP1. On Aug. 11, 1926, Budd wrote the following to Abbott: "I am, of course, greatly pleased to know that you believe in the soundness of the work the Great Northern Railway has undertaken and is carrying on in bettering its public relations."

26. The newspaper clippings cited are in GNP1.

27. Mills to Budd, May 1, 1925, GNP1. It is true (and scarcely surprising) that various local entrepreneurs and organizations tried to cash in on what looked so clearly like a good thing. See the letter from the Commercial Club of Sheridan, Wyoming, to Governor Sorlie of North Dakota, June 30, 1925, pleading for a side trip to Sheridan and to the old site of Fort Phil Kearny, scene of the Wagon Box Fight and the Fetterman Massacre (in GNP1). It is a tribute to Budd's politesse that the pitch was sent to Sorlie rather than to Budd.

28. *Great Northern Semaphore,* Aug. 1925, p. 6.

29. Budd to Davis, May 15, 1926, in Great Northern Papers, file PSF 11620, Minnesota Historical Society, Manuscripts Division, St. Paul, Minnesota (referred to hereafter as GNP2).

30. Morison, "Recent Historical Expeditions in the Northwest," typescript, 8 pp., GNP2. For a representative letter of appreciation, see D. W. Greenburg (of the Midwest Refining Company, Casper, Wyo.) to Budd, Aug. 17, 1926, GNP2.

31. Blegen, "General Comment," in "The Columbia River Historical Expedition," *Minnesota History* 7 (Sept. 1926): 249.

32. Some interest was expressed in holding a "reunion" in St. Paul for "veterans" of the two expeditions. See Edward F. Flynn to Ralph Budd, Jan. 15, 1927, GNP2.

33. Kaplan, "R. T. H. Halsey: An Ideology of Collecting American Decorative Arts," 45–53.

34. *New York Times,* Feb. 25, 1937, p. 5; Walter Rendell Storey, "Colonial Styles Are Revealed in New Copies," Ibid., May 16, 1937, sec. 8, p. 14.

35. Wendell D. Garrett, "Wallace Nutting," *Dictionary of American Biography*, suppl. 3 (New York, 1973), 567; *New York Times*, Oct. 12, 1984, p. B10.

36. *New York Times*, April 30, 1939, sec. 1, p. 4.

37. Quoted in Godfrey Hodgson, *America in Our Time* (Garden City, N.Y., 1972), 10.

38. Anthony DePalma, "A Colonial Shopping Village," *New York Times*, Aug. 21, 1985, p. D22.

39. Thomas J. Lueck, "More Corporations Becoming Working Museums," *New York Times*, Sept. 15, 1985, p. A60; Moscow, *Rockefeller Inheritance,* 232, 248–49, 333–35.

40. For an interesting case that required a ten-year struggle to resolve, see the story about the Lit Brothers' department store, "Supporters Save Historic Building in Philadelphia," *New York Times*, Jan. 19, 1986, p. A38.

Chapter 5
The Enduring Challenges and Changing Role of Cultural Institutions

1. See Michael Wallace, *Mickey Mouse History and Other Essays on American Memory* (Philadelphia, 1996); Edward A. Chappell, "Social Responsibility and the American History Museum," *Winterthur Portfolio* 24 (Winter 1989): 247–65; *Journal of American Culture* 12 (Summer 1989), a special issue devoted to relationships between historians and museum professionals in the United States.

2. Jane S. Becker and Barbara Franco, eds., *Folk Roots, New Roots: Folklore in American Life* (Lexington, Mass., 1988), 39–40; Allen Eaton, *Immigrant Gifts to American Life* (New York, 1932).

3. Steven K. Hamp and Michael J. Ettema, "To Collect or Educate? Some History Museums Discover They Can't Do One Without the Other," *Museum News* 68 (Sept./Oct. 1989): 41–44.

4. Rossiter Howard, "Changing Ideals of the Art Museum," *Scribner's Magazine* 71 (Jan. 1922): 125–26. See also Howard Greenfield, *The Devil and Dr. Barnes: Portrait of an American Art Collector* (New York, 1987), 73–74, 103–4, 113–14.

5. Howard, "Changing Ideals of the Art Museum," 127–28. For context, see Paul J. DiMaggio, "Progressivism and the Arts," *Society* 25 (July 1988): 70–75; DiMaggio, "Constructing an Organizational Field as a Professional Project: The Case of U.S. Art Museums, 1920–1940," in Walter W. Powell and Paul J. DiMaggio, eds., *The New Institutionalism in Organizational Analysis* (Chicago, 1991), 267–92.

6. Calvin Tomkins, *Merchants and Masterpieces: The Story of the Metropolitan Museum of Art* (New York, 1970), 272, 277.

7. See Mary Kupiec Cayton, "The Making of an American Prophet: Emerson, His Audiences, and the Rise of the Culture Industry in Nineteenth-Century America," *American Historical Review* 92 (June 1987): 597–620, esp. 604–15; David S. Reynolds, *Beneath the American Renaissance: The Subversive Imagination in the Age of Emerson and Melville* (New York, 1988), 4, 24.

8. Richard F. Bach, "Museums and the Factory: Making the Galleries Work for the Art Trades," *Scribner's Magazine* 71 (June 1922): 766–68.

9. Joseph Downs, "The History of the American Wing," *Magazine Antiques* 50 (Oct. 1946): 235.

10. Ford's interview with S. J. Woolf, *New York Times*, Jan. 12, 1936, sec. 7, p. 1.

11. The decentralization of American museums in the twentieth century is an implicit theme in Nathaniel Burt, *Palaces for the People: A Social History of the American Art Museum* (Boston, 1977), ch. 5; and for Rockefeller's bequest, see the *New York Times*, July 21, 1978, p. B2.

12. See Michael Kammen, *Mystic Chords of Memory: The Transformation of Tradition in American Culture* (New York, 1991), ch. 17; Robert G. Hartje, *Bicentennial USA: Pathways to Celebration* (Nashville, 1973), chs. 4–7; *The Bicentennial of the United States of America: A Final Report to the People* (Washington, D.C., 1977), esp. vols. 3–5.

13. Antoinette J. Lee, "Discovering Old Cultures in the New: The Role of Ethnicity," in Robert E. Stipe and A. J. Lee, eds., *The American Mosaic: Preserving a Nation's Heritage* (Washington, D.C., 1987), 191–92.

14. *U.S. Statutes at Large*, vol. 86, 92nd Congress (1972), pp. 346–48; *New York Times*, Jan. 28, 1974, p. 11.

15. Joy B. Dunn, "A New Vision: The Valentine, Museum in a House," *History News* 44 (July 1989): 25–27.

16. See John R. Gillis, *Youth and History: Tradition and Change in European Age Relations, 1770–Present* (New York, 1974); and for a fine description of the rise of multiculturalism during the 1930s, set in its historical context, see Richard Weiss, "Ethnicity and Reform: Minorities and the Ambience of the Depression Years," *Journal of American History* 66 (Dec. 1979): 566–85. For a very recent example of museum exhibits devoted to the history of homelife, see Suzanne Slesin, "Lasting Visions of the Home," *New York Times*, Sept. 13, 1990, pp. C1 and C6.

17. See Adamic, *Dinner at the White House* (New York, 1946), 66; Adamic, *A Nation of Nations* (New York, 1945); Weiss, "Ethnicity and Reform: Minorities and the Ambience of the Depression Years," 568–69.

18. "John Cotton Dana and the Newark Museum," *Newark Museum Quarterly* 30, nos. 2 and 3 (Spring–Summer 1979): 40–42.

19. See Michael R. Weisser, *A Brotherhood of Memory: Jewish Landsmanshaftn in the New World* (New York, 1985); David L. Lewis, *When Harlem Was in Vogue* (New York, 1981); Greenfeld, *The Devil and Dr. Barnes*, 58–60.

20. See Kammen, *Mystic Chords of Memory: The Transformation of Tradition in American Culture*, chs. 18–19. For an early example of collaboration between CBS, the Metropolitan Museum of Art, and the Museum of Modern Art, see Gilbert Seldes, "Television and the Museums," *Magazine of Art* 37 (May 1944): 178–79.

21. See V. Sofka, *Museology and Identity: Basic Papers, ICOFOM Study Series no. 10* (Buenos Aires, 1986), esp. 135–39 and 189–92.

Chapter 6
Myth, Memory, and Amnesia in American Historical Art

1. See David Levin, *History as Romantic Art: Bancroft, Prescott, Motley, and Parkman* (Stanford, Calif., 1959); Arthur M. Schlesinger, Jr., "The Historian as Artist," *Atlantic Monthly* (July 1963): 35–40; Peter Gay, *Style in History* (New York, 1974).

2. *In This Academy: The Pennsylvania Academy of the Fine Arts, 1805–1976* (Washington, D.C., 1976), 101, 110.

3. See Daniel J. Boorstin, *The Genius of American Politics* (Chicago, 1953); Irvin G. Wyllie, *The Self-Made Man in America: The Myth of Rags to Riches* (New Brunswick, N.J., 1954); John G. Cawelti, *Apostles of the Self-Made Man* (Chicago, 1965); Henry Nash Smith, *Virgin Land: The American West as Symbol and Myth* (Cambridge, Mass., 1950).

4. See Michael Kammen, *A Season of Youth: The American Revolution and the Historical Imagination* (New York, 1978), 96–100 and figs. 22–27.

5. See Michael Kammen, *Mystic Chords of Memory: The Transformation of Tradition in*

American Culture (New York, 1991), 53, 240–42; Brian W. Dippie, *Custer's Last Stand: The Anatomy of an American Myth* (Missoula, Mont., 1976); Michael Kowalewski, "Imagining the California Gold Rush: The Visual Legacy," *California History* 71 (Spring 1992): 60–73.

6. Ralph Ellison, "Going to the Territory" (1979), in Ellison, *Going to the Territory* (New York, 1986), 123–24.

7. For an interesting contrast, see Joany Hichberger, "Old Soldiers," in *Patriotism: The Making and Unmaking of British National Identity*, ed. Raphael Samuel (London, 1989), III: 50–63. Hichberger finds that paintings of aged war veterans enjoyed considerable vogue in England for many decades after 1815. A prime example is David Wilkie's *Chelsea Pensioners Receiving the London Gazette Extraordinary of Thursday June 22nd 1815 Announcing the Battle of Waterloo*, first exhibited at the Royal Academy in 1822. Wilkie's painting emphasized working-class men, the "worthy poor," responding in a patriotic manner to the great victory. For the political complexities of what could (and could not) be shown in paintings of this sort, see 53–54.

8. David M. Potter, "The Historian's Use of Nationalism and Vice Versa," in Potter, *The South and the Sectional Conflict* (Baton Rouge, 1968), 68–83.

9. Mark Twain, *Life on the Mississippi* (1883; rpt., New York, 1961), 254–55.

10. Michael Kammen, *Meadows of Memory: Images of Time and Tradition in American Art and Culture* (Austin, Tex., 1992), 138.

11. Ibid., xv.

12. Robert Penn Warren, *The Legacy of the Civil War* (Cambridge, Mass., 1961), 100.

Chapter 7
The Problem of American Exceptionalism: A Reconsideration

1. Ian Tyrrell, "American Exceptionalism in an Age of International History," with a critique by Michael McGerr and a rejoinder by Tyrrell, *American Historical Review* 96 (Oct. 1991): 1031–72; Byron Shafer, ed., *Is America Different? A New Look at American Exceptionalism* (Oxford, 1991); Sanford M. Jacoby, ed., *Masters to Managers: Historical and Comparative Perspectives on American Employers* (New York, 1991), esp. ch. 8 by Jacoby, "American Exceptionalism Revisited: The Importance of Management"; Gary Marks, *Unions in Politics: Britain, Germany, and the United States in the Nineteenth and Early Twentieth Centuries* (Princeton, 1989), ch. 6, "American Exceptionalism in Comparative Perspective"; David Hamer, *New Towns in the New World: Images and Perceptions of the Nineteenth-Century Urban Frontier* (New York, 1990), a comparative study of New Zealand, Australia, the United States, and Canada.

2. For some citations of their work, in addition to those mentioned in note 1 above, see Daniel Bell, " 'American Exceptionalism' Revisited: The Role of Civil Society," *Public Interest* 95 (Spring 1989): 38–56; Mona Harrington, *The Dream of Deliverance in American Politics* (New York, 1986), esp. ch. 1, "The Promise and the Myth": Samuel P. Huntington, *American Politics: The Promise of Disharmony* (Cambridge, Mass., 1981), esp. ch. 2, "The American Creed and National Identity"; Alex Inkeles, "The American Character," *Center Magazine* (Nov./Dec. 1983): 25–39; Alan F. J. Artibise, "Exploring the North-American West: A Comparative Urban Perspective," *American Review of Canadian Studies* 14 (Spring 1984): 29–43; John P. Roche, "Immigration and Nationality: A Historical Overview of United States Policy," in Uri Ra'anan and Roche, eds., *Ethnic Resurgence in Modern Democratic States: A Multidisciplinary Approach to Human Resources and Conflict* (New York, 1980), 30–76.

3. Richard J. Oestreicher, *Solidarity and Fragmentation: Working People and Class Consciousness in Detroit, 1875–1900* (Urbana, Ill., 1986); Kathleen Neils Conzen, "Mainstream and Side Channels: The Localization of Immigrant Cultures," *Journal of American Ethnic History* 11 (Fall 1991): 5–20; James M. McPherson, "Antebellum Southern Exceptionalism: A New Look at an Old Question," *Civil War History* 29 (Sept. 1983): 230–44; Carl L. Becker, "Kansas," in *Everyman*

His Own Historian: Essays on History and Politics (New York, 1935), 5, 28.

4. Quoted in Richard White, *Inventing Australia: Images and Identity, 1688–1980* (Sydney, 1981), 49; James Baldwin, *Nobody Knows My Name: More Notes of a Native Son* (New York, 1961), 17, 117, 123.

5. Marks, *Unions in Politics*, xiii, xvi, 223 n. 42.

6. Ibid., 210, 212, 217–19, 231–34.

7. Jacoby, "American Exceptionalism Revisited: The Importance of Management," 173–200, esp. 177, 184, 187, 200, quotation at 199.

8. Ibid., 173, 176, 178–79, 182. See also Olivier Zunz, *Making America Corporate, 1870–1920* (Chicago, 1990), which examines the social characteristics and values of people who participated in the formation of corporate bureaucracies.

9. V. P. Bynack, "Noah Webster's Linguistic Thought and the Idea of an American National Culture," *Journal of the History of Ideas* 45 (Jan. 1984): 99–114; Alan D. Aberback, "A Search for an American Identity," *Canadian Review of American Studies* 2 (Fall 1971): 76–88; William Findley, *History of the Insurrections, in the Four Western Counties of Pennsylvania* (Philadelphia, 1796), vi. See also Arthur H. Shaffer, *To Be an American: David Ramsay and the Making of the American Consciousness* (Columbia, S.C., 1991).

10. See Michael Kammen, *A Season of Youth: The American Revolution and the Historical Imagination* (New York, 1978), 7–9, 24; Henry Adams, *History of the United States during the Administrations of Thomas Jefferson and James Madison* (New York, 1889), I: ch. 6, "American Ideals"; James Chace, "Dreams of Perfectibility: American Exceptionalism and the Search for a Moral Foreign Policy," in Leslie Berlowitz et al., eds., *America in Theory* (New York, 1988), 249–61; Nick Salvatore, "Some Thoughts on Class and Citizenship in America in the Late Nineteenth Century," in Marianne Debouzy, ed., *In the Shadow of the Statue of Liberty: Immigrants, Workers and Citizens in the American Republic, 1880–1920* (Paris, 1988), 226–27.

11. James T. Schleifer, *The Making of Tocqueville's Democracy in America* (Chapel Hill, 1980), 50, 58–59; Patrice Higonnet, *Sister Republics: The Origins of French and American Republicanism* (Cambridge, Mass., 1988), 5.

12. R. Laurence Moore, *European Socialists and the American Promised Land* (New York, 1970), 4–5; Daniel Bell, *The Winding Passage: Essays and Sociological Journeys, 1960–1980* (Cambridge, Mass., 1980), 256; Robert P. Frankel, "British Observers of America, 1890–1950" (Ph.D. diss., Harvard University, 1989), 152, 261, 274, 286–87, 298–308.

13. F. R. Leavis, "The Americanness of American Literature" (1952), in William Wasserstrom, ed., *Van Wyck Brooks: The Critic and His Critics* (Port Washington, N.Y., 1979), 157–67; Edmund Wilson, *Patriotic Gore: Studies in the Literature of the American Civil War* (New York, 1962), 491; Denis W. Brogan, "The Character of American Life," in David H. Burton, ed., *American History—British Historians: A Cross-Cultural Approach to the American Experience* (Chicago, 1976), 11, 14, 20; Christopher Thorne, *Border Crossings: Studies in International History* (Oxford, 1988), 5; Stuart M. Blumin, *The Emergence of the Middle Class: Social Experience in the American City, 1760–1900* (New York, 1989), 293 (citing a contrast made by Jürgen Kocka).

14. [John Knapp], "National Poetry," *North American Review* 8 (Dec. 1818): 169–76; Robert G. Athearn, *The Mythic West in Twentieth-Century America* (Lawrence, Kans., 1986), 81. See also Roderick Nash, *Wilderness and the American Mind*, 3rd edition (New Haven, 1982), 261.

15. T. H. Breen, ed., *Shaping Southern Society: The Colonial Experience* (New York, 1976), 131; James Lemon, *The Best Poor Man's Country: A Geographical Study of Early Southeastern Pennsylvania* (Baltimore, 1972); Sacvan Bercovitch, *The Puritan Origins of the American Self* (New Haven, 1975), esp. ch. 3.

16. James Russell Lowell, "The Rebellion: Its Causes and Consequences," *North American Review* 99 (July 1864): 254; Robert R. Hubach, "Three Uncollected St. Louis Interviews of Walt Whitman," *American Literature* 14 (May 1942): 144–45; Michael Kammen, *Meadows of Memory:*

Images of Time and Tradition in American Art and Culture (Austin, Tex., 1992), xiii, 133–34, 160–62; James H. Duff et al., *An American Vision: Three Generations of Wyeth Art* (Boston, 1987), 80, 84.

17. Bernard DeVoto reviewed Seldes, *Mainland*, in *The Saturday Review* 14 (Oct. 3, 1936): 7; and see Seldes, *Mainland* (New York, 1936), 415; Seldes, *The Public Arts* (New York, 1956), 284–85. See also John A. Kouwenhoven, *The Beer Can by the Highway: Essays on What's "American" about America* (Garden City, N.Y., 1961), a collection of pieces written mostly during the 1950s.

18. Gertrude Stein, *Four in America* (New Haven, 1947), xv–xvi; Thornton Wilder, "Toward an American Language," *Atlantic Monthly* 190 (July 1952): 29–37; and Clement Greenberg, "'American-Type' Painting," in William Phillips and Philip Rahv, eds., *The Partisan Review Anthology* (New York, 1962), 165–78.

19. Carl L. Becker, "Frederick Jackson Turner," in Becker, *Everyman His Own Historian: Essays on History and Politics* (New York, 1935), 216–17; Turner to Haskins, May 6, 1925, Haskins Papers, box 17, Mudd Library, Princeton University; Donald L. Miller, *Lewis Mumford: A Life* (New York, 1989), 132, 231–32; Ellen Nore, *Charles A. Beard: An Intellectual Biography* (Carbondale, Ill., 1983), 124, and chs. 8–9 generally.

20. William H. Nolte, ed., *H. L. Mencken's Smart Set Criticism* (Washington, D.C., 1987), 3; J. E. Spingarn, "Criticism in the United States," in Irving Babbitt, et al., *Criticism in America: Its Function and Status* (New York, 1924), 292–93; Thomas Craven, "American Men of Art," *Scribner's Magazine* 92 (Nov. 1932): 262–63.

21. Seldes, *Mainland*, 6. Seldes asserted that the meaning of America was not simply part of the meaning of Europe (8), a point that echoed John Crowe Ransom's concern for "the meaning of European history" and "Europeanism." See Twelve Southerners, *I'll Take My Stand: The South and the Agrarian Tradition* (New York, 1930), 4–5.

22. Bell, *The Winding Passage*, 254, Ralph G. Martin, *Henry and Clare: An Intimate Portrait of the Luces* (New York, 1991), 172. See also Neal Gabler, *An Empire of Their Own: How the Jews Invented Hollywood* (New York, 1988), 1; David A. Hollinger, *In the American Province: Studies in the History and Historiography of Ideas* (Baltimore, 1985), 162–64.

23. Kouwenhoven, *The Beer Can by the Highway*, 30–31; Allen F. Davis, "The Politics of American Studies," *American Quarterly* 42 (Sept. 1990): 360, 370; Karen J. Winkler, "Organization of American Historians Backs Teaching of Non-Western Culture and Diversity in Schools," *Chronicle of Higher Education* (Feb. 6, 1991): A7.

24. Thomas Wentworth Higginson, "Americanism in Literature," *The Atlantic* 25 (Jan. 1870): 63; Leon Samson, "Americanism as Surrogate Socialism," in John Laslett and Seymour Martin Lipset, eds., *Failure of a Dream? Essays in the History of American Socialism* (New York, 1974), 426; Roy Rosenzweig, " 'United Action Means Victory': Militant Americanism on Film," *Labor History* 24 (Spring 1983): 274–88.

25. Irving Howe, *Socialism and America* (New York, 1985), 133–34; "American Culture is Called Unique," *New York Times*, April 26, 1937, p. 3. For an extraordinary echo of Overstreet in 1992, see Lewis H. Lapham (the editor), "Who and What Is American?," *Harper's* 284 (Jan. 1992): 49.

26. Bell, "The End of American Exceptionalism," *Public Interest* 41 (Fall 1975): 193–224, reprinted in Bell, *The Winding Passage*, 245–71; Campbell, "The American Past as Destiny," in Burton, ed., *American History—British Historians*, 51–72, esp. 64–66. Contrast Bell's position in 1975 with his exceptionalist emphasis in *The End of Ideology: On the Exhaustion of Political Ideas in the Fifties* (New York, 1962), part I generally and esp. 113 and 310.

27. Laurence Veysey, "The Autonomy of American History Reconsidered," *American Quarterly* 31 (Fall 1979): 455–77, esp. 458. It should be noted that Seymour Martin Lipset and Reinhard Bendix, *Social Mobility in Industrial Society* (Berkeley, 1959), sought to show that all

industrial societies have had approximately the same rates of mobility. Therefore the notion of a uniquely "open" American society cannot explain why our political history has been different, that is, no significant socialist persuasion. See also David A. Hollinger's complaint that historians of the United States "remain too concerned . . . with the uniqueness of American history and not enough with the place of American intellectual history in the history of the West. . . ." In John Higham and Paul K. Conkin, eds., *New Directions in American Intellectual History* (Baltimore, 1979), 63.

28. Sean Wilentz, *Chants Democratic: New York City & the Rise of the American Working Class, 1788–1850* (New York, 1984); Wilentz, "Against Exceptionalism: Class Consciousness and the American Labor Movement, 1790–1920," *International Labor and Working Class History* 26 (Fall 1984): 1–24; Eric Foner, "Why Is There No Socialism in the United States?," *History Workshop Journal* 17 (Spring 1984): 74–76.

29. William C. Spengemann, *A Mirror for Americanists: Reflections on the Idea of American Literature* (Hanover, N.H., 1989), esp. 13. For the opposite perspective, see George Watson (an Australian), "The Americanness of American Poetry," *Virginia Quarterly Review* 65 (Winter 1989): 81–93; Jeffrey H. Richards, *Theater Enough: American Culture and the Metaphor of the World Stage, 1607–1789* (Durham, 1991), esp. xii, 179, 182–83.

30. Jack P. Greene, *Pursuits of Happiness: The Social Development of Early Modern British Colonies and the Formation of American Culture* (Chapel Hill, 1988), 175; J. G. A. Pocock, "Between Gog and Magog: The Republican Thesis and the *Ideologia Americana*," *Journal of the History of Ideas* 48 (April 1987): 325.

31. Hall lectured at Cornell on April 3, 1974. Cf. Hall, *Worlds of Wonder, Days of Judgement: Popular Religious Belief in Early New England* (New York, 1989), esp. 4–6, 18, 212. For an early critique of exceptionalism from the perspective of American religion, see Winthrop S. Hudson, "How American is Religion in America?," in Jerald C. Brauer, ed., *Reinterpretation in American Church History* (Chicago, 1968), 153–67, esp. 156, 166–67.

32. Wilentz, *Chants Democratic*, esp. 142, 156–57, 238; Foner, "Why Is There No Socialism in the United States?," in Jean Heffer and Jeanine Rovet, eds., *Why Is There No Socialism in the United States?* (Paris, 1988), 61, 63–64.

33. Alan Dawley, "E. P. Thompson and the Peculiarities of the Americans," *Radical History Review* 19 (Winter 1978–79): 33–59, esp. 34–35, 56–57; Dawley, "Farewell to 'American Exceptionalism,'" in Heffer and Rovet, eds., *Why Is There No Socialism in the United States?*, 311–15. In his recent book, *Struggles for Justice: Social Responsibility and the Liberal State* (Cambridge, Mass., 1991), 10–11, Dawley presents his most strident attack upon American exceptionalism.

34. Zolberg, "The Roots of American Exceptionalism," in Heffer and Rovet, eds., *Why is There No Socialism in the United States?*, 105–6; Zolberg, "How Many Exceptionalisms?," in Ira Katznelson and Zolberg, eds., *Working-Class Formation: Nineteenth-Century Patterns in Western Europe and the United States* (Princeton, 1986), 427–28, 454–55.

35. Dwight Macdonald, *Discriminations: Essays & Afterthoughts, 1938–1974* (New York, 1974), 255; Macdonald, "The String Untuned" (1962), in Macdonald, *Against the American Grain* (New York, 1962), 315; Irving Horowitz, ed., *Power, Politics, and People: The Collected Essays of C. Wright Mills* (New York, 1963), 228; and Mills, *White Collar: The American Middle Classes* (New York, 1951), xi, 3–4.

36. Giles Gunn, *The Culture of Criticism and the Criticism of Culture* (New York, 1987), 161–62; Marian J. Morton, *The Terrors of Ideological Politics: Liberal Historians in a Conservative Mood* (Cleveland, 1972).

37. Mike Davis, *Prisoners of the American Dream: Politics and Economy in the History of the US Working Class* (London, 1986), Myra Jehlen, *American Incarnation: The Individual, the Nation, and the Continent* (Cambridge, Mass., 1986).

38. Bailyn, *The Peopling of British North America: An Introduction* (New York, 1986), 60,

81–83, 85, 114, 118, 123; Bailyn, *The Origins of American Politics* (New York, 1968), 92, 96.

39. Butler, *Awash in a Sea of Faith: Christianizing the American People* (Cambridge, Mass., 1990), esp. 162–63, 174, 212. See also Leonard W. Levy, *Original Intent and the Framers' Constitution* (New York, 1988), 193; Nathan Hatch, *The Democratization of American Christianity* (New Haven, 1990), 210.

40. Leon D. Epstein, *Political Parties in the American Mold* (Madison, 1986), 3–4; Harold M. Hyman, *American Singularity: The 1787 Northwest Ordinance, the 1862 Homestead and Morrill Acts, and the 1944 G.I. Bill* (Athens, Ga., 1986), 11, 13. The roster of American writers who have been perfectly sanguine about using the word "unique" is diverse and spans many decades. It includes Randolph Bourne in "Trans-National America" (1916), Gilbert Seldes in *Mainland* (1936) and *The Public Arts* (1956), Daniel Bell in some of the essays collected in *The End of Ideology* (1962), James Baldwin in some of the pieces collected in *Nobody Knows My Name* (1961), and Gary Marks in *Unions in Politics* (1989), xvi.

41. David S. Reynolds, *Beneath the American Renaissance: The Subversive Imagination in the Age of Emerson and Melville* (New York, 1988), 8, 170, 198–99, 340, 442, 452, 460.

42. Ibid., 190, 203, 277, 291, 364, 445, 448–49, 489–90, 496. For some of Reynolds's predecessors, see Leo Marx, "The Vernacular Tradition in American Literature," in Joseph J. Kwiat and Mary C. Turpie, eds., *Studies in American Culture* (Minneapolis, 1960), 109–22; Roy Harvey Pearce, *The Continuity of American Poetry* (Princeton, 1961), 379 n. 4; and Leslie Fiedler, *The Return of the Vanishing American* (New York, 1968), preface, n.p.

43. Jerrold Hirsch, "Folklore in the Making: B. A. Botkin," *Journal of American Folklore* 100 (Jan. 1987): 6–7; Bert Feintuch, ed., *The Conservation of Culture: Folklorists and the Public Sector* (Lexington, Ky., 1988), 55; Alan Dundes, "The American Concept of Folklore," *Journal of the Folklore Institute* 3 (Dec. 1966): 237.

44. Mary Ryan, "The American Parade: Representations of the Nineteenth-Century Social Order," in Lynn Hunt, ed., *The New Cultural History* (Berkeley, 1989), 132, 134; Kathleen Neils Conzen, "Ethnicity as Festive Culture: Nineteenth-Century German Americans on Parade," in Werner Sollors, ed., *The Invention of Ethnicity* (New York, 1989), 44–76; David Glassberg, *American Historical Pageantry: The Uses of Tradition in the Early Twentieth Century* (Chapel Hill, 1990), 111, 149–50.

45. Loren Baritz, *The Good Life: The Meaning of Success for the American Middle Class* (New York, 1989), xi–xii; Mary C. Waters, *Ethnic Options: Choosing Identities in America* (Berkeley, 1990), 148, 166; Robert Anthony Orsi, *The Madonna of 115th Street: Faith and Community in Italian Harlem, 1880–1950* (New Haven, 1985); Barry D. Karl and Stanley N. Katz, "Foundations and Ruling Class Elites," *Daedalus* 116 (Winter 1987): 36–39.

46. Wyn Wachhorst, *Thomas Alva Edison: An American Myth* (Cambridge, Mass., 1981), 120. In Nathan Reingold, *Science, American Style* (New Brunswick, N.J., 1991), the author explicitly rejects "any assumption of American singularity" (17), in an essay prepared in 1976, yet titles another essay "Science and Technology in the American Idiom" (1970), and still another one "European Models and American Realities" (1987). The introduction to this volume does not indicate that a well-modulated emphasis upon exceptionalism characterizes several of the essays. *Yankee Enterprise: The Rise of the American System of Manufactures* (Washington, D.C., 1981), edited by Otto Mayr and Robert C. Post, offers essays initially presented at a 1978 symposium held at the National Museum of American History. Although the editors acknowledge that many of the phenomena discussed had Old World origins, they find "these circumstances" to have been "anomalous" there, "while in America, by contrast, techniques of quantity production—and extension of the techniques to an ever broader range of products—became fundamentals in the nation's social and economic history" (xi). Although the contributors to the volume vary in their emphases, all agree that foreign visitors to the United States believed that they were witnessing a new and different system in terms of its component elements. In the

closing essay Neil Harris asserts the following: "If the American experience was not unique, it did offer, so far as historians of consumption are concerned, special circumstances" (190).

47. Lee Clark Mitchell, *Witnesses to a Vanishing America: The Nineteenth-Century Response* (Princeton, 1981), 20–21; Barbara J. Howe, "Women in Historic Preservation: The Legacy of Ann Pamela Cunningham," *Public Historian* 12 (Winter 1990): 34; Daniel J. Czitrom, *Media and the American Mind from Morse to McLuhan* (Chapel Hill, 1982), 31, 58, 113, 191; Stephen E. Weil, *Rethinking the Museum and Other Meditations* (Washington, D.C., 1990), 143; Richard E. Neustadt and Ernest May, *Thinking in Time: The Uses of History for Decision-Makers* (New York, 1986), xv.

48. Marianne Debouzy, "La Classe ouvrière américaine: Recherches et problèmes," *Le Mouvement social* 102 (Jan. 1978): 3–7.

49. See Laurence R. Veysey, *The Communal Experience: Anarchist and Mystical Counter-Cultures in America* (New York, 1973), 7; and see his critical response to Carl Degler's presidential address, "In Pursuit of an American History," in *American Historical Review* 92 (Oct. 1987): 1081–82; and Iriye, "The Internationalization of History," *American Historical Review* 94 (Feb. 1989): 1–10, esp. 3–4.

50. C. Vann Woodward, *The Future of the Past* (New York, 1989), 81, 168–69; Carl Degler, "Comparative History: An Essay Review," *Journal of Southern History* 34 (Aug. 1968): 427. Rebecca J. Scott has also remarked of the comparative method that it has "certain obvious advantages for the highlighting of crucial differences. . . ." Scott, "Exploring the Meaning of Freedom: Postemancipation Societies in Comparative Perspective," in Scott et al., *The Abolition of Slavery and the Aftermath of Emancipation in Brazil* (Durham, N.C., 1988), 2.

51. There is actually a fourth category that is quite important and revealing because it, too, generally reinforces a sense of American distinctiveness. I have in mind a cluster of highly empirical works that compare selected issues and themes in three societies that one might expect to be more alike than they are like any others. See, for example, Seymour Martin Lipset, *Continental Divide: The Values and Institutions of the United States and Canada* (New York, 1990); Richarde M. Merelman, *Partial Visions: Culture and Politics in Britain, Canada, and the United States* (Madison, Wis., 1991); Walter Kendrick, *The Secret Museum: Pornography in Modern Culture* (New York, 1987), 135, 142–43, 150, 158–59; and Howard M. Leichter, *Free to Be Foolish: Politics and Health Promotion in the United States and Great Britain* (Princeton, 1991), esp. 5, 211. John Harmon McElroy, *Finding Freedom: America's Distinctive Cultural Formation* (Carbondale, Ill., 1989), builds on comparisons between the United States, Brazil, Canada, and Spanish America.

52. For the relentless litany of differences, see Kolchin, *Unfree Labor: American Slavery and Russian Serfdom* (Cambridge, Mass., 1987), xii, 43, 45–46, 50–51, 57–58, 78, 83, 85, 98, 117, 140, 148–49, 155–58, 169, 178, 218–19, 222, 234–35, 239, 276–78, 290, 352, 355–57, 361–62, 374–75, quotation at 362.

53. Woodward, *The Future of the Past* (New York, 1989), 44, 198–99; Scott, "Exploring the Meaning of Freedom: Postemancipation Societies in Comparative Perspective," in Scott et al., *The Abolition of Slavery*, 2, 5, 6, 9, 19. See also Scott, "Comparing Emancipations: A Review Essay," *Journal of Social History* 20 (Spring 1987): 565–83.

54. Gerber, *The Making of an American Pluralism: Buffalo, New York, 1825–60* (Urbana, 1989), esp. chs. 3–5, and 9.

55. When contrasting British and American conditions, David Montgomery suggested that the most effective deterrent during the pre-Civil War era to the maturation of class consciousness and creation of a labor party in the United States was the "ease with which American working men entered elective office." Montgomery, *Beyond Equality: Labor and the Radical Republicans, 1862–1872* (New York, 1967), 215.

56. Ira Berlin, "Herbert G. Gutman and the American Working Class," in Gutman, *Power*

& Culture: Essays on the American Working Class (New York, 1987), 25, 28, 29, 34, 36, and 198.

57. Veysey, "The Autonomy of American History Reconsidered," 467, 469, 477; Aristide Zolberg, "The Roots of American Exceptionalism," in Heffer and Rovet, eds., *Why Is There No Socialism in the United States?*, 110, 112–14.

58. Irving Howe, *Socialism and America* (San Diego, 1985), 128–29; Davis, *Prisoners of the American Dream*, 41, 43.

59. Zolberg, "The Roots of American Exceptionalism," 114–15; Chandler, *The Visible Hand: The Managerial Revolution in American Business* (Cambridge, Mass., 1977), 64, 93, quotation at 205. See also Alfred D. Chandler, Jr., *Scale and Scope: The Dynamics of Industrial Capitalism* (Cambridge, Mass., 1990), which highlights differences among the business systems that developed in the United States, Great Britain, and Germany, ca. 1880 to 1940; and also Howe, *Socialism and America*, 121–22, and especially Richard Rose, "How Exceptional Is the American Political Economy?," *Political Science Quarterly* 104 (Spring 1989): 91–115.

60. Kathryn K. Sklar, "A Call for Comparisons," *American Historical Review* 95 (Oct. 1990): 1109–14, esp. 1111; Carl N. Degler, *At Odds: Women and the Family in America from the Revolution to the Present* (New York, 1980), 290. See also Elizabeth H. Pleck, "Women's History: Gender as a Category of Historical Analysis," in James B. Gardner and George R. Adams, eds., *Ordinary People and Everyday Life: Perspectives on the New Social History* (Nashville, 1983), 52–53. Donald Meyer, *Sex and Power: The Rise of Women in America, Russia, Sweden, and Italy* (Middletown, Conn., 1987), strongly emphasizes distinctive national patterns derived from cultural differences. He believes that under the impact of democratic capitalism in the nineteenth century, only in the United States did a separate sphere of behavior and activity emerge for women. That "separate sphere" in America would be crucial in providing a stimulus for the growth of a feminist movement and for individual self-realization. Meyer's rejection of any universal explanation for the subordination of women, and his insistence upon national particularity, disturbed some prominent reviewers of the book. Meyer acknowledges on pp. xxv–xxvi that his project reinforces the penchant for American exceptionalism.

61. See, for example, Orsi, *The Madonna of 115th Street*, 55, 95, 107–12. Orsi also happens to make the intriguing point that during the decades ca. 1890–1910, the Vatican regarded Catholicism in the United States as deviant and problematic. At stake, in key respects, was a conflict between the Marian Catholicism advocated by Pope Leo XIII and a form of modernism supported by the Irish clergy in the United States who tended to be assimilationist. (See ibid., 62–63.)

62. Richard Waterhouse, *From Minstrel Show to Vaudeville: The Australian Popular Stage, 1788–1914* (New South Wales, 1990), xi, xiii, 14–16, 28, 38, 139–41; Ian Tyrrell's response to Michael McGerr, *American Historical Review* 96 (Oct. 1991); 1068–70; John Agnew, *The United States in the World-Economy: A Regional Geography* (Cambridge, 1987), 15.

63. See, for example, Dorothy Ross, *The Origins of American Social Science* (New York, 1991), xvii; John Rickard, *Australia: A Cultural History* (London, 1988), xi; Charles S. Maier, *The Unmasterable Past: History, Holocaust, and German National Identity* (Cambridge, Mass., 1988), 108; Dawley, "Farewell to 'American Exceptionalism,'" in Heffer and Rovet, eds., *Why Is There No Socialism in the United States?*, 312.

64. Veysey's letter to the Editor, *American Historical Review* 92 (Oct. 1987): 1081–82.

65. E. P. Thompson, "The Peculiarities of the English," in Ralph Miliband and John Saville, eds., *The Socialist Register 1965* (New York, 1965), 311–59, esp. 323, 329–30; Linda Colley, "Whose Nation? Class and National Consciousness in Britain, 1750–1830," *Past and Present* 113 (Nov. 1986): 97–117. For additional statements of British exceptionalism, see Gareth Stedman Jones, *Languages of Class: Studies in English Working Class History, 1832–1982* (Cambridge, 1983), 2, 4; Paul Fussell, *The Great War and Modern Memory* (New York, 1975), 232–35, 245–46.

66. Jerrold Seigel, "Politics, Memory, Illusion: Marx and the French Revolution," in François

Furet and Mona Ozouf, eds., *The French Revolution and the Creation of Modern Political Culture*, vol. 3: *The Transformation of Political Culture, 1789–1848* (Oxford, 1989), 636; Theodore Zeldin, *France, 1848–1945: Politics and Anger* (New York, 1979), 1–2; Roger Chartier, *Cultural History: Between Practices and Representations* (Ithaca, 1988), ch. 8; James H. Billington, *The Icon and the Axe: An Interpretive History of Russian Culture* (New York, 1966); George Seldes, *Witness to a Century: Encounters with the Noted, the Notorious, and the Three SOBs* (New York, 1987), 285.

67. Gordon A. Craig, *The Germans* (New York, 1982), 25, 184; George L. Mosse, *Masses and Man: Nationalist and Fascist Perceptions of Reality* (New York, 1980), 21–51.

68. Blackbourn and Eley, *The Peculiarities of German History: Bourgeois Society and Politics in Nineteenth-Century Germany* (New York, 1984), 1–35, 41–42.

69. Ibid., 45–46, 83–84, 89, 123, 133.

70. Isaiah Berlin, *Vico and Herder: Two Studies in the History of Ideas* (New York, 1976), 145, 153.

71. Both Ian Tyrrell and Michael McGerr acknowledge this in "American Exceptionalism in an Age of International History," *American Historical Review* 96 (Oct. 1991): 1049, 1063, and 1066. See also Samuel P. Huntington, *American Politics: The Promise of Disharmony* (Cambridge, Mass., 1981), 36; Mona Harrington, *The Dream of Deliverance in American Politics* (New York, 1986), 8–9, 14; and Michael Kammen, *Mystic Chords of Memory: The Transformation of Tradition in American Culture* (New York, 1991), esp. chs. 2 and 3.

72. The closest thing that we have at present is Aristide R. Zolberg's long essay "How Many Exceptionalisms?," in Katznelson and Zolberg, eds., *Working-Class Formation*, 397–455. See also the essays in Peter Boerner, ed., *Concepts of National Identity: An Interdisciplinary Dialogue* (Baden-Baden, 1986); and Richard O. Curry and Lawrence B. Goodheart, eds., *American Chameleon: Individualism in Trans-National Context* (Kent, Ohio, 1991), esp. 3, 10–19, which vigorously reaffirms American exceptionalism based upon extended comparisons with Great Britain, France, and Germany.

73. See (for the cultural) William A. White, "Tradition and Urban Development: A Contrast of Chicago and Toronto in the Nineteenth Century," *Old Northwest* 8 (Fall 1982): 245–72, and (for the political) David Hamer, *New Towns in the New World: Images and Perceptions of the Nineteenth-Century Urban Frontier* (New York, 1991), esp. 231–32, a comparison of New Zealand, Australia, the United States, and Canada.

74. Richard White, *Inventing Australia: Images and Identity, 1688–1980* (Sydney, 1981), 63, 64, 81, 83, long quotation at 63. See also Hamer, *New Towns in the New World*, 226, 228–29; John Carroll, ed., *Intruders in the Bush: The Australian Quest for Identity* (Melbourne, 1982), esp. ch. 14, "National Identity"; and William M. Johnston, "A Nation Without Qualities: Australia and Its Quest for a National Identity," in Boerner, ed., *Concepts of National Identity: An Interdisciplinary Dialogue*, 177–86.

75. Chace, "Dreams of Perfectibility: American Exceptionalism and the Search for a Moral Foreign Policy," in Berlowitz et al., eds., *America in Theory*, 249–61; Howe, *Socialism and America*, 136, 138–39. For the formation and role of a comparable myth in Dutch history, see Simon Schama, *The Embarrassment of Riches: An Interpretation of Dutch Culture in the Golden Age* (New York, 1987), 7–8, 24, 54, 82, 125, 256, 283, 285, 287. Cf. the interesting poem by Douglas Le Pan, "The Country Without a Mythology," in A. J. M. Smith, ed., *The Book of Canadian Poetry*, 3rd edition (Chicago, 1957), 422–23.

76. Catherine Collomp, "Unions, Civics, and National Identity: Organized Labor's Reaction to Immigration, 1881–1897," *Labor History* 29 (Fall 1988): 450–74. Collomp's point is strongly supported by Zolberg, "How Many Exceptionalisms?," 427–28; and by Marks, *Unions in Politics*, 210, 212.

77. For examples of Wilson's many speeches, see Arthur S. Link, ed., *The Papers of Woodrow Wilson* (Princeton, 1966–), XII: 265, XIV: 365–78, XV: 160, 165, 168, XVI: 285–86, 340–41,

XVIII: 550, XIX: 112; Cohen, *Making a New Deal: Industrial Workers in Chicago, 1919–1930* (Cambridge, 1990), 165 and 432 n. 14. It is interesting and noteworthy that "Americanisation" became a pejorative phrase in British public discourse during the nineteenth century.

78. Gerstle, *Working-Class Americanism: The Politics of Labor in a Textile City, 1914–1960* (Cambridge, 1989), chs. 1, 2.

79. Ibid., 6–8, 12, chs. 5, 9. See also Thomas Göbel, "Becoming American: Ethnic Workers and the Rise of the CIO," *Labor History* 29 (Spring 1988): 173–98, esp. 198.

80. Clifford Geertz, *The Interpretation of Cultures: Selected Essays* (New York, 1973), ch. 8.

81. Quoted in Howe, *Socialism and America*, 107.

82. Gerstle, *Working-Class Americanism*, 178, 179, 182, 187.

83. Henry Nash Smith, *Virgin Land: The American West as Symbol and Myth* (1950; rpt. Cambridge, Mass., 1970), 150.

84. In 1899 the Pope explicitly condemned the special heresy of "Americanism," by which he meant democracy and its traditions. In 1918 Van Wyck Brooks referred to Americanism pejoratively because "the world" equated it with "the worship of size, mass, quantity, and numbers." Thirty-five years later Edmund Wilson defined Americanism as an affection for and partiality toward the United States. He then suggested that "it has been made to serve some very bad causes, and is now a word to avoid." See Sigmund Skard, *The American Myth and the European Mind: American Studies in Europe, 1776–1960* (Philadelphia, 1961), 53–54; Van Wyck Brooks, *Three Essays on America* (New York, 1934), 127; Edmund Wilson, "The United States," in Wilson, *A Piece of My Mind: Reflections at Sixty* (New York, 1956), 32–35.

85. See Sheila Jasanoff, "American Exceptionalism and the Political Acknowledgment of Risk," *Daedalus* 119 (Fall 1990): 61–81; Mary Ann Glendon, *Rights Talk: The Impoverishment of Political Discourse* (New York, 1991); Anthony Lewis, "Justice Black and the First Amendment," *Alabama Law Review* 38 (Winter 1987): 289–306.

86. Gerstle, *Working-Class Americanism*, 187, 195, 218. Aristide Zolberg points out that the labor movement in the United States was not *so* different from Europe in 1886 or 1936, but very different in 1956. "The Roots of American Exceptionalism," 101.

87. See, for example, Gordon S. Wood, *The Creation of the American Republic, 1776–1787* (Chapel Hill, 1969), ix and ch. 2, "Republicanism"; Daniel T. Rodgers, "Republicanism: The Career of a Concept," *Journal of American History* 79 (June 1992): 11–38; Ross, *The Origins of American Social Science*, 23–30; Rudolph Vecoli, " 'Free Country': The American Republic Viewed by the Italian Left, 1880–1920," in Marianne Debouzy, ed., *In the Shadow of the Statue of Liberty: Immigrants, Workers and Citizens in the American Republic, 1880–1920* (Paris, 1988), 35–36.

88. Vecoli, "The American Republic Viewed by the Italian Left," 37–53; Olivier Zunz, *Making America Corporate, 1870–1920* (Chicago, 1990), a work that responds to the question: How did corporate capitalism succeed in creating a new work culture and new living patterns? Also Barry D. Karl, *The Uneasy State: The United States from 1915 to 1945* (Chicago, 1983); and for reasons peculiar to their region and sensibility, unregenerate Southern spokesmen also found this phrasing both plausible and lamentable. See John Crowe Ransom's essay in Twelve Southerners, *I'll Take My Stand: The South and the Agrarian Tradition* (New York, 1930), 17.

89. See Godfrey Hodgson, *America in Our Time* (Garden City, N.Y., 1976); Stanley Hoffman, *Gulliver's Troubles; or, The Setting of American Foreign Policy* (New York, 1968); Studs Terkel, *The Great Divide: Second Thoughts on the American Dream* (New York, 1988).

90. See Daniel T. Rodgers, *Contested Truths: Keywords in American Politics since Independence* (New York, 1987), esp. ch. 1, and 91; Rob Kroes, ed., *High Brow Meets Low Brow: American Culture as an Intellectual Concern* (Amsterdam, 1988), esp. 145; and John Lukacs, "American History: The Terminological Problem," *American Scholar* 61 (Winter 1992): 17–32.

91. Carl Degler, "In Pursuit of an American History," *American Historical Review* 92 (Feb.

1987): 1–12 esp. 2, 4, 7. See also Miles Orvell, *The Real Thing: Imitation and Authenticity in American Culture, 1880–1940* (Chapel Hill, 1989), xxv–xxvi, 4; James Guimond, *American Photography and the American Dream* (Chapel Hill, 1991), 12, 103.

92. See Bruce M. Stave, "A Conversation with Eric Monkkonen," *Journal of Urban History* 22 (Jan. 1996): 236, 239.

93. See Bluestein, "Folk and Pop in American Culture," *Journal of American Culture* 13 (Summer 1990): 21.

94. April 29, 1996, pp. 9–10.

Chapter 8
Some Patterns and Meanings of Memory Distortion in American History

1. See Andrew Delbanco, "The Puritan Errand Re-viewed," *Journal of American Studies* 18 (Dec. 1984): 343–60; Delbanco, *The Puritan Ordeal* (Cambridge, Mass., 1989); Francis J. Bremer, *Puritan Crisis: New England and the English Civil Wars, 1630–1670* (New York, 1989), chs. 2–6; Stephen Foster, *The Long Argument: English Puritanism and the Shaping of New England Culture, 1570–1700* (Chapel Hill, 1991); Virginia D. Anderson, *New England's Generation: The Great Migration and the Formation of Society and Culture* (New York, 1991), ch. 1.

2. Perry Miller, *The New England Mind from Colony to Province* (Cambridge, Mass., 1953), book I; David D. Hall, *The Faithful Shepherd: A History of the New England Ministry in the Seventeenth Century* (Chapel Hill, 1972), chs. 2–5; Edmund S. Morgan, *Visible Saints: The History of a Puritan Idea* (New York, 1963); Patrick Collinson, *The Puritan Character: Polemics and Polarities in Early Seventeenth-Century English Culture* (Los Angeles, 1989).

3. Perry Miller, *Errand into the Wilderness* (Cambridge, Mass., 1956), 48–98.

4. Ibid., 184–203; Perry Miller, *Nature's Nation* (Cambridge, Mass., 1967), 90–120.

5. Whitney R. Cross, *The Burned-Over District: The Social and Intellectual History of Enthusiastic Religion in Western New York, 1800–1850* (Ithaca, 1950), chs. 1, 4, 5; Donald G. Mathews, *Religion in the Old South* (Chicago, 1977); Nathan Hatch, *The Democratization of American Christianity* (New Haven, 1989).

6. Herbert G. Gutman, *Work, Culture, and Society in Industrializing America: Essays in American Working-Class and Social History* (New York, 1976), 69.

7. Herbert G. Gutman, *Power and Culture: Essays on the American Working Class* (New York, 1987), ch. 12; for the same phenomenon in Canada, see Iwona Irwin-Zarecka, *Frames of Remembrance: The Dynamics of Collective Memory* (New Brunswick, 1994), 59–60.

8. Peter Kivisto and Dag Blanck, eds., *American Immigrants and Their Generations: Studies and Commentaries on the Hansen Thesis after Fifty Years* (Urbana, 1990); Jane Marie Pederson, *Between Memory and Reality: Family and Community in Rural Wisconsin, 1870–1970* (Madison, 1992), ch. 2. See also Studs Terkel, *Hard Times: An Oral History of the Great Depression* (New York, 1970): Dorothy Spruill Redford, *Somerset Homecoming: Recovering a Lost Heritage* (New York, 1988).

9. See Wilbur Zelinsky, *Nation into State: The Shifting Symbolic Foundations of American Nationalism* (Chapel Hill, 1988); Michael Kammen, *Mystic Chords of Memory: The Transformation of Tradition in American Culture* (New York, 1991); John Bodnar, *Remaking America: Public Memory, Commemoration, and Patriotism in the Twentieth Century* (Princeton, 1992).

10. Edmund Wilson, *Patriotic Gore: Studies in the Literature of the American Civil War* (New York, 1962); Gaines M. Foster, *Ghosts of the Confederacy: Defeat, the Lost Cause, and the Emergence of the New South, 1865 to 1914* (New York, 1987).

11. Daniel Aaron, *The Unwritten War: American Writers and the Civil War* (New York, 1973).

12. Kammen, *Mystic Chords of Memory*, chs. 4 and 12; and see Thomas J. Pressly, *Americans Interpret Their Civil War* (Princeton, 1954); Robert Penn Warren, *The Legacy of the Civil War*

(Cambridge, Mass., 1961).

13. Henry Steele Commager, ed., *Documents of American History* (New York, 1962), 174; Felix Gilbert, *To the Farewell Address: Ideas of Early American Foreign Policy* (Princeton, 1961).

14. Walter LaFeber, *Inevitable Revolutions: The United States in Central America* (New York, 1983), chs. 1 and 2; LaFeber, *The American Age: United States Foreign Policy at Home and Abroad since 1750* (New York, 1989), chs. 8–11.

15. See *New York Times*, Feb. 17, 1980, p. A18; Ibid., Feb. 19, 1985, p. A14; ibid., Feb. 17, 1987, p. A18.

16. Charles A. Radin, "Japan Official Retracts Statements on WWII," *Boston Globe*, May 7, 1994, p. 2; and see G. Cameron Hurst III, *Weaving the Emperor's New Clothes: The Japanese Textbook "Revision" Controversy* (Hanover, N.H., 1982); Stefan Tanaka, *Japan's Orient: Rendering Pasts into History* (Berkeley, 1993), 228–83.

17. John R. Howe, "Republican Thought and the Political Violence of the 1790s," *American Quarterly* 19 (Summer 1967): 147–65.

18. Commager, ed., *Documents of American History*, 187, 188.

19. Michael Kammen, "Changing Presidential Perspectives on the American Past," *Prologue: Quarterly of the National Archives* 25 (Spring 1993): 55.

20. Commager, ed., *Documents*, 100.

21. David M. Potter, *Lincoln and His Party in the Secession Crisis* (New Haven, 1942); William W. Freehling, *Prelude to Civil War: The Nullification Controversy in South Carolina, 1816–1836* (New York, 1966).

22. Kenneth M. Stampp, "The Concept of a Perpetual Union," *Journal of American History* 65 (June 1978): 5–33.

23. Commager, ed., *Documents*, 82–84; Stampp, "The Concept of a Perpetual Union," 6–7, 10–11.

24. Commager, ed., *Documents*, 511; Garry Wills, *Lincoln at Gettysburg: The Words That Remade America* (New York, 1992).

25. Samuel Lubell, *The Future of American Politics* (New York, 1952), chs. 4 and 5; Albert Haworth Jones, *Roosevelt's Image Brokers: Poets, Playwrights, and the Use of the Lincoln Symbol* (Port Washington, N.Y., 1974); Nancy J. Weiss, *Farewell to the Party of Lincoln: Black Politics in the Age of FDR* (Princeton, 1983), 28–29, 91–92, 224–25.

26. Merrill D. Peterson, *The Jefferson Image in the American Mind* (New York, 1960), ch. 7.

27. Kammen, *Mystic Chords of Memory: The Transformation of Tradition in American Culture*, 658–62.

28. Garry Wills, *Reagan's America: Innocents at Home* (Garden City, N.Y., 1987), chs. 38–41.

29. Seymour Martin Lipset, *The First New Nation: The United States in Historical and Comparative Perspective* (New York, 1963); Fred Somkin, *Unquiet Eagle: Memory and Desire in the Idea of American Freedom, 1815–1860* (Ithaca, 1967); Michael Kammen, *A Season of Youth: The American Revolution and the Historical Imagination* (New York, 1978).

30. Enrique Florescano, *Memory, Myth, and Time in Mexico from the Aztecs to Independence* (Austin, Tex., 1994); John L. Greenway, *The Golden Horns: Mythic Imagination and the Nordic Past* (Athens, Ga., 1977); Maurice Agulhon, *Marianne into Battle: Republican Imagery and Symbolism in France, 1789–1880* (Cambridge, 1981).

31. Emilia Viotti da Costa, *The Brazilian Empire: Myths and Histories* (Chicago, 1985), ch. 9; Roy Porter, ed., *Myths of the English* (Cambridge, 1992); George L. Mosse, *Fallen Soldiers: Reshaping the Memory of the World Wars* (New York, 1990); Herman Lebovics, *True France: The Wars over Cultural Identity, 1900–1945* (Ithaca, 1992); Yael Zerubavel, *Recovered Roots: Collective Memory and the Making of Israeli National Tradition* (Chicago, 1995).

32. Bernard Lewis, *History—Remembered, Recovered, Invented* (Princeton, 1975); Eric Hobsbawm and Terence Ranger, eds., *The Invention of Tradition* (Cambridge, 1983), ch. 7;

Charles S. Maier, *The Unmasterable Past: History, Holocaust, and German National Identity* (Cambridge, Mass., 1988); Amatzia Baram, *Culture, History and Ideology in the Formation of Ba'thist Iraq, 1968–1989* (New York, 1991); Deborah Lipstadt *Denying the Holocaust: The Growing Assault on Truth and Memory* (New York, 1993).

33. Anaïs Nin, *Incest: From a Journal of Love: The Unexpurgated Diary of Anaïs Nin, 1932–1934* (New York, 1992), 110.

34. Michael Kammen, *The Lively Arts: Gilbert Seldes and the Transformation of Cultural Criticism in the United States* (New York, 1996), ch. 11.

35. Allen Tate, *Memoirs and Opinions* (Chicago, 1975), ix.

36. Allen Tate, "A Southern Mode of the Imagination," in Joseph J. Kwiat and Mary C. Turpie, eds., *Studies in American Culture: Dominant Ideas and Images* (Minneapolis, 1960), 96–108, esp. 99; Radcliffe Squires, *Allen Tate: A Literary Biography* (New York, 1971), ch. 1.

37. Quoted in Gilbert Seldes, *The Stammering Century* (New York, 1928), 224.

Chapter 9
History Is Our Heritage: The Past in Contemporary American Culture

1. David Lowenthal, *Possessed by the Past: The Heritage Crusade and the Spoils of History* (New York, 1996); see Robert Hewison, *The Heritage Industry: Britain in a Climate of Decline* (London, 1987); and *British Heritage*, a popular magazine that began publication in 1979. Scotland offers The [Robert] Burns Heritage Trail (Alloway to Dumfries), Linlithgow Heritage Trail, and Dunfermline Heritage, which includes the burial place of Robert the Bruce and the birthplace of Andrew Carnegie. Examples in Canada include Heritage Park in Calgary and Heritage Collection at the Whyte Museum of the Canadian Rockies in Banff, both located in Alberta. See also Siegfried Lenz, *The Heritage: The History of a Detestable Word* (New York, 1981), a German novel whose original title (1978) literally translated as "The Homeland Museum." The book's principal theme is the huge chasm between Germany's perception of past and present, a gap caused by the Nazis' warped use of the concepts of "homeland," heritage, and history to legitimize nationalistic xenophobia and the doctrine of racial purity.

2. See *Preservation News*, Sept. 1986, pp. 7, 11; proclamation issued by Governor Cuomo on Dec. 18, 1987.

3. *Los Angeles Times*, Dec. 23, 1976, p. 6.

4. Ibid., p. 4.

5. *New York Times*, Nov. 8, 1987, p. 62.

6. Ibid., Sept. 8, 1985, p. A78.

7. See Carl Becker, *Everyman His Own Historian: Essays on History and Politics* (New York, 1935), 247–48.

8. *Smithsonian*, Dec. 1985, p. 143. Precedents for this attitude reach back many decades. See fig. 2.1 on page 74 in this book.

9. *Preserving Our Heritage Through "Living History"* (Green Bay, Wis., n.d.).

10. Michael Wallace, "Reflections on the History of Historic Preservation," in *Presenting the Past: Essays on History and the Public*, ed. Susan Porter Benson et al. (Philadelphia, 1986), 177.

11. See Lynne V. Cheney, *American Memory: A Report on the Humanities in the Nation's Public Schools* (Washington, D.C., 1987); Merrill Peterson, *The Humanities and the American Promise: Report of the Colloquium on the Humanities and the American People* (Austin, Tex., 1987); Diane Ravitch and Chester E. Finn, Jr., *What Do Our 17-Year-Olds Know?* (New York, 1987).

12. *New York Times*, Dec. 20, 1975, p. 26. See the 1987 prospectus for the Minnetrista Cultural Center in Muncie, Indiana: "Preserving the Heritage of East Central Indiana."

13. Claudia J. Hoone, "Planning for Local Heritage Projects," *Hoosier Heritage* 3 (March 1986); Joan R. Challinor and Wilcomb E. Washburn, "Five Ways We Can Hail Columbus,"

Washington Post, Oct. 11, 1987, p. II5. See also "The National Park Service and Historic Preservation," a special issue of the *Public Historian* 9 (Spring 1987); Betty Shaw, "Interpreting Our Outdoor Heritage," *Museum News* 44 (June 1966): 24–28.

14. The letter is undated. Wallace Stegner, ed., *The Letters of Bernard DeVoto* (New York, 1975), 285. See also George Jean Nathan and H. L. Mencken, *The American Credo: A Contribution Toward the Interpretation of the National Mind*, 2nd edition (New York, 1921), 69–70; John Higham, "Beyond Consensus: The Historian as Moral Critic," *American Historical Review* 67 (April 1963): 615–16.

15. Bemis to Brooks, June 12, 1953, Brooks Papers, Van Pelt Library (Rare Book Collection), University of Pennsylvania, Philadelphia. See also Perry Miller, *Errand into the Wilderness* (Cambridge, Mass., 1956), viii–ix.

16. Countee Cullen, *On These I Stand* (New York, 1947), 24–28. It may be instructive, though not entirely attractive, to contemplate a letter that Herbert Hoover wrote in 1912: "In these days of stifling struggle our people need something to bring back to them the heritage, not only of the combat of immediate fathers in the upbuilding of the West, but also to bring to the people that they have a heritage of race." Quoted in Robert W. Rydell, *All the World's a Fair: Visions of Empire at American International Expositions, 1876–1916* (Chicago: 1984), 208.

17. See Herbert G. Gutman, "Historical Consciousness in Contemporary America," in *Power & Culture: Essays on the American Working Class*, ed. Ira Berlin (New York, 1987), 395–412; Henry F. May, *Coming to Terms: A Study in Memory and History* (Berkeley, Calif., 1987), esp. xi, 146; William Maxwell, *Ancestors* (New York, 1971).

18. *U.S.A. Weekend, Ithaca Journal*, May 23, 1986; and a personal visit by the author in July 1986.

19. See Ron Powers, *White Town Drowsing* (Boston: 1986), esp. 19, 69, 108, 111, 206, 257, 267, 271–72, 274, 277, 287. For the failure of a Mark Twain Heritage Theme Park to develop, as planned, near Hannibal, Missouri, see 115, 128–37.

20. See Merritt Roe Smith, *Harpers Ferry Armory and the New Technology: The Challenge of Change* (Ithaca, N.Y., 1977); Richard N. Current, *Northernizing the South* (Athens, Ga., 1983), 85, 97, 103–5; Neil Harris, "Cultural Institutions and American Modernization," *Journal of Library History* 16 (Winter 1981): 43; and T. J. Jackson Lears, *No Place of Grace: Antimodernism and the Transformation of American Culture, 1880–1920* (New York, 1981).

21. See "Overrated & Underrated Americans," *American Heritage* 39 (July 1988): 48–63.

22. William K. Stevens, "National Trauma Played Out Again at Gettysburg," *New York Times*, June 27, 1988, p. A10.

23. See Michael Kammen, *Selvages & Biases: The Fabric of History in American Culture* (Ithaca, N.Y., 1987), 287–89.

Index

Credits